CONTENTS

CONTENTS

ACKNOWLEDGEMENTS

We are indebted to the following people for permission to reproduce copyright material:

The British Broadcasting Corporation for fig. 4.1 from page 27 of *Mathematics in Action: BBC Television for Schools (Summer 1968)* © The British Broadcasting Corporation 1966.

PREFACE

Operational Research is now widely used in business, industry and government to assist managers in making decisions. This book provides an introduction to the subject for students in universities, polytechnics and colleges who are following courses in engineering, technology, science or the social sciences. It should also prove useful to those in the professions who bear managerial responsibilities.

I have interpreted Operational Research broadly and included chapters on the time value of money, and probability and statistics, as well as the usual topics of network analysis, linear programming, queueing, stock control and games theory.

I have drawn on everyday experiences to illustrate the principles involved and I have indicated the wide ranging applications of the various techniques. The text contains a number of examples with detailed solutions and each chapter ends with a set of problems and answers. I hope that these features will make the book especially useful to those who are studying with little tutorial assistance or by distance learning.

The books listed at the ends of the chapters are recommended to those readers who wish to explore particular topics in greater depth.

In my experience many students are daunted by advanced mathematics. Here the treatment is as simple as possible, and the main algebraic results and formulae are explained in Appendix A. The arithmetic can prove tedious, however, and I have included a number of BASIC computer programs to speed the calculations. These should suit all machines that can use BASIC and they are well within the capacity of the humblest home computer. Appendix B explains the few minor changes that may be needed on some machines. The listings must be carefully typed but the effort is well worthwhile and the computation time in many examples is reduced to a few seconds.

Tables of present value factors, one-tail areas of the normal curve and random numbers are collected in Appendix C. Together the appendices should help to make the book self-contained.

Every book of this kind must owe a great deal to the writings of others and I have derived much benefit from the works of those authors who are cited in the bibliographies.

I shall always be grateful to Professor John Crank who, twenty-five years ago, encouraged me to develop my teaching in this field; and to John Cain who gave me the opportunity to reach a wide audience through television.

I am also indebted to my colleagues for many lively and fruitful discussions on the teaching of Operational Research and to my students who have followed, with patience and good humour, the fluctuating fortunes of the Tardy Timepiece Company and its kindly chairman, Sir Tempus Tardy. These are chronicled within the pages that follow.

Finally, my thanks are due to the Publishers for their care in all aspects of the book's production.

The responsibility for errors is mine alone, however, and I shall gratefully acknowledge any corrections or comments.

Syd Urry

Bridport
October 1990

1 MODELLING

'The student of arithmetic who has mastered the first four rules of his art, and successfully striven with money sums and fractions, finds himself confronted by an unbroken expanse of questions known as problems. These are short stories of adventure and industry with the end omitted, and though bearing a strong family resemblance, are not without a certain element of romance.

The characters in the plot of a problem are three people called A, B and C.'

Stephen Leacock, Literary Lapses. A, B and C

1.1 WHAT OPERATIONAL RESEARCH IS ABOUT

At some stage in our mathematical studies we meet problems such as the following: A train travels between two towns 240 km apart. What is the journey time if an increase of 15 km per hour in the average speed would result in a saving of 32 minutes?

We soon learn that in every question of this kind, there is just enough information to find the answer; furthermore, there is only one right answer. Such problems seem to bear little relevance to our everyday lives; after all, if we need to know the duration of a real train journey we can look it up in the timetable!

Suppose, in contrast, I am planning a journey from London to Paris and I want to know how long it will take and how much it will cost. I shall first have to choose whether to travel by air, by train and ferry, or by some other means. However, my choice may well be affected by factors such as time and cost. When there are several possibilities it helps to show the figures in some compact form, and Table 1.1 gives the travelling times and single fares for some of the many ways in which my journey can be made. The costs are 1989 values and are subject to inflation – like all such values in this book. For simplicity the costs and times are rounded to the nearest whole numbers. Note, too, that the figures for the car journey can only be approximate.

Table 1.1 London–Paris journey times and costs

Mode of travel	Centre to centre time (hours)	Single journey cost (£)	Comfort rating
① Air (from Heathrow)	3	65	8
② Rail and hovercraft (first class)	6	59	7
③ Rail and hovercraft (standard class)	6	46	5
④ Coach and ship	10	25	4
⑤ Car and ferry	9	100	9

The time and cost figures (by public transport) will be the same for all travellers, but in the last column I have given my personal comfort 'ratings' on a scale of 1–10. Your assessment may differ from mine and we must always be prepared for differences of opinion in practical examples. A table is not the only way in which the information can be shown and it is often easier to make decisions from a graphics display. In Fig. 1.1, for instance, the horizontal and vertical axes represent cost and time. Each mode of travel is then represented by a point whose coordinates give the two values for that mode. The points are numbered for ease of reference to Table 1.1. They do not lie on a simple curve; slower journeys are generally cheaper but there can be exceptions.

At this stage I might set limits to the time and money I am prepared to spend on the journey. For example, I might not be able to spare more than 8 hours for the journey. This rules out modes ④ and ⑤. I could also set a cost limit, say £60.00, and this would eliminate modes ① and ⑤. Such limitations are called *constraints* and, in the present example, they are represented by vertical and horizontal lines on the diagram. Together with the coordinate axes they form a rectangle within which the method of travel must be selected. This rectangle is called the *feasible region* and the points that lie within it represent feasible solutions.

Depending on the values of the constraints there can be several feasible solutions, there can be just one or there can be none; in the present example there are two, modes ② and ③.

If there are two or more feasible solutions I am free to choose the one that gives me the greatest comfort on my journey. Comfort is then said to be the *objective*, and the feasible solution that gives the best value of the objective is called the *optimum solution*. In the present example we only have to examine the comfort ratings of the feasible solutions. In this

Figure 1.1

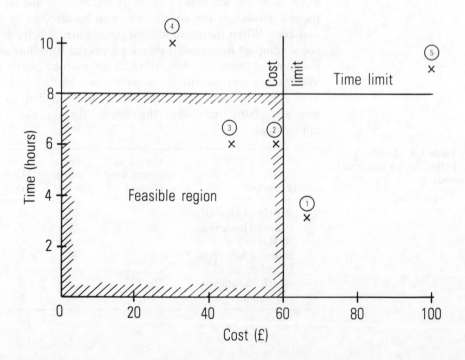

example it is mode ②, rail and hovercraft with a first class ticket. In later chapters we shall meet problems with two or more optimal solutions.

Although this first example is very elementary, it has several features that are typical of operational research (OR) problems. There are constraints – limitations of resources such as money, time, personnel, manufacturing capacity – and these define a feasible region within which solutions have to be found. We set an objective – comfort in the present case, but usually some other form of benefit such as financial profit or least cost – and we look for the best value of that objective. It is this process of optimization – finding the best solution from several possible ones – that distinguishes operational research work from the kind of example I quoted at the beginning of this chapter. Hence the subtitle of this book.

1.2 DEFINING OPERATIONAL RESEARCH

It has been claimed that some aspects of OR were understood from the time of the Industrial Revolution, but it is generally agreed that the main development of the subject began during the Second World War when mathematicians and scientists were recruited to help in making the best use of scarce resources. It was this research into military operations that gave the subject its name, but it became clear that the techniques had many applications and OR is now widely used in industry, business and government. It is a rapidly growing subject with no universally agreed definition. Indeed, it was stated in one early book on the subject[1] that 'those who seek here for a precise definition of operational research will be disappointed'. However, there are a number of characteristics that are common to most OR problems:

- they are concerned with planning and predicting;
- they are described and analysed in numerical terms;
- there are constraints such as limitations of resources;
- there are objectives to be optimized;
- there are uncertainties.

The definition adopted by the Operational Research Society (UK) includes the following: 'The distinctive approach is to develop a scientific model of the system incorporating measurements of factors, such as chance and risk, with which to predict and compare the outcomes of alternative strategies or controls.'

Whatever its definition, OR has become an important management tool. This book presents a broad introduction. Theory is kept to a minimum and the emphasis is on applications.

1.3 OPERATIONAL RESEARCH AND MANAGEMENT

Managers have to take decisions and provide leadership. The process of decision-making can be divided into three stages:

1   Collecting data, identifying constraints and setting objectives;

2   Analysing the problem, given the data, constraints and objectives;

3   Interpreting the results of the analysis and selecting a course of action.

Operational research is concerned mainly with the second stage. It does not replace the manager who remains responsible for the other two stages and who has the additional task of implementing the chosen course of action. Nor are the three stages always independent of one another. Often there is feedback and the initial results of the analysis can lead to changes in the constraints or objectives. The manager must also assign values to those factors that may be difficult to quantify. The comfort ratings in Table 1.1 reflect personal preferences and the values set by different travellers may vary considerably.

Some of these considerations are beyond the scope of this book and, in the examples that follow, details of the constraints and objectives will always be given.

1.4 CALCULATIONS AND COMPUTERS

Some OR books are highly mathematical but this one requires no more than a knowledge of arithmetic, elementary algebra and simple graphical methods. The arithmetic of OR can be tedious, however, and a pocket calculator is essential for some of the examples. We shall need a few mathematical results and formulae in later chapters and these are summarized in Appendix A.

In practice, many OR calculations are so lengthy that computers offer the only practical means of carrying them out. As an introduction to the use of computers several BASIC program listings are included in the text. These are not substitutes for the wide range of powerful commercial and public domain software that is now available, but they give an indication of the savings in time that can be achieved by using computers. You do not require a powerful machine to use the programs in this book. They were developed on a very cheap model – the Acorn Electron – and they should run satisfactorily on all home and personal computers that can use BASIC. No programming experience is required and, even if you are new to computers, you should have little difficulty in using them. Appendix B gives more details, including the amendments that may be needed on some machines.

Some calculations lead to very large numbers and there are several ways of expressing them. In the past it was usual to show the digits in groups of three, starting from the decimal point and (in English-speaking countries) separated by commas. This convention is still widely used for sums of money, e.g. £87,000,000 and $403,100,000. It is now recommended[2] that the groups of three are separated only by spaces and this style is followed throughout the text of this book. For numbers between 1000 and 9999 the space is often omitted, but it should be retained where columns of figures have to be totalled. Neither commas nor spaces should be used with data input to computers.

When a number has several trailing zeros it is convenient to use 'scientific' notation. For instance, the sums of money given in the last paragraph can be expressed as £8.7×10^7 and $\$4.031 \times 10^8$. Most computers will accept and display such numbers in the form 8.7E7 and 4.031E8 (no spaces). For very small numbers we can use negative indices so that 0.0000372 can be written as 3.72×10^{-5} or, on a computer, 3.72E−5. See Appendix A for more details.

Negative quantities are normally indicated by minus signs so that, in a table of profits, a loss of 5780 will be shown as − 5780. This style is followed throughout this book, but in balance sheets you may come across brackets instead, e.g. (5780).

1.5 MODELS

The concept of a model is fundamental to OR. By 'model' we mean some representation – usually on paper – that possesses some of the features of the project or system we are trying to understand and control. It can appear as a table of values, a graph, a network or a set of mathematical equations and, by experimenting with the model, we can predict to some extent how the real system will behave. Figure 1.1 is a very simple example of a model. In an elementary way it tells us something about the time and cost of the journey and it enables us to make certain decisions about it.

No model can reproduce every feature of the original, however, and we must never lose sight of the approximations that are inherent in its construction. Computers may enable us to find answers rapidly, and with apparent precision, but the value of these answers is limited by the accuracy of the original data, and the extent to which the model reproduces the behaviour of the system itself. The adage 'garbage in, garbage out' should be heeded in all OR work! In practice every model should be tested against known conditions before it is used to predict the outcome of an untried course of action.

We use two fundamental types of model in operational research and their differences can be illustrated by another travel example. Suppose we are planning to drive from, say, Exeter to Edinburgh and we are interested in the distance and time of the journey. If we have a map or network diagram showing the intermediate distances along the possible routes, we can determine the total distance of a particular route by adding together the values for all its segments. Provided we make no arithmetical errors, we shall obtain the same result each time we carry out the calculation and we would expect good agreement with the distance we measured on the journey itself. Such a model is said to be *deterministic*.

If, however, we attempted to do a similar calculation for the time of the journey we would know that the answer could only be approximate and that the actual time would vary from one occasion to another. In these circumstances we can only talk about average or probable values. A model of this kind is called *stochastic* or *probabilistic*. It may be convenient to categorize OR problems as deterministic or probabilistic, but in practice there is rarely such a clear-cut distinction. The same difficulty is encountered in the natural world and this has led to the development of the new mathematics of chaos.[3]

Financial considerations are the basis of many OR problems and the rest of this chapter is devoted to some cost models that represent conditions (at least approximately) that often occur in practice.

1.6 FIXED AND VARIABLE COSTS

Most householders are familiar with electricity, gas and telephone bills. They usually show charges of two kinds. There is a fixed or standing charge that is made whatever the usage, and a variable charge that depends on the number of units used. If the cost of every unit is the same then the variable cost is found by multiplying this cost by the number of units. In mathematical terms, if c is the standing charge, x the number of units and m the cost of each, the variable charge is mx and the total bill y is given by

$$y = mx + c \qquad\qquad\qquad [1.1]$$

A graph of y against x is a straight line (Fig. 1.2), and Eq. 1.1 is described as a linear relationship between x and y (see section A.7). Such relationships play an important part in OR and they form the basis of linear programming (see Chs 4 and 5). The constant c is the intercept on the y-axis, that is the value of y when $x = 0$. The coefficient m is the slope of the line.

Figure 1.2

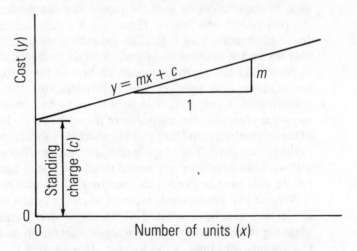

The value m, the extra cost for each additional unit, is often called the marginal cost. The assumption that it is constant leads to a model that is a good approximation to many practical systems. Motoring costs are typical of this pattern. Motor tax, insurance and, to some extent, depreciation are independent of the mileage. (It is true that a car with a very low mileage will have a slightly smaller depreciation than the 'average for the year' but, for most cars, age is the prime factor.)

In contrast, the cost of petrol, servicing and replacing items such as tyres, is likely to be proportional to the distance covered.

Manufacturing costs can be looked at in the same way. There are fixed overheads (rent, rates, insurance, heating and other services) and variable costs (such as raw materials and components) that depend on the number of units of production. The category into which labour costs are placed can be a matter for debate.

Example 1.1

A motorist drives 15 000 miles each year and finds that the annual costs under various headings are as follows:

	£		£
Tax	100	Servicing	160
Insurance	220	Depreciation	1200
Petrol	960	Motoring club subscription	40
Tyres	80		

Derive a cost model in terms of a weekly fixed or standing charge together with a mileage cost and use it to answer the following questions:

(a) What is the weekly cost for a mileage of 400?
(b) What is the annual cost with a mileage of 12 000?
(c) The motorist's employer pays an allowance of 20p per mile for business journeys. What is the smallest annual mileage for which this allowance will cover all costs?
(d) The motorist is offered a similar car on lease at a weekly rental of £40.00 to cover all costs except petrol. Under what conditions would it pay to lease rather than own the car?

Solution
If the tax, insurance, depreciation and motoring club subscription are taken as fixed costs, there is an annual standing charge of (100 + 220 + 1200 + 40) = £1560 or 1560/52 = £30.00 per week.

The remaining items (petrol, tyres and servicing) are the variable costs and total £1200 for 15 000 miles or 1200/15 000 = £0.08 (or 8p) per mile.

The cost model is therefore £30.00 per week + £0.08 per mile.

This result is shown graphically in Fig. 1.3.

Figure 1.3

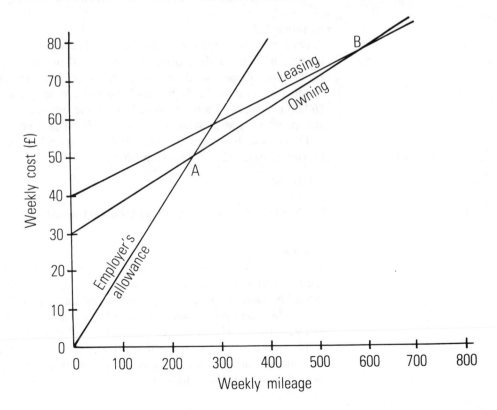

(a) The weekly cost for 400 miles is £(30 + 0.08 × 400) = **£62.00**.
(b) The annual cost for 12 000 miles is £(30 × 52 + 0.08 × 12 000) = **£2520**.
(c) Since the employer pays mileage only, the sum received by the motorist is shown in Fig. 1.3 by a straight line through the origin. With 400 miles, for example, the payment would be 400 × 0.20 = £80.00. The mileage at which the allowance just covers all costs is given by point A, the intersection of this line with the one representing cost. It corresponds to a weekly mileage of 250, or 250 × 52 = **13 000** annually.

The result can also be obtained algebraically. If x is the weekly break even mileage then the employer's allowance is £0.20x and the weekly cost is £(30 + 0.08x). Equating these two expressions,

$$0.20x = 30 + 0.08x$$

from which

$$x = 250$$

as before.

(d) From the data given in the question, the petrol cost is £960 for 15 000 miles, or 960/15 000 = £0.064 per mile. This result, together with the weekly rental of £40.00, establishes another straight line (Fig. 1.3) intersecting the first at B. This point corresponds to a weekly mileage of 625 or an annual figure of 625 × 52 = **32 500**. Below this mileage it is cheaper to own the car, but leasing would pay if the motorist covered more miles than this each year.

The same result can be obtained by equating the expressions for the weekly leasing cost, £(40 + 0.064x), and the owning cost, £(30 + 0.08x).

Example 1.2
A craft workshop making lampshades finds that the number it can sell varies linearly with the selling price. It can sell 10 per week if the price is set at £8.00, but 50 per week if the price is reduced to £4.00. The marginal production cost is £2.00 for each lampshade and there are overheads of £60.00 per week. Show graphically how the income (or revenue), total cost and profit vary with sales in the range 10–70 per week.

Determine the level of sales and corresponding selling price that will maximize each of the following objectives:

(a) revenue,
(b) profit,
(c) level of production (without incurring a loss).

Solution
The variation of price with sales is shown in Fig. 1.4. In practice the relationship is not likely to be linear over a wide range of sales and we should be cautious when using data of the kind given in the question. If we accept the assumption, however, we obtain Table 1.2. As the sales per week figure increases, the price decreases in a uniform way; revenue (or income) is the product of sales and selling price, and the total manufacturing cost is the sum of the overheads (constant at £60.00) and the variable cost (the marginal cost of £2.00 multiplied by the sales figure).

Figure 1.4

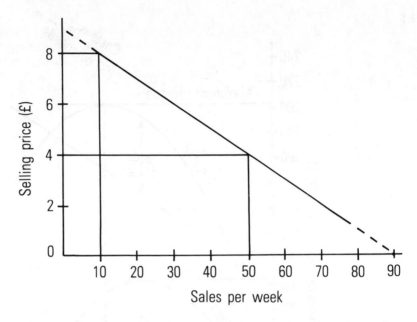

Table 1.2 Revenue
and profit from
lampshade
manufacturing

Sales per week	10	20	30	40	50	60	70
Selling price (£)	8.00*	7.00	6.00	5.00	4.00*	3.00	2.00
Revenue (income) (£)	80	140	180	200	200	180	140
Cost (£)	80	100	120	140	160	180	200
Profit (£)	0	40	60	60	40	0	− 60

* Value given in the question

The required graphs are shown together in Fig. 1.5. That for total manufacturing cost is a straight line, but those for revenue and profit are curves with maximum values at certain intermediate levels of sales.

The answers called for at the end of the question can be obtained by noting the symmetry of the curves and interpolating within Table 1.2.

(a) The maximum revenue corresponds to sales of **45 per week** and this figure is achieved when the price is set at **£4.50**.
(b) Maximum profit is obtained at a lower level of sales, **35 per week**, and a corresponding price of **£5.50**.
(c) The greatest level of sales that can be achieved without incurring a loss is the upper of the two values at which the profit is zero. From Table 1.2 this is seen to be **60** with a selling price of **£3.00**.

These results (which can also be obtained by algebra and calculus) show that the best course of action may be different for different objectives – a common feature of OR problems. Note that the conditions for maximum profit are not the same as those for maximum revenue. Profit is often the selected objective but there may be others. In the present example, for instance, the workshop might be a non-profit making enterprise with the aim of employing as many people as possible. In this case objective (c) would be selected.

Figure 1.5

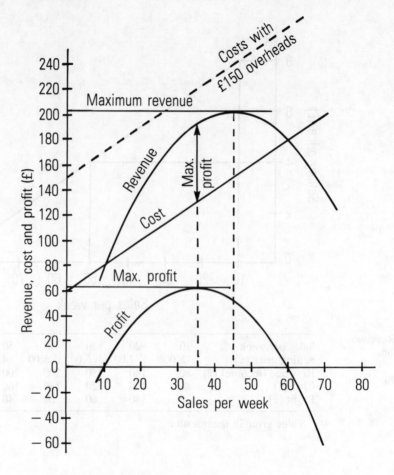

1.7 COMPUTER PROGRAM FOR LINEAR SALES/PRICE RELATIONSHIP

The theory of the last example is the basis of the computer program shown in Fig. 1.6. It uses the assumptions that the relationships between sales and price, and between total cost and number of items produced, are both linear. It can determine:

(a) the maximum revenue, the corresponding sales and selling price;
(b) *either* the range of sales for which the operation is profitable, the maximum profit and the corresponding sales and price; *or* if there is no profitable level of sales, the minimum loss to be sustained, and the corresponding sales and price;
(c) the price, total cost, revenue and profit for any chosen sales figure.

Lines 10–50 print the heading and lines 60–100 call for the initial data. Lines 110–120 then determine the slope and intercept values for the straight-line relationships.

Line 180 calculates the sales for maximum revenue, the results being printed in lines 200–210. Lines 220–230 determine two parameters X and Y that give the range of profitable sales in the form $X \pm \sqrt{Y}$. Line 240 finds the level of sales for maximum profit.

Figure 1.6

```
10 PRINT "--------------------------------"
20 PRINT "REVENUE AND PROFIT ANALYSIS FOR"
30 PRINT "LINEAR PRICE/SALES RELATIONSHIP"
40 PRINT "--------------------------------"
50 PRINT
60 PRINT "ENTER DATA:"
70 PRINT "FIRST PRICE AND CORRESPONDING SALES"
80 INPUT P1,S1
90 PRINT "SECOND PRICE AND CORRESPONDING SALES"
100 INPUT P2,S2
110 M1=(P2-P1)/(S2-S1)
120 K1=(P1*S2-P2*S1)/(S2-S1)
130 PRINT "FIXED OVERHEADS"
140 INPUT K2
150 PRINT "MARGINAL COST"
160 INPUT M2
170 PRINT
180 S=INT(0.5-K1/(2*M1))
190 GOSUB 450
200 PRINT "MAXIMUM REVENUE IS ";R;" WITH"
210 PRINT "SALES OF ";S;" AND PRICE OF ";P
220 X=(M2-K1)/(2*M1)
230 Y=X*X+K2/M1
240 S=INT(X+0.5)
250 GOSUB 450
260 PRINT
270 IF Y<0 THEN PRINT "NO PROFITABLE RANGE OF SALES":GOTO 320
280 PRINT "OPERATION PROFITABLE FOR SALES"
290 PRINT "BETWEEN ";-INT(SQR(Y)-X);" AND ";INT(X+SQR(Y))
300 PRINT "MAXIMUM PROFIT IS ";Z;" AT SALES"
310 GOTO 330
320 PRINT "MINIMUM LOSS IS ";-Z;" AT SALES"
330 PRINT "OF ";S;" AND A PRICE OF ";P
340 PRINT
350 PRINT "ANOTHER SALES FIGURE? (0 TO FINISH)"
360 INPUT S
370 IF S=0 THEN GOTO 430
380 S=INT(S+0.5)
390 GOSUB 460
400 PRINT "PRICE = ";P;"    TOTAL COST = ";S*M2+K2
410 PRINT "REVENUE = ";R;"    PROFIT = ";Z
420 GOTO 340
430 PRINT "--------------------------------"
440 END
450 REM     CALCULATE PRICE, REVENUE AND PROFIT
460 P=INT(100*(M1*S+K1)+0.5)/100
470 R=S*P
480 Z=INT(100*(R-S*M2-K2)+0.5)/100
490 RETURN
```

Lines 270–340 print the profitable range of sales and lines 350–410 will then determine the price, revenue, cost and profit corresponding to any specified level of sales. The subroutine in lines 450–490 calculates the price, revenue and profit for a given sales figure, and is used several times.

Results are expressed to the nearest whole number of sales and to an accuracy of 0.01 for monetary values, using the INTeger routine.

The printout shown in Fig. 1.7 was obtained by running the program with the data of Example 1.2 and selecting a sales figure of 20. Check the rest of Table 1.2 by entering other sales values in the range 10–90.

It is clear from Fig. 1.5 that the profitable range of sales is bounded by the intersections of the cost line with the revenue curve. With higher overheads or marginal costs there may be no such intersections, and the program responds by determining the minimum loss and the sales figure at which it occurs. Run the program again with the overheads increased to £150.00. This corresponds to the broken line at the top of Fig. 1.5.

It is possible for the cost line to be tangential to the curve and this leads to a single break-even level of sales. The program can easily be extended to respond appropriately. Change the overheads to £122.50 to see the answers produced by the program as it stands.

Figure 1.7

```
---------------------------------
REVENUE AND PROFIT ANALYSIS FOR
LINEAR PRICE/SALES RELATIONSHIP
---------------------------------

ENTER DATA:
FIRST PRICE AND CORRESPONDING SALES
?8
?10
SECOND PRICE AND CORRESPONDING SALES
?4
?50
FIXED OVERHEADS
?60
MARGINAL COST
?2

MAXIMUM REVENUE IS 202.5 WITH
SALES OF 45 AND PRICE OF 4.5

OPERATION PROFITABLE FOR SALES
BETWEEN 10 AND 60
MAXIMUM PROFIT IS 62.5 AT SALES
OF 35 AND A PRICE OF 5.5

ANOTHER SALES FIGURE? (0 TO FINISH)
?20
PRICE = 7      TOTAL COST = 100
REVENUE = 140    PROFIT = 40

ANOTHER SALES FIGURE? (0 TO FINISH)
?0
-----------------------------------------
```

1.8 INVERSE COSTS

It is often the case in business, industry and government that an increase in spending under one heading can lead to savings under another. The more we spend on the maintenance of equipment such as vehicles and machine tools the smaller should be our losses arising from breakdowns. If, as a nation, we increase our spending on health screening we can expect to reduce the costs of treating certain diseases. Some examples, such as the costs of safety measures and accidents in the construction industry, have been studied in detail.[4] There are many other examples – more money spent on roads should lead to lower transport costs, more on the prevention of fire and crime should reduce losses from these causes.

Figure 1.8

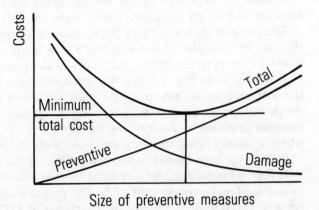

The precise relationship between the two categories of cost will vary from one example to another but the general tendencies are shown in Fig. 1.8. In this diagram the costs are plotted vertically, and the horizontal axis represents the size of the safety or precautionary measures. This could be the number of maintenance staff employed, the hours spent on safety training or the number of health screening units. If very little is spent on prevention we can expect the costs of breakdown to be high. Conversely, an increase in the preventive spending is likely to bring about a reduction in the breakdown costs.

If we plot the sum of the two costs we obtain the dish-shaped curve at the top of the diagram and there will be a point where this total is a minimum. In terms of total cost this represents an optimum solution, but there are two complicating factors.

One is the difficulty of assessing costs and benefits. We can estimate the cost of a road improvement scheme, but what value do we place on the lives of accident victims?

The other complication arises when the costs under the two headings are not borne by the same organization. It would be reasonable to expect that an increase in the number of firemen and fire-fighting equipment would result in smaller insurance claims for fire damage. However, the fire service is maintained from public funds but the claims are borne by the insurance companies. In this sense neither agency bears the total cost. However, the insurance claims are met ultimately from the premiums paid by policyholders who, as taxpayers, also pay for the fire service. In eighteenth-century England the fire insurance companies themselves provided the fire service – but only to the homes of those policyholders whose houses were distinguished by firemarks. If all the costs are the responsibility of one agency there is an incentive to minimize the total. In the eighteenth century, however, the concepts of OR might not have been widely understood!

In some systems it is a good approximation to take the two costs as being inversely proportional – if one is doubled the other is halved, and so on. Under these conditions, it can be shown that the minimum total cost occurs when the separate amounts are equal. The next example is of this kind. It is a cost model that we shall meet again in stock control analysis (Ch. 8).

Example 1.3

The damage from fires in Midshire is estimated to cost £12 million annually and the present expenditure on the fire service is £2 million. Research has indicated that the costs under the two headings are inversely proportional. On this basis draw up a table showing how the costs vary when the expenditure on the fire service is increased through the range £2–12 million.

What is the minimum total cost?

Solution

It is convenient to take steps of £2 million in the given range. The results are shown in Table 1.3 and the minimum total cost is seen to be in the region of £10 million.

It can also be seen from Table 1.3 that the product of each pair of costs is 24 (working in units of £ million). If the two values are equal when the total is a minimum then each will be $\sqrt{24}$, that is, 4.9 approximately. Hence the

Table 1.3 Fire
prevention and damage
costs (£ million)

Cost of fire service	2	4	6	8	10	12
Cost of fire damage	12	6	4	3	2.4	2
Total cost	14	10	10	11	12.4	14

total cost is likely to be least when the expenditure on the fire service is increased to £4.9 million. Under these conditions the cost of damage would also be £4.9 million, giving a total of **£9.8 million**.

1.9 MATHEMATICAL RESULTS FOR INVERSE COSTS MODEL

Suppose that, in Fig. 1.9, x is the horizontal variable and the cost y, plotted upwards, is made up of two elements, one proportional, and one inversely proportional, to x. These are given by ax and b/x respectively, where a and b are constants with positive values. These separate costs are represented by a straight line through the origin ($y = ax$) and a curve ($y = b/x$) as shown in the diagram.

Figure 1.9

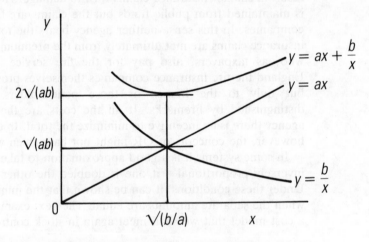

It follows that the total cost is given by

$$y = ax + \frac{b}{x} \qquad [1.2]$$

and this is represented by the upper curve in Fig. 1.9.

The result should be compared with Eq. 1.1. It can be shown by differentiating Eq. 1.2 that the minimum value of y occurs when $x = \sqrt{(b/a)}$. Each term on the right-hand side of the equation is then equal to $\sqrt{(ab)}$ and the corresponding minimum total cost is $2\sqrt{(ab)}$.

1.10 DEPRECIATION

Much of the equipment we use at work and in the home reduces in value year by year and this depreciation of our assets can represent a considerable

Figure 1.10

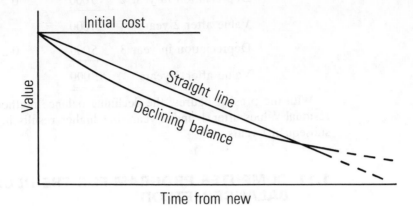

proportion of our total costs. The process of allowing for this reduction in value is generally known as 'writing down'. There are two models that are widely used in calculating the amounts involved and they are illustrated in Fig. 1.10.

The straight-line method is based on the assumption that the reduction in value is the same each year. It makes the arithmetic very simple but it is unrealistic in many cases. A new £10 000 car may reduce in value to £8000 in its first year, but we would not expect it to fall from £2000 to zero in the fifth year.

In practice, the reduction in value is likely to be smaller year by year and a common assumption is to take it as a fixed percentage of the value at the beginning of the year. This model is known as the *declining balance* or *reducing balance* method. As the diagram shows, the straight-line method leads to a zero value after a finite number of years – and a negative one if taken further! With the declining balance method some (positive) value always remains.

Example 1.4

A machine tool costs £30 000 when new. Calculate its written-down values after 1, 2 and 3 years using:

(a) the straight-line method with an annual depreciation of £5000;
(b) the declining balance method with an annual depreciation of 20 per cent.

Solution

The calculations are set out below with all values in £. In (b), the reduction in value each year is $20/100 = 0.2$ of the value at the beginning of that year.

	(a)		(b)
Capital cost	30 000		30 000
Depreciation in year 1	5 000	$0.2 \times 30000 =$	6 000
Value after 1 year	25 000		24 000

Depreciation in year 2	5 000	$0.2 \times 24\,000 =$	4 800
Value after 2 years	20 000		19 200
Depreciation in year 3	5 000	$0.2 \times 19\,200 =$	3 840
Value after 3 years	15 000		15 360

With the present figures, the declining balance method has led to lower residual values after 1 and 2 years but higher results in the third (and all subsequent) years.

1.11 COMPUTER PROGRAM FOR THE DECLINING BALANCE METHOD

The four quantities – initial cost, number of years, annual percentage depreciation and final value – are linked by the computer program given in Fig. 1.11. If three of the four are entered, the fourth is calculated. The program will also print a table showing the depreciation and end-of-year values for the intermediate years.

Lines 50–130 call for the data, the 'wild' value −99 being used to identify the unknown quantity. This quantity is then determined by one of the lines 140–170 and the answer is printed by one of the lines 180–210. Line 230 offers the option of intermediate values which, if required, are determined and printed by lines 260–330. Common or natural logarithms may be used in line 150. The keyword will be LOG, LN or LOG10 depending on your computer.

Figure 1.11

```
10  PRINT "---------------------------------------"
20  PRINT "DECLINING-BALANCE METHOD"
30  PRINT "---------------------------------------"
40  PRINT
50  PRINT "INPUT DATA (-99 IF UNKNOWN)"
60  PRINT "INITIAL COST:"
70  INPUT C1
80  PRINT "NUMBER OF YEARS:"
90  INPUT N
100 PRINT "ANNUAL PERCENTAGE DEPRECIATION:"
110 INPUT D
120 PRINT "FINAL VALUE:"
130 INPUT C2
140 IF C1=-99 THEN C1=C2/(1-D/100)^N:GOTO 180
150 IF N=-99 THEN N=LN(C2/C1)/LN(1-D/100):GOTO 190
160 IF D=-99 THEN D=100*(1-(C2/C1)^(1/N)):GOTO 200
170 IF C2=-99 THEN C2=C1*(1-D/100)^N:GOTO 210
180 PRINT "INITIAL COST = ";INT(C1+0.5):GOTO 220
190 PRINT "NUMBER OF YEARS = ";INT(10*N+0.5)/10:GOTO 220
200 PRINT "ANNUAL DEPRECIATION = ";INT(100*D+0.5)/100;" PERCENT":GOTO 220
210 PRINT "FINAL VALUE = ";INT(C2+0.5)
220 PRINT
230 PRINT "INTERMEDIATE VALUES? (Y/N)"
240 INPUT Q$
250 IF Q$="N" THEN GOTO 340
260 PRINT
270 PRINT "YEAR";TAB(6);"DEPRECIATION";TAB(20);"END-OF-YEAR VALUE"
280 PRINT
290 FOR I=1 TO INT(N)
300 C=C1*(1-D/100)
310 PRINT TAB(1);I;TAB(9);INT(C1-C+0.5);TAB(24);INT(C+0.5)
320 C1=C
330 NEXT I
340 PRINT "---------------------------------------"
350 END
```

Monetary values are shown to the nearest integer (whole number) value, the period to the nearest 0.1 of a year and the annual percentage depreciation to the nearest 0.01 per cent. The display shown in Fig. 1.12 was obtained using an initial value of £40 000, declining to £6000 over a period of 6 years, the percentage depreciation being the unknown quantity.

Figure 1.12

```
----------------------------------------
DECLINING-BALANCE METHOD
----------------------------------------

INPUT DATA (-99 IF UNKNOWN)
INITIAL COST:
?40000
NUMBER OF YEARS:
?6
ANNUAL PERCENTAGE DEPRECIATION:
?-99
FINAL VALUE:
?6000
ANNUAL DEPRECIATION = 27.11 PER CENT

INTERMEDIATE VALUES? (Y/N)
?Y

YEAR  DEPRECIATION  END-OF-YEAR VALUE

 1       10843          29157
 2        7904          21253
 3        5761          15492
 4        4200          11292
 5        3061           8231
 6        2231           6000
----------------------------------------
```

1.12 PROJECT COSTS AND THE S-CURVE

In some activities, income and expenditure flow at a reasonably constant rate. A successful shopkeeper who sells day-to-day necessities to regular customers, and who pays suppliers promptly, can expect a steady flow of income and expenditure. In contrast, the rate of spending on a large one-off building project is not likely to remain constant from beginning to end. In many cases it follows a pattern known as the S-curve (Fig. 1.13). The rate of spending is slow to start with, rises to a level that remains approximately the same for a considerable period and then tails off at the end.

This pattern has been widely studied,[5-7] and it has been found that many projects, notably in the construction industry, divide into three phases, of approximately equal durations. It seems that a quarter of the total expenditure is incurred in each of the first and last phases, when the spending rate is growing and declining respectively. The balance of the spending takes place at a constant rate during the middle phase. Figure 1.13 shows these proportions with a smooth transition at each phase boundary. The corresponding mathematical equations are incorporated in the computer program of Fig. 1.14. Given the total project sum and a specified number of (equal) periods, the program determines the expenditure in each period, the cumulative amount at the end of each period and its proportion of the total as a percentage.

Lines 10–40 print the heading and 50–60 call for the data. Lines 90–110 then print the table heading. The calculations are carried out, and the results displayed, in lines 120–220. The proportions of total time and total

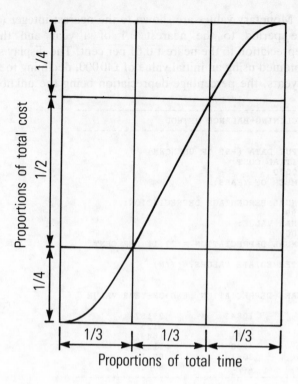

Figure 1.13

cost are denoted by X and Y, and lines 140, 150 and 160 correspond in turn to the three phases of the project.

Monetary values are shown to the nearest whole number and percentages to 0.01. Figure 1.15 shows the results for a 16-month project costing £275 000.

Figure 1.14

```
10 PRINT "----------------------------------------"
20 PRINT "S-CURVE ANALYSIS"
30 PRINT "----------------------------------------"
40 PRINT
50 PRINT "ENTER TOTAL COST AND NUMBER OF PERIODS"
60 INPUT C,N
70 PRINT
80 C1=0
90 PRINT "PERIOD";TAB(8);"PERIOD";TAB(16);"CUMULATIVE";TAB(28);"PERCENTAGE"
100 PRINT "NO.";TAB(8);"COST";TAB(16);"COST";TAB(28);"OF TOTAL"
110 PRINT
120 FOR I=1 TO N
130 X=I/N
140 Y=9*X*X/4
150 IF X>(1/3) THEN Y=(6*X-1)/4
160 IF X>(2/3) THEN Y=(18*X-9*X*X-5)/4
170 C2=INT(Y*C+0.5)
180 C1=C2-C1
190 C3=INT(1E4*Y+0.5)/100
200 PRINT TAB(1);I;TAB(8);C1;TAB(16);C2;TAB(28);C3
210 C1=C2
220 NEXT I
230 PRINT "----------------------------------------"
240 END
```

Figure 1.15

```
-----------------------------------------
S-CURVE ANALYSIS
-----------------------------------------
ENTER TOTAL COST AND NUMBER OF PERIODS
?275000
?16

PERIOD   PERIOD   CUMULATIVE   PERCENTAGE
NO.      COST     COST         OF TOTAL

1        2417     2417         0.88
2        7251     9668         3.52
3        12085    21753        7.91
4        16919    38672        14.06
5        21753    60425        21.97
6        25513    85938        31.25
7        25781    111719       40.63
8        25781    137500       50
9        25781    163281       59.38
10       25782    189063       68.75
11       25512    214575       78.03
12       21753    236328       85.94
13       16919    253247       92.09
14       12085    265332       96.48
15       7251     272583       99.12
16       2417     275000       100
-----------------------------------------
```

1.13 PROJECT INVESTMENT DECISIONS

Many industrial and business projects require the expenditure of capital at the beginning, with the prospect of producing income (or revenue) for several years to come. Sometimes the initial expenditure is a single payment, as in the purchase of a machine tool or a delivery van. In other cases, such as the Channel Tunnel, it can be spread over several years. Once a decision is made to go ahead with a project of this kind it cannot be reversed – at least, not without incurring considerable losses.

One criterion for making investment decisions is the *payback method*. This is a long-established technique and is still widely used. It is calculated as

$$\text{Payback period} = \frac{\text{Investment}}{\text{Annual return}}$$

The payback period is therefore a measure of how many years it takes for the project to 'break even'. Projects with short payback periods are obviously attractive to most entrepreneurs, but there are other considerations. The payback method takes no account of earnings after the original investment has been recovered nor of the resale values of plant and equipment. The financial risk associated with the project should also be taken into account. A long payback period may be acceptable if the project is likely to remain successful for many years.

An alternative to the payback method is the *accounting rate of return*. This is defined as

$$\text{Accounting rate of return} = \frac{\text{Annual profit}}{\text{Capital investment}}$$

and is usually expressed as a percentage. The definition is not precise because the profit may be reckoned before or after tax is paid, and may or may not allow for depreciation. The profit is usually calculated as an annual average. The accounting rate of return should not be confused with the internal rate of return (see section 2.17).

The accounting rate of return method is superficially attractive because it suggests a direct comparison with the cost of borrowing money, or the return on investment, but this is not realistic. Cash received at some future date must be 'discounted' to allow for the time value of money; this is the subject of Chapter 2.

Example 1.5
The owner of a rural service station proposes to install a car wash at an outright cost of £30 000.

(a) What is the expected payback period, assuming a net income of £0.50 per car with an average of 200 cars per week throughout?
(b) If, in the event, the annual profits for the first 5 years are £7000, £5000, £4000, £6000 and £5000, what is the average accounting rate of return?

Solution
Since there are 52 weeks in the year,

(a)   Annual return $= 52 \times 200 \times 0.50 = £5200$
              Payback period = investment/annual return
                             $= 30\,000/5200 = \textbf{5.77 years}$

(b) Using the figures given in the question,

$$\text{Average annual profit} = \frac{7000 + 5000 + 4000 + 6000 + 5000}{5}$$

$$= £5400$$

and accounting rate of return is

Annual profit/capital investment $= 5400/30\,000$
$$= \textbf{0.18} \text{ or } \textbf{18 per cent}$$

1.14 REPLACEMENT ANALYSIS

Suppose an organization has a permanent need for an item of equipment, such as a vehicle or machine tool, that wears out over a period of several years. In the first year or two, depreciation is likely to be high but maintenance costs should be low. Towards the end of its useful life, the rate of depreciation may be slow but heavy repair bills can arise. A full analysis must take account of inflation and the time value of money (Ch. 2), but an indication of the optimum replacement interval is given by averaging the net costs on an annual basis.

In contrast, some components (such as light bulbs) fail suddenly. At home we usually wait until failure occurs before replacing them. In a hospital or factory, however, it may prove cheaper to replace them on a routine basis before they reach the age when failures are expected. Decisions in these circumstances will depend on considerations of probability (see Ch. 6).

Example 1.6

It is anticipated that, in a machine shop, there is a permanent requirement for a particular machine tool, whose capital cost is £20 000. The following table shows the estimated maintenance costs and resale values for the first 8 years of its life:

Year	1	2	3	4	5	6	7	8
Maintenance (£)	600	800	1000	2000	3500	5000	7000	9000
Resale value (£)	15 000	11 000	8000	7000	6000	5000	4000	3000

At what intervals should the tool be replaced, ignoring the effects of inflation and the time value of money?

Solution

Table 1.4 shows the costs for life periods of 1–8 years. Column ② shows the depreciation, found by subtracting the resale values from the original capital cost of £20 000. The yearly maintenance costs are given in column ③ and the cumulative total in column ④.

Table 1.4 Replacement analysis for machine tool (values in £)

Year	① Value	② Depreciation	③ Yearly maintenance	④ Cumulative maintenance	⑤ Life cost	⑥ Annual equivalent
0	20 000	—	—	—	—	—
1	15 000	5 000	600	600	5 600	5600
2	11 000	9 000	800	1 400	10 400	5200
3	8 000	12 000	1000	2 400	14 400	4800
4	7 000	13 000	2000	4 400	17 400	4350
5	6 000	14 000	3500	7 900	21 900	4380
6	5 000	15 000	5000	12 900	27 900	4650
7	4 000	16 000	7000	19 900	35 900	5129
8	3 000	17 000	9000	28 900	45 900	5737

Column ⑤ shows the life costs, obtained by adding the values in columns ② and ④. The average annual costs are obtained by dividing the values in ⑤ by the numbers of years, and the results are shown in ⑥. They are the annual costs of operating the tool on a permanent basis, subject to the constraints and approximations mentioned in the question.

It can be seen that the minimum annual cost (£4350) is obtained by replacing the tool **every 4 years**. In practice other considerations, such as the advent of an improved model, may influence the decision.

1.15 SUMMARY

Operational research is concerned with optimization in the field of management – finding the best course of action among all the possible options. Generally there are constraints, such as limitations on the time and money available, and these define a region that contains the feasible solutions. The optimal solution is then the one that leads to the best value of the specified objective.

Modelling is an essential part of OR work. The characteristics of the system under consideration are represented by mathematical relationships in the form of equations, graphs, networks or tables of values, and this model is used to predict the outcome of selected strategies. The approximations inherent in the model and the limitations on the data must always be taken into account.

Operational research assists, but does not replace, the manager who remains responsible for identifying the constraints and resources, setting the objectives and implementing the chosen course of action.

REFERENCES

1. Eddison R T, Pennycuick K, Rivett B H P 1962 *Operational Research* English Universities Press
2. British Standard BS 1957: 1953 *Presentation of Numerical Values*
3. Stewart I 1990 *Does God Play Dice?* Penguin
4. Fellows R, Langford D, Newcombe R, Urry S 1983 *Construction Management in Practice* Longman Scientific and Technical Ch 5 (see 1990 reprint)
5. Fellows R, Langford D, Newcombe R, Urry S 1983 *Construction Management in Practice* Longman Scientific and Technical Ch 9 (see 1990 reprint)
6. Pilcher R 1973 *Appraisal and Control of Project Costs* McGraw-Hill pp 169–75, 248–51
7. Wearne S H (ed) 1974 *Control of Engineering Projects* Edward Arnold Ch 5

BIBLIOGRAPHY

Bronson R 1982 *Operations Research* Schaum's Outline Series, McGraw-Hill

Burley T A, O'Sullivan G 1986 *Work Out Operational Research* Macmillan

Cohen S S 1985 *Operational Research* Edward Arnold

Lucey T 1982 *Quantitative Techniques* 2nd edn D P Publications

Makower M S, Williamson E 1985 *Operational Research* 4th edn, Teach Yourself Books, English Universities Press

Mole R H 1987 *BASIC Business Analysis and Operations Research* Butterworths

Moore P G 1976 *Basic Operational Research* 2nd edn Pitman

Palmer C, Innes A E 1980 *Operational Research by Example* Macmillan

Singh J 1971 *Operations Research* Penguin

Stainton R S 1977 *Operational Research and its Management Applications* Macdonald and Evans

Thierauf R J, Klekamp R C 1975 *Decision Making through Operations Research* 2nd edn Wiley

Whitaker D 1984 *OR on the Micro* Wiley

White D J 1985 *Operational Research* Wiley

Wicks C T, Yewdall G A 1971 *Operational Research* Pan Piper

PROBLEMS

1. The Tardy Timepiece Company is planning the production of its new quartz analogue watch for the Christmas market. It will be available in two versions – the Apollo for men and the Daphne for women. The company estimates that it could sell a maximum of 8000 Apollos and 6000 Daphnes. In the time available, however, it can only manufacture a combined total of 10 000 watches. Show these constraints on a diagram similar to Fig. 1.1, the axes representing the numbers of Apollos and Daphnes. Mark the feasible region.

Show that each of the following production schedules satisfies the marketing and manufacturing constraints and find the corresponding total profits, the profit margin being £2.00 on each Apollo and £3.00 on each Daphne.

(a) 5000 Apollos, 5000 Daphnes;
(b) 7000 Apollos, 2500 Daphnes;
(c) 8000 Apollos, 1500 Daphnes.

How many of each should be manufactured for maximum total profit and what is the corresponding profit?
Answer (a) £25 000; (b) £21 500; (c) £20 500. 4000 Apollos and 6000 Daphnes; £26 000.

2. A planning problem involving two quantities x and y is subject to the following constraints:

(a) x must not exceed 8;
(b) y must not exceed $2x$;
(c) $x(y - 1)$ must not exceed 18;
(d) x and y are both positive.

Draw axes for x and y on squared paper, taking the range 0 to 10 for each variable. Add the constraint lines and mark the feasible region. State whether the following solutions are feasible:
 (i) $x = 6$, $y = 4$;
 (ii) $x = 4$, $y = 6$;
 (iii) $x = 7$, $y = 3.6$;
 (iv) $x = 5.6$; $y = 4.2$.
What is the greatest feasible value of $(x + 2y)$?
Answer (i) yes; (ii) no; (iii) no; (iv) yes. 16.3 (when $x = 3.26$ and $y = 6.52$).

3. A telephone customer pays a standing charge of £14.00 per quarter plus 5 p (£0.05) per unit. Draw a graph showing how the total quarterly bill varies for the range 0–1000 units. What is the average cost per unit (reckoned as total cost/number of units) if the quarterly usage is (a) 100 units, (b) 500 units, (c) 1000 units?
Answer (a) £0.19; (b) £0.078; (c) £0.064.

4. A householder compares the costs of (town) gas and electricity. Gas is supplied at a cost of 0.4 p (£0.004) for each megajoule (MJ) of energy, together with a standing charge of £10.00. For electricity the figures are 1.4 p (£0.014) and £7.00. Draw graphs on the same axes showing the total quarterly bills for the two fuels, for energy consumptions in the range 0–5000 MJ.

Heating costs must take account of the thermal efficiencies of the appliances used. Suppose the efficiency of gas appliances is taken as 50 per cent; on this basis the cost of gas per useful MJ is 0.8 p (£0.008). Add a graph to your diagram to show the total quarterly gas bill for a useful energy range of 0–5000 MJ. Under what circumstances is gas then the cheaper fuel?
Answer   Gas is cheaper if the (useful) energy requirement exceeds 500 MJ per quarter.

5.   Suppose, in the previous question, the householder already uses electricity for cooking, lighting and power, and is considering which fuel to use for heating. It is reasonable to omit the electricity standing charge from the calculations, since this has already been accepted for lighting and power. Draw a graph on the same axes as before to show the electricity costs, ignoring the standing charge. Under what circumstances is gas now the cheaper fuel?
Answer   Gas is cheaper if the quarterly (useful) energy requirement exceeds 1667 MJ.

6.   A heating contractor quotes £1300 for the installation of a gas central heating system and £700.00 for an equivalent electrical system. The annual running costs are estimated to be £300.00 and £420.00 respectively. Show, by means of graphs, how the total expenditure (installation plus running costs) varies with the life of the system, in the range 0–10 years. On the basis of total cash paid, when does the gas system prove cheaper?
Answer   After 5 years.

7.   A computer software company carries out market research to predict the sales of its new game 'Zapper'. It finds that sales of 70 a week can be expected if the price is set at £8.00, but only 50 a week if the price is £10.00. The manufacturing cost is £5.00 per game plus overheads of £120.00 per week. Assuming a linear sales/price relationship, find:

(a) the maximum revenue;
(b) the range of sales for which Zapper is profitable;
(c) the maximum profit.

Find also the cost and profit for various sales levels in the profitable range. What is the maximum percentage profit (defined as profit/revenue) and at what level of sales is this achieved? How does it compare with the percentage profit at (i) maximum profit and (ii) maximum revenue or turnover?
Answer   (a) £562.50; (b) 14–86; (c) £130.00; 27.3 per cent with sales of 41; (i) 26.0 per cent; (ii) 12.0 per cent.

8.   Midshire is investigating the costs of maintaining stocks of stationery at County Hall. If items are bought in large batches the holding costs (storage, insurance, etc.) are high, but few orders have to be placed and ordering costs are low. On the other hand, small batches reduce holding costs but necessitate frequent orders so that ordering costs become high. At present, headed notepaper is bought in batches of 400 reams and, at this level, the annual holding cost is £120.00 and the annual ordering cost is £270.00. It is assumed that the annual holding and ordering costs are proportional to, and inversely proportional to, the batch size respectively. What is the minimum total cost of stocking this item, and to what level should the batch size be changed? Use the method of section 1.8 or the results obtained in section 1.9.

Answer   £360.00; 1200 (see Ch. 8 for a more detailed treatment of stock control).

9.   The inverse costs model has parallels in other fields. The total drag of an aircraft is made up of the *form* drag, which is proportional to the square of the speed, and the *induced* drag, which is inversely proportional to the square of the speed. In a particular plane the form drag is 6250 N (newtons) and the induced drag is 2560 N when the speed is 200 knots. What is the minimum total drag for this aircraft, and at what speed does it occur?

Answer   8000 N; 160 knots.

10.   A machine tool costing £45 000 when new has a written-down value of £3000 after 8 years.

(a) What is the annual depreciation by the straight-line method?
(b) What is the annual percentage depreciation by the declining-balance method?

Find also the written-down value after 5 years by each method.

Answer   (a) £5250; (b) 28.72 per cent; £18 750; £8282.

11.   Find, for the declining-balance method, how many years it takes for the written-down value to become one-quarter of the original cost, if the annual depreciation is (a) 5 per cent, (b) 10 per cent, (c) 15 per cent, (d) 20 per cent.

For what annual depreciation does the value fall to one-half of the original cost in 5 years?

Answer   (a) 27; (b) 13.2; (c) 8.5; (d) 6.2; 12.94 per cent.

12.   The contract for the Port Bredy link road has been awarded at a price of £2 760 000 and the project is expected to take 19 months to complete. Use the computer program of Fig. 1.14 to predict, on the basis of the S-curve, the value of the work to be done in months 7 and 15.

What is the expected value of the work to be done in the first year of the contract?

Answer   £215 983; £154 820; £1 924 737.

13.   Use the S-curve computer program with 20 periods and any convenient total cost to estimate the percentage of that cost incurred up to each of the following stages of the project:

(a) 10 per cent of the total time;

(b) a quarter of the time;

(c) 95 per cent of the time.

Answer   (a) 2.25; (b) 14.06; (c) 99.44.

14.   A lamp manufacturer offers a fluorescent replacement for existing light bulbs, and claims that it gives as much light as an ordinary 100 W bulb, using only one-fifth the energy. Details of the two types are as follows:

	Ordinary Bulb	New Bulb
Energy consumption	100 W	20 W
Running time on 1 unit of electricity	10 hours	50 hours
Purchase price	£0.45	£13.50
Life	1000 hours	6000 hours

If the cost of electricity is £0.06 per unit and the lamps are switched on for 1000 hours a year, what is the payback period for investing in the new type?

Answer   About 2.5 years.

15.   Estimate the accounting rate of return for each of the following projects:

(a) a toll bridge, costing £24 million, with an expected traffic flow of 12 000 vehicles a day, each yielding £0.60 net;

(b) a new 60-bedroom hotel, costing £1 800 000, with an expected occupancy rate of 75 per cent and a profit margin of £14.00 per day for each occupied room;

(c) a 300-seat airliner, costing £20 million, making an average of two flights a day each 85 per cent full, with a net profit of £18.00 per passenger.

Answer   (a) 10.95 per cent; (b) 12.78 per cent; (c) 16.75 per cent.

16.   A transport manager keeps records of the maintenance costs of a particular type of van. The annual costs for the first 6 years are found to be £500, £500, £2000, £3500, £5000 and £6000 respectively. The cost of the van when new is £16 000 and depreciation is reckoned at 40 per cent annually. If there is a permanent need for this type of vehicle, when should it be replaced? Use the declining-balance method of depreciation and ignore inflation and the time value of money.

Answer   After 4 years.

2   THE TIME VALUE OF MONEY

'A dollar today is worth more than a dollar tomorrow.'

Wall Street epigram

2.1 PRESENT AND FUTURE VALUES

Borrowing and lending money is a familiar feature of everyday life. Bank loans, mortgages, credit cards and hire-purchase enable us to buy expensive items now and spread the cost over several months or years. We have to pay interest, of course, and the total amount repaid may be considerably more than the sum originally borrowed. Industry, too, relies on borrowed capital to finance many of its projects, and the rate of interest on the loan is often referred to as the cost of capital.

If we have cash to spare, we can deposit it in a bank, a building society or in National Savings where it will earn interest for us. The sum of money invested at the beginning is known as the *principal* and the corresponding sum available at the end is often called the *terminal value*. For positive interest rates the terminal value will always be greater than the principal. This means that a fixed bill in the future can be met by investing a smaller sum now, the amount depending on the interest rate and when the bill is to be paid.

Today's equivalent of a future payment is called its *present value* (or *present worth*). In business and industry, projects are often assessed by reducing future expenditure and income to their equivalent present values. This process is known as *discounting* and the method of accounting based on it is usually called *discounted cash flow*. The interest rate used in the calculations is given the name *discount rate*.

The applications of present value techniques range from personal borrowing, such as house mortgages, to the financing of major construction projects like the Channel Tunnel. The equations that relate the principal and the terminal value of a cash investment can also be used for finding the present value of a future payment.

2.2 SIMPLE AND COMPOUND INTEREST

Interest rates are usually expressed as percentages, written 'per annum' or p.a. Suppose I invest the sum of £500 at 8 per cent p.a. for 3 years. In the first year the interest will amount to 8 per cent of £500, which is £40. The outcome in later years depends on the terms of the investment. With simple interest the amount is always based on the original investment – £500 in the present case. If I leave the interest in the account I shall have £540 after 1 year, £580 after 2 years and £620 after 3 years as shown in Table 2.1.

Table 2.1 Simple and compound interest. All values in £

	Simple interest	Compound interest
Principal	500.00	500.00
First year's interest	40.00	$0.08 \times 500.00 =$ 40.00
Total after 1 year	540.00	540.00
Second year's interest	40.00	$0.08 \times 540.00 =$ 43.20
Total after 2 years	580.00	583.20
Third year's interest	40.00	$0.08 \times 583.20 =$ 46.66
Total after 3 years	620.00	629.86

With *compound interest* the amount to be added is based on the total investment (principal + interest) and the interest increases year by year. The details are shown in Table 2.1. The total interest over 3 years is £129.86 with compounding, compared with £120.00 by the simple interest method. Unless otherwise stated, compounding is assumed throughout this book.

2.3 COMPOUND INTEREST LAW

The type of compound interest calculation shown in Table 2.1 occurs so frequently that it is worth establishing a general formula. Although the interest rate is usually given as a percentage it is convenient to express it as a decimal so that 15 per cent, for example, is entered as 0.15 and 8.5 per cent as 0.085. On this basis let:

$$PV = \text{principal or present value;}$$
$$FV = \text{terminal or future value;}$$
$$i = \text{annual interest rate (expressed as a decimal).}$$
$$n = \text{number of years.}$$

The interest added at the end of the first year is therefore $PV \times i$, and we have:

$$\text{Total amount at the end of 1 year} = PV + PV \times i$$
$$= PV.(1 + i)$$

This result shows that the value at the end of the first year is $(1 + i)$ times that at the beginning. The factor $(1 + i)$ is the same for later years and the final value after n years is therefore:

$$FV = PV.(1 + i)(1 + i)(1 + i). . .n \text{ times}$$

or

$$FV = PV.(1 + i)^n$$

a formula known as the *compound interest law*.

The expression $(1 + i)^n$ is called the *compound amount factor* and is denoted in this book by F_1. Thus:

$$F_1 = (1 + i)^n \qquad [2.1]$$

where F_1 is the amount to which unit sum (£1 or $1) will grow. It is used to calculate the future equivalent of a given sum today. It can be evaluated using a scientific or financial calculator, or obtained from published tables.[1] The computer program given in section 2.8 will print such a table for any chosen interest rate. In most examples, n is the number of years, but the formula can be applied to other periods (such as half-years, quarters or months) if interest is added more frequently. The value of i must correspond to the period under consideration.

Example 2.1
The sum of £2000 is invested at 12 per cent p.a. for 5 years. Calculate the total amount in the account at the end of this period when interest is added under each of the following conditions:

(a) simple interest only;
(b) compound interest added annually;
(c) compound interest added half-yearly.

Solution
For interest at 12 per cent, $i = 12/100 = 0.12$.

(a) In this case the interest is based on the original sum of £2000 throughout. Working in £,

$$\begin{aligned}
\text{Interest for each year} &= 0.12 \times 2000 = 240 \\
\text{Total interest over 5 years} &= 5 \times 240 = 1200 \\
\text{Final value} &= 2000 + 1200 = \mathbf{£3200}
\end{aligned}$$

(b) In the notation given above, PV = 2000, $i = 0.12$ and $n = 5$. Using Eq. 2.1, or from tables, the compound amount factor is

$$F_1 = (1 + i)^n = (1 + 0.12)^5 = 1.7623$$

and

$$\begin{aligned}
FV = PV \times F_1 &= 2000 \times 1.7623 \\
&= \mathbf{£3525} \text{ (to the nearest £)}
\end{aligned}$$

(c) In this case, interest is added at the rate of 6 per cent every half-year, 10 times in all. Putting $i = 0.06$ and $n = 10$ in Eq. 2.1, the factor F_1 becomes 1.7908 and the final amount is

$$FV = 2000 \times 1.7908 = \mathbf{£3582} \text{ (again to the nearest £)}$$

The last answer shows that the growth in value of the investment is greater if interest is added every 6 months rather than annually. With interest added quarterly or monthly the increase would be greater still. The limiting case in which interest is added continuously is considered in section 2.19.

2.4 REPEATED PAYMENTS AND SINKING FUNDS

Some investments require a series of equal payments. Suppose an annual payment A is made n times. The first payment will gain interest for $n - 1$ years and, from the compound interest law, its final value, FV, will be $A(1 + i)^{n-1}$. For the second and third payments the corresponding final values will be $A(1 + i)^{n-2}$ and $A(1 + i)^{n-3}$. The nth payment will attract no interest and its FV is therefore A. The total FV is given by

$$\text{FV} = A(1 + i)^{n-1} + A(1 + i)^{n-2} + A(1 + i)^{n-3} + \ldots + A$$

This is a *geometric series* (or *progression*) and it is shown in Appendix A that its sum is given by

$$\text{FV} = A[(1 + i)^n - 1]/i$$

The value obtained by putting $A = 1$ is called the *uniform series compound amount factor*, denoted in this book by F_2. Thus

$$F_2 = [(1 + i)^n - 1]/i \qquad [2.2]$$

This result, like that for F_1, may be applied to monthly or quarterly periods provided the corresponding interest rate is used. The uniform series result has a number of practical applications. If a series of equal contributions is made to a savings scheme or a pension fund with a guaranteed rate of interest, the factor F_2 can be used to predict the total sum available at the end. The same considerations apply when money is set aside at regular intervals to finance the replacement of an asset at the end of its expected life. A fund set up for this purpose is called a *sinking fund*.

Values of F_2 can be calculated from Eq. 2.2 or read from tables.[1] The computer program introduced in section 2.8 includes a routine for generating such tables.

Example 2.2
What annual payment should be made into a sinking fund to finance the replacement of a factory at an estimated cost of £2 500 000 in 8 years time? Take interest at 7 per cent.

Solution
From Eq. 2.2 or tables, the uniform series compound amount factor for $i = 0.07$ and $n = 8$, is

$$F_2 = [(1 + i)^n - 1]/i = [(1 + 0.07)^8 - 1]/0.07 = 10.2598$$

The final value FV is £2 500 000 and therefore:

$$2\,500\,000 = A \times F_2$$

from which

$$A = 2\,500\,000/10.2598$$
$$= \textbf{£243 670}$$

2.5 PRESENT VALUE FACTOR

The compound interest law $FV = PV.(1 + i)^n$ can be rearranged to give the equivalent value today of expenditure in the future. It becomes

$$PV = \frac{FV}{(1 + i)^n}$$

If we put $PV = 1$ this result gives the present value of unit sum (£1 or $1) to be paid or received in the future. Denoting this factor by F_3,

$$F_3 = \frac{1}{(1 + i)^n} \qquad\qquad [2.3]$$

This is known as the *present value* (or present *worth*) *factor* and it is used to find today's equivalent of a single payment, made or received, in the future. It can be seen from Eqs 2.1 and 2.3 that $F_3 = 1/F_1$.

   Table C.1 gives values of this factor for interest rates between 1 and 20 per cent, and values of n up to 80.

2.6 PRESENT VALUE AND DECISION-MAKING

The concept of present value is widely used in choosing between different ways of carrying out a project. The present value of all expenditure, during the expected life of the project, is used as a basis for comparing competing schemes. A full analysis should take account of inflation and the possible resale or scrap value of equipment at the end of the project.

Example 2.3
A householder is looking at ways of producing domestic hot water and considers two possibilities – an electric immersion heater having an installation cost of £160 and estimated annual fuel bills of £200, and a gas boiler with an installation cost of £760 and annual fuel bills of £80.
   Compare the two systems on the basis of (a) total expenditure, and (b) present value, over a 5-year period. Take interest at 9 per cent.

Solution
(a) The outgoings consist of the installation (or capital) cost together with the fuel bills for 5 years. The total amounts are as follows:

   For the immersion heater, $160 + 5 \times 200 = $ **£1160**
   For the gas boiler, $760 + 5 \times 80 = $ **£1160**

   On this basis the total cash paid is the same for both systems and there is nothing to choose between them.
   (b) The present values of all the fuel bills are given in Table 2.2. The present value factors can be calculated using Eq. 2.3, or read from tables, and they are the same for both systems since they depend only on i and n. The PV amounts are rounded to the nearest £; in practice, there are so many uncertainties that greater accuracy is not justified.
   The present value of the installation cost equals the cost itself since it is incurred at the outset. Hence the present value of all the costs during the

5-year period becomes

For the immersion heater, 160 + 777 = **£937**

For the gas boiler, 760 + 311 = **£1071**

Table 2.2 Present
value of fuel bills. All
values to the nearest £

Year	PV factor F_3	Immersion heater ($200 p.a.)	Gas-fired boiler ($80 p.a.)
1	0.9174	183	73
2	0.8417	168	67
3	0.7722	154	62
4	0.7084	142	57
5	0.6499	130	52
		777	311

On the basis of present value, therefore, the immersion heater is cheaper over the 5-year period. The outcome may be different for other periods. For 7 or more years the gas-fired boiler has the smaller PV. In practice the choice may be influenced by other considerations including the cost and ease of maintenance, the inflation of fuel prices and existing energy use, such as cooking and space heating.

2.7 PRESENT VALUE FACTOR FOR REPEATED PAYMENTS

In the solution to the last problem, separate present value calculations were made for each of the annual payments. When the same payment is made for a number of years in succession the arithmetic can be simplified by using another factor F_4 that allows for multiple payments. If we apply Eq. 2.3 n times taking values of n from 1 to n itself, we obtain the following result:

$$F_4 = \frac{1}{(1 + i)^1} + \frac{1}{(1 + i)^2} + \frac{1}{(1 + i)^3} + \frac{1}{(1 + i)^4} \cdots$$

$$+ \frac{1}{(1 + i)^n}$$

This is another geometric series and it is shown in Appendix A that its sum may be written

$$F_4 = \frac{1}{i}\left[1 - \frac{1}{(1 + i)^n}\right] \qquad [2.4]$$

This is the *uniform series present value factor*. The total present value of all the payments is obtained by multiplying it by one of them. With the data of Example 2.3, $i = 0.09$ and $n = 5$, and Eq. 2.4 gives the following result:

$$F_4 = \frac{1}{0.09}\left[1 - \frac{1}{(1 + 0.09)^5}\right] = 3.8897$$

This result is confirmed by adding the five separate factors in Table 2.2. The sum of these factors is 3.8896, the difference in the last figure being due to rounding.

It is clear from Eqs 2.3 and 2.4 that the factors F_3 and F_4 are closely related, F_3 being equal to the second term within the curly brackets of F_4. Hence:

$$F_4 = (1 - F_3)/i \qquad [2.5]$$

It follows from Eq. 2.4 that the value of F_4 increases as n increases. The limiting value, as n tends towards infinity, is $1/i$. This is the present value factor for a series of equal payments continued for ever, or in perpetuity, as it is often known.

Values of F_4 are tabulated in Table C.2.

Example 2.4
A motorist buys a new car for £8000 and intends to keep it for 5 years. If the resale value at the end of that time is expected to be £3000 and the annual running costs (apart from depreciation) are £2000, what is the net present value of the life costs? Take interest at 8 per cent.

Solution
In the notation of section 2.3, $n = 5$ and $i = 0.08$. Hence, from Eq. 2.3 or by reference to tables, the present value factor for a single payment is

$$F_3 = \frac{1}{(1 + i)^n} = \frac{1}{(1 + 0.08)^5} = 0.6806$$

This factor applies to the resale value. From Eq. 2.4, or more easily from Eq. 2.5, the factor for repeated payments is

$$F_4 = (1 - 0.6806)/0.08 = 3.9927$$

This result is used to obtain the present value of the running costs. The present value of the purchase price equals that price, since it is incurred at the outset. Collecting results,

PV of purchase price		= £8 000
PV of resale value	= 0.6806 × 3000	= £2 042
PV of running costs	= 3.9927 × 2000	= £7 985
Net PV of life costs	= 8000 − 2042 + 7985	= **£13 943**

If this sum were placed in a bank or other account which paid 8 per cent interest on the investment (and charged the same rate on overdrafts), it would just be sufficient to meet the costs over the 5-year period. After the purchase price was paid the balance would be £5943. In the first year, 8 per cent interest would be added and £2000 would be withdrawn for running costs. In the later years, interest would be smaller but the running costs would be the same. In year 5 the account would be in deficit and the interest would increase the debt. The running costs in the last year would further increase the deficit to £3000 and this would be met by the cash received from the sale of the car. In practice, the calculation would be more complicated because the running costs would arise at frequent intervals and not at the end of each year.

2.8 COMPUTER PROGRAM FOR GENERATING TABLES OF TIME-VALUE FACTORS

The listing shown in Fig. 2.1 is the first part of a comprehensive program for performing time-value calculations. You are recommended to test and save it before adding the remaining sections. When complete, the program will generate tables of time-value factors, and carry out individual calculations for single and repeated payments.

The notation is given in lines 10–30, and lines 40–140 print the heading and the main menu. Lines 150–170 direct the program to the required option. The first option is the only one that can be used with the present listing, but the other two lines are included in preparation for the later stages.

Figure 2.1

```
10 REM    P,F     PRESENT, FUTURE VALUES
20 REM    I,N     INTEREST RATE, NUMBER OF PERIODS
30 REM    A       AMOUNT PER PERIOD
40 PRINT "----------------------------------------"
50 PRINT "TIME VALUE OF MONEY"
60 PRINT "----------------------------------------"
70 PRINT:PRINT "OPTIONS:"
80 PRINT "TABLE OF FACTORS...............1"
90 PRINT "SINGLE PAYMENT CALCULATION.....2"
100 PRINT "REPEATED PAYMENT CALCULATION...3"
110 PRINT
120 INPUT "INPUT CHOICE BY NUMBER ",C
130 IF C<>1 AND C<>2 AND C<>3 THEN GOTO 110
140 PRINT
150 IF C=1 THEN GOSUB 300
160 IF C=2 THEN GOSUB 600
170 IF C=3 THEN GOSUB 900
200 REM    CLOSING STATEMENT
210 PRINT
220 INPUT "ANOTHER CALCULATION (Y/N)",Q$
230 IF Q$="Y" OR Q$="y" THEN GOTO 70
240 PRINT "----------------------------------------"
250 END
300 REM    TABLE OF FACTORS
310 PRINT "ENTER PERCENTAGE RATE, NUMBER OF PERIODS"
320 INPUT I,M
330 PRINT:PRINT "TABLE OF FV AND PV FACTORS FOR ";I;"%"
340 I=I/100
350 PRINT
360 PRINT "NO.OF FV OF 1   FV OF     PV OF 1    PV OF"
370 PRINT "PERI-           1 PER                1 PER"
380 PRINT "ODS             PERIOD               PERIOD"
390 D=5
400 FOR N=1 TO M
410 IF D>4 THEN PRINT:D=0
420 GOSUB 2000
430 X=F1:GOSUB 2100:F1=X
440 X=F2:GOSUB 2100:F2=X
450 X=F3:GOSUB 2100:F3=X
460 X=F4:GOSUB 2100:F4=X
470 PRINT TAB(1);N;TAB(6);F1;TAB(15);F2;TAB(24);F3;TAB(33);F4
480 D=D+1
490 NEXT N
500 RETURN
2000 REM    FACTORS
2010 F1=(1+I)^N
2020 F2=(F1-1)/I
2030 F3=1/F1
2040 F4=(1-F3)/I
2050 RETURN
2100 REM    ROUNDING CALCULATION
2110 IF X>1000 THEN X=INT(X+0.5):GOTO 2150
2120 IF X>100 THEN X=INT(100*X+0.5)/100:GOTO 2150
2130 IF X>10 THEN X=INT(1000*X+0.5)/1000:GOTO 2150
2140 X=INT(10000*X+0.5)/10000
2150 RETURN
```

Lines 200–250 offer the choice of a further calculation or of quitting.

Lines 300–500 form the subroutine for generating the table of factors. The percentage interest rate and maximum number of periods are called for in lines 310–320, the interest rate being converted to a decimal in line 340. Lines 330 and 360–380 print the table heading. The values are calculated and rounded with two further subroutines and printed at line 470. The format is designed for a 40-column display; if your computer is limited to 32 columns, you should make some abbreviations in the table heading, and reductions in the TAB values of line 470.

Lines 390, 410 and 480 improve the legibility of the table by ensuring a gap between each block of five lines.

Lines 2000–2050 form the subroutine for calculating the four factors, and each result is rounded by means of the subroutine given in lines 2100–2150. Values below 10 are shown to four decimal places, those between 10 and 100 to three places, and those between 100 and 1000 to two. Values above 1000 are displayed as integers (whole numbers).

Figure 2.2

```
----------------------------------------
TIME VALUE OF MONEY
----------------------------------------

OPTIONS:
TABLE OF FACTORS...............1
SINGLE PAYMENT CALCULATION.....2
REPEATED PAYMENT CALCULATION...3

INPUT CHOICE BY NUMBER ?1

ENTER PERCENTAGE RATE, NUMBER OF PERIODS
?12.25
?10

TABLE OF FV AND PV FACTORS FOR 12.25%

NO.OF FV OF 1  FV OF     PV OF 1  PV OF
PERI-          1 PER              1 PER
ODS            PERIOD             PERIOD

  1   1.1225   1         0.8909   0.8909
  2   1.26     2.1225    0.7936   1.6845
  3   1.4144   3.3825    0.707    2.3916
  4   1.5876   4.7969    0.6299   3.0214
  5   1.7821   6.3845    0.5611   3.5826

  6   2.0004   8.1666    0.4999   4.0825
  7   2.2455   10.167    0.4453   4.5278
  8   2.5205   12.412    0.3967   4.9245
  9   2.8293   14.933    0.3534   5.278
 10   3.1759   17.762    0.3149   5.5929

ANOTHER CALCULATION (Y/N)?N
----------------------------------------
```

Figure 2.2 shows the printout obtained by running the program with an interest rate of 12.25 per cent, and a maximum of 10 periods. Try other interest rates and numbers of periods, and check the results against published tables or individual answers found with a calculator. When you are satisfied that the program is working correctly, SAVE it to disc or cassette.

2.9 COMPUTER PROGRAM FOR SINGLE PAYMENT CALCULATIONS

If three of the four quantities PV, FV, i and n are given, the fourth can be calculated, using the compound interest law. When i and n are known the relationships $FV = PV \times F_1$ and $PV = FV \times F_3$ are used. Rearranging the compound interest law, section 2.3, we obtain

$$(1 + i)^n = \frac{FV}{PV} \tag{2.6}$$

Taking logs of both sides,

$$n.\log(1 + i) = \log(FV/PV) \quad \text{or} \quad n = \frac{\log(FV/PV)}{\log(1 + i)}$$

In the computer program FV and PV are denoted by F and P, and n and i are replaced by upper case (capital) letters. Since the interest rate is entered as a percentage i is replaced by I/100. Some computers do not recognize LOG and require LN instead. With these changes the last result becomes

$$N=LN(F/P)/LN(1+I/100)$$

If the interest rate is the unknown quantity Eq. 2.6 is rearranged to make i the subject. Taking the $1/n$th power of each side,

$$1 + i = \left(\frac{FV}{PV}\right)^{1/n} \quad \text{or} \quad i = \left(\frac{FV}{PV}\right)^{1/n} - 1$$

or, in computer notation,

$$I=(F/P)^{\wedge}(1/N)-1$$

The last result gives I as a decimal and it is multiplied by 100 to give the interest rate as a percentage.

Figure 2.3

```
600 REM    SINGLE PAYMENT CALCULATION
610 PRINT "ENTER THE FOLLOWING QUANTITIES IN THE"
620 PRINT "ORDER GIVEN (USE -99 FOR THE UNKNOWN)"
630 PRINT "PV,FV,PER CENT INTEREST,NO. OF PERIODS"
640 INPUT P,F,I,N
650 IF P<>-99 AND F<>-99 AND P>=F THEN PRINT "ERROR! PV MUST BE LESS THAN FV
GOTO 630
660 IF I=-99 THEN I=(F/P)^(1/N)-1:GOSUB 1500:GOTO 710
670 IF N=-99 THEN N=LN(F/P)/LN(1+I/100):GOSUB 1400:GOTO 710
680 I=I/100:GOSUB 2000
690 IF P=-99 THEN P=F3*F:GOSUB 1600:GOTO 710
700 IF F=-99 THEN F=F1*P:GOSUB 1700
710 RETURN

1400 REM    N RESULT
1410 PRINT "NUMBER OF PERIODS = ";INT(10*N+0.5)/10
1420 RETURN
1500 REM    I RESULT
1510 PRINT "INTEREST RATE = ";INT(10000*I+0.5)/100;" PER CENT"
1520 RETURN
1600 REM    PV RESULT
1610 X=P:GOSUB 2100
1620 PRINT "PRESENT VALUE (PV) = ";X
1630 RETURN
1700 REM    FV RESULT
1710 X=F:GOSUB 2100
1720 PRINT "FUTURE VALUE (FV) = ";X
1730 RETURN
```

The listing given in Fig. 2.3 incorporates these results and it should be added to the previous one (Fig. 2.1). See Appendix B for details of program merging.

Lines 600–640 call for the values of three of the four quantities PV, FV, i and n. When running the program, use the wild value -99 to indicate the unknown quantity. Line 650 halts the program if PV is given a greater value than FV.

Line 660 determines the value of i, if it is the unknown quantity, and calls up a subroutine to print the result. Line 670 carries out similar processes when n is the unknown.

If i and n are both specified, lines 660–670 are bypassed. Line 680 then converts the interest rate from a percentage to a decimal and uses the subroutine at line 2000 to compute the four factors.

Line 690 calculates the value of PV, if it is the unknown, and uses a subroutine to print the result. Line 700 carries out the corresponding steps for FV. In all cases the subroutine ends at line 710 and the program returns to the closing section at line 200 in the earlier listing.

The subroutines 1400–1420, 1500–1520, 1600–1630 and 1700–1730 print the results for n, i, PV and FV respectively. The number of periods n is shown to one place of decimals and the percentage interest rate to two places. The values of PV and FV are rounded by the subroutine at lines 2100–2150 before being displayed.

Figure 2.4

```
----------------------------------------
TIME VALUE OF MONEY
----------------------------------------

OPTIONS:
TABLE OF FACTORS...............1
SINGLE PAYMENT CALCULATION.....2
REPEATED PAYMENT CALCULATION...3

INPUT CHOICE BY NUMBER ?2

ENTER THE FOLLOWING QUANTITIES IN THE
ORDER GIVEN (USE -99 FOR THE UNKNOWN)
PV,FV,PER CENT INTEREST,NO. OF PERIODS
?4000
?20000
?-99
?25
INTEREST RATE = 6.65 PER CENT

ANOTHER CALCULATION (Y/N)?N
----------------------------------------
```

The printout in Fig. 2.4 was obtained when the program was run to find the interest rate required for a lump sum investment of £4000 to grow to £20 000 in 25 years.

If the program is used to find the number of periods, the answer will not normally be a whole number. In practice, the exact time at which a loan or investment ends will depend on the detailed terms of the contract.

As before, it is advisable to check and save the program before continuing with the final section.

2.10 COMPUTER PROGRAM FOR REPEATED PAYMENT CALCULATIONS

The program is completed by adding the lines needed for repeated payment calculations. These are given in Fig. 2.5. If the amount per period A, the interest rate i and the number of periods n are all given, the program will compute both PV and FV. If PV or FV is given, together with two of the three quantities A, i and n, the program will calculate the third. Some of the results are obtained directly from the factors F_2 and F_4, but the determination of n and i require new results or methods. Using the result $PV = F_4 \times A$ and Eq. 2.4 the number of periods can be expressed in terms of PV, A and i by the following formula (shown in conventional and computer notation):

$$n = \frac{\log[1/(1 - i \times PV/A)]}{\log(1 + i)}$$

and

$$N=LN(1/(1-I*P/A))/LN(1+I)$$

Common or natural logarithms may be used but the interest rate must first be converted from a percentage to a decimal. This is allowed for in the computer listing. The corresponding result with FV instead of PV takes the forms:

$$n = \frac{\log(1 + i \times FV/A)}{\log(1 + i)}$$

and

$$N=LN(1 + I*F/A)/LN(1+I)$$

It is not possible to transform Eqs 2.2 and 2.4 to make i the subject and the program uses a searching technique. This is explained in the description that follows.

Lines 900–940 ask whether one or neither of the quantities PV and FV is given. If either is given the program jumps at line 950 to 1040. Otherwise lines 970–980 call for the values of A, n and i. These are used in line 990 to determine the four factors, by means of the subroutine in lines 2000–2050. The values of PV and FV are computed in line 1000 from the factors F_4 and F_2, the results being rounded and displayed in lines 1010–1020, using the subroutines in the earlier listings. At line 1030 the program jumps to 1390 and returns to the main program.

Lines 1040–1070 establish which of the three quantities A, n and i is the unknown and the values of the other two. If A is unknown, line 1080 obtains the values of the factors from the usual subroutine. If FV is also unknown the program jumps from line 1090 to 1250.

Lines 1100–1120 perform the calculations when PV is given. If A is unknown, its value is calculated and displayed by line 1130, using the appropriate subroutines, and the program returns to the closing section via line 1390. If n is the unknown quantity, a check is made in line 1140 and the program halts if A is too small. Otherwise the value of n is calculated and displayed in line 1150, and the program returns to the closing section.

Lines 1160–1230 determine the interest rate using a trial-and-error method. It consists of setting a range of values within which the answer must lie, testing the midpoint of this range and then taking the upper or lower

Figure 2.5

```
900 REM    REPEATED PAYMENT CALCULATIONS
910 PRINT "WHICH OF THESE IS GIVEN?"
920 INPUT "PV,FV,NEITHER (P/F/N)  ",R$
930 PRINT
940 IF R$<>"P" AND R$<>"F" AND R$<>"N" THEN GOTO 920
950 IF R$<>"N" THEN GOTO 1040
970 PRINT "ENTER AMOUNT PER PERIOD, NUMBER OF"
980 INPUT "PERIODS,PERCENTAGE INTEREST",A,N,I
990 I=I/100:GOSUB 2000:PRINT
1000 P=A*F4:F=A*F2
1010 X=P:GOSUB 2100:GOSUB 1600
1020 X=F:GOSUB 2100:GOSUB 1700
1030 GOTO 1390
1040 REM    INPUT TWO OF A,N,I
1050 PRINT "ENTER AMOUNT PER PERIOD,"
1060 PRINT "NUMBER OF PERIODS, PERCENTAGE"
1070 INPUT "INTEREST (-99 FOR UNKNOWN)  ",A,N,I
1080 IF A=-99 THEN I=I/100:GOSUB 2000
1090 IF R$="F" THEN GOTO 1250
1100 REM    CALCULATIONS GIVEN P AND TWO OF A,N,I
1110 INPUT "PRESENT VALUE (PV)  ",P
1120 PRINT
1130 IF A=-99 THEN A=P/F4:GOSUB 1800:GOTO 1390
1140 IF N=-99 AND P>(100*A/I) THEN PRINT "ERROR! AMOUNT TO SMALL TO ACHIEVE PV"
:GOTO 1040
1150 IF N=-99 THEN I=I/100:N=LN(1/(1-I*P/A))/LN(1+I):GOSUB 1400:GOTO 1390
1160 REM    ITERATION FOR I, GIVEN P,A,N
1170 L=0:U=A/P
1180 I=(L+U)/2:GOSUB 2000
1190 IF ABS(F4-P/A)<(0.0001*F4) THEN GOTO 1220
1200 IF F4<P/A THEN U=(L+U)/2:GOTO 1180
1210 L=(L+U)/2:GOTO 1180
1220 GOSUB 1500
1230 GOTO 1390
1250 REM    CALCULATIONS GIVEN F AND TWO OF A,N,I
1260 INPUT "FUTURE VALUE (FV) ",F
1270 PRINT
1280 IF A=-99 THEN A=F/F2:GOSUB 1800:GOTO 1390
1290 IF N=-99 AND F<A THEN PRINT "ERROR! AMOUNT IS GREATER THAN FV":GOTO 1040
1300 IF N=-99 THEN I=I/100:N=LN(1+I*F/A)/LN(1+I):GOSUB 1400:GOTO 1390
1310 REM    ITERATION FOR I GIVEN F,A,N
1320 L=0:U=10
1330 I=(L+U)/2:GOSUB 2000
1340 IF ABS(F2-F/A)<(0.0001*F2) THEN GOTO 1370
1350 IF F2<F/A THEN L=(L+U)/2:GOTO 1330
1360 U=(L+U)/2:GOTO 1330
1370 GOSUB 1500
1390 RETURN

1800 REM    AMOUNT PER PERIOD RESULT
1810 X=A:GOSUB 2100
1820 PRINT "AMOUNT PER PERIOD = ";X
1830 RETURN
```

half of the range depending on whether the midpoint is found to be too low or too high. The process is repeated until the relevant factor (F_4 in the present case) is sufficiently close to the required value. In line 1170 the lower and upper limits (L and U) are set at 0 and A/PV respectively. The interest rate cannot exceed the latter value, which corresponds to an infinite number of periods. Line 1180 obtains the factors for the midpoint of this range and line 1190 compares F_4 with the required value. If the difference is sufficiently small, the program jumps to line 1220, the result is printed and the program returns to the closing section. If not, line 1200 checks whether the current value of F_4 is too low; if so, the interest rate is too high, the lower half of the range is selected, and the process is repeated. Otherwise, line 1210 selects the upper half of the range. The program cycles until the condition in line 1190 is met and the answer is displayed.

Lines 1250–1390 carry out all the calculations described above, but with the present value PV replaced by the final or future value FV. In the interest rate calculation, line 1320 sets the initial upper limit at 10 (i.e. 1000 per cent). This will cover all realistic examples, but data leading to a higher value would cause the computer to loop endlessly in the search for an answer.

Lines 1800–1830 round and display answers for the amount per period.

Figure 2.6

```
-----------------------------------------
TIME VALUE OF MONEY
-----------------------------------------

OPTIONS:
TABLE OF FACTORS...............1
SINGLE PAYMENT CALCULATION.....2
REPEATED PAYMENT CALCULATION...3

INPUT CHOICE BY NUMBER ?3

WHICH OF THESE IS GIVEN?
PV,FV,NEITHER (P/F/N)  ?F

ENTER AMOUNT PER PERIOD,
NUMBER OF PERIODS, PERCENTAGE
INTEREST (-99 FOR UNKNOWN)  ?15000
?8
?-99
FUTURE VALUE (FV) ?200000

INTEREST RATE = 14.21 PER CENT

ANOTHER CALCULATION (Y/N)?N
-----------------------------------------
```

Figure 2.6 shows the printout obtained when the program was run to determine the interest rate required if equal payments of £15 000 are to meet a £200 000 bill after eight periods.

After checking, the complete program should be saved for future use. It will be of use in nearly all time-value examples involving single or equal repeated payments. The remaining sections of this chapter are concerned with applications of the time-value concept.

2.11 MORTGAGE REPAYMENTS

A mortgage is a loan used to buy property and granted on the security of that property. It is usually repaid by equal monthly instalments that cover both interest and principal. This is known as a repayment mortgage. In the early years the interest on the outstanding debt accounts for a large proportion of the repayments, but the interest decreases as the debt is reduced. Towards the end of the mortgage term a large part of the payments is devoted to reducing the debt.

Mortgage contracts of this kind are an example of present value and the equivalent uniform series amount. These two quantities are related by the factor F_4. The figures quoted by building societies, banks and mortgage companies may differ slightly from the values obtained from this factor because of variations in the way interest is added. A more detailed treatment[2] is needed to cope with interest changes during the life of the mortgage.

An alternative to the repayment mortgage is the endowment mortgage, offered by some insurance companies. Under this arrangement, a life policy is taken out with an assured sum equal to the loan. The borrower pays interest on the loan, together with the insurance premiums, but the debt is not reduced during the life of the policy. The mortgage is redeemed when the policy matures, using the money paid out under the terms of the policy. Repayments are usually higher with an endowment mortgage, but it does provide insurance cover and there may be tax benefits.

Example 2.5

A house-buyer takes a £40000 repayment mortgage at 11 per cent over 20 years. What are the monthly repayments, and the total cash repaid during the mortgage term? What would be the repayment period if the interest rate were changed to (a) 10 per cent, (b) 12 per cent, (c) 13 per cent, the repayments being unaltered?

Solution

From Eq. 2.4 or tables, the appropriate factor, with $i = 0.11$ and $n = 20$, is

$$F_4 = 7.9633$$

With this figure the annual repayment becomes

$$A = \text{PV}/F_4 = 40\,000/7.9633 = \textbf{£5023}$$

which is equivalent to approximately £419 per month. The result can also be obtained by using the repeated payments option in the computer program given in the previous sections.

The total cash repaid during the mortgage term is $5023 \times 20 = £100\,460$, a considerable increase on the sum originally borrowed. However, the rise in property values has generally outstripped such increases in recent decades, to the benefit of the borrower. In addition, a proportion of the repayments may qualify for tax relief.

In the second part of the question, the present value and annual payment are unaltered so that the factor remains at 7.9633. It is therefore necessary to find the value of n corresponding to this figure, with the new interest rates.

(a) With an interest rate of 10 per cent, the tables show that the factor 7.9633 corresponds to a value of n between 16 and 17. Using the computer program with PV = 40000, $A = 5023$ and 10 per cent interest, the number of periods is found to be **16.7**.

(b) The corresponding result for 12 per cent interest is just under 28 from tables, and **27.5** using the computer program. In this example, therefore, a reduction of 1 per cent in the interest rate reduces the term by a little over 3 years, but an increase of the same amount adds nearly 8 years.

(c) An examination of the tables shows that, with interest at 13 per cent, the factor never reaches the required value. If the computer program is used with this interest rate, an error message appears. The explanation is that, at the 13 per cent rate, the interest in the first year amounts to $0.13 \times 40\,000 = £5200$ and this is greater than the repayment for the year. The debt therefore increases year by year. In practice the mortgagee may accept the arrangement, at least in the short term, because the value of the property may be increasing faster than the debt. Furthermore, most borrowers move house before the mortgage term is completed, redeeming the existing mortgage and starting another in the process.

2.12 ANNUITIES

An annuity is simply a series of equal annual payments. However, the term is commonly used for the payments made by an insurance company to a retired person for the rest of his or her life, in return for a lump sum at the beginning of the contract. In practice the payments are usually paid monthly, in order to provide a steady income.

This is another example of a uniform series equivalent to a capital sum. The sums involved depend on the expectation of life of the person concerned, and the interest rate used in the calculations.

Example 2.6
A retired man is offered an annuity, equivalent to £110 a month, in return for a lump sum payment of £10000. What is the corresponding expectation of life on this basis, taking interest at 6 per cent p.a.? What monthly payment could a woman expect in return for the same lump sum if her life expectancy is 14 years?

Solution
The annual income from the annuity is $A = 110 \times 12 = £1320$ and the present value PV is £10000. Hence the uniform series present value factor is

$$F_4 = \text{PV}/A = 10\,000/1320 = 7.5758$$

From tables the corresponding number of periods, with 6 per cent interest, is between 10 and 11. The value obtained with the computer program is **10.4**.

The increased expectation of life in the case of the woman leads to a smaller monthly income. With $n = 14$ and $i = 0.06$ the value of F_4 is 9.295 and the income is $10\,000/9.295 = $ **£1076** annually or approximately £90 per month.

2.13 REPLACEMENT ANALYSIS WITH DISCOUNTED CASH FLOW

The problem of finding the best time for the replacement of equipment was introduced in section 1.15. No allowance was made for the time value of money and, in Example 1.6, comparisons were made on the basis of the average annual cash expenditure.

To allow for the cost of capital, each item of expenditure is replaced by its present value and the net life totals are replaced by their annual equivalents.

Example 2.7

Repeat Example 1.6 allowing for the time value of money. Take the cost of capital as 9 per cent.

Solution

Table 2.3 Replacement analysis. All values to the nearest £ (PV = present value)

The various costs and their present value equivalents are shown in Table 2.3, cash sums being rounded to the nearest £.

① Year	② PV factor single payment	③ PV factor repeated payment	④ Cash spent	⑤ PV of cash spent ② × ④	⑥ Cumulative PV of cash spent	⑦ Resale value	⑧ PV of resale value ② × ⑦	⑨ Net life PV ⑥ − ⑧	⑩ Equiv. sum p.a. ⑨ ÷ ③
0	1	—	20 000	20 000	20 000	—	—	—	—
1	0.9174	0.917	600	550	20 550	15 000	13 761	6 789	7 403
2	0.8417	1.759	800	673	21 223	11 000	9 259	11 964	6 802
3	0.7722	2.531	1 000	772	21 995	8 000	6 178	15 817	6 249
4	0.7084	3.240	2 000	1 417	23 412	7 000	4 959	18 453	5 695
5	0.6499	3.890	3 500	2 275	25 687	6 000	3 899	21 788	5 601
6	0.5963	4.486	5 000	2 981	28 668	5 000	2 982	25 686	5 726
7	0.5470	5.033	7 000	3 829	32 497	4 000	2 188	30 309	6 022
8	0.5019	5.535	9 000	4 517	37 014	3 000	1 506	35 508	6 415

The present value factors for single and repeated payments, F_3 and F_4, are given in columns ② and ③. Note that $F_3 = 1$ at year 0. Column ④ shows the cash payments and column ⑤ the corresponding present values, obtained by multiplying the quantities in columns ② and ④. The cumulative total of these amounts is shown in column ⑤.

The resale values are shown in column ⑦, and their present values, obtained by multiplying them by the factors in column ②, are given in column ⑧. The net life present values are obtained by subtracting the values in column ⑧ from those in column ⑥, and are displayed in column ⑨.

Finally, these net life values are divided by the factors in column ③ to give the equivalent annual amounts, column ⑩. The values in this column are the annual payments that would cover the costs in perpetuity, for the various replacement intervals.

The results show that the minimum equivalent annual cost (£5601) is obtained with replacement every **5 years**. This differs from the answer (4 years) obtained in Example 1.6 when the cost of capital was ignored.

2.14 COMPUTER SPREADSHEET FOR REPLACEMENT ANALYSIS

A spreadsheet is a chart containing rows and columns of rectangular slots in which the results of calculations can be displayed. The value in one slot may be related to the values in others by a formula and a change in one item may therefore affect several others. In a computer spreadsheet these recalculations are carried out automatically for the whole chart. This is particularly useful in replacement analysis where, for example, a change in the cost of capital affects every other value.

Spreadsheets are available for most computers and on some machines they are built in or 'bundled'. Some can accommodate hundreds of rows and columns but the present application requires fewer than 20. The details vary from one spreadsheet to another but most have the following properties:

1. Rows are numbered (1, 2, 3 . . .), columns are lettered (A, B, C . . .) and slots are known by their column and row references. Slot D5 is therefore in the fourth column and the fifth row.
2. A slot may contain a label, a numerical value or a formula.
3. A formula may be specified in terms of other slots. If D5 contains the formula B5 + C5, for example, the contents of B5 and C5 will be added and displayed in D5.
4. It is often necessary to use related formulae in a whole column or row of slots, a process known as *replication*. Suppose D5 is to contain the formula B5 + C5, D6 is to be B6 + C6 and so on. With most spreadsheets there is a procedure whereby the first formula can be automatically adapted to the other slots.
5. Calculation is normally carried out from left to right starting with the first row. The value in a particular slot may therefore be affected by a calculation that comes later. To allow for this the computer repeats the process until no further changes are detected.
6. The labels and formulae for a particular application can be SAVEd to disc or tape and, for new examples, only the numerical values have to be entered.

Most spreadsheets offer additional features. The calculations for a whole sheet may take several seconds and this can be frustrating if the computer recalculates every time a value is entered; some programs therefore offer the possibility of suspending calculations until all the data are entered. With some spreadsheets, there is a choice of brackets or minus signs for negative values, and it is usually possible to specify the number of decimal places in the results. Some are also capable of displaying results in the form of bar charts, pie charts or graphs.

Table 2.4 gives a set of labels and formulae for a replacement analysis spreadsheet. It offers the following possibilities:

1. Expenditure can be in the form of individual payments and/or repeated annual amounts, with or without an annual percentage increase.
2. Depreciation can be specified as individual amounts or an annual percentage, using the declining-balance method.

It is convenient to use the columns for the years, rather than the rows. The year numbers are shown in slots B1, C1, D1 . . ., starting with year 0. A maximum of 20 years will be sufficient for all the examples in this book. The slots in column A contain labels identifying the data and results. Abbreviate these if the slot width is limited. To improve the screen display, rows 9 and 12 are left empty, as are rows 2 and 5 (apart from the labels in the first column).

The formulae for columns B, C, D and E are given in the appropriate slots. Those for F and other columns are obtained by replication. To extend the analysis to 20 years replicate from column F to V. Slots that are left blank are automatically set at zero by the computer. For this reason, B8

Table 2.4 Computer spreadsheet for replacement analysis

	A	B	C	D	E	F
1		YEAR 0	YEAR 1	YEAR 2	YEAR 3	YEAR 4
2	EXPENDITURE					
3	—INDIVIDUAL PAYMENTS					
4	—REPEATED PAYMENTS %/1ST YR			C4*(1+B4/100)	D4*(1+B4/100)	replicate
5	DEPRECIATION					
6	—INDIVIDUAL AMOUNTS					
7	—DECLINING %		B3*(1−B7/100)	C7*(1−B7/100)	D7*(1−B7/100)	replicate
8	COST OF CAPITAL %	1	B8/100	B8/100	B8/100	replicate
9						
10	PV FACTOR (SINGLE PAYMENT)	1	B10/(1+C8)	C10/(1+D8)	D10/(1+E8)	replicate
11	PV FACTOR (REPEATED PAYMENT)		(1−C10)/C8	(1−D10)/D8	(1−E10)/E8	replicate
12						
13	PV OF CURRENT YEAR'S COSTS	B3	C10*(C3+C4)	D10*(D3+D4)	E10*(E3+E4)	replicate
14	PV OF ALL COSTS TO DATE	B3	B14+C13	C14+D13	D14+E13	replicate
15	DEPRECIATION TO DATE		B15+C6	C15+D6	D15+E6	replicate
16	RESALE VALUE		C7−C15	D7−D15	E7−E15	replicate
17	PV OF RESALE VALUE		C10*C16	D10*D16	E10*E16	replicate
18	NET PV OF LIFE PAYMENTS		C14−C17	D14−D17	E14−E17	replicate
19	EQUIVALENT ANNUAL COST		C18/C11	D18/D11	E18/E11	replicate

must be given a non-zero value, say 1; otherwise division by zero will occur in row 11. When the spreadsheet is used to analyse a particular example, entering the appropriate cost of capital will override this value.

To use the spreadsheet, first enter the capital cost in B3, and other specified payments in C3 onwards. For repeated payments enter the annual percentage increase in B4 (zero if the amounts are constant) and the value for the first year in C4.

Depreciation details are entered in rows 6 and 7. If individual amounts are specified, these are entered in C6, D6, E6 . . . . If, instead, an annual percentage depreciation is given, this is entered in B7. Finally the cost of capital, also as a percentage, is entered in B8.

When run, the sheet will display the intermediate answers in rows 13–17. Row 18 gives the net present value of the life payments for the various replacement intervals, and line 19 the corresponding annual equivalent costs.

Example 2.8

A delivery van costs £15 000 when new and it is estimated that running costs will be £3000 in the first year, rising by 15 per cent annually thereafter. If there is a permanent need for a vehicle of this type, at what intervals should it be replaced? Take depreciation at 30 per cent p.a. and the cost of capital at 12 per cent.

Investigate the effects of changes in the rate of depreciation and the cost of capital.

Figure 2.7

```
.........................................A ......B......C
......1                                   YEAR 0  YEAR 1
......2 EXPENDITURE
......3 --INDIVIDUAL PAYMENTS             15000
......4 --REPEATED PAYMENTS %/1ST YR         15    3000
......5 DEPRECIATION
......6 --INDIVIDUAL AMOUNTS
......7 --DECLINING %                        30
......8 COST OF CAPITAL %                    12
```

Solution

With the spreadsheet layout given in Table 2.4, the capital cost (15 000) is entered in B3. The annual percentage increase in running costs (15) is entered in B4 and the first year amount (3000) in C4. The annual percentage depreciation (30) and percentage cost of capital (12) are placed in B7 and B8 respectively. The top left-hand corner of the spreadsheet, with these values entered, is shown in Fig. 2.7.

Figure 2.8 shows the results up to year 8. In this example the sheet has been set to round money values to the nearest whole number and the PV factors in lines 10 and 11 to four places of decimals. The minimum value in row 19 is found to be 7611 and this corresponds to year 6, although the result is almost the same for year 7.

The power of the spreadsheet becomes apparent in the second part of the question. A change in the rate of depreciation or the cost of capital is made by altering the contents of a single slot. Reducing the rate of depreciation from 30 to 20 per cent changes the optimum replacement period to 5 years. Increasing it to 40 per cent leads to an optimum interval of 7 years.

The result is not highly sensitive to changes in the cost of capital. With

Figure 2.8

	A	B YEAR 0	C YEAR 1	D YEAR 2	E YEAR 3	F YEAR 4	G YEAR 5	H YEAR 6	I YEAR 7	J YEAR 8
1										
2	EXPENDITURE									
3	--INDIVIDUAL PAYMENTS	15000								
4	--REPEATED PAYMENTS %/1ST YR	15	3000	3450	3967	4563	5247	6034	6939	7980
5	DEPRECIATION									
6	--INDIVIDUAL AMOUNTS									
7	--DECLINING %	30	10500	7350	5145	3601	2521	1765	1235	865
8	COST OF CAPITAL %	12	0	0	0	0	0	0	0	0
9										
10	PV FACTOR (SINGLE PAYMENT)	1.0000	0.8929	0.7972	0.7118	0.6355	0.5674	0.5066	0.4523	0.4039
11	PV FACTOR (REPEATED PAYMENT)		0.8929	1.6901	2.4018	3.0373	3.6048	4.1114	4.5638	4.9676
12										
13	PV OF CURRENT YEAR'S COSTS	15000	2679	2750	2824	2900	2977	3057	3139	3223
14	PV OF ALL COSTS TO DATE	15000	17679	20429	23253	26153	29130	32187	35326	38549
15	DEPRECIATION TO DATE		0	0	0	0	0	0	0	0
16	RESALE VALUE		10500	7350	5145	3601	2521	1765	1235	865
17	PV OF RESALE VALUE		9375	5859	3662	2289	1431	894	559	349
18	NET PV OF LIFE PAYMENTS		8304	14570	19591	23864	27699	31293	34767	38200
19	EQUIVALENT ANNUAL COST		9300	8621	8157	7857	7684	7611	7618	7690

Note: In this example rows 10 and 11 have been formatted to display four places of decimals. All other values are rounded to the nearest whole number. As a result the value 0.12 stored in slots C8, D8 . . . . . . J8 is shown as 0 interest reduced to 9 per cent the optimum interval is still 6 years; at 15 per cent it is increased to 7 years.

2.15 HIRE-PURCHASE

Under most hire-purchase agreements all the interest is added at the beginning of the contract. It is usually calculated by applying the quoted rate to the total sum borrowed for each year of the agreement. For example, with a 3-year agreement and interest at 9 per cent, a charge of 27 per cent is added at the outset. The total debt is then repaid in equal monthly instalments, 36 in this case.

This method of calculating interest leads to higher charges than would be the case with a bank loan at the same rate. In many instances the effective rate (known as the annual percentage rate, APR) is almost twice the nominal hire-purchase rate.

Example 2.9
A motorist buys a new car costing £6400 on hire purchase over 3 years, using his existing vehicle as a deposit of £2500. Interest is charged at the rate of 8 per cent and the agreement calls for 36 equal instalments, commencing 1 month from the date of purchase. Find:

(a) the amount of each instalment;
(b) the effective annual interest rate.

Solution
(a) After allowing for the deposit, the sum borrowed is $6400 - 2500 = £3900$ to which is added a total of 24 per cent interest.

$$
\begin{aligned}
\text{Total interest} &= 3900 \times (24/100) = \text{£}936 \\
\text{Total sum to be repaid} &= 3900 + 936 &= \text{£}4836 \\
\text{Monthly instalment} &= 4836/36 &= \textbf{£134.33}
\end{aligned}
$$

(b) The true compound interest rate is that which gives a present value of £3900 for a series of 36 payments, each of £134.33. Using the computer program, these values lead to a rate of 1.21 per cent per month. The corresponding value per annum is found by compounding this rate 12 times. Putting $n = 12$ and $i = 0.0121$ in Eq. 2.1 the factor for 1 year is

$$F_1 = (1 + 0.0121)^{12} = 1.1553$$

This corresponds to the annual factor $(1 + i)$ where i is the annual rate, and the true interest rate is therefore 0.1553 or **15.53 per cent** p.a. Since the monthly rate is rounded to two decimal places by the computer program, this result is slightly inaccurate. If the computer program is adjusted to give four decimal places, the monthly rate becomes 1.2126 per cent and the corresponding annual rate is 15.56 per cent.

2.16 INFLATION

So far in this chapter no allowance has been made for the increases in future prices due to inflation. The effect of such price rises is to reduce the purchasing power of an investment. Suppose a sum of money is invested at an interest rate i (decimal not percentage) and the inflation rate is r (also a decimal). In each period the monetary value of the investment increases by the factor $1 + i$, but the purchasing power is reduced by the factor $1 + r$. At the end of each period, therefore, the effective value of the investment is $(1 + i)/(1 + r)$ times that at the beginning. This is equal to $(1 + i')$ where i' is the effective interest rate (again expressed as a decimal). Hence:

$$1 + i' = \frac{1 + i}{1 + r}$$

and

$$i' = \frac{1 + i}{1 + r} - 1 = \frac{1 + i - (1 + r)}{1 + r} = \frac{i - r}{1 + r}$$

If r is small compared to 1 this result is approximately $i - r$, but the error increases with increasing r. With interest at 6 per cent ($i = 0.06$) and inflation at 2 per cent ($r = 0.02$) the effective interest rate is approximately 4 per cent ($i' = 0.04$) and, more accurately using the above result, 3.92 per cent. With interest and inflation at 20 and 16 per cent respectively, the approximate result is still 4 per cent, but the more accurate value is 3.45 per cent.

Since inflation rates cannot be predicted accurately, the approximate result ($i - r$) is commonly used.

2.17 NET PRESENT VALUE AND INTERNAL RATE OF RETURN

Two traditional investment criteria — the payback period and the accounting rate of return — were introduced in section 1.14. Neither allows for the time value of money and they have been largely replaced by other measures of financial performance.

One is the net present value (NPV) in which all the payments associated with a project are converted to their present value equivalents. Income is treated as positive and expenditure as negative. If the NPV of all the payments is positive, the project may be acceptable. Net present value alone, however, does not give a measure of the relative profitability of different projects. A large project could have the same NPV as a small one, but might require a much greater capital investment. One way of meeting this objection is to express the NPV as a percentage of the present value of the cash outflow. This is often called the *profitability index* and projects with low values are likely to be looked at with caution.

An alternative is the internal rate of return (IRR). This is defined as the discount rate at which the NPV is zero. If the IRR is greater than the cost of capital the outgoings are covered and, in this sense, the project is acceptable.

The IRR is a relative index and therefore useful in comparing projects of different sizes. There are complications, however. There may not be a unique value of the IRR. A project can have several values, or none at all. A detailed treatment of NPV and IRR can be found in specialist texts such as those by Mole[2] and Ayres.[3]

In general, it is necessary to take each cash payment separately when calculating NPV and IRR. An exception is the case where all the capital expenditure occurs at the beginning and income is in the form of a series of equal payments. Under these conditions the NPV and IRR values can be found using the methods given earlier in this chapter.

Example 2.10

A property developer estimates that the construction of a new shopping precinct will have a capital cost of £5.1 million and will produce a net income of £1.1 million a year for the next 10 years. Find:

(a) the net present value of the project taking the cost of capital as 12 per cent;
(b) the profitability index;
(c) the internal rate of return.

Solution

(a) The present value of the income can be found using the uniform series present value factor F_4. From Eq. 2.4, with $i = 0.12$ and $n = 10$, or from tables, its value is 5.650. Hence the present value of the income is given by

$$PV = A \times F_4 = 1\,100\,000 \times 5.65 = £6\,215\,000$$

This result can also be obtained directly using the computer program given earlier. The present value of the expenditure is taken as the capital cost itself since this is incurred at the beginning. In practice, building will take several months and there will be no income during construction. This should be taken into account when assessing the present values. On the basis of instant availability, however,

$$NPV = 6\,215\,000 - 5\,100\,000 = \textbf{£1\,115\,000}$$

(b) Relating this result to the present value of the capital expenditure, we have:

$$\text{Profitability index} = \frac{NPV}{PV \text{ of cash outflow}} = \frac{1\,115\,000}{5\,100\,000}$$

$$= 0.2186 \text{ or } \textbf{21.86 per cent}$$

(c) For the NPV to be zero, the present value of the income will just equal that of the outflow — the capital expenditure in the present case. From the relationship $PV = A \times F_4$, the corresponding value of the uniform series present value factor is

$$F_4 = \frac{PV}{A} = \frac{5\,100\,000}{1\,100\,000} = 4.6364$$

Table C.2 shows that, with $n = 10$, the discount or interest rate that gives this value is approximately 17 per cent. Running the computer program with

PV = 5 100 000, A = 1 100 000 and n = 10, gives the value of i as 17.13 per cent. Thus the IRR is **17.13 per cent**.

2.18 FINANCIAL BONDS AND COUPONS

A bond is effectively a receipt for a fixed-term loan that pays specified sums of money to the lender at regular intervals. These sums are quoted as percentages and were originally paid in exchange for coupons cut from the bond document. The percentage is therefore known as the coupon rate, or simply the coupon. Some bonds repay their face value at the end; others have no value at the end and the principal or face value is said to be amortized. Bonds are called short-term if they mature in less than 5 years, medium-term if between 6 and 15 years.

Suppose a 5-year bond has a face value of £1000 and pays a coupon of 6 per cent on a semi-annual basis with no amortization of principal. The lender will receive 6 per cent of £1000, i.e. £60, every half-year, 10 times in all. Note that the final payment includes the return of the principal, and is therefore £1060. Altogether the lender receives £1600 during the life of the bond.

The initial present value of all the money received can be found by adding the values for the regular payments and for the return of the principal. Suppose these are calculated using a discount rate equal to the coupon, i.e. 6 per cent for 10 periods. From Table C.1 the single payment present value factor is 0.5584 and the present value of the £1000 received at the end is therefore £558.40. The corresponding factor for the uniform series (10 equal payments of £60 at 6 per cent) is 7.360 and the present value of all the coupon payments is therefore 7.360 × £60 = £441.60. The total present value is therefore 558.40 + 441.60 = £1000, exactly the same as the principal or face value. This is always the case if the discount rate equals the coupon, a result that can be proved from Eq. 2.5. Suppose V is the face value and i the coupon per period. Each coupon payment is then iV and the present value of the series is $F_4 \times iV$. The present value of the terminal repayment V is $F_3 \times V$ and, using Eq. 2.5, we have:

$$\begin{aligned}
\text{Present value} &= F_4 \times iV + F_3 \times V \\
&= [(1 - F_3)/i] \times iV + F_3 \times V \\
&= V
\end{aligned}$$

If the interest rate used for discounting differs from the coupon, the purchase price will not be equal to the face value of the bond.

Example 2.11
A 4-year bond, with a face value of £1000 and no amortization, pays a coupon of 11 per cent half-yearly. What is its selling price if the yield (or discount rate) is taken to be

(a) 10 per cent;
(b) 12 per cent?

Solution

The payments to the lender are £110 for each of eight periods, and £1000 at the end. Their present values can be obtained using the computer program or from the factors F_3 and F_4. These can be taken from Tables C.1 and C.2 or calculated from Eqs 2.3 and 2.4.

(a) With interest at 10 per cent, the factors are $F_3 = 0.4665$ and $F_4 = 5.3349$. Hence the appropriate selling price, given by the total present value, is

$$PV = 0.4665 \times 1000 + 5.3349 \times 110 = \textbf{£1053.34}$$

(b) For 12 per cent, the factors are $F_3 = 0.4039$ and $F_4 = 4.9676$, and the selling price becomes

$$PV = 0.4039 \times 1000 + 4.9676 \times 110 = \textbf{£950.34}$$

These answers show that, with a discount rate or yield below the coupon, a bond should sell above its face value, i.e. at a premium. Conversely, a discount rate above the coupon should reduce the selling price below the face value.

The reverse problem of finding the discount rate corresponding to a given selling price requires a trial-and-error solution. A computer program for this purpose can be written using a successive halving technique similar to that in the listing given in Fig. 2.5.

2.19 CONTINUOUS COMPOUNDING

In the solution to Example 2.1 it was shown that 6 per cent interest compounded every half-year resulted in a higher terminal value than 12 per cent once a year. Compounding at 1 per cent each month leads to a higher value still. With a scientific or financial calculator you can quickly see the effect of compounding more frequently.

Suppose an investment yields a fixed rate of 9 per cent p.a. for four years. With $i = 0.09$ and $n = 4$ the compound amount factor, Eq. 2.1, is

$$F_1 = (1 + i)^n = (1 + 0.09)^4 = 1.4116$$

With interest added every month the interest rate per period is 0.75 per cent and there are 48 periods in all. Thus $i = 0.0075$ and $n = 48$, giving the value:

$$F_1 = (1 + 0.0075)^{48} = 1.4314$$

Try the effect of adding interest daily, taking 365 days in a year. The value of i is now 0.09/365 and the number of periods $n = 4 \times 365$. With these values the factor becomes 1.4333 to four decimal places.

It is shown in Appendix A that with interest added continuously at the rate of i per period the factor for n periods is given by the exponential function:

$$F_1 = e^{in}$$

where e is the number 2.718 . . ., the base of natural logarithms.

To obtain the other factors, F_2, F_3 and F_4, it is only necessary to replace the term $(1 + i)^n$ by e^{in} each time it occurs. Note that the factors F_2 and F_4 now apply to a continuous flow of cash rather than a series of equal payments. If a table of values is needed it is only necessary to change line 2010 in the computer program to the following:

2010 F1=EXP(I*N)

This is sufficient for option 1, but further amendments are necessary if the program is required to perform all the possible calculations for continuous compounding within options 2 and 3.

Example 2.12

A shop is rented on a 7-year lease and the expected profit on sales is £12 000 a year. What are the present and final values of this profit if it is treated as a continuous inflow of cash and the discount rate is taken as 11 per cent p.a., compounded continuously?

Solution

Replacing $(1 + i)^n$ by e^{in} in Eq. 2.4, and with $i = 0.11$ and $n = 7$, the present value factor is

$$F_4 = \frac{1}{i}\left(1 - \frac{1}{e^{in}}\right) = \frac{1}{0.11}\left(1 - \frac{1}{e^{0.11 \times 7}}\right) = 4.882$$

Hence the present value = $4.882 \times 12\,000 =$ **£58 580**.

With the same modifications and values in Eq. 2.2 the final value factor is

$$F_2 = [e^{in} - 1]/i = [e^{0.11 \times 7} - 1]/0.11 = 10.543$$

and the final value is $10.543 \times 12\,000 =$ **£126 520**.

The second result can also be obtained from the first, using the relationship:

$$FV = PV \times F_1 = PV \times e^{in} = 58\,580 \times e^{0.11 \times 7} = £126\,520$$

2.20 SUMMARY

The interest paid on a cash investment means that a sum of money today is worth more than the same sum in the future. Conversely, a payment to be made or received at a later date has a lower equivalent now. The compound amount, and uniform series compound amount, factors can be used to find the future (or terminal) values of single and repeated payments.

The reverse process of finding the present value of future cash flows is known as discounting and is widely used in project decision-making. With two or more competing schemes, the NPV provides a rational basis for comparison. In replacement analysis, the NPV of the life costs of an item of equipment is determined for various replacement intervals. By finding the equivalent annual values, the most economical life can be determined.

Several criteria are used for investment analysis. The payback period, and accounting rate of return, methods ignore the time value of money, and are of limited value. The NPV method produces a result that is not related to the size of the project in terms of expenditure. The profitability index, defined as the ratio of the NPV to the PV of the expenditure, provides a more rational basis. The internal rate of return, defined as the discount rate at which the NPV is zero, enables a comparison to be made with prevailing interest rates.

The present value of a uniform series of payments in the future is the basis of calculations on repayment mortgages and annuities. The use of a computer or financial calculator greatly speeds the calculations, particularly the determination of interest rate for a given uniform series.

To allow for inflation, at least approximately, interest is reduced by the rate of inflation. As with other techniques of operational research, the usefulness of the results is limited by the accuracy of the data, and interest rates can change considerably during the period under consideration.

REFERENCES

1. Fellows R, Langford D, Newcombe R, Urry S 1983 *Construction Management in Practice* Longman Scientific and Technical Appendix C pp 326–36 (see reprint 1990)
2. Mole R H 1985 *Basic Investment Appraisal* Butterworths pp 53–62
3. Ayres F *Mathematics of Finance* Schaum's Outline Series, McGraw-Hill

BIBLIOGRAPHY

Merrett A J, Sykes A 1973 *The Finance and Analysis of Capital Projects* 2nd edn Longman
Pilcher R, 1973 *Appraisal and Control of Project Costs* McGraw-Hill

PROBLEMS

1. An investor deposits £5000 in an account that pays 8 per cent interest per annum. If the money is left in the account for 4 years, what will be the final value assuming:

(a) simple interest;
(b) compound interest added once a year;
(c) compound interest added half-yearly;
(d) compound interest added quarterly?

Answer (a) £6600; (b) £6802; (c) £6843; (d) £6864.

2. A building society offers annual interest to savers of 9 per cent, compounded half-yearly. What is the equivalent annual compound rate?
Answer 9.20 per cent.

3. A self-employed computer consultant pays £150 a month into a pension fund. If interest is added annually at the rate of 7 per cent, what total sum will be available after 25 years?
Answer £113 848.

4. A bus operator expects to replace each vehicle (costing £80 000) every 5 years. What annual payment should be made to a sinking fund to meet this cost if interest is taken at 11 per cent?
Answer   £12 846.

5. A government savings bond is sold for £500 with the guarantee that it will be worth £700 after 5 years. What is the equivalent annual rate of interest?
Answer   6.96 per cent.

6. What is the present worth of:

(a) a single payment of £8000 made after 6 years;
(b) payments of £5000, £10 000 and £15 000 made after 4, 7 and 11 years respectively;
(c) an annual payment of £3000 for the next 12 years?

Take interest at 9 per cent.
Answer   (a) £4770; (b) £14 825; (c) £21 482.

7. To save money on fuel, a householder considers spending £4000 on double glazing, loft insulation and cavity wall filling. What annual reduction in fuel bills would justify this expenditure over (a) 10 years, (b) 15 years, with interest taken at 7 per cent?
Answer   (a) £570; (b) £440.

8. A motorist is offered a new car on hire-purchase, the terms being £2000 deposit and 36 monthly payments of £190. The cash price is £6750. What is the rate of interest per month and the effective rate per annum?
Answer   2.12 per cent; 28.63 per cent.

9. A transport manager considers two types of van (petrol and diesel) for a team of service engineers. The petrol van costs £12 000 and has an estimated annual running cost of £2500. For the diesel van the figures are £14 000 and £2000. It is expected that each van will have a useful life of 8 years, after which it can be sold for 15 per cent of the original cost. What is the net present worth of the life costs for each type? Take interest at 12 per cent.
Answer   Petrol, £23 692; diesel £23 087.

10. The purchasers of a starter home are offered a £40 000 repayment mortgage with interest at 11 per cent. What would be the monthly repayment and the total sum repaid if the mortgage term were (a) 20 years, (b) 30 years, (c) 40 years.
Answer   (a) £419, £100 460; (b) £383, £138 030; (c) £372, £178 760.

11. A householder has a mortgage with 17 years to run. The outstanding debt is £50 000 and the current rate of interest is 11 per cent. If the interest rate is increased to 12 per cent find:

(a) the increase in the monthly repayment needed to complete the mortgage in the same period (17 years),

(b) the extension of the period that keeps the monthly repayment at its present amount.

Answer   (a) £33.27; (b) 3.9 years.

12.   Two types of boiler are considered for a factory heating installation. The system is due to be replaced in 10 years' time. Type A has a capital cost of £25 000 and an estimated fuel cost of £1000 per annum. For B the figures are £22 000 and £1100.

Depreciation for both types is 25 per cent per annum of the value at the beginning of the year. The maintenance costs for A and B in the first year are estimated to be £600 and £800 respectively, both figures increasing at the rate of 10 per cent per annum thereafter.

On the basis of this information, and taking the cost of capital as 15 per cent, which type should be selected?

Answer   Type B (net NPV = £32 956 against £33 977 for A).

13.   On reaching retirement a man is offered an annuity of £4000 for a capital payment of £30 000. If interest is reckoned at 7 per cent, what life expectancy does this represent?

Answer   11 years.

14.   An insurance company offers a woman an annual pension of £3000 in return for a sum of £60 000 to be paid from the sale of her house when she dies. If the pension is calculated on a life expectancy of 15 years, what rate of interest does it represent?

Answer   3.98 per cent.

15.   A building contractor has a permanent need for an earth-moving machine, having a capital cost of £24 000. The annual fuel cost is £2000 and the maintenance charge is estimated at £1000 in the first year, rising at the rate of 25 per cent annually thereafter.

If the capital cost is written off over 8 years on a straight-line basis and the cost of capital is reckoned at 16 per cent, at what intervals should the machine be replaced and what is the corresponding annual equivalent cost? Consider periods up to 12 years.

Answer   Within the 8-year period the optimum replacement period is 6 years, the corresponding equivalent annual cost being £9551. There can be no further depreciation after year 8 and, if the analysis is extended to 12 years, the optimum period is found to be 10 years, with a corresponding annual cost of £9520.

16.   A heavy engineering company analyses the records of maintenance costs and depreciation of its machine tools. It finds that for a machine with a capital cost P the maintenance cost in year t of its life can be expressed as:

$$0.025P(3 + 1.5^t)$$

and the resale value at the end of year t is given by

$$P e^{-0.25t}$$

The cost of capital to the company is assessed at 10 per cent.

Determine the optimum replacement time for the machine tools, considering periods up to 8 years.

Hint. Take a convenient value of P, such as £10 000. The expression for maintenance cost is equivalent to a fixed annual amount together with a sum that increases at the rate of 50 per cent annually. The formula for the resale value corresponds to a constant percentage depreciation.

Answer Every 4 or 5 years. The equivalent annual sum is about $0.3837P$ in both cases.

17. A car dealer offers hire-purchase on the basis of 20 per cent deposit and 36 equal monthly instalments, calculated at an annual flat rate of 11 per cent. If a motorist buys a car costing £9000 on these terms, what are the monthly instalments, and the true monthly and annual rates of interest?
Answer £266, 1.63 and 21.42 per cent.

18. A retailer offers 'low interest' hire-purchase at the flat rate of 2 per cent p.a. with 24 equal monthly instalments. If the cost of capital is 9 per cent what cash discount does this offer represent?
Answer 4.81 per cent.

19. A company is offered a 5-year maintenance contract on a new computer system with a choice of terms:

(i) a monthly payment of £48, guaranteed for the whole period;
(ii) a single payment of £2500 at the beginning.

Which is better if the cost of capital is assumed to be 10 per cent per annum throughout and inflation is taken as (a) 6 per cent, (b) 2 per cent?
Answer (a) (ii) is better; (b) (i) is better.

20. The contract price for a new toll bridge is £4.8 million and the expected annual revenue is £830 000. Calculate:

(a) the payback period;
(b) the accounting rate of return.

Find also, on the basis of a 10-year period,

(c) the NPV taking the cost of capital as 10 per cent;
(d) the corresponding profitability index;
(e) the IRR.

Answer (a) 5.78 years; (b) 17.29 per cent; (c) £300 400; (d) 6.26 per cent; (e) 11.43 per cent.

21. The following questions refer to a bond with a face value of £1000, repaid in full at the end of the term.

(a) If the term is 4 years and the coupon rate is 7 per cent payable every 6 months, what is the total present value of all the coupon payments and the present value of the bond itself at the end? Take the discount rate as equal to the coupon rate.
(b) Repeat (a) for the same coupon but a discount rate of 6 per cent (per 6 months).

(c) What should be the selling price of a 5-year bond with a coupon of 8 per cent payable every 6 months if the discount rate is 9 per cent?

(d) If a 3-year bond with a 6-monthly coupon rate of 7 per cent sells for £1040, what is the effective discount rate? (Use a trial-and-error method.)

Answer   (a) £418, £582; (b) £435, £627; (c) £936; (d) 6.18 per cent.

3 CRITICAL PATH ANALYSIS

'There must be a beginning of any great matter, but the continuing until the end until it be thoroughly finished yields the true glory.'
Sir Francis Drake *Dispatch to Sir Francis Walsingham, 17 May 1587*

3.1 THE MANAGEMENT OF TIME

Chapters 1 and 2 were concerned with money and the financing of projects. In this chapter we consider project time. Time and money are often closely related and delay in completing an undertaking can prove costly. Techniques for planning and controlling the progress of projects are therefore of considerable interest. One group of techniques has proved particularly useful and they are known by names such as *critical path analysis*, *network analysis* and *critical path method*. Their success with major projects in the 1960s, such as the construction of the London Underground Victoria Line,[1] has led to their widespread use as a management tool. One particular technique, known as programme evaluation and review technique (PERT), incorporates a statistical analysis of the time estimates (see section 3.12).

Experience alone will often enable us to predict the total time needed to carry through a project of a familiar type, but a detailed analysis is required whenever the nature or size of the work is novel. The general approach is to break the project down into separate jobs, or activities as they are usually called, and to estimate the duration of each. The total time needed to complete all the tasks is normally less than the sum of these durations because there will be periods when two or more activities can proceed in parallel.

3.2 ACTIVITY ANALYSIS

In a major undertaking, such as the Channel Tunnel, many thousands of separate jobs can be identified but the principles can be illustrated by everyday examples with just a few. Consider the following story:

Example 3.1
Jenny and Paul have decided to change their car. In order to give themselves the widest possible choice of model and colour, they intend to buy a brand new vehicle. Furthermore, they believe it will pay them to sell their existing car privately through an advertisement in a local paper, and seek a discount on the new one. They have set a limit on the amount they

will spend on the new car, and they know how much they can expect from the sale of the old one. They plan to cover the difference with a bank loan.

They are told that it will take 7 days for the advertisement to appear, and probably a further 4 days to sell their present car. They are advised by the bank that a loan can be arranged in 3 days. They are allowing 6 days to take test drives, read manufacturers' catalogues and study consumer magazines, and another 2 days to negotiate a discount once they have decided which model they want.

How long will it take to complete these steps?

Solution

The first stage in the analysis is to identify the separate activities, determine the order in which they take place and note the time required for each. It is convenient to adopt brief names for the activities and, denoting the existing and new vehicles by CAR1 and CAR2 respectively, the list becomes:

Activity number	Activity name	Duration (days)	
1	ADVERTISE	7	
2	SELL CAR1	4	(must follow activity 1)
3	RAISE LOAN	3	
4	PICK CAR2	6	
5	HAGGLE	2	(must follow activity 4)

This list is not exhaustive. For instance, the dealer may not have the chosen model and colour in stock and this could lead to delay. For the moment, however, let us find how long it will take to carry out the five activities listed. The sum of their durations is 22 days, but this is not relevant because some of the activities can be carried out in parallel. Others must follow a sequence as indicated by the statements in brackets. Selling their present car (activity 2) can only begin when the advertisement appears and it therefore follows activity 1.

The solution is completed in the next section.

3.3 BAR CHARTS AND NETWORKS

It is useful to show the activities on a diagram and two types are commonly used. One is the *bar chart* (or *Gantt chart*), Fig. 3.1(a), in which each activity is represented by a horizontal line or rectangle. The time-scale is shown on the horizontal axis, and the length of each bar is proportional to the duration of the activity it represents. In the present case the axis is marked in days, but it is often convenient to show dates. Activities 1, 3 and 4 can all start at time zero but activity 2 must wait for 1 to be finished, and 5 must follow 4.

From the diagram it is clear that all the activities can be completed in **11 days**. It can also be seen that this time is set by the first two activities. With the present figures, the other three activities would have time to spare. The activity RAISE LOAN, for instance, could be delayed by 8 days without affecting the completion of the project. The bar chart is useful in showing the relative times required for the various activities, but it does not

Figure 3.1

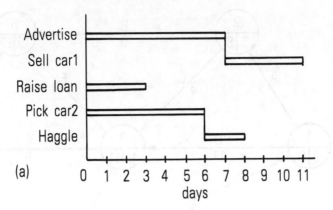

(a)

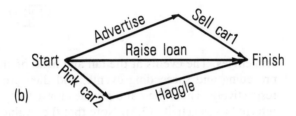

(b)

show clearly the sequence in which they must take place.

To overcome this disadvantage, we use a network (Fig. 3.1(b)). In this diagram, each activity is represented by an arrow showing how it leads to others. For example, the head of the arrow ADVERTISE coincides with the tail of the arrow SELL CAR1. In a network of this kind the lengths of the lines are not proportional to the durations of the activities. The longest line in the present case (RAISE LOAN) corresponds to one of the shortest durations (3 days). Moreover, the slopes of the arrows are of no significance.

Bar charts and networks each have their advantages and it is possible to combine them in one diagram.[2]

3.4 PROPERTIES OF NETWORKS

Figure 3.2 shows a network, or *arrow diagram*, with 10 activities A, B, C . . . K and 6 junctions. The numbers on the arrows are the times required for the various activities in some convenient units (hours, days, weeks). The junctions are shown as circles, each divided into a semicircle and two quadrants. The form of presentation may vary slightly from one book to another, but the fundamental rule for constructing a network is that all the activities approaching a junction must be completed before any activity leaving it can commence.

The term *node* is commonly used for a junction on a network diagram. In the present case it represents a point in time at which activities can begin or end, and is called an *event*. The diagram is therefore known as an event-on-node network. The events are referred to by numbers shown in the

Figure 3.2

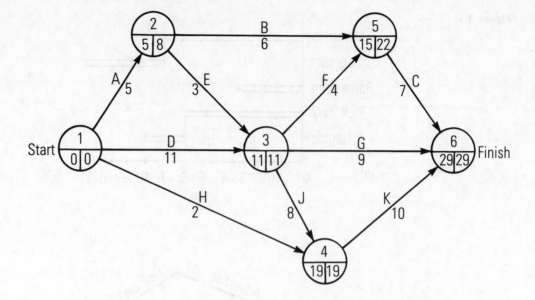

semicircles. The events at the tail and head of an activity arrow are called its preceding and succeeding events, and they are usually denoted by i and j respectively. Thus, the i and j values for activity F are 3 and 5, and it can be referred to as activity (3,5). Note that the i value for one activity can be the j value for another. For some computer programs, the event numbers must be chosen so that the j value is greater than the i value for every activity. This convention is followed throughout this book. Furthermore, some programs will not accept zero as an event number.

The network has one starting-point, one finishing-point and no loose ends. It is usually drawn so that progress is from left to right. As in Fig. 3.2, there may be several paths through the diagram from start to finish. Each one can be identified by the activities along it, or by the numbers of the events through which it passes. For instance, the path containing activities D, F and C can be referred to by its event numbers ①–③–⑤–⑥. Note that a path through a network can only pass through an event along its route once; there can be no loops.

Each of the paths through the network has its own duration. In the case of Fig. 3.2, there are eight possible routes and, with the times shown for the individual activities, their durations range from 12 to 29 units. Check this for yourself by listing the paths ABC, AEFC, . . . and summing the times required for the activities along each one.

Every activity must be completed and it is the path with the longest duration that gives the minimum time for completing the project. In the present example, it is defined by activities D, J, K or events ①–③–④–⑥. This is called the *critical path* and the activities along it are called the *critical activities*. Any delay in one of these will delay the completion of the project. The other activities have time to spare and this slack time is called *float*. There are several kinds of float and the distinctions are given in section 3.6.

3.5 EARLIEST AND LATEST TIMES

In most projects we need to know the earliest times at which activities can begin and the latest times by which they must be finished. The values are usually shown in the lower quadrants of the event circles. In the left-hand quadrant of each event we record the earliest time by which all the activities approaching it can be completed.

Suppose (Fig. 3.2) we take the starting time for the project as zero. This is shown in the left-hand quadrant for event ①. Event ② can then be reached at time 5, the duration of activity A, (1,2). Event ③ is approached by two activities, E and D, and these give arrival times of $5 + 3 = 8$ and $0 + 11 = 11$ respectively. The greater value, 11, is recorded at event ③ and the procedure is repeated for events ④ and ⑤. These are found to have earliest times of 19 and 15 units respectively. The final event ⑥ is approached by three activities, C, G and K, whose earliest arrival times at ⑥ are 22, 20 and 29 respectively. The greatest of these, 29, is recorded. It confirms the result found earlier by considering all the possible paths through the network.

The right-hand quadrants are used to show the latest times by which activities must be completed. If we are trying to complete the project in the shortest possible time, we use the minimum project time as the latest time for the final event. In the present example this gives us 29 for the right-hand quadrant of event ⑥. Working backwards along activity C, the corresponding value at event ⑤ is $29 - 7 = 22$ and, along activity K, the value at event ④ is $29 - 10 = 19$.

For event ③ we have to consider three possibilities. Along activity F it is $22 - 4 = 18$, along G it is $29 - 9 = 20$ and along J it is $19 - 8 = 11$. We record the least of these results, 11, and then repeat the process for events ② and ①. You are advised to check the results for yourself. You will find that for each critical activity (D, J and K in this example):

(a) the earliest and latest times of the preceding event are equal;
(b) the earliest and latest times of the succeeding event are equal; and
(c) the activity time t is the difference between its i and j times.

All three conditions are necessary. The first two are satisfied by activities G and H, but they are not critical because they do not meet condition (c).

3.6 FLOAT

Non-critical activities have spare time, or float, and this can be defined in a number of ways.

Total float is the amount by which the maximum possible time available for an activity exceeds the time needed to perform it. In the network of Fig. 3.2, activity B could start at time 5 (provided A were completed at the earliest time) and finish as late as time 22. The maximum time available is therefore $22 - 5 = 17$ units and, since 6 units are needed for the activity, the total float is $17 - 6 = 11$. This spare time is only available once; if it were all applied to activity B, activities A and C would have to be carried out in the minimum times.

The definition given above for total float is universally agreed, but for other forms of float the definitions may vary from one author to another. The following have been widely accepted, however.[2,3]

Free float is the spare time available if the activity can start at the earliest time, but must finish by the earliest time of the succeeding event. In the case of activity B, therefore, the free float is $(15 - 5) - 6 = 4$.

Interfering float is the difference between the total float and the free float. For activity B it is $11 - 4 = 7$. The result can also be obtained as the difference between the earliest and latest times of the succeeding event; in the present case, $22 - 15 = 7$.

Independent float can be regarded as the spare time available for an activity which does not affect activities that come earlier or later. It is obtained by subtracting the activity time from the difference between its latest i time and earliest j time. Activity B, for instance, could start at time 8 and finish by time 15 without affecting any other activity. Its independent float is therefore $(15 - 8) - 6 = 1$. It is possible for independent float to be negative.

The results for the activities in Fig. 3.2 are collected in Table 3.1.

Table 3.1 Network analysis results

Activity	i	j	t	Total float	Free float	Interfering float	Independent float
A	1	2	5	3	0	3	0
B	2	5	6	11	4	7	1
C	5	6	7	7	7	0	0
D	1	3	11	Critical			
E	2	3	3	3	3	0	0
F	3	5	4	7	0	7	0
G	3	6	9	9	9	0	0
H	1	4	2	17	17	0	17
J	3	4	8	Critical			
K	4	6	10	Critical			

3.7 NETWORK CONSTRUCTION

So far in this chapter we have been analysing existing networks. This is essentially an exercise in arithmetic and it can easily be carried out by a computer. A suitable program is given in section 3.9.

Before it can be analysed, however, the network must be drawn and, in many examples, this is the more difficult task. Furthermore, it is not easily implemented on a computer.

Initially the data are likely to be given in a written or verbal report rather than a table of values. In this case we must first identify all the activities that contribute to the project, and determine how each follows one or more others. The durations of the activities may be noted at this stage, but they do not affect the construction of the network. This must be drawn so that the arrows indicate the sequences in which the activities take place. Figure 3.3 shows various ways in which four activities, A, B, C and D, might be linked. At Fig. 3.3(a), there are two separate relationships; activity A must be completed before B can commence and C must be finished before D can

Figure 3.3

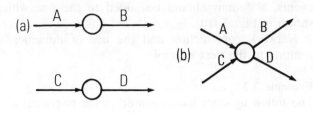

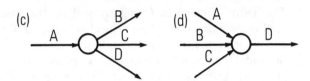

begin. The logic represented at Fig. 3.3(b) is that neither B nor D can begin until both A and C are completed.

The numbers of activities arriving at and departing from a particular event may not be equal. In some cases, as at Fig. 3.3(c), several activities can commence when one ends; or, as at Fig. 3.3(d), one activity may have to wait for the completion of several others.

3.8 DUMMY ACTIVITIES

Figure 3.3 does not include all the possible sequences of four activities. Suppose that B depends on the completion of A only but D requires the completion of A and C. This is achieved in Fig. 3.4(a) by the introduction of an extra activity called a *dummy*. This arrangement meets the required logic because B can start as soon as A ends, whereas D depends on the completion of C and the dummy, and the dummy depends on the completion of A. A dummy activity is shown by a broken line and it has zero duration. It does not add directly to the project time, therefore, but it establishes an additional path or paths through the network and this can affect the results.

Figure 3.4

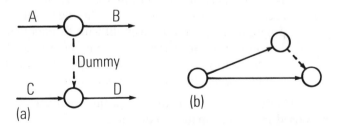

The analysis of a network containing dummies is carried out in exactly the same way as before. A dummy can have a value for each of the forms of float defined in section 3.6, or it may be a critical activity and lie on the critical path. If two activities have the same preceding and succeeding events, a dummy should be added to the one with the shorter time, as shown in Fig. 3.4(b).

Network construction and the use of dummies are illustrated in the solution to the next example.

Example 3.2
The following story has appeared in the pages of the *Midshire Gazette*:

NEW FACTORY FOR INDUSTRIAL ESTATE
Adrian Quill-Penn, Business Correspondent
The Tardy Timepiece Company will be the first firm to come to the Ambridge Industrial Estate. The chairman, Sir Tempus Tardy, yesterday announced a major diversification programme. Production of sundials at the old Clerkenwell works will be phased out and the company will move to Ambridge where two factory units will be built, one for the manufacture of scientific and sports timing equipment and the other for producing a range of quartz watches and clocks.

A new technical and administrative office block is already being planned and building will commence in 3 months' time. It will then be possible to plan the two production units. The planning of each unit will take about 8 months but, by the use of industrialized building techniques, each building contract (including the office block) should require no more than 6 months.

The scheme, said Sir Tempus, has the full support of the unions. Staff will be given every assistance in moving and a retraining programme has already been agreed. This will cover the latest techniques in electronics, fibre-optics and lasers. When the technical and administrative personnel have moved their present accommodation will be used for the retraining programmes.

In reply to a question Sir Tempus explained that there would be two retraining programmes, each lasting nine months, one for each section of the works. 'I am confident,' he concluded, 'that we shall be in full production on the new site in 2½ years' time.'

An editorial in the same issue, though welcoming the development as a much-needed boost for light industry in the area, expressed doubts about the time-scale of 2½ years. It asked:

Is Sir Tempus justified in this forecast? We must allow two months for each of the three moves to the new site. Furthermore, building programmes are notoriously difficult to maintain. An extension of only 1 month to each of the three contracts would delay the completion of the project by 3 months. Would it not be desirable to try and reduce the planning times for the two stages of the factory?

Construct a network for the project and use it to answer the questions posed in the newspaper's editorial.

Solution
The details of the story, as given in the question, can be interpreted in more than one way. In practice, such ambiguities should be resolved in discussions with the persons responsible for the various activities. For the present

solution, the following interpretation is used.

The project comprises three stages of planning, three building contracts, three moves to the new accommodation and two retraining programmes – 11 activities in all. No building can be started until its planning is completed. It is assumed, too, that only one building can be planned at a time, only one built at a time, and only one move made at a time. Furthermore, each of the two moves to the factory units can only take place when the unit is finished and the corresponding training programme completed. These relationships are shown in Table 3.2 which gives the duration and preceding activities for each of the 11 activities.

Table 3.2 Factory relocation project

Activity number	Activity name	Preceding activities	Duration (months)
1	PLAN OFFCE	—	3
2	PLAN UNIT1	1	8
3	PLAN UNIT2	2	8
4	B'LD OFFCE	1	6
5	MOVE OFFCE	4	2
6	B'LD UNIT1	2, 4	6
7	B'LD UNIT2	3, 6	6
8	RETRAIN 1	5	9
9	RETRAIN 2	8	9
10	MOVE UNIT1	5, 6, 8	2
11	MOVE UNIT2	7, 9, 10	2

The durations are in months and include the values suggested in the editorial for each of the moves. As is often the case in practice, the report contains some details, such as the content of the training programmes, that are irrelevant to the task in hand!

The activities are referenced by number to facilitate a computer analysis, but letters (A, B, C, . . .) are sometimes more convenient, especially if there is the possibility of confusing activities and events. The numbering is arranged so that preceding activities all have lower values than the current one; this is a requirement of some critical path computer programs. Each activity is also given a name and this is abbreviated to 10 characters in the present case, to suit the screen display of the computer program given later.

Figure 3.5

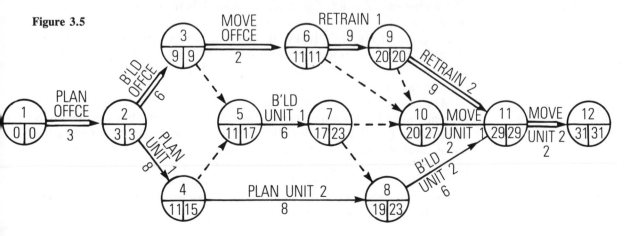

There are many ways of drawing the network and one possibility is shown in Fig. 3.5. It uses six dummies, giving a total of 17 activities in all. When drawing a network you may find that several attempts are needed to represent correctly the sequences of the activities. Check that your network correctly represents all the precedence relationships. For example, activity 11 (MOVE UNIT2) depends on the completion of activities 7, 9 and 10, and this is represented by the arrows converging at event ⑪.

The names and durations of the activities are shown on the arrows, and the events are numbered so that the j value is greater than the i value for every activity. With these details, and noting that the duration of every dummy is zero, the earliest and latest event times are calculated, the results being shown in the quadrants of the node circles, as before.

The project time is found to be 31 months, the critical path being ①–②–③–⑥–⑨–⑪–⑫ in terms of events. The critical activities are 1, 4, 5, 8, 9 and 11.

The points raised in the newspaper editorial can now be dealt with. From the network the project time is **31 months** and the forecast of 2½ years made by Sir Tempus is a good approximation. On the question of building delays, an extension of 1 month to the office contract would certainly prolong the project but the other two contracts are not on the critical path. They have total floats of 6 and 4 months respectively and a delay of 1 month in each would not postpone the finishing date. Conversely, a reduction in the planning times for these units would not shorten the project because these activities (2 and 3) are not critical.

Although only 11 activities were identified in this example (apart from the dummies) the method of solution is the same for large projects. All the activities that contribute to the project must be identified, together with details of the preceding activities, and a network drawn to show the logical sequences, using dummies as needed. There can only be one starting-point and one finishing-point, and no other loose ends. The earliest and latest times for each event can then be found using the method given in section 3.5.

3.9 COMPUTER PROGRAM FOR NETWORK ANALYSIS

The arithmetic needed for analysing a network is straightforward, but it can be tedious. Many computer programs are available for the task and a simple one is given in Fig. 3.6. To avoid fatigue it can be typed in sections. For example, lines 10–420 together with lines 1000–1090 can be typed and test run, using data from one of the examples in this chapter, before the rest of the program is added.

Mistakes can easily be made when long lists of data are entered and the program includes a routine for amending items before the calculation is carried out. This facility is also offered at the end of the program so that the names and durations of the activities can be modified. When using the program it is essential to include the dummies in the list of activities.

Lines 10–100 print the heading and a reminder of the notation.

Lines 110–180 call for the numbers of activities and events, and set up arrays for the various quantities to be stored.

Figure 3.6

```
 10 PRINT "---------------------------------------"
 20 PRINT "CRITICAL PATH ANALYSIS"
 30 PRINT "---------------------------------------"
 40 PRINT
 50 PRINT "NOTATION:"
 60 PRINT "PRECEDING EVENT (TAIL)...........I"
 70 PRINT "SUCCEEDING EVENT (HEAD)..........J"
 80 PRINT "ACTIVITY DURATION................T"
 90 PRINT "NOTE:  J MUST BE GREATER THAN I"
100 PRINT
110 PRINT "INPUT NUMBER OF ACTIVITIES"
120 PRINT "(INCLUDING DUMMIES):"
130 INPUT A
140 PRINT "INPUT NUMBER OF EVENTS:"
150 INPUT N
160 REM     ACTIVITY AND EVENT ARRAYS
170 DIM N$(A):DIM P(A):DIM S(A):DIM T(A)
180 DIM E(N):DIM L(N):DIM X(N,N)
190 REM     CALL FOR DATA
200 PRINT "FOR EACH ACTIVITY INPUT NAME (MAXIMUM"
210 PRINT "10 CHARACTERS), I, J AND T"
220 PRINT
230 FOR I=1 TO A
240 GOSUB 1060
250 NEXT I
260 PRINT
270 REM    DISPLAY DATA
280 PRINT "ACTIVITY         I    J    T"
290 PRINT
300 FOR I=1 TO A
310 PRINT TAB(1);I;TAB(4);N$(I);TAB(16);P(I);TAB(20);S(I);TAB(24);T(I)
320 NEXT I
330 PRINT
340 REM    AMEND DATA
350 PRINT "TO CHANGE AN ENTRY INPUT ITS NUMBER"
360 PRINT "(0 TO CONTINUE):"
370 INPUT I
380 IF I=0 THEN GOTO 420
390 PRINT "INPUT REVISED NAME, I, J, AND T"
400 GOSUB 1060
410 GOTO 260
420 REM    STORE DURATION TIMES
430 FOR I=1 TO N
440 E(I)=0
450 FOR J=1 TO N
460 X(I,J)=-1
470 NEXT J
480 NEXT I
490 FOR K=1 TO A
500 I=P(K)
510 J=S(K)
520 X(I,J)=T(K)
530 NEXT K
540 REM    CALCULATE EARLIEST TIMES
550 FOR I=1 TO N-1
560 FOR J=I+1 TO N
570 IF X(I,J)=-1 THEN GOTO 600
580 IF E(J)>E(I)+X(I,J) THEN GOTO 600
590 E(J)=E(I)+X(I,J)
600 NEXT J
610 NEXT I
620 REM    CALCULATE LATEST TIMES
630 FOR I=1 TO N
640 L(I)=E(N)
650 NEXT I
660 FOR J=N TO 2 STEP -1
670 FOR I=N-1 TO 1 STEP -1
680 IF X(I,J)=-1 THEN GOTO 710
690 IF L(I)<L(J)-X(I,J) THEN GOTO 710
700 L(I)=L(J)-X(I,J)
710 NEXT I
720 NEXT J
730 PRINT
740 REM    DISPLAY RESULTS
750 PRINT "RESULTS:"
760 PRINT "MINIMUM PROJECT TIME = ";E(N)
770 PRINT
780 PRINT "CRITICAL ACTIVITIES   I   J   T"
790 PRINT
```

```
 800 FOR I=1 TO A
 810 IF T(I)<>(L(S(I))-E(P(I))) THEN GOTO 830
 820 PRINT TAB(1);I;TAB(4);N$(I);TAB(22);P(I);TAB(25);S(I);TAB(28);T(I)
 830 NEXT I
 840 PRINT
 850 PRINT "PE = PRECEDING EVENT"
 860 PRINT "SE = SUCCEEDING EVENT"
 870 PRINT "ET = EARLIEST TIME"
 880 PRINT "LT = LATEST TIME"
 890 PRINT
 900 PRINT "ACTIVITY      I  J  T  -PE-- -SE-- TOTAL"
 910 PRINT "NO.NAME              ET LT ET LT FLOAT"
 920 FOR I=1 TO A
 930 PRINT TAB(0);I;TAB(3);N$(I);TAB(14);P(I);TAB(17);S(I);TAB(20);T(I);TAB(23)
;E(P(I));TAB(26);L(P(I));TAB(29);E(S(I));TAB(32);L(S(I));TAB(36);(L(S(I))-E(P(I)
)-T(I))
 940 NEXT I
1000 PRINT:PRINT "CHANGE DATA? (Y/N)"
1010 INPUT Q$
1020 IF Q$="N" OR Q$="n" THEN GOTO 1040
1030 GOTO 260
1040 PRINT "-------------------------------------"
1050 END
1060 REM   INPUT ACTIVITY DATA
1070 PRINT "---ACTIVITY NO. ";I;":"
1080 INPUT N$(I),P(I),S(I),T(I)
1090 RETURN
```

Lines 190–250 ask for the details of each activity, using the subroutine in lines 1060–1080. All the data are then displayed by lines 260–330, and lines 340–410 provide the opportunity to change the details of any items before the calculation is carried out.

Lines 420–530 store the durations. This section includes a commonly used device to identify the links between events. We first suppose that every event is linked to every other event with a duration of −1. This value is replaced by the true duration for each link that coincides with an activity. In the subsequent calculations, links with durations of −1 are then ignored.

Lines 540–610 calculate the earliest times for the events and lines 620–720 the latest times.

The remaining lines present the results, including the minimum project time, a list of critical activities and a table showing the earliest and latest times of the preceding and succeeding events for every activity. The table also displays the total float for each activity. It is arranged in a 40-column format and this limits the number of details that can be displayed. Furthermore, the layout will be distorted if any of the time values exceed 999 units.

Lines 1000–1030 offer the option of returning to the original table of activities and changing their durations. If this is declined the program ends at line 1050.

Figure 3.7 shows part of the screen display that was obtained when the program was run for the factory relocation problem of Example 3.2 using the activity names listed in Table 3.2 and the event numbers of Fig. 3.5. The data entry is displayed here for the first activity only; note that there are 17 activities in all, including the six dummies. The computer may take a few seconds to carry out the calculations if there are many activities. The number of activities is limited by the memory of the computer, but a 32 k machine should be able to deal with at least 40.

Use the program to check the answers for the networks shown in Figs 3.1 and 3.2. Then take the 'change data' option at the end of a program run to see the effect of modifying activity durations.

```
----------------------------------------
CRITICAL PATH ANALYSIS                          71
----------------------------------------
```

Figure 3.7

```
NOTATION:
PRECEDING EVENT (TAIL)............I
SUCCEEDING EVENT (HEAD)..........J
ACTIVITY DURATION.................T
NOTE:  J MUST BE GREATER THAN I

INPUT NUMBER OF ACTIVITIES
(INCLUDING DUMMIES):
?17
INPUT NUMBER OF EVENTS:
?12
FOR EACH ACTIVITY INPUT NAME (MAXIMUM
10 CHARACTERS), I, J AND T

---ACTIVITY NO. 1:
?PLAN OFFCE
?1
?2
?3
---ACTIVITY NO. 2:
?

ACTIVITY          I    J    T

 1   PLAN OFFCE   1    2    3
 2   PLAN UNIT1   2    4    8
 3   PLAN UNIT2   4    8    8
 4   B'LD OFFCE   2    3    6
 5   MOVE OFFCE   3    6    2
 6   B'LD UNIT1   5    7    6
 7   B'LD UNIT2   8   11    6
 8   RETRAIN 1    6    9    9
 9   RETRAIN 2    9   11    9
10   MOVE UNIT1  10   11    2
11   MOVE UNIT2  11   12    2
12   DUMMY 1      3    5    0
13   DUMMY 2      4    5    0
14   DUMMY 3      6   10    0
15   DUMMY 4      7   10    0
16   DUMMY 5      7    8    0
17   DUMMY 6      9   10    0

TO CHANGE AN ENTRY INPUT ITS NUMBER
(0 TO CONTINUE):
?0
RESULTS:
MINIMUM PROJECT TIME = 31

CRITICAL ACTIVITIES   I   J   T

 1   PLAN OFFCE       1   2   3
 4   B'LD OFFCE       2   3   6
 5   MOVE OFFCE       3   6   2
 8   RETRAIN 1        6   9   9
 9   RETRAIN 2        9  11   9
11   MOVE UNIT2      11  12   2

PE = PRECEDING EVENT
SE = SUCCEEDING EVENT
ET = EARLIEST TIME
LT = LATEST TIME

ACTIVITY        I   J   T  -PE--  -SE--  TOTAL
NO.NAME                    ET LT  ET LT  FLOAT
 1  PLAN OFFCE   1   2   3   0  0   3  3    0
 2  PLAN UNIT1   2   4   8   3  3  11 15    4
 3  PLAN UNIT2   4   8   8  11 15  19 23    4
 4  B'LD OFFCE   2   3   6   3  3   9  9    0
 5  MOVE OFFCE   3   6   2   9  9  11 11    0
 6  B'LD UNIT1   5   7   6  11 17  17 23    6
 7  B'LD UNIT2   8  11   6  19 23  29 29    4
 8  RETRAIN 1    6   9   9  11 11  20 20    0
 9  RETRAIN 2    9  11   9  20 20  29 29    0
10  MOVE UNIT1  10  11   2  20 27  29 29    7
11  MOVE UNIT2  11  12   2  29 29  31 31    0
12  DUMMY 1      3   5   0   9  9  11 17    8
13  DUMMY 2      4   5   0  11 15  11 17    6
14  DUMMY 3      6  10   0  11 11  20 27   16
15  DUMMY 4      7  10   0  17 23  20 27   10
16  DUMMY 5      7   8   0  17 23  19 23    6
17  DUMMY 6      9  10   0  20 20  20 27    7

CHANGE DATA? (Y/N)
?N
----------------------------------------
```

Figure 3.8

```
 900 PRINT "ACTIVITY          I    J    T    --PE--  --SE--   TOTAL   FREE  INTERFERING
INDEPENDENT"
 910 PRINT "NO.NAME                             ET  LT  ET  LT  FLOAT  FLOAT FLOAT
FLOAT"
 920 FOR I=1 TO A
 930 TF=(L(S(I))-E(P(I))-T(I))
 940 FF=(E(S(I))-E(P(I))-T(I))
 950 IN=TF-FF
 960 IND=(E(S(I))-L(P(I))-T(I))
 970 PRINT TAB(0);I;TAB(3);N$(I);TAB(15);P(I);TAB(19);S(I);TAB(23);T(I);TAB(27)
;E(P(I));TAB(31);L(P(I));TAB(35);E(S(I));TAB(39);L(S(I));TAB(43);TF;TAB(50);FF;T
AB(56);IN;TAB(68);IND
 980 NEXT I
```

If your computer offers a screen display of 80 columns the program can easily be extended to show the free, interfering and independent floats as well as the total float. Lines 900–940 should be replaced by the listing given in Fig. 3.8. On most computers the new lines will overwrite the existing ones. The four kinds of float (total, free, interfering and independent) are represented by the variables TF, FF, IN and IND. Figure 3.9 shows the extended table of results for the factory relocation example.

Figure 3.9

```
PE = PRECEDING EVENT
SE = SUCCEEDING EVENT
ET = EARLIEST TIME
LT = LATEST TIME
```

ACTIVITY NO.NAME		I	J	T	--PE-- ET	LT	--SE-- ET	LT	TOTAL FLOAT	FREE FLOAT	INTERFERING FLOAT	INDEPENDENT FLOAT
1	PLAN OFFCE	1	2	3	0	0	3	3	0	0	0	0
2	PLAN UNIT1	2	4	8	3	3	11	15	4	0	4	0
3	PLAN UNIT2	4	8	8	11	15	19	23	4	0	4	-4
4	B'LD OFFCE	2	3	6	3	3	9	9	0	0	0	0
5	MOVE OFFCE	3	6	2	9	9	11	11	0	0	0	0
6	B'LD UNIT1	5	7	6	11	17	17	23	6	0	6	-6
7	B'LD UNIT2	8	11	6	19	23	29	29	4	4	0	0
8	RETRAIN 1	6	9	9	11	11	20	20	0	0	0	0
9	RETRAIN 2	9	11	9	20	20	29	29	0	0	0	0
10	MOVE UNIT1	10	11	2	20	27	29	29	7	7	0	0
11	MOVE UNIT2	11	12	2	29	29	31	31	0	0	0	0
12	DUMMY 1	3	5	0	9	9	11	17	8	2	6	2
13	DUMMY 2	4	5	0	11	15	11	17	6	0	6	-4
14	DUMMY 3	6	10	0	11	11	20	27	16	9	7	9
15	DUMMY 4	7	10	0	17	23	20	27	10	3	7	-3
16	DUMMY 5	7	8	0	17	23	19	23	6	2	4	-4
17	DUMMY 6	9	10	0	20	20	20	27	7	0	7	0

3.10 ACTIVITY-BASED PROGRAMS

In order to obtain the data in the form required by the computer program of Fig. 3.6 we must first draw the network. With a complex project this may be difficult. Furthermore, it usually requires the introduction of dummy activities. To avoid these complications we need a program that uses data in the form of Table 3.2, that is, a list of activities and their durations, together with details of the activities that must precede them. The listing given in Fig. 3.10 is a simple program of this kind; it determines the minimum project time and critical activities without the need for a network or dummy activities. It requires no information about the events.

Lines 10–80 define the arrays and print the heading.

Lines 90–190 call for the number of activities and set the initial values of certain elements at zero.

Figure 3.10

```
10 REM   N$(),D()   NAME, DURATION
20 REM   P()         PRECEDING ACTIVITIES
30 REM   X(),Y()     START, FINISH TIMES
40 REM   C()         CRITICAL ACTIVITIES
50 PRINT "----------------------------------------"
60 PRINT "CRITICAL PATH (ACTIVITY-BASED)"
70 PRINT "----------------------------------------"
80 PRINT
90 PRINT "INPUT NUMBER OF ACTIVITIES"
100 INPUT N
110 DIM N$(N):DIM D(N):DIM P(N,N)
120 DIM X(N):DIM Y(N):DIM Z(N):DIM C(N)
130 FOR I=1 TO N
140 C(I)=0
150 FOR J=1 TO N
160 P(I,J)=0
170 NEXT J
180 NEXT I
190 PRINT
200 PRINT "PRECEDING ACTIVITIES MUST HAVE LOWER"
210 PRINT "REFERENCE NUMBERS THAN CURRENT ACTIVITY"
220 PRINT
230 PRINT "FOR EACH ACTIVITY, INPUT NAME (UP TO"
240 PRINT "10 CHARACTERS), DURATION AND THE"
250 PRINT "NUMBERS OF THE PRECEDING ACTIVITIES"
260 PRINT
270 FOR I=1 TO N
280 GOSUB 520
290 NEXT I
300 PRINT
310 PRINT "CHECK TABLE OF ACTIVITIES AND NOTE THE"
320 PRINT "NUMBER OF ANY ITEM TO BE CHANGED:"
330 PRINT
340 PRINT TAB(1);"NO.";TAB(4);"NAME";TAB(15);"DURA-";TAB(21);"PRECEDING"
350 PRINT TAB(15);"TION";TAB(21);"ACTIVITIES"
360 FOR I=1 TO N
370 PRINT TAB(1);I;TAB(4);N$(I);TAB(15);D(I);
380 C=21
390 FOR J=1 TO I
400 IF P(I,J)=0 THEN GOTO 430
410 PRINT TAB(C);P(I,J);
420 C=C+3
430 NEXT J
440 NEXT I
450 PRINT:PRINT
460 PRINT "TO CHANGE AN ENTRY ENTER THE"
470 PRINT "ACTIVITY NUMBER (-99 TO CONTINUE)"
480 INPUT I
490 IF I=-99 THEN GOTO 670
500 GOSUB 520
510 GOTO 300
520 REM    DATA INPUT
530 PRINT
540 PRINT "ACTIVITY NO. ";I
550 PRINT "---NAME"
560 INPUT N$(I)
570 PRINT "---DURATION"
580 INPUT D(I)
590 PRINT "---PRECEDING ACTIVITY NUMBERS"
600 PRINT "   (0 IF NONE OR TO FINISH)"
610 J=1
620 INPUT P(I,J)
630 IF P(I,J)=0 THEN GOTO 660
640 J=J+1
650 GOTO 620
660 RETURN
670 REM    FIND MINIMUM PROJECT TIME
680 T=0
690 FOR I=1 TO N
700 IF P(I,1)=0 THEN Y(I)=D(I)
710 NEXT I
720 I=1
730 X(I)=0
740 IF P(I,1)=0 THEN GOTO 790
750 FOR J=1 TO I
760 IF P(I,J)=0 THEN GOTO 780
770 IF X(I)<Y(P(I,J)) THEN X(I)=Y(P(I,J)):Z(I)=P(I,J)
780 NEXT J
790 Y(I)=X(I)+D(I)
800 IF T<Y(I) THEN T=Y(I)
```

```
810 IF I<N THEN I=I+1:GOTO 730
820 REM     FIND CRITICAL PATH
830 A=1
840 FOR I=1 TO N
850 IF Y(I)=T THEN C(A)=I
860 NEXT I
870 IF X(C(A))=0 THEN GOTO 910
880 C(A+1)=Z(C(A))
890 A=A+1
900 GOTO 870
910 REM    DISPLAY RESULTS
920 PRINT:PRINT "THE CRITICAL ACTIVITIES IN ORDER ARE:"
930 PRINT
940 PRINT "NO. NAME        START FINISH DURATION"
950 PRINT "               TIME   TIME"
960 PRINT
970 FOR I=A TO 1 STEP -1
980 PRINT TAB(1);C(I);TAB(4);N$(C(I));TAB(15);X(C(I));TAB(21);Y(C(I));TAB(28);
D(C(I))
990 NEXT I
1000 PRINT
1010 PRINT "THE MINIMUM PROJECT TIME IS ";T
1020 PRINT
1030 PRINT "----------------------------------------"
1040 END
```

Lines 200–300 call for the data, one activity at a time, using the subroutine in lines 520–660.

Lines 310–450 present all the data in a table and lines 460–510 offer the chance of amending individual entries, again using the subroutine in lines 520–660.

Lines 670–810 determine the minimum project time T. Initially, T is set at zero. The earliest starting time for each activity is determined by reference to the finishing times of its preceding activities, and its own finishing time is then found by adding its duration. If T is less than its finishing time then T is made equal to it. By repeating the process for all the activities, the earliest finishing time for the whole project is found.

Lines 820–900 determine which activities are on the critical r ..l – in reverse order.

Lines 910–1040 then display the critical activities (in the correct sequence), together with the duration of the critical path.

Figure 3.11 shows part of the screen display that was obtained when the program was run for the data of Example 3.2, as displayed in Table 3.2. It first asks for the number of activities and the response is now 11 (no dummies being required). It then calls for data on each activity in turn and the printout shows the responses for activities 1, 2 and 11. For activity 1 there is no preceding activity so the response to the third question is 0. For activity 2 there is one preceding activity, 1, and the corresponding reply is 1, then 0. Activity 11 has three preceding activities and the response is therefore 7, 9, 10 and 0.

After the table of activities has been checked the wild value − 99 is entered. The computer then displays the sequence of critical activities and the minimum project time.

The program could be extended to calculate the earliest and latest times of the preceding and succeeding events, and the various floats for the non-critical activities, but this would lengthen it considerably. In exceptional cases there may be two paths having the same minimum project time; as it stands, the program identifies one only.

Figure 3.11

```
----------------------------------------
CRITICAL PATH (ACTIVITY-BASED)
----------------------------------------

INPUT NUMBER OF ACTIVITIES
?11
PRECEDING ACTIVITIES MUST HAVE LOWER
REFERENCE NUMBERS THAN CURRENT ACTIVITY

FOR EACH ACTIVITY, INPUT NAME (UP TO
10 CHARACTERS), DURATION AND THE
NUMBERS OF THE PRECEDING ACTIVITIES


ACTIVITY NO. 1
---NAME
?PLAN OFFCE
---DURATION
?3
---PRECEDING ACTIVITY NUMBERS
   (0 IF NONE OR TO FINISH)
?0

ACTIVITY NO. 2
---NAME
?PLAN UNIT1
---DURATION
?8
---PRECEDING ACTIVITY NUMBERS
   (0 IF NONE OR TO FINISH)
?1
?0



ACTIVITY NO. 11
---NAME
?MOVE UNIT2
---DURATION
?2
---PRECEDING ACTIVITY NUMBERS
   (0 IF NONE OR TO FINISH)
?7
?9
?10
?0

CHECK TABLE OF ACTIVITIES AND NOTE THE
NUMBER OF ANY ITEM TO BE CHANGED:

   NO.NAME        DURA- PRECEDING
                  TION  ACTIVITIES
   1  PLAN OFFCE 3
   2  PLAN UNIT1 8      1
   3  PLAN UNIT2 8      2
   4  B'LD OFFCE 6      1
   5  MOVE OFFCE 2      4
   6  B'LD UNIT1 6      2  4
   7  B'LD UNIT2 6      3  6
   8  RETRAIN 1  9      5
   9  RETRAIN 2  9      8
   10 MOVE UNIT1 2      5  6  8
   11 MOVE UNIT2 2      7  9  10

TO CHANGE AN ENTRY ENTER THE
ACTIVITY NUMBER (-99 TO CONTINUE)
?-99

THE CRITICAL ACTIVITIES IN ORDER ARE:

NO. NAME        START FINISH DURATION
                TIME  TIME

   1  PLAN OFFCE 0      3      3
   4  B'LD OFFCE 3      9      6
   5  MOVE OFFCE 9      11     2
   8  RETRAIN 1  11     20     9
   9  RETRAIN 2  20     29     9
   11 MOVE UNIT2 29     31     2

THE MINIMUM PROJECT TIME IS 31

----------------------------------------
```

3.11 PRECEDENCE DIAGRAMS

An alternative form of the network diagram is sometimes used, in which the nodes represent the activities and the arrows show the order in which one activity follows another. The diagram does not show events. It is known as an *activity-on-node* or *precedence diagram*.

Figure 3.12

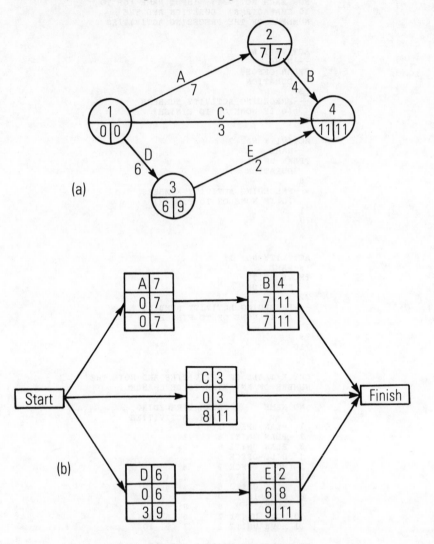

(a)

(b)

Figure 3.12 compares the two forms of network for the car purchase exercise of Example 3.1. Figure 3.12(a) shows the event-on-node diagram with the five activities identified by the letters A, B, C, D and E. The corresponding precedence diagram is shown at (b). Each activity is represented by a box divided into six elements. The first two elements are the activity identification letter and duration. The next two show its earliest start and finish times, and the last two are the latest start and finish times. All the information relating to an activity is therefore assembled at one node, instead of two as previously.

The powerful commercial and public domain programs now available eliminate the need for drawing networks. These programs can accept data in the form of precedence statements and they can print bar charts and detailed tabulations of the results, often with the option of including calendar dates.

3.12 UNCERTAINTIES IN TIME ESTIMATES

Critical path, or network, analysis is concerned with forecasting and is therefore subject to uncertainty. At the start of a project the durations of the various activities can only be estimates. The results of the calculations must be interpreted in terms of probability rather than certainty. (The concept of probability is discussed in Ch. 6.) The extended version of network analysis that allows for uncertainties in the durations of activities is known as Programme Evaluation and Review Technique (PERT).

This allows for the range of times that might be needed for each activity if it were carried out, say, 100 times. Suppose that:

m = the most likely duration of the activity;
a = the optimistic value, the shortest time that could be expected if everything went well;
b = the pessimistic value, the longest time that could be expected.

If it is assumed that the durations of many trials conform to a statistical pattern known as the *beta distribution*, then the mean value t is given by:

$$t = \frac{a + 4m + b}{6}$$

Furthermore, the spread of the results is represented by the quantity $(b - a)/6$. This is the *standard deviation* for the distribution (see Ch. 6). Bui[4] gives a computer program for PERT analysis based on these relationships and the use of random numbers. The application of probability theory to network analysis is described in a paper by Mitchell and Willis.[5]

3.13 SUMMARY

Critical path method is widely used to plan and control the progress of complex projects that depend on contributions from many people. The analysis falls into two parts – establishing the order in which the various activities take place, and calculating the final and intermediate times for the project. The analysis pin-points those activities that must not be delayed if the project is to finish on time. These are the critical activities and together they form the critical path. The method also determines the spare time (or float) for the other activities.

The project can be represented by a network in which the activities are shown as arrows, and the events – points in time at which activities begin or end – as the nodes. The earliest and latest times for each event are calculated from the durations of the individual activities – a simple task for a computer.

In practice, the details of the project are normally expressed in the form of precedence statements and, in a 'hand' solution, it is first necessary to draw a network. This usually requires the use of dummy activities. Computer programs are available that accept the information in the form of precedence statements, thus eliminating the need for networks and the introduction of dummy activities.

REFERENCES

1. Dunton C E, Kell J, Morgan H D 1965 Victoria Line: experimentation, design, programming, and early progress *Proceedings of the Institution of Civil Engineers* **31** pp 1–24
2. Nuttall J F, Jeanes R E 1963 The critical path method, *The Builder* 14 and 21 June
3. British Standard 4335: 1987 *Glossary of Terms used in Project Network Techniques* British Standards Institution
4. Bui T 1982 *Executive Planning with BASIC* Sybex, Ch 5
5. Mitchell G, Willis M J 1973 The determination of realistic probability levels for project completion dates *Aeronautical Journal* December

BIBLIOGRAPHY

Battersby A 1970 *Network Analysis for Planning and Scheduling* 3rd edn Macmillan

Lang D 1977 *Critical Path Analysis* 2nd edn Teach Yourself Books, English Universities Press

Lockyer K G 1984 *Critical Path Analysis and other Project Network Techniques* Pitman

PROBLEMS

1. Figure 3.13 shows a network with 12 activities (A, B, C . . . M) and 7 events. The figures on the arrows are the durations of the activities in some convenient units. Activity E is a dummy. Number the events, using the rule that *j* must be greater than *i* for each activity.

Figure 3.13

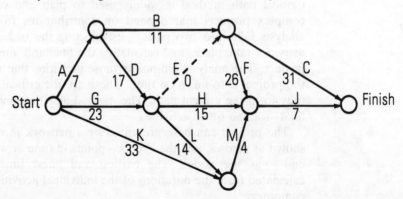

How many paths are there through the network and what are their durations? Find the minimum project time, the critical activities and the total float for each non-critical activity.

What are the critical activities and minimum project time if:

(a) the dummy is removed;
(b) the duration of M is increased to 15 units.

Answer 11 paths with durations of 44, 45, 46, 48, 49 (twice), 51, 54, 55, 56 and 57 units. Minimum project time is 57 units. Critical activities are A, D, E, F and J. Total floats on other activities: B, 6; C, 2; G, 1; H, 11; K, 13; L, 8; M, 8. (a) A, B, F and J; 51 units. (b) A, D, L, M and J; 60 units.

2. Figure 3.14 shows a network with 14 events. Letter the activities, locate the critical path, and calculate the minimum project time.

Figure 3.14

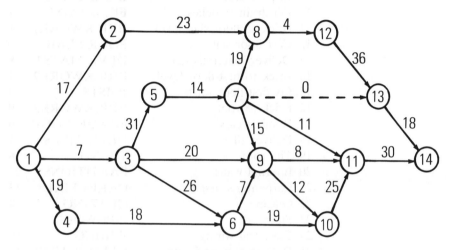

Calculate the total, free, interfering and independent float for each of the activities (2,8), (7,13) and (4,6).

Answer Critical path ①-③-⑤-⑦-⑨-⑩-⑪-⑭. Minimum project time, 134 units. The floats, in the order stated, are: (2,8), 36, 31, 5 and −5; (7,13), 64, 59, 5 and 59; (4,6), 23, 0, 23 and −23.

3. The following table gives the preceding and succeeding event numbers (*i* and *j*) and durations (*t*) for a project with 17 activities. Find the minimum project time, locate the critical path and calculate the total and independent floats for activities (6,9) and (8,9).

i	1	2	2	3	3	5	5	4	4	6	6	6	7	7	9	10	8
j	2	3	4	5	6	6	8	6	10	7	8	9	10	11	11	11	9
t	5	11	6	19	8	16	3	21	18	14	7	0	12	20	13	10	9

Answer 87 units. ①-②-③-⑤-⑥-⑦-⑩-⑪. For (6,9), 23 and 16. For (8,9), 7 and −7.

4. The major activities in constructing a detached house are listed below, together with their durations and preceding activities. The details will vary considerably with the size, form of construction and design, and the list could be extended to include pre-contract work such as sketch plans, working drawings, planning permission and building regulations approval. Some 10-character abbreviations for the activities are suggested for use with the computer programs given in Figs 3.6 and 3.10.

Activity	Abbreviation	Duration (days)	Preceding activities
1 Clear site	CLEAR SITE	3	—
2 Deliver materials (1)	DLVR MATS1	12	—
3 Level site	LEVEL SITE	2	1
4 Dig foundations	EXCAVATE	5	3
5 Lay foundations	LAY FNDTNS	8	2, 4
6 Inspect foundations	INS FNDTNS	2	5
7 Dig drains trenches	DIG DRAINS	4	1
8 Lay drains	LAY DRAINS	9	2, 7
9 Inspect drains	INS DRAINS	2	8
10 Fill drain trenches	FIL DRAINS	1	6, 9
11 Brick to floor slab level	BRICKWORK1	5	2, 6
12 Cast floor slab	POUR SLAB	6	2, 11
13 Deliver materials (2)	DLVR MATS2	8	2
14 Brick to first-floor level	BRICKWORK2	17	12, 13
15 Fix first-floor joists	JOISTS	4	13, 14
16 Brick to roof	BRICKWORK3	19	13, 15
17 Roof carcass	FRAME ROOF	9	13, 16
18 Deliver tiles	DLVR TILES	7	13
19 Tile roof	TILING	8	17, 18
20 Internal walls	PARTITIONS	23	13, 19
21 Carpenter's first fix	CARPS FIX1	13	13, 20
22 Glazing	GLAZING	4	21
23 Pipework	PIPEWORK	17	21
24 Electrical wiring	WIRING	9	21
25 Deliver plumber's fittings	DLVR PLUMB	11	19, 23
26 Deliver electrical fittings	DLVR ELECT	6	19, 23
27 Plastering	PLASTERING	23	23, 24
28 Carpenter's second fix	CARPS FIX2	27	21, 27
29 Fix plumbing fittings	PLUMB FIT	12	25, 27
30 Fix electrical fittings	ELECT FIT	5	26, 27
31 Floor finishing	FLOOR FNSH	3	28
32 Fix gutters	GUTTERS	4	19, 25
33 Internal decorating	INT DECOR	20	22, 28, 29, 31
34 External painting	EXT DECOR	12	22, 28, 32, 33
35 Clear site and turf lawn	LANDSCAPE	10	10, 32
36 Lay drive	LAY DRIVE	3	35
37 Clean and hand over	HANDOVER	4	34, 36

Determine:

(a) the minimum project time;
(b) the critical activities;
(c) the time at which the house becomes 'dry' (roof completed);
(d) the periods for which the carpenters are required on site (activities 17, 20 and 28).

Answer (a) 232 days; (b) Nos. 2, 5, 6, 11, 12, 14, 15, 16, 17, 19, 20, 21, 23, 27, 28, 31, 33, 34, 37; (c) day 90; (d) days 73–82, 113–126, 166–193.

5. Figure 3.15 relates to an urban redevelopment scheme, the present and proposed land use being as follows:

(a) A is a cleared site, ready for building;
(b) B, C, D and E contain derelict industrial buildings and some old housing whose occupants are to be relocated on A and B (at twice the present density);
(c) F is an old school, which is to be replaced by a new one on C;
(d) D, E and F will be used for widening the main road and providing amenity land.

Figure 3.15

The building programmes for areas A and B are each divided in half (each half requiring 11 months) and, as each half is completed, families from one of the areas B, C, D and E can be rehoused. It is anticipated that each move to the new areas will take 1 month. The new school on C is designed to use an industrial building system and will take 8 months to build.

Building can only take place on one site at a time. Demolition is to be carried out by contract and 2 months is required for clearing each area, only one being dealt with at a time.

The road widening and landscaping is to be carried out in a single 4-months contract.

List the activities to be carried out, together with their durations and preceding activities, draw a network and determine the time to complete the project. What are the critical activities?

Answer There are 16 activities (5 stages of building, 5 demolition contracts, 5 moves and the road widening/landscaping). More than one order of building is possible, but the critical activities are the various building stages followed by the moving of the school, the clearance of F and the road widening. Project time, 59 months.

6. Analyse each of the following projects, listing 10–20 major activities and their preceding activities. Estimate the duration of each activity and determine the project time and critical activities.

(a) staging a musical play;
(b) planning an overseas holiday;
(c) organizing an excursion for a school group.

4   LINEAR PROGRAMMING – TRANSPORTATION

'Alia tentanda via est – Another route must be found.'

Virgil *Georgics, Book 3*

4.1 RESOURCE ALLOCATION

Most organizations face the task of dividing their available resources among a number of products or services. A large car manufacturer produces several different models, a major transport undertaking operates various routes and an arable farmer may grow several crops.

Each has to decide how to allocate resources (such as money, materials, personnel or land) so as to achieve the best outcome. What we mean by best depends on the circumstances; it might be least cost, maximum profit, shortest distance or minimum time.

Many problems of this kind are examples of *linear programming*. In this context, programming means scheduling or planning, not computer programming. Computers are often programmed to solve linear programming problems, but the two ideas are separate. The term 'linear' is used because the algebraic equations that arise are linear in the mathematical sense, that is, they do not include terms containing x^2, x^3 or other powers of x. Graphical solutions are possible in some examples (see Ch. 5) and the graphs are straight lines. Linear programming is a special case of *mathematical programming* which allows for these higher powers.

The main concepts and theorems of linear programming appeared in the 1940s, and the subject has since grown rapidly so that there is now a vast literature on the subject. Many of the publications are highly mathematical but the basic ideas are simple and, in practice, the calculations can be delegated to computers.

4.2 TRANSPORTATION AND MIXTURE EXAMPLES

Linear programming problems can be considered under two headings – transportation and mixture. Transportation examples include the scheduling of goods and vehicles of all kinds, the allocation of personnel and machines to various tasks and the planning of factory production. Mixture problems arise when an organization has to allocate resources to several products or services.

The transportation problem can be thought of as a special case of linear programming and it is convenient to deal with it first. Chapter 5 covers the generalized mixture type of problem.

4.3 FEASIBLE SOLUTIONS

The meaning of feasibility in the context of transportation can best be explained by a numerical example. The following problem is one that might arise in airline operations. It is concerned only with the movement of aircraft and does not take into account complicating factors such as the availability of crews, the traffic demand on the various routes or the servicing requirements of the planes.

Figure 4.1
(© The British
Broadcasting
Corporation 1966)

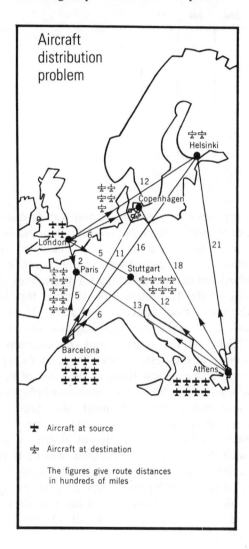

Aircraft distribution problem

Example 4.1

A charter airline has 24 planes of the same type. At the end of a weekend operation the planes are located as follows:

4 in London; 12 in Barcelona; 8 in Athens.

For the next stage of operation the planes are required in four other cities as follows:

2 in Helsinki; 5 in Copenhagen; 10 in Paris; 7 in Stuttgart.

Find a feasible schedule and show it on a suitable matrix.

Solution
Figure 4.1 shows a map locating the starting-points, or sources as they are called, and the destinations. With three sources and four destinations there are 12 possible routes in all.

Figure 4.2

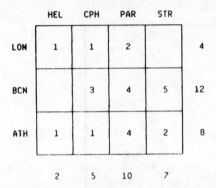

	HEL	CPH	PAR	STR	
LON	1	1	2		4
BCN		3	4	5	12
ATH	1	1	4	2	8
	2	5	10	7	

For our purposes a map is not the best way of displaying the information and it will prove more convenient to show the data in rows and columns on a *matrix*, *array* or *tableau*, as in Fig. 4.2. The rows are used for the sources and the columns for the destinations. In the present case, they are identified by the standard airline abbreviations for the names of the cities. Each cell represents one of the 12 routes. For example, the third cell in the second row gives the route from Barcelona to Paris. If we enter the number of planes on each route in the corresponding cell, the row totals must equal the numbers available at the sources and the columns must add up to the numbers required at the destinations. These totals represent the constraints in the problem. and we show them at the ends of the rows and columns.

A *feasible solution* is a list of the numbers of planes on the various routes, satisfying these constraints. We must also take note of the practical considerations; we cannot have fractional or negative numbers of aircraft! To find a feasible solution we merely put positive whole numbers (integers) in the cells such that the rows and columns add up to the totals given. There are many feasible solutions in problems of this kind. In the present example, for instance, there are 1925 possibilities altogether. Figure 4.2 shows one; it has no particular merit and you should have no difficulty in finding others. Note that some routes are not used at all. Do not use zeros; it is better to leave such cells blank.

4.4 BASIC FEASIBLE SOLUTIONS

Empty cells are called *free*, those with planes allocated to them are said to be *occupied*. The number of occupied cells can vary from one feasible solution to another but it is always possible to find solutions that do not require more than a certain critical number.

Figure 4.3

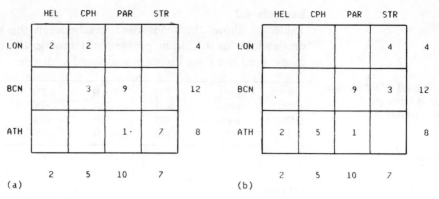

(a)	HEL	CPH	PAR	STR	
LON	2	2			4
BCN		3	9		12
ATH			1·	7	8
	2	5	10	7	

(b)	HEL	CPH	PAR	STR	
LON				4	4
BCN			9	3	12
ATH	2	5	1		8
	2	5	10	7	

This is illustrated by Fig. 4.3(a), which is obtained as follows. Begin with the top left-hand cell, and place in it the largest possible number. The row and column totals for this cell are 4 and 2 respectively and neither can be exceeded; we therefore enter 2. This completes the requirements of the first column (destination) so we move to the second column. The largest number that can be entered is again 2, since this completes the total for the first row. The first row and first column are now accounted for and we turn to the second cell in the second row. The greatest possible value here is now 3, which completes the requirements for the second column. The remaining cells are dealt with in the same way and, in the present problem, six cells are occupied altogether. This particular result, starting with the top left-hand cell, is called the *northwest corner solution*.

Figure 4.3(b) shows the result of starting in the top right-hand corner and moving left and downwards. Again six cells are occupied.

In these two solutions, each entry has been chosen so as to complete the total for a row or column – except the last, which accounts for both a row and a column. If there are m rows and n columns, therefore, solutions can always be found with not more than $m + n - 1$ occupied cells. In some examples feasible solutions can be found with fewer occupied cells (see section 4.9). The quantity $m + n - 1$ is called the *critical number*. A *basic feasible solution* is defined as one which conforms to the pattern of each entry completing one row or column (except the last) and occupies the critical number of routes. In the airline problem, $m = 3$ and $n = 4$ so that the critical number is $3 + 4 - 1 = 6$, and this is confirmed by the solutions shown in Fig. 4.3(a) and (b).

The constraints in Example 4.1 are satisfied by all the solutions shown in Figs. 4.2 and 4.3. They are all feasible, therefore, but that shown in Fig. 4.2 is not a basic feasible solution since it uses more than the critical number of occupied cells.

4.5 TOTAL COST

So far we have not considered the *cost* of the operation. If the cost (or distance) for one vehicle on each of the routes is given the total cost (or distance) of each feasible solution can be found.

Example 4.2
Table 4.1 shows the flying distances between the starting-points and the destinations for the airline problem of Example 4.1, rounded to hundreds of miles. Find the total distance associated with your solution.

Table 4.1 Distances by air in miles (to the nearest hundred)

	HEL	CPH	PAR	STR
LON	1200	600	200	500
BCN	1600	1100	500	600
ATH	2100	1800	1300	1200

Solution
It is convenient to add the information on distances to the matrix. This is done in Fig. 4.4 for the solution of Fig. 4.2. The distances are shown in the corners of the cells, in units of 100 miles. Although the figures represent distances in this example, they are generally referred to as the 'costs' in transportation problems. The form of presentation makes it easy to calculate the total cost. Working in units of 100 miles, there is one plane on the London–Helsinki route flying 12 units, one on the 6-unit London–Copenhagen route, two on the 2-unit London–Paris route, and so on. The total distance or 'cost' C is therefore given by:

$$C = 1 \times 12 + 1 \times 6 + 2 \times 2 + 3 \times 11 + 4 \times 5 + 5 \times 6$$
$$+ 1 \times 21 + 1 \times 18 + 4 \times 13 + 2 \times 12$$
$$= \mathbf{220\ units}$$

If you carry out similar calculations for the solutions shown in Fig. 4.3(a) and (b) you will find that the corresponding total distances are 211 and 228 units respectively.

Figure 4.4

	HEL	CPH	PAR	STR	
LON	12 / 1	6 / 1	2 / 2	5	4
BCN	16 / 3	11 / 4	5 / 5	6 / 5	12
ATH	21 / 1	18 / 1	13 / 4	12 / 2	8
	2	5	10	7	

4.6 THE STEPPING-STONE METHOD

In most transportation examples the objective is least total cost (or distance). In the airline problem we already have solutions with total costs of 228, 220 and 211 units. The last figure represents a considerable saving over the first and, by trying more solutions, we could probably achieve smaller totals. However, the problem has hundreds of feasible solutions and we could spend many hours finding them. Furthermore, we should not know for certain when we had reached the minimum.

A more systematic approach is to start with one feasible solution and modify it to obtain another with a lower total cost. The set of rules for modifying the solution is called an algorithm and we apply it again and again until no further improvement is possible, a process known as *iteration*.

The most popular algorithm for solving transportation problems is the *stepping-stone* (or *distribution*) method, put forward by Hitchcock[1] in 1941. It is best explained by reference to a numerical problem, such as Example 4.2.

It is necessary to start with a basic feasible solution. Any will do but the northwest corner solution of Fig. 4.3(a) has a lower total distance (211 units) than the others considered so far. It is reproduced as Fig. 4.5(a).

We then consider the free or empty cells one at a time. Take the Barcelona–Helsinki cell, for instance, and try the effect of putting one plane on this route. For the moment it is convenient to indicate this change by a $\oplus$ sign. Such a change will upset the totals for the Barcelona row and the Helsinki column. We can compensate by subtracting a plane from each of the routes Barcelona–Copenhagen and London–Helsinki as indicated by the $\ominus$ signs. Finally, to restore the totals for the London row and the Copenhagen column we add a plane to the London–Copenhagen route. Taken together, the four changes make no difference to the row and column totals since each affected row and column contains one $\oplus$ and one $\ominus$. The modified solution would still be feasible therefore.

What is the effect on total distance? Putting a plane on the Barcelona–Helsinki route increases the total distance by 16 units, subtracting one from the Barcelona–Copenhagen route reduces the total by 11, adding one from London to Copenhagen adds 6 and removing one from London to Helsinki saves 12. The net change is $+16 - 11 + 6 - 12$, a reduction of 1 unit. Making these changes will therefore result in an improvement. Furthermore, they can be made for a second plane. It is not possible to add and subtract more than two planes, however, because the London–Helsinki route has only two planes initially.

If the changes are made for two planes we obtain the basic feasible solution shown in Fig. 4.5(b). As before there are six occupied cells, but the total distance is reduced to 209 units.

The four cells involved in a rearrangement do not always form a square. Take the Athens–Helsinki route, for example. Putting a plane on this route cannot be compensated by removing one from the Athens–Copenhagen route since this is a free, unoccupied cell. The $\oplus$ and $\ominus$ adjustments are therefore made at the corners of a rectangle, as shown. The effect on total distance is $+21 - 13 + 5 - 16$, a net change of -3. Again the modification is beneficial but the adjustments can only be made for one plane since the Athens–Paris cell then becomes empty. The result of this modification is shown in Fig. 4.5(c) and the saving of 3 units reduces the total distance to 206 units.

In contrast, using the Athens–Copenhagen route would now increase the total distance. The $\oplus$ and $\ominus$ markers, Fig. 4.5(c), form a square but the net change in total distance is $+18 - 11 + 16 - 21 = +2$. This possibility is therefore discarded.

Sometimes the $\oplus$ and $\ominus$ adjustments cannot be made using a square or rectangle of cells. To test the London–Stuttgart route (Fig. 4.5(d)) it is

Figure 4.5

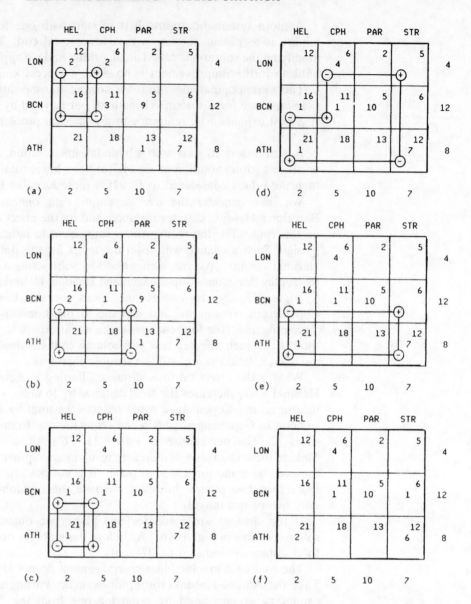

necessary to compensate with ⊖ markers in the London–Copenhagen and Athens–Stuttgart cells. The circuit of adjustments can only be made by using six occupied cells altogether, as shown. The resulting solution would still be a basic feasible one with six occupied routes because each row and column involved in the rearrangement would carry both a ⊕ and a ⊖. The change in total distance would then be $+5 - 6 + 11 - 16 + 21 - 12 = +3$, an increase of 3 units. This amendment would not be beneficial and is therefore abandoned.

In this configuration there is one cell that offers an improvement. It is Barcelona–Stuttgart and the amendments are shown in Fig. 4.5(e). The change in total distance is $+6 - 16 + 21 - 12 = -1$. The move can only be made for one plane and the resulting solution is shown in Fig. 4.5(f). The total distance is now **205 units** (20 500 miles). The allocations are: London–Copenhagen, 4; Barcelona–Copenhagen, 1; Barcelona–Paris, 10; Barcelona–Stuttgart, 1; Athens–Helsinki, 2; Athens–Stuttgart, 6.

If you test all the free cells at this stage you will find that no further improvement is possible. Of all the hundreds of feasible solutions this one gives the smallest total distance. It is called the optimal solution.

In this example the optimal solution contains a few surprises. It does not use the shortest route, London–Paris, at all but it includes two planes on the longest route, Athens–Helsinki. Furthermore, Stuttgart receives six of its required seven planes on the longest of the three routes approaching it. We could hardly have expected this outcome on first seeing the data.

The general method is to begin with a basic feasible solution and then to test the effect of adding a plane to one of the free routes. The cell is linked to occupied cells using horizontal and vertical paths; in chess, these are rook (or castle) moves. If alternate + and − changes round the circuit lead to a reduction in total cost or distance the adjustments are made for as many vehicles as possible. The optimal solution is reached when there is no free cell whose use would lead to a reduction in total cost.

If a stage is reached when there is no free cell that would give a reduction, but there is one whose use would neither increase nor decrease the total cost, there are at least two optimal solutions.

4.7 SHADOW COSTS

In the example just completed there were six unoccupied or free cells at every stage. It may be necessary to test all of them in turn before we find one that leads to an improvement. Furthermore, a cell that does not offer an improvement at one stage may do so after further iterations. We can only be sure that we have reached an optimal solution when none of the free elements leads to a reduction in total cost or distance.

With six free elements this work may be manageable, but consider a larger example with, say, eight sources and six destinations. Its matrix will contain 48 cells and, by the $m + n - 1$ rule, basic feasible solutions will occupy 13 of them. Hence, up to 35 cells have to be tested to find an improved solution or confirm that the current solution is optimal.

The work can be shortened by a technique known as the method of *shadow costs* (or method of *potentials*). It enables us to see in a single display the change in total cost or distance arising from the use of any of the free cells.

Figure 4.6

(a)   (b)

The method can be explained by reference to the airline problem. Suppose we have arrived at the solution shown in Fig. 4.5(b). It is reproduced as Fig. 4.6(a). The method enables us to construct a second matrix (Fig. 4.6(b)) showing, for each free cell, the change in total cost of allocating one plane to that route. The algorithm is as follows:

(a) Enter the cost values for the occupied routes. These are the circled values in Fig. 4.6(b).
(b) Assign u- and v-values to the rows and columns, chosen so that each value of $(u + v)$ equals the cost for the corresponding cell. The u- and v-values are called the *shadow costs*.
(c) For each free cell, subtract $(u + v)$ from its cost (or distance).
(d) The value obtained is the change in total cost that would result from the allocation of one vehicle to this route.

The first shadow cost is chosen arbitrarily. It can be a u- or a v-value. Whatever choice we make, the final values in the matrix will be the same. Suppose (Fig. 4.6(b)) we take the u-value for the first row as 4. Since the value of $(u + v)$ for the second cell of this row is 6, the v-value for the second column must be 2. For the second cell of the second row the $(u + v)$ total is 11. Since $v = 2$, the value of u for the second row is 9. For the first cell in the second row, $u + v = 16$ and, since $u = 9$, the v-value for the first column is 7. Similarly, for the third cell in the same row, $u + v = 5$ and v is therefore -4. It follows that the u-value for the third row must be 17 in order that $u + v = 13$ for the third cell, and the v-value for the fourth column is -5 to give 12 in the fourth cell.

We can now complete the matrix. For each free cell we subtract the value of $(u + v)$ from the corresponding cost. In row 1, the first cell becomes $12 - (4 + 7) = 1$, the third cell is $2 - [4 + (-4)] = 2$ and the fourth cell is $5 - [4 + (-5)] = 6$. The remaining free cells are completed in the same way.

As a check, repeat the process starting with a different choice for the first shadow cost. You will find that the u- and v-values will change but the elements in the matrix will be unaltered. Note that the shadow costs, and the values in the matrix, may be positive, negative or zero.

A free cell with a negative value is one that would lead to a reduction in cost or distance. In Fig. 4.6(b) there are two, the Athens–Helsinki and Athens–Copenhagen routes. Either could be used but the first leads to a greater reduction. Furthermore, the use of the Athens–Copenhagen route leads to a complication in that two cells would become empty at the same time and the solution, though feasible, would not be a basic feasible one. This matter is taken up in section 4.9.

You are advised to construct a shadow cost matrix for each step in the solution of the airline problem given earlier. Refer to the solutions shown in Fig. 4.5(a), (c) and (f). In the final matrix all the values in the free cells are positive, confirming that no further improvement can be made and that the solution is optimal.

The shadow cost method identifies every free cell that offers an improvement and the reduction in total cost or distance that its use would produce. However, the amendments to the solution must still be made using the stepping-stone technique.

4.8 UNBALANCED SUPPLY AND DEMAND

In the airline problem of Example 4.1 the total number of aircraft available at the sources, 24, was equal to the total required at the destinations. Suppose, however, the number available is greater than the number required. We can allow for the difference by introducing a fictitious 'dummy' destination to which the excess planes are sent, as shown in Fig. 4.7(a). The details are explained in the solution to the next example. The distance or cost of each route leading to the dummy is taken to be zero. The analysis is carried out in the same way as before and, in the optimal solution, planes destined for the dummy remain, in fact, at their sources.

If the demand exceeds the total available, a dummy source can be introduced. The requirements at the destinations can no longer be met in full, but we can ensure that the allocation of the planes available is made as economically as possible.

Example 4.3
Find the optimal solution for the airline problem of Examples 4.1 and 4.2 with the numbers of planes available increased to: 6 in London; 14 in Barcelona; 12 in Athens.

Solution
Figure 4.7(a) shows the northwest corner solution extended to include the dummy destination. In the rest of this diagram the basic feasible solutions are shown on the left, the various cities now being identified by their initial letters. The corresponding shadow cost matrices appear on the right. With three rows and five columns the critical number is $3 + 5 - 1 = 7$. Each basic feasible solution therefore occupies seven cells.

In each shadow cost calculation the arbitrary first choice is taken as $u = 0$ in row 1. The northwest corner solution, repeated in Fig. 4.7(b), involves a total distance of 175 units (17 500 miles). The corresponding shadow cost matrix is given in Fig. 4.7(c). Two free cells, BH and AH, have negative values and the use of either would lead to a reduction; AH shows the greater saving and this one is chosen for the first iteration. The changes affect six cells and the improved solution is given in Fig. 4.7(d).

The next shadow cost matrix (Fig. 4.7(e)) contains no negative values and the solution is therefore optimal. However, the value in cell LP is zero, indicating that another solution exists with the same total distance. The stepping-stone details are shown in Fig. 4.7(d) and the second optimal solution is given in Fig. 4.7(f). The shadow cost matrix for this solution is given in Fig. 4.7(g). It confirms that this solution is optimal.

The optimal allocations are therefore:

LH, 1; LC, 5; BP, 10; BS, 4; AH, 1; AS, 3

and

LC, 5; LP, 1; BP, 9; BS, 5; AH, 2; AS, 2.

The corresponding total distance is **173 units** (17 300 miles) and, in both optimal solutions, eight of the planes at Athens remain there.

Figure 4.7

	HEL	CPH	PAR	STR	Dummy	
LON	12 / 2	6 / 4	2	5	0	6
BCN	16	11 / 1	5 / 10	6 / 3	0	14
ATH	21	18	13	12 / 4	0 / 8	12
(a)	2	5	10	7	8	32

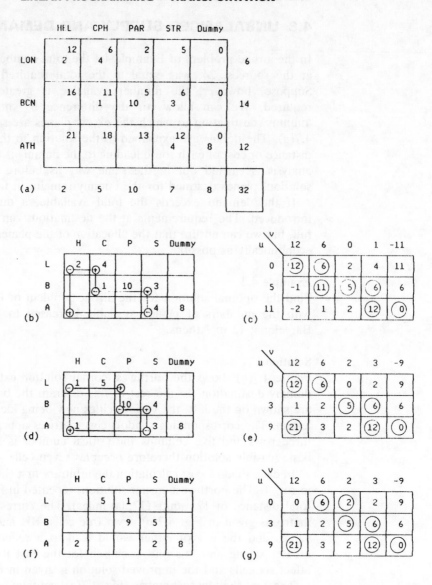

4.9 DEGENERATE SOLUTION

In some examples a feasible solution may arise that uses fewer routes than the critical number $(m + n - 1)$. Such a solution is said to be *degenerate* and it may occur at any stage of the analysis.

We can only use the method of shadow costs if the number of occupied cells is equal to the critical number. We therefore convert the degenerate solution to a basic feasible one, by bringing in one or more cells with zero allocations. These must be chosen from the cells that were occupied in the previous basic feasible solution. If the next solution is also degenerate the process is repeated.

A degenerate solution can arise in the airline problem of Examples 4.1 and 4.2. Consider the basic feasible solution of Fig. 4.5(b). It is repeated in

Figure 4.8

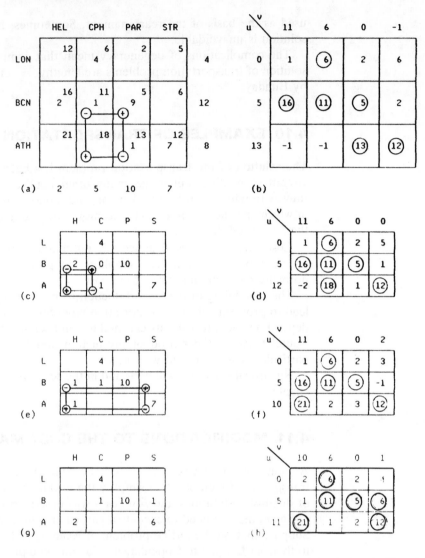

Fig. 4.8(a) with the corresponding shadow cost matrix shown in Fig. 4.8(b). Two cells, Athens–Helsinki and Athens–Copenhagen, lead to reductions in the total distance and, in the earlier analysis, the Athens–Helsinki route was used as the basis of the stepping-stone adjustments.

Suppose, however, the Athens–Copenhagen (AC) route is used, as indicated in Fig. 4.8(a). Putting a plane on this route leads to a reduction in the total distance, but it causes two cells (BC and AP) to become empty simultaneously. As a result, the next solution uses five routes only and is therefore degenerate. We can convert it to a basic feasible solution by incorporating BC or AP through a zero allocation. If we choose BC we obtain the solution shown in Fig. 4.8(c). The shadow cost matrix is obtained in the usual way (Fig. 4.8(d)) and it contains one cell with a negative value, AH. Using this route, and making amendments to the related cells by the stepping-stone method, leads to the basic feasible solution of Fig. 4.8(e).

The optimal solution of Fig. 4.8(g) is obtained after one more iteration. Degeneracy can usually be avoided by a judicious choice of the cell to be used as the basis of the rearrangment. Sometimes, however, a degenerate solution is unavoidable.

The complications of degeneracy mean that computer programs for the solution of transportation problems are lengthy. A very efficient one is given by Bunday.[2]

4.10 EXAMPLES OF TRANSPORTATION PROBLEMS

The solution of the transportation problem has been described in terms of aircraft scheduling, but it has many other applications. The allocation of railway freight wagons, oil-tankers or school buses can also lead to examples in which specified numbers have to move from sources to destinations with the least total distance.

Cost often replaces distance. A purchaser may be offered goods at different prices by different suppliers. In placing contracts the aim will normally be to minimize the total cost.

The scheduling of factory production to meet changing demand can also lead to problems of the transportation type. Storage and overtime costs will depend on the interval between making and selling the goods, so that each 'route' between the period of production and that of selling will have a particular cost associated with it.

Numerical examples will be found in the set of problems at the end of this chapter.

4.11 MODIFICATIONS TO THE COST MATRIX

A number of devices are used to extend the applications of the transportation method or to simplify the arithmetic. One of these – the use of dummy destinations and sources – was described in section 4.8.

Sometimes we need to exclude a particular route; this is easily dealt with. Suppose that, in the airline problem of Example 4.1, no planes are allowed to fly from London to Copenhagen. To eliminate planes from this route, we need only increase its distance from 6 units to a very high, fictitious value, say 1000. The usual methods of solution can then be applied and this route will not appear in the optimal solution.

It is often beneficial to modify the matrix of cost elements. We first note that every row and column involved in a stepping-stone circuit contains one $\oplus$ and one $\ominus$ adjustment. The net change due to these two adjustments will be unaltered if every element in the row (or column) is increased or decreased by the same amount. The generalization of this idea leads to the following theorem:

The optimal solution is unchanged if all the cost elements in a particular row or column are increased or decreased by the same amount.

To illustrate the use of this theorem, consider the cost matrix for the airline problem of Example 4.2.

The original values are shown in Fig. 4.9(a). It is convenient to reduce the elements to their lowest possible values, while avoiding negative

Figure 4.9

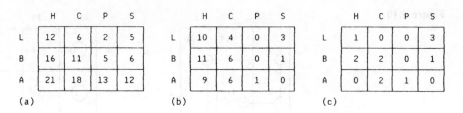

	H	C	P	S
L	12	6	2	5
B	16	11	5	6
A	21	18	13	12

(a)

	H	C	P	S
L	10	4	0	3
B	11	6	0	1
A	9	6	1	0

(b)

	H	C	P	S
L	1	0	0	3
B	2	2	0	1
A	0	2	1	0

(c)

quantities. We first subtract from all the elements in each row the lowest value in that row. In the present case the lowest value in the first row is 2, in the second is 5 and in the third is 12. If we subtract these amounts from all the elements on a row-by-row basis we obtain the matrix of Fig. 4.9(b). It contains three zeros, two being in the same column. The first and second columns contain no zeros, their least values being 9 and 4 respectively. If we reduce the other elements in these columns by these amounts, we arrive at the matrix of Fig. 4.9(c).

If you rework the problem using the elements in this matrix, you will obtain the same optimal solution as before. Note, however, that the total distance for the optimal solution must be found using the original values.

4.12 THE ASSIGNMENT PROBLEM

A special case of transportation is the assignment of personnel or machines to different tasks on a one-to-one basis. As in the earlier sections of this chapter, the solution is discussed in terms of a numerical example.

Example 4.4
Three machine tools are available for producing three different components on a one-to-one basis. The time in minutes required by each machine for each component is given in the following table:

		Component		
		1	2	3
	A	13	14	10
Machine	B	11	16	15
	C	17	12	9

Find the minimum total time required and the corresponding assignments.

Solution
This example can be regarded as a transportation problem in which each source and each destination has one vehicle, and the machine times are taken to be the costs or distances.

Figure 4.10(a) shows a solution in which machines A, B and C are assigned to components 1, 2 and 3 respectively. It is convenient to denote the cells by their row and column references so that these assignments use cells A1, B2 and C3. With three rows and three columns the critical number is $3 + 3 - 1 = 5$. However, only three routes can be used and every

Figure 4.10

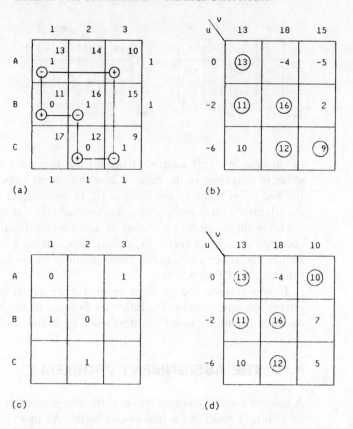

(a)   (b)

(c)   (d)

feasible solution is degenerate. To achieve a basic feasible solution, two zeros are added to the table. Their locations must be chosen to conform with the property of a basic feasible solution, namely that each entry must complete the requirements for one row or column. We cannot put the zeros in A2 and B1 since this combination would imply that the allocation in A1 does not complete a row or column. Several legitimate possibilities exist and the cells B1 and C2 are selected in this solution.

The shadow cost matrix for this solution is obtained in Fig. 4.10(b), starting with the arbitrary u-value of zero for row 1. Two cells contain negative values and either may be used as the basis of a stepping-stone circuit. If we select A3 the amendments involve six cells of which three, A1, B2 and C3, become empty. Two must be retained if the next solution is to be a basic feasible one and A1 and B2 are selected here. Figure 4.10(c) shows the resulting solution and Fig. 4.10(d) the corresponding shadow cost matrix.

One cell, A2, contains a negative value and this suggests that there might be a better solution. However, the use of A2 would necessitate the reduction of the allocations in A1 and B2, and this is impossible since they both have zero values.

The solution of Fig. 4.10(c) is therefore optimal. It allocates machine A to component 3, machine B to component 1, and machine C to component 2. The total machine time is 10 + 11 + 12 = **33 minutes**.

4.13 THE HUNGARIAN METHOD

The stepping-stone method is not very efficient when applied to assignment problems because the solution is degenerate at every stage. Algorithms have been devised especially for the assignment problem and the best known is the Hungarian method published by Kuhn[3] in 1955. As before, it is best explained by reference to a numerical example.

Example 4.5
Five managers (A, B, C, D and E) are to be placed in charge of five projects. The managers differ in ability and experience, and the projects vary in type and complexity. The suitability of each manager for each project is assessed on a numerical scale with a maximum of 50 points, and the results are as follows:

		Project				
		1	2	3	4	5
	A	43	27	31	17	41
	B	37	44	26	22	40
Manager	C	24	42	35	19	32
	D	46	30	40	36	18
	E	21	37	39	42	19

To which project should each manager be assigned to achieve the highest total points score, and what is the corresponding total?

Solution
The question asks for the highest total score but the transportation problem uses techniques for minimization. We therefore subtract every element in the matrix from the maximum score of 50. The results are shown in Fig. 4.11(a). A solution that minimizes the total score for this matrix will give the maximum with the original figures. This step is omitted, of course, if we are seeking a minimum points score.

The purpose of the remaining steps is to obtain a matrix containing zeros through which the assignments can be made, but without introducing negative elements. This is achieved by repeated applications of the theorem introduced in section 4.11. The steps are:

(a) *The smallest element in each row is subtracted from every element in that row.* In Fig. 4.11(a) the smallest row elements are 7, 6, 8, 4 and 8. This step leads to the matrix of Fig. 4.11(b).

(b) *The smallest element in each column is subtracted from every element in that column.* Columns 1, 2 and 4 already contain zeros; only columns 3 and 5 require modification. Their smallest elements are 3 and 2, and the result of this step is given in Fig. 4.11(c).

(c) *The zeros in the matrix are covered by the minimum number of horizontal and vertical lines. If this number equals the number of rows (or columns) the assignments can now be made; continue with step (e). If not, continue with step (d).* In the present case, four lines are sufficient to cover the zeros (one possibility is shown). We therefore proceed to (d).

Figure 4.11

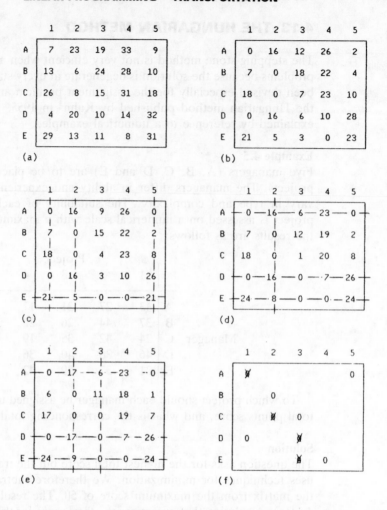

(d) *Select the smallest uncovered element. Subtract it from all the uncovered elements, and add it to those that are covered twice. Leave unaltered those that are covered once. Return to (c).* In Fig. 4.11(c) the smallest uncovered element is 3. Using this value the modifications lead to Fig. 4.11(d). Four lines are again sufficient to cover all the zeros (one possible configuration is shown). The lowest uncovered element is now 1 and the modifications result in the matrix of Fig. 4.11(e). This time, a minimum of five lines is needed to cover all the zeros and we continue to step (e).

(e) *Select an element of zero value for each assignment.* If a row or column contains only one zero it must be used. This may remove other zeros from consideration so that there is only one optimal solution. In some cases, however, a choice may remain and there can be two or more optimal solutions. Figure 4.11(f) shows the zeros in the present case. There are single zeros in row B, column 4, and column 5. These must be used and the zeros in A1, C2 and E3 are therefore eliminated. Manager C must therefore be assigned to project 3 and D must undertake project 1.

The assignments are therefore **A to 5; B to 2; C to 3; D to 1; E to 4**. The points total must be calculated from the original values given in the question. It is $41 + 44 + 35 + 46 + 42 =$ **208**.

The analysis is easily modified if there are more managers than projects. We increase the number of columns to equal the number of rows, taking all the elements in the additional columns to be zero. We then carry out the same steps as before and, in the optimum solution, managers assigned to the dummy projects are omitted from the schedule.

An alternative to the Hungarian algorithm, devised by Mack[4] and known as the Bradford method, is described in the book by Bunday.[5]

4.14 COMPUTER PROGRAM FOR THE ASSIGNMENT PROBLEM

The Hungarian method is not easily implemented on a computer. A simple alternative for small problems is given in Fig. 4.12. It is limited to seven assignments because its running time increases rapidly with the number of rows and columns.

It is written in BBC BASIC and employs a recursive technique that is only available on BBC and Acorn machines, and the Cambridge Z88. This is used to generate all the feasible solutions which are then examined in turn. For n assignments the number of feasible solutions is $n!$ so that with $n = 3$, 4 and 5 there are 6, 24 and 120 feasible solutions respectively. A computer can deal with these in a few seconds, but larger problems take noticeably longer. On the Acorn Electron, for example, a relatively slow machine by today's standards, six assignments (720 feasible solutions) take nearly one minute and for seven (5040 feasible solutions) the running time is several minutes.

Lines 10–80 display the heading, call for the number of assignments and set up arrays. Line 90 defines a string variable used in the permutations.

Lines 110–140 establish whether the problem is one of maximization or minimization. If maximization is chosen the initial total points value T is set at zero. If minimization, T is given a very large value, 10^{10}.

Lines 150–400 call for the cost elements one at a time, display the complete matrix and offer the chance of amending entries. Note that the rows are denoted by letters (A, B, C . . .) to be consistent with the notation of Figs 4.10 and 4.11, but for amending entries the row numbers must be used.

Lines 410–460 display a heading for the results and line 470 initiates the PROCedure for generating the feasible solutions.

Lines 490–530 print the optimum points score and close the program.

Lines 530–620 define the PROCedure for permuting the assignments, calling up a further PROCedure at line 560 for showing the results.

Lines 630–720 define the PROCedure for the display which is then shown on the screen by lines 730–780 if it represents an improvement.

Figure 4.13 shows the printout that was obtained when the program was run with the data of the machine assignment problem of Example 4.3.

A longer but very efficient program based on Mack's Bradford method is given by Bunday.[6] This does not limit the number of assignments and finds

Figure 4.12

```
10 REM    N         NUMBER OF ROWS, COLUMNS
20 REM    X(R,C) ELEMENT AT ROW R, COLUMN C
30 PRINT "------------------------------------"
40 PRINT "ASSIGNMENTS"
50 PRINT "------------------------------------"
60 PRINT
70 INPUT "NUMBER OF ASSIGNMENTS (2-7)";N
80 DIM X(N,N):DIM Y(N):DIM R$(N)
90 A$=LEFT$("1234567",N)
100 PRINT
110 INPUT "MAXIMISE OR MINIMISE (MAX/MIN)";Q$
120 IF Q$="MAX" OR Q$="max" THEN Z=1:T=0:GOTO 150
130 IF Q$="MIN" OR Q$="min" THEN Z=-1:T=1E10:GOTO 150
140 GOTO 100
150 PRINT:PRINT "ENTER THE VALUE OF EACH ELEMENT":PRINT
160 FOR I=1 TO N
170 READ R$(I)
180 FOR J=1 TO N
190 PRINT "ROW ";R$(I);" COLUMN ";J
200 INPUT X(I,J)
210 NEXT J
220 PRINT
230 NEXT I
240 PRINT "CHECK THE TABLE OF VALUES:"
250 PRINT
260 FOR I=1 TO N
270 FOR J=1 TO N
280 PRINT TAB(4*J);X(I,J);
290 NEXT J
300 PRINT
310 NEXT I
320 PRINT
330 PRINT "TO CHANGE A VALUE ENTER THE ROW AND"
340 PRINT "COLUMN NUMBERS (0,0 TO CONTINUE)"
350 INPUT R,C
360 IF R=0 OR C=0 THEN GOTO 410
370 PRINT
380 PRINT "PRESENT VALUE IS ";X(R,C)
390 INPUT "ENTER NEW VALUE";X(R,C)
400 GOTO 240
410 PRINT "ROW-";
420 FOR I=1 TO N
430 PRINT TAB(3*I+2);R$(I);
440 NEXT I
450 PRINT TAB(3*N+8);"TOTAL POINTS"
460 PRINT:PRINT "COL:"
470 PROCperm(A$,"")
480 PRINT
490 IF Z=1 THEN PRINT "THE MAXIMUM TOTAL POINTS SCORE IS ";T
500 IF Z=-1 THEN PRINT "THE MINIMUM TOTAL POINTS SCORE IS ";T
510 PRINT:PRINT "------------------------------------"
520 END
530 DEFPROCperm(A$,U$)
540 LOCAL I,B$,V$
550 L=LEN A$
560 IF L=1 PROCdisp:ENDPROC
570 FOR I=1 TO L
580 V$=U$+MID$(A$,I,1)
590 B$=LEFT$(A$,I-1)+MID$(A$,I+1)
600 PROCperm(B$,V$)
610 NEXT I
620 ENDPROC
630 DEFPROCdisp
640 U$=U$+A$
650 R=0
660 FOR J=1 TO N
670 Y(J)=VAL(MID$(U$,J,1))
680 R=R+X(J,Y(J))
690 NEXT J
700 IF Z=1 AND R>=T THEN T=R:GOSUB 730
710 IF Z=-1 AND R<=T THEN T=R:GOSUB 730
720 ENDPROC
730 REM  DISPLAY RESULTS
740 FOR J=1 TO N
750 PRINT TAB(3*J+2);Y(J);
760 NEXT J
770 PRINT TAB(3*N+8);T
780 RETURN
790 DATA A,B,C,D,E,F,G
```

Figure 4.13

```
------------------------------------
ASSIGNMENTS
------------------------------------

NUMBER OF ASSIGNMENTS (2-7)?3

MAXIMISE OR MINIMISE (MAX/MIN)?MIN

ENTER THE VALUE OF EACH ELEMENT

ROW A COLUMN 1
?13
ROW A COLUMN 2
?14
ROW A COLUMN 3
?10

ROW B COLUMN 1
?11
ROW B COLUMN 2
?16
ROW B COLUMN 3
?15

ROW C COLUMN 1
?17
ROW C COLUMN 2
?12
ROW C COLUMN 3
?9

CHECK THE TABLE OF VALUES:

     13  14  10
     11  16  15
     17  12   9

TO CHANGE A VALUE ENTER THE ROW AND
COLUMN NUMBERS (0,0 TO CONTINUE)
?0
?0
ROW- A  B  C      TOTAL POINTS

COL:
      1  2  3       38
      2  1  3       34
      3  1  2       33

THE MINIMUM TOTAL POINTS SCORE IS 33

------------------------------------
```

an optimum solution for large problems in a few seconds. If there are two or more optimal solutions it displays only one, however, whereas the program given above shows them all.

4.15 CONSTRAINT EQUATIONS AND THE OBJECTIVE FUNCTION

The algorithms used in the solution of the transportation problem are expressed in terms of tables and matrices. The problems can also be formulated in terms of linear equations. Suppose, in the airline problem of Examples 4.1 and 4.2, the numbers of planes on the London–Helsinki, London–Copenhagen, London–Paris . . . routes are denoted by the variables x_{LH}, x_{LC}, x_{LP} . . ., there being 12 altogether.

Each constraint can be represented by a linear equation. For instance, the variables for the routes starting from London, x_{LH}, x_{LC}, x_{LP} and x_{LS} must add up to 4, since this is the number of planes available there. Similarly, the variables associated with the routes from Barcelona must total 12, and for Athens it is 8. These source constraints therefore lead to the equations:

$$x_{LH} + x_{LC} + x_{LP} + x_{LS} = 4$$
$$x_{BH} + x_{BC} + x_{BP} + x_{BS} = 12$$
$$x_{AH} + x_{AC} + x_{AP} + x_{AS} = 8$$

The requirements at the four destinations can be represented by further equations, each containing the variables for routes approaching the corresponding city. These are:

$$x_{LH} + x_{BH} + x_{AH} = 2$$
$$x_{LC} + x_{BC} + x_{AC} = 5$$
$$x_{LP} + x_{BP} + x_{AP} = 10$$
$$x_{LS} + x_{BS} + x_{AS} = 7$$

In all we have 7 simultaneous equations and 12 variables (or unknowns). It follows that there are many feasible solutions, even though the variables are restricted to positive integer values. Of these, we are seeking the one that minimizes the total distance.

The total distance (or cost) to be minimized is called the *objective function* and it is usually denoted by z. It can be expressed in terms of the same variables. Since the London–Helsinki distance is 12 units the total for all the planes on this route is $12x_{LH}$. For Copenhagen it is $6x_{LC}$, and so on. Hence, for all the routes,

$$z = 12x_{LH} + 6x_{LC} + 2x_{LP} + 5x_{LS} + 16x_{BH} + 11x_{BC} + 5x_{BP}$$
$$+ 6x_{BS} + 21x_{AH} + 18x_{AC} + 13x_{AP} + 12x_{AS}$$

The optimum solution is the one that minimizes z. The constraint equations and the objective function are all linear in form – hence the term linear programming. The transportation problem is usually tackled by the iterative methods described in the earlier sections. It is a special case of linear programming and the general form includes inequalities as well as equations. This is the subject of Chapter 5.

The assignment problem is a restricted case of transportation in which the right-hand side of each constraint equation is 1 and the value of each variable is therefore 0 or 1.

4.16 SUMMARY

Transportation problems are concerned with the scheduling of vehicles or other units from sources to destinations. The numbers available at the sources and required at the destinations constitute constraints, and the total cost or distance is the objective function that has to be optimized.

The general method of solution is to begin with an arbitrary feasible solution and improve it step by step until the optimum is attained. The stepping-stone method is used to make the adjustments, and the routes that can lead to improvements are identified by means of shadow costs. The techniques require the allocations to form a basic feasible solution and this can be achieved by setting each variable to a value which completes a row or column total and making use of $m + n - 1$ routes, where m and n are the numbers of rows and columns. Solutions that use fewer routes are said to be degenerate.

If supply and demand are not equal, we introduce a dummy destination or source to account for the difference. All routes to or from the dummy are taken as having zero cost or distance.

The assignment problem is a case of transportation in which every source and destination has one vehicle or unit. Special algorithms, such as the Hungarian method, are more efficient than the shadow cost and stepping-stone methods.

REFERENCES

1. Hitchcock F L 1941 The distribution of a product from several sources to numerous localities *Journal for Mathematics and Physics* **20:** 224
2. Bunday D B 1984 *Basic Linear Programming* Edward Arnold p. 89
3. Kuhn H W 1955 The Hungarian method for the assignment problem *Nav. Res. Logistics Quarterly* **2:** 83
4. Mack C 1969 The Bradford method for the assignment problem *The New Journal of Statistics and Operational Research* **1** (1): 17
5. Bunday D B 1984 *Basic Linear Programming* Edward Arnold p. 106
6. Bunday D B 1984 *Basic Linear Programming* Edward Arnold pp 107–11

BIBLIOGRAPHY

Dantzig G 1963 *Linear Programming and Extensions* Princeton University Press

Kreko B 1968 *Linear Programming* (English translation) Pitman

Loomba N P 1964 *Linear Programming, an Introductory Analysis* McGraw-Hill

Taha H A 1987 *Operations Research* 4th edn Collier-Macmillan

Vajda S 1973 *Planning by Mathematics* 2nd edn Pitman

PROBLEMS

1. Figure 4.14(a) shows a transportation problem with three sources, A, B and C, and four destinations, P, Q, R and S.

Figure 4.14

	P	Q	R	S	
A					11
B					4
C					16
	6	2	18	5	31

(a)

	P	Q	R	S
A	10	18	9	20
B	8	14	22	7
C	11	6	15	5

(b)

(i) Obtain the northwest corner solution.

(ii) The cost matrix is shown in Fig. 4.14(b). What is the cost of the northwest corner solution?

(iii) Find the optimum solution and the minimum cost.

Answer   (i) AP, 6; AQ, 2; AR, 3; BR, 4; CR, 11; CS, 5.

(ii) 401.

(iii) AR, 11; BP, 4; CP, 2; CQ, 2; CR, 7; CS, 5. Cost = 295.

2. Repeat Problem 1 with the quantities available at the sources increased to 12 at A, 8 at B, and 20 at C.

Answer   (i) AP, 6; AQ, 2; AR, 4; BR, 8; CR, 6; CS, 5; C/DUMMY, 9.

(ii) 423.

(iii) AR, 12; BP, 6; B/DUMMY, 2; CQ, 2; CR, 6; CS, 5; C/DUMMY, 7. Cost = 283.

3. Solve the transportation problem of Fig. 4.15.

Figure 4.15

	1	2	3	4	5	6	7	8	
1	7	12	23	2	14	8	16	5	11
2	4	20	17	8	16	26	13	7	18
3	10	11	9	19	3	18	5	24	4
4	21	26	14	2	20	17	25	6	13
5	18	7	5	17	10	19	21	9	8
	7	3	5	10	2	9	6	12	54

Answer   Optimal solution is degenerate. $x_{16} = 9$, $x_{18} = 2$, $x_{21} = 7$, $x_{27} = 4$, $x_{28} = 7$, $x_{35} = 2$, $x_{37} = 2$, $x_{44} = 10$, $x_{48} = 3$, $x_{52} = 3$, $x_{53} = 5$. Cost = 311.

4. Three foundries A, B and C can produce a certain casting in the following maximum quantities per week:

A, 6; B, 8; C, 18.

The casting is required at four assembly plants in the following numbers per week:

P, 4; Q, 3; R, 9; S, 10.

The relative costs of transporting each casting between the foundries and the assembly plants are shown in the following table:

	P	Q	R	S
A	8	4	7	6
B	12	5	9	10
C	11	2	15	3

Find the schedule that minimizes the total transport cost, and state the production rates required at A, B and C. What is the corresponding transport cost?

Answer AP, 4; AR, 2; BR, 7; B/DUMMY, 1; CQ, 3; CS, 10; C/DUMMY, 5. Production rates: A, 6; B, 7; C, 13. Cost = 145.

5. A raw material is available from four chemical plants in the following quantities, in tonnes per week:

A, 80; B, 40; C, 140; D, 180.

The material is required at four processing plants in the following quantities, also in tonnes per week:

K, 160; L, 60; M, 20; N, 200.

(a) Show, on a suitable matrix, a feasible allocation based on multiples of 20 tonnes.
(b) The material is carried in 20-tonne lorries, the transport cost in £ per return lorry-journey for the various routes, being given in the following table:

	K	L	M	N
A	27	9	17	39
B	45	13	19	37
C	33	31	15	23
D	11	27	29	5

Calculate the total weekly transport cost for the allocations you have made.
(c) Find the optimal solution and the corresponding minimum cost.

Answer (a) Northwest corner solution is AK, 4; BK, 2; CK, 2; CL, 3; CM, 1; CN, 1; 9 (in multiples of 20 tonnes). (b) £440. (c) AK, 3; AL, 1; BL, 2; CM, 1; CN, 6; DK, 5; DN, 4; £344.

6. The following table shows the positions of wagons at the end of a week's operation of a containerization service.

Depot	A	B	C	D	E	F	G
Number of wagons at depot	5	2	9	14	10	4	22
Number required for following week	10	15	6	8	6	18	3

The wagons are to be redistributed during the weekend in readiness for the next week's schedule. The distance (in km) chart for the various routes is given below.

	A	B	C	D	E	F	G
A	—						
B	40	–					
C	320	330	—				
D	290	340	10	—			
E	80	30	270	260	—		
F	70	90	200	220	50	—	
G	130	70	350	370	40	90	—

Obtain a feasible routeing arrangement and calculate the total wagon-kilometres involved.

Find the optimal solution and the corresponding minimum total wagon-kilometres.

Answer Note that C, D, E and G are effectively sources and A, B and F are net destinations. With the rows and columns in these orders, the northwest corner solution is CA, 3; DA, 2; DB, 4; EB, 4; GB, 5; GF, 14; the corresponding total distance is 4630 wagon-kilometres.

The optimal solution is CF, 3; DF, 6; EA, 4; GA, 1; GB, 13; GF, 5; the minimum total distance is 3730 wagon-kilometres.

7. (a) In the development of a satellite town four new residential areas are planned. It is expected that these will have the following secondary school populations:

A, 120; B, 60; C, 210; D, 270.

These populations are to be accommodated by the expansion of four existing schools. The numbers of places to be provided are:

P, 240; Q, 90; R, 30; S, 300.

Show, in a suitable table, a feasible allocation arrangement based on multiples of 30.

School buses are to be provided, each carrying 30 students, between the residential areas and the schools. The expected journey times in minutes are given below:

	P	Q	R	S
A	25	7	15	33
B	46	14	20	37
C	34	32	16	24
D	12	28	30	18

(b) Calculate the total bus-minutes for the arrangement you have selected.

(c) Modify the solution to reduce this total to the minimum.

(d) It has been decided that no student should spend more than 35 minutes on the journey. What is now the optimal solution and the corresponding total of bus-minutes?

Answer (a) In units of 30 the northwest corner solution is AP, 4; BP, 2; CP, 2; CQ, 3; CR, 1; CS, 1; DS, 9; (b) 558 bus-minutes; (c) AP, 1; AQ, 3; BR, 1; BS, 1; CS, 7; DP, 7; DS, 2. 391 bus-minutes; (d) AP, 2; AQ, 2; BQ, 1; BR, 1; CS, 7; DP, 6; DS, 3. 392 bus-minutes.

8. A sudden strike by the pilots of the Royal Ruritanian Airline has left its fleet of 24 jumbo jets grounded in the following cities (with their crews):

5 in New York; 8 in Athens; 11 in London.

An early settlement of the dispute is expected and, to restart operations, the aircraft will be required at the following airports:

2 in Madrid; 7 in Rome; 9 in Tripoli; 6 in Zenda.

How should the planes be allocated so that the total aircraft-miles will be as small as possible? The route distances in miles are given in the following table:

	Madrid	Rome	Tripoli	Zenda
New York	3600	4300	4700	4100
Athens	1500	700	1200	500
London	800	900	1500	600

What is the total aircraft-miles corresponding to this schedule?
Answer New York–Madrid, 2; New York–Tripoli, 3; Athens–Rome, 2; London–Rome, 5; London–Zenda, 6. Total distance = 38 000 miles.

9. The Tardy Timepiece Company is launching its new atomic chronometer at the beginning of August. Market research shows that sales will increase rapidly as Christmas approaches. The expected monthly orders are 2000 in August, 4000 in September, 5000 in October and 7000 in November. Under normal working conditions the production capacity is 4000 per month, at a unit cost of £20. If overtime is worked an additional 1000 can be made, at a cost of £22 each.

Stocks not sold within the month of manufacture can be stored at a cost of £1 each per month. In addition, chronometers in store must be reinspected after 2 months at a cost of £1 each.

Figure 4.16 shows a table for displaying production schedules, the row and column totals being given in thousands. It is equivalent to a

Figure 4.16

Month of production:	Month of sale: August	September	October	November	Dummy	
August normal	20	21	23	24	0	4000
August overtime	22	23	25	26	0	1000
September normal		20	21	23	0	4000
September overtime		22	23	25	0	1000
October normal			20	21	0	4000
October overtime			22	23	0	1000
November normal				20	0	4000
November overtime				22	0	1000
	2000	4000	5000	7000	2000	

transportation matrix in which the production months and the selling months are the sources and destinations. Each 'route' has a cost made up of the unit production cost (regular or overtime), together with the storage and reinspection costs, if appropriate. A route for which the selling month is earlier than the production month must, of course, be excluded by being given a very high cost value.

How should the production be scheduled in order to minimize the total cost?

Answer There are many optimal solutions, each with a total cost of £370 000. They all include the manufacture of 4000 units in August and again in September, no overtime being worked in these months. These quantities satisfy the needs for August and September, with 2000 being carried forward for sale in October.

In October, the maximum production (regular and overtime) is required. Of the 5000 units produced, 3000 are sold during the month and 2000 are carried forward for sale in November. It makes no difference whether the units carried forward come from the regular or overtime working; hence there are many optimal solutions. Again in November the maximum production is required in order to satisfy the demand.

10. An alternative to the northwest corner method for a first basic feasible solution is the 'lowest costs first' rule. We select the cell of least cost and assign to it the maximum number of units, subject to the row and column totals. This removes one row or one column and the rule is applied to the cells that remain. The process is repeated until all the rows and columns are accounted for.

Find the 'lowest costs first' solution for the airline problem of Examples 4.1 and 4.2.

Answer LP, 4; BP, 6; BS, 6; AH, 2; AC, 5; AS, 1. Distance = 218 units.

11. Using the data of Example 4.2 find the solution that would maximize the total aircraft-miles and the corresponding total distance.

Answer LS, 4; BH, 2; BC, 5; BP, 2; BS, 3; AP, 8. 23 900 miles (239 units).

12. Solve each of the following assignment problems for both minimum and maximum total scores:

(a)
17	11	14
9	7	12
15	6	10

(b)
15	12	9	17
6	11	10	14
8	18	5	16
3	13	8	19

(c)
65	64	60	62	60
61	61	64	60	58
61	59	54	62	48
57	61	56	56	54
63	59	64	57	55

(d)
68	64	71	52	73	58
50	41	72	86	68	83
84	34	74	81	37	73
51	41	84	38	64	74
40	51	57	61	82	75
60	54	59	55	76	46

Answer (all assignments expressed as row/column numbers).

(a) Minimum: 13, 21, 32.   Total = 29.
Maximum: 12, 23, 31.   Total = 38.
(b) Minimum: 12, 24, 33, 41. Total = 34.
Maximum: 11, 23, 32, 44. Total = 62.
(c) Minimum: 13, 22, 35, 41, 54. Total = 283.
Maximum: Two optimal solutions. 11, 25, 34, 42, 53, and 15, 23, 34, 42, 51. Total = 310.
(d) Minimum: Two optimal solutions. 13, 22, 35, 44, 51, 66, and 16, 22, 35, 44, 51, 63. Total = 273.
Maximum: 12, 24, 31, 43, 56, 65. Total = 469.

13. A major food retailer is expanding its operations in Midshire. It plans to build four superstores and has obtained tenders from four contractors in the region. The sums in millions of £ are shown below:

	Superstore			
	1	2	3	4
Contractor 1	1.73	1.27	1.69	1.96
Contractor 2	1.78	1.28	1.67	2.01
Contractor 3	1.68	1.34	1.59	2.11
Contractor 4	1.72	1.29	1.52	1.89

The company has decided that each contractor shall be limited to one store. How should the four contracts be assigned in order to minimize the total cost? What is the optimum cost?
Answer Contractors 1, 2, 3 and 4 should be assigned to stores 4, 2, 1 and 3 respectively. Total cost £6.44 million.

14. A fifth contractor is invited to tender for the construction of the four stores in the previous question. If this contractor quotes sums, in £ million, of 1.65, 1.33, 1.53 and 1.90 respectively for the four stores, how should the contracts be assigned, and what is now the minimum total cost?
Answer Two optimal solutions. Both omit contractor 2, and assign contractors 1 and 3 to stores 2 and 1 respectively. Contractors 4 and 5 undertake stores 4 and 3 respectively, or 3 and 4. Total cost £6.37 million.

15. Five precision components are to be shaped using five machine tools, one being assigned to each. The machining times, in minutes, are given in the following table:

	Component				
	1	2	3	4	5
Machine tool 1	27	21	20	39	36
Machine tool 2	30	25	22	24	25
Machine tool 3	26	36	22	36	23
Machine tool 4	43	34	21	23	39
Machine tool 5	40	34	22	23	39

How should the machine tools be assigned so that the total machining time will be as small as possible, and what is the corresponding minimum total time?

How are the answers modified if a sixth machine tool, capable of completing each of the components in 23 minutes, becomes available?

Answer The five machine tools should be assigned to components 2, 5, 1, 3 and 4 respectively. Total machining time, 116 minutes. With the sixth machine available, tool number 2 is not used and the others are assigned to components 2, 5, 3, 4 and 1 respectively; total time = 111 minutes.

5 LINEAR PROGRAMMING – GRAPHICAL AND SIMPLEX METHODS

'Simplex munditiis – Simply but with style.'

Horace *Odes, Book 1*

5.1 CONSTRAINTS AND BOUNDARIES

In the transportation problem (Ch. 4) the constraints are the numbers of vehicles or other units at the sources and destinations. Each constraint can be expressed as an equation (section 4.15) and a feasible solution is a set of values satisfying these equations. These are constraints of the 'equal-to' type.

We now extend the analysis to include constraints that are upper or lower boundaries. These are 'less-than-or-equal-to' or 'more-than-or-equal-to' constraints and they are expressed as inequalities rather than equations.

Example 5.1
A publisher is bringing out the autobiography of a controversial politician and is confident that the entire first printing can be sold if there is no delay in publication. It has been decided that hardback and paperback versions will appear simultaneously and the project is subject to the following constraints:

(a) The printing department can produce a maximum of 10 000 copies, hardback or paperback.
(b) The binding department could manage 12 000 paperback copies alone or 8000 hardbacks alone, or proportions of these two amounts that total 1.
(c) The warehouse could dispatch a maximum of 15 000 paperback copies or 9000 hardbacks, or proportions of each totalling 1.
(d) There are advance orders for 2000 paperback copies and 1000 hardbacks that must be fulfilled from the first printing.
(e) At least a quarter of the total copies must be hardback.

Under these conditions, which of the following production schedules are feasible?

 (i) 3000 paperbacks and 6000 hardbacks;
 (ii) 5000 paperbacks and 5000 hardbacks;
 (iii) 7000 paperbacks and 3000 hardbacks;
 (iv) 8000 paperbacks and 2000 hardbacks.

If the profit on each paperback copy is 30 p, and on each hardback is 36 p, what is the total profit for those of the above schedules that are feasible?

111

Solution

A feasible solution is a production schedule – the numbers of paperback and hardback copies – that satisfies all the constraints specified in the question. Testing the four pairs of values in turn we have:

(i) (a) Printing requirement = 3000 + 6000 = 9000 copies, which is within that department's capacity.

   (b) The proportion of the binding department's capacity required for the paperbacks is 3000/12 000 = 0.25. For the hardbacks it is 6000/8000 = 0.75. Adding these results, 0.75 + 0.25 = 1, and the department's capacity is therefore just sufficient.

   (c) The corresponding proportions for the warehouse are 3000/15 000 = 0.2 and 6000/9000 = 0.667. These total 0.867 and the schedule is therefore within the capacity of this department.

   (d) The schedule is clearly sufficient to cover the advance orders.

   (e) A quarter of the total number of copies (9000) is 2250. The schedule includes 6000 hardbacks, thus meeting the requirement.

   Since all the constraints are met, this schedule is a **feasible** solution.

(ii) (a) This schedule leads to a total of 10 000 copies and is therefore a possible one for the printing department.

   (b) The total proportion of the binding capacity required by this schedule is 5000/12 000 + 5000/8000 = 1.042. This exceeds the capacity of this department and the schedule is **not feasible**.

(iii) (a) The total number of copies = 10 000 and the printing constraint is therefore satisfied.

   (b) The required proportion of the binding capacity is 7000/12 000 + 3000/8000 = 0.958.

   (c) The required proportion of the warehouse capacity is 7000/15 000 + 3000/9000 = 0.800.

   (d) The advance orders are covered by this schedule.

   (e) A quarter of the total number of copies (10 000) is 2500 so that the hardback number exceeds the required minimum.

   Since all the constraints are met, the schedule is **feasible**.

(iv) If you test this schedule against the constraints you will find that it meets all the constraints except (e). The solution is therefore **not feasible**.

Of the four schedules given in the question, (i) and (iii) are feasible. The corresponding profits are as follows:

(i) profit = 3000 × 30 + 6000 × 36 = 306 000 p
   = **£3060**

(iii) profit = 7000 × 30 + 3000 × 36 = 318 000 p
   = **£3180**

There are many examples of this kind in industry and business, in which resources have to be divided among two or more products. They are sometimes called 'mixture' problems and the usual aim is to obtain the schedule that leads to maximum profit. We shall return to this in section 5.3.

5.2 GRAPHIC REPRESENTATION

It is convenient to represent the constraints by graphs and Fig. 5.1 shows the outcome for the data of Example 5.1.

Figure 5.1

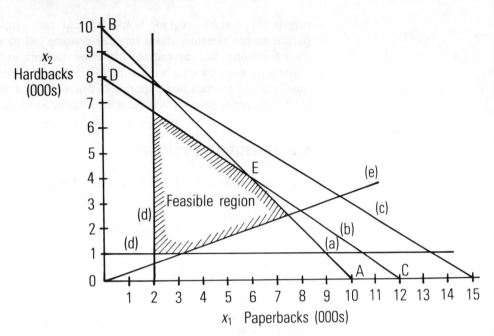

The horizontal and vertical axes represent the numbers of paperback and hardback copies and each point on the diagram corresponds to a particular production schedule. It is usual to denote the variables by x_1 and x_2 (rather than x and y).

The capacity of the printing department is sufficient for a maximum of 10 000 paperback copies (provided there are no hardbacks) or 10 000 hardbacks (and no paperbacks). These two possibilities are represented by points A and B respectively. There are many other combinations that use the full printing capacity, such as 1000 hardbacks and 9000 paperbacks, 2500 hardbacks and 7500 paperbacks, and so on. The corresponding points all lie on the straight line AB, and this represents constraint (a). Every feasible solution lies on or below this line.

In the same way, constraint (b) (a maximum of 12 000 paperbacks or 8000 hardbacks) is represented by the line CD. Schedules that satisfy both (a) and (b) lie within or on the perimeter of the quadrilateral OAED. The line representing constraint (c) (15 000 paperbacks or 9000 hardbacks) is entirely outside this quadrilateral and it does not restrict the production schedules further.

The advance orders given in (d) constitute two more constraints since they are linked by 'and' rather than 'or'. The minimum number of paperbacks is given by the vertical line that cuts the horizontal axis at 2000, and the minimum hardback requirement by the horizontal line cutting the vertical axis at 1000.

Constraint (e) requires the hardbacks to be at least one-quarter of the total. If the total is 4000, the hardbacks must be at least 1000, leaving 3000 paperbacks. Similarly, with 6000 paperbacks there must be at least 2000 hardbacks. These combinations are represented by points on the line through the origin whose slope is 1/3. Feasible solutions are located to the left (anticlockwise) of this line.

Together, the constraint lines define the hatched area on the diagram and this is the feasible region. Solutions that fall within the area or on its perimeter are feasible, those that fall outside fail to satisfy one or more of the constraints. We can therefore use the diagram to test for feasibility. For a given production schedule we locate the point whose coordinates are the numbers of hardback and paperback copies. If it is within the feasible region (or on its perimeter), it is a feasible solution; otherwise it is not.

5.3 MAXIMUM PROFIT

Each feasible solution leads to a particular level of profit. In Example 5.1 the profits associated with the production schedules (i) and (iii) are £3060 and £3180 respectively. The feasible region of Fig. 5.1 is reproduced in Fig. 5.2 and we could seek the schedule giving maximum profit by testing more points within or on the edge of it. This would not take long in the present case, but it is worth seeking a more systematic method.

Figure 5.2

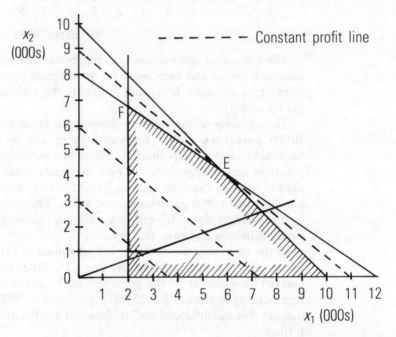

To do this we consider various profit levels and determine the combinations of paperbacks and hardbacks that produce them. Suppose we look for a profit of 108 000 p (this figure is a convenient multiple of 30 and 36). To achieve it with paperbacks alone we should need 108 000/30 = 3600 copies. With hardbacks and no paperbacks, we should require 108 000/36 = 3000 copies. These two schedules are represented by points on the horizontal and vertical axes at values of 3600 and 3000 respectively. Furthermore, the same level of profit would be obtained for all schedules on the line joining these points. This is shown by the lowest of the broken lines in Fig. 5.2.

If we repeat the process for a higher level of profit, say 216 000 p, we obtain a parallel constant profit line further from the origin.

For the maximum profit, therefore, we seek the line which has the same slope and intersects the feasible region as far as possible from the origin. From the diagram it is the one through E and this point represents the schedule leading to the greatest profit. From a scale drawing, or by calculation, its coordinates are $x_1 = 6000$ and $x_2 = 4000$. The optimum schedule is therefore 6000 paperbacks and 4000 hardbacks. Hence

$$\text{Maximum profit} = 6000 \times 30 + 4000 \times 36 = 324\,000\,\text{p}$$
$$= \textbf{£3240}$$

Compare this result with those for schedules (i) and (iii). Note that this profit, obtained from a mixture of paperback and hardback copies, is greater than we would obtain by concentrating on one or the other.

With different unit profits the optimum schedule might not correspond to the point E. However, the maximum total profit normally occurs at one of the vertices of the feasible region. To find the maximum profit we only need to test these vertices.

It may happen that the constant profit lines are parallel to one side of the feasible region. For example, if the unit profits on paperbacks and hardbacks were 24 and 36 p respectively the constant profit lines would be parallel to the side EF. All points along EF would then lead to the same maximum profit (£2880).

There is a further consideration to be taken into account. In most production problems practical values must be whole numbers. We cannot sell a fraction of a book!

5.4 ALGEBRAIC FORMULATION

In the transportation problem the constraints lead to equations in which expressions containing the x variables are equal to specified values. In the mixture problem the constraints are usually expressed, not in terms of 'equal to', but as 'not more than' or 'not less than'. For these relationships we use the symbols $\leqslant$ and $\geqslant$, meaning 'less than or equal to' and 'more than or equal to'. In computer programs we have to use the double symbols $<=$ and $>=$.

Suppose, in Example 5.1, we take x_1 and x_2 to be the numbers of paperback and hardback copies. Neither can be negative and we indicate this by putting $x_1 \geqslant 0$ and $x_2 \geqslant 0$, or simply

$$x_1, x_2 \geqslant 0$$

Constraint (a) specifies that the total number of copies cannot exceed 10 000. This is shown as

$$x_1 + x_2 \leqslant 10\,000$$

Using the figures specified in constraint (b), the proportion of the total binding capacity used for hardbacks is $x_1/12\,000$, and for paperbacks it is $x_2/8000$. The sum of these two fractions cannot be greater than 1, and we can therefore write

$$\frac{x_1}{12\,000} + \frac{x_2}{8000} \leqslant 1$$

or, on multiplying through by 24 000,

$$2x_1 + 3x_2 \leqslant 24\,000$$

For constraint (c) the corresponding result is

$$\frac{x_1}{15\,000} + \frac{x_2}{9\,000} \leqslant 1$$

or, on multiplying through by 45 000,

$$3x_1 + 5x_2 \leqslant 45\,000$$

The advance orders (d) lead to two more inequalities:

$$x_1 \geqslant 2000 \quad \text{and} \quad x_2 \geqslant 1000$$

The policy expressed in (e) requires that at least one-quarter of the total copies must be hardbacks. In symbols, this becomes

$$x_2 \geqslant \tfrac{1}{4}(x_1 + x_2)$$

or

$$4x_2 \geqslant x_1 + x_2$$

and

$$x_1 - 3x_2 \leqslant 0$$

With the unit profits of 30 and 36 pence for the paperbacks and hardbacks respectively the total profit z (in pence) is given by

$$z = 30x_1 + 36x_2$$

This is the objective (or target) function that has to be maximized. Collecting the results, we can express the problem in symbols as

$$\text{Maximize } z = 30x_1 + 36x_2$$

subject to

$$
\begin{aligned}
x_1, x_2 &\geqslant 0 \\
x_1 + x_2 &\leqslant 10\,000 \\
2x_1 + 3x_2 &\leqslant 24\,000 \\
3x_1 + 5x_2 &\leqslant 45\,000 \\
x_1 &\geqslant 2000 \\
x_2 &\geqslant 1000 \\
x_1 - 3x_2 &\leqslant 0
\end{aligned}
\qquad [5.1]
$$

All these relationships are linear in form and bear some resemblance to those for the transportation problem given in section 4.15. The main difference is the use of the 'greater than' and 'less than' statements in place of 'equal to' relationships. The transportation problem can therefore be regarded as a special case of linear programming. However, its importance has merited the development of the special techniques described in Chapter 4.

5.5 SLACK VARIABLES

In solving the transportation problem we started with a basic feasible solution and improved it by a series of transformations, until we reached the optimum. We can adopt a similar approach in tackling problems such as the book production example. The method can best be explained by reference to a numerical example, and it is convenient to start with a simplified version of Example 5.1 in which the constraints (d) and (e) are absent. Figure 5.3 shows the corresponding graphical representation of the problem, and the effect on the algebraic formulation is to remove the last three inequalities in Eq. 5.1.

Figure 5.3

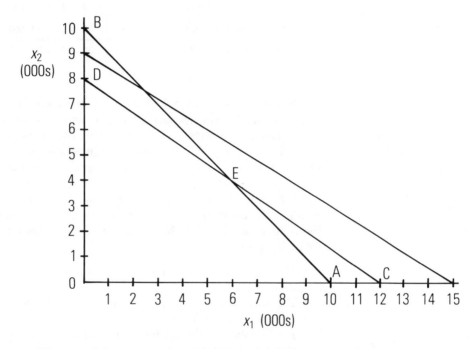

The remaining constraints (a), (b) and (c) give three of the less-than-or-equal-to statements of Eq. 5.1. We first convert these inequalities to equations by adding variables u_1, u_2 and u_3 to the expressions on the left-hand side. Thus:

$$\begin{aligned}
u_1 + x_1 + x_2 &= 10\,000 \\
u_2 + 2x_1 + 3x_2 &= 24\,000 \\
u_3 + 3x_1 + 5x_2 &= 45\,000
\end{aligned}$$

[5.2]

These additional variables represent the unused capacities of the various departments. For example, if $x_1 = 4000$ and $x_2 = 3000$ we have $u_1 = 3000$, $u_2 = 7000$ and $u_3 = 18\,000$. These new variables are called *slack* (or *dual*) variables.

From the nature of the problem the u variables, like the x variables, must be positive or zero. All the variables in the equations are therefore described as non-negative and this condition will be assumed throughout.

5.6 SIMPLEX TABLE

It is convenient for what follows to rearrange the objective function in the first line of Eq. 5.1 in the form

$$-z + 30x_1 + 36x_2 = 0$$

If this result is combined with those of Eq. 5.2 we obtain the set of equations shown in Fig. 5.4(a).

Figure 5.4

$u_1 + x_1 + x_2 = 10\,000$

$u_2 + 2x_1 + 3x_2 = 24\,000$

$u_3 + 3x_1 + 5x_2 = 45\,000$

$-z + 30x_1 + 36x_2 = 0$

(a)

	x_1	x_2	
u_1	1	1	10 000
u_2	2	3	24 000
u_3	3	5	45 000
$-z$	30	36	0

(b)

The equations in Fig. 5.4(a) enable us to determine u_1, u_2, u_3 and z when x_1 and x_2 are known. In particular, if x_1 and x_2 are both zero, $u_1 = 10\,000$, $u_2 = 24\,000$, $u_3 = 45\,000$ and $z = 0$. This trivial solution is represented by the origin O in Fig. 5.3. No books are produced, no resources are used and the profit is zero. The variables u_1, u_2 and u_3 are then said to be basic or incorporated, and x_1 and x_2 are free or not incorporated.

This solution can be represented by the table of Fig. 5.4(b), which contains the coefficients of x_1 and x_2 from the four equations, together with the values on the right-hand side of each equation. The table has the following properties:

(a) The variables incorporated in the solution are shown in the left-hand column.
(b) The variables not incorporated in the solution are shown in the top row and are equal to zero.
(c) The number in the bottom right-hand corner equals the value of the objective function z, with the sign changed.

This method of displaying the solution enables us to make transformations that lead to improvements in the value of z. It is known as the *simplex table*. When the top row contains only the x variables it corresponds to the origin of the graph O (Fig. 5.2), and is known as the *initial solution*.

5.7 TRANSFORMATION OF THE SIMPLEX TABLE

The initial solution produces no profit ($z = 0$). To improve on this we need to incorporate x_1 or x_2, that is, transfer one of them from the top of the table, where it has zero value, to the left-hand column where it will be equal to the value in the right-hand column of the same line. To see how this can be done and how the other elements are affected, we rearrange the four equations of Fig. 5.4(a). From the first of these we obtain

$$x_1 = 10\,000 - u_1 - x_2$$

Substituting this expression for x_1 in the other equations leads to the following set:

$$u_2 + 2(10\,000 - u_1 - x_2) + 3x_2 = 24\,000$$
$$u_3 + 3(10\,000 - u_1 - x_2) + 5x_2 = 45\,000$$
$$-z + 30(10\,000 - u_1 - x_2) + 36x_2 = 0$$

On removing the brackets and rearranging the expression for x_1 we obtain the new set of equations in Fig. 5.5(a).

Figure 5.5

(a)

$x_1 + u_1 + x_2 = \quad 10\ 000$

$u_2 - 2u_1 + x_2 = \quad 4\ 000$

$u_3 - 3u_1 + 2x_2 = \quad 15\ 000$

$-z - 30u_1 + 6x_2 = -300\ 000$

(b)

	u_1	x_2	
x_1	1	1	10 000
u_2	-2	1	4 000
u_3	-3	2	15 000
$-z$	-30	6	-300 000

The corresponding simplex table is shown alongside the equations (Fig. 5.5(b)), and if you compare it with the previous one, you will find that u_1 and x_1 have exchanged positions; x_1 is now incorporated and u_1 is said to have been 'driven out'. As before, the variables in the left-hand column take the values in the right-hand column, so that $x_1 = 10\,000$, $u_2 = 4000$ and $u_3 = 15\,000$. The variables in the top row are not incorporated, and this means that u_1 and x_2 are zero. Furthermore, the profit z is 300\,000 pence at this stage.

We can interpret this solution graphically. It corresponds to point A in Fig. 5.3. This point is on the printing constraint line, confirming that there is no spare printing capacity ($u_1 = 0$), but below the other two constraint lines, u_2 and u_3 having positive values. The profit arises entirely from the paperback production, 30 pence on each of 10\,000 copies.

5.8 BASIC FEASIBLE SOLUTIONS

In the transportation problem a basic feasible solution is one that uses the critical number of routes, $m + n - 1$, where m and n are the numbers of rows and columns. Each route corresponds to one of the x variables and, in the transformation from one basic feasible solution to another, the number of basic variables remains the same. There is a parallel in moving from one simplex table to another. In the transformation from the table of Fig. 5.4(b) to that of Fig. 5.5(b) we exchange a basic or incorporated variable, u_1, for a free or non-incorporated one, x_1. The element in the table corresponding to the row and column of these two variables is called the pivot. In the present case the pivot is in the u_1 row and x_1 column of Fig. 5.4(b).

Each simplex table, and each basic feasible solution, corresponds to a vertex of the feasible region. If a problem has a single optimal solution it will occur at one of these vertices. However, as explained at the end of section 5.3 it is possible for a range of optimal solutions to occur, corresponding to one side of the feasible region.

5.9 THE SIMPLEX METHOD

In section 5.7 the transformation from the table of Fig. 5.4(b) to that of Fig. 5.5(b) was made by first rearranging the equations. The following algorithm enables us to make the change without reference to the equations. The steps are as follows:

1. Select a column with a positive element in the bottom row.
2. Divide the other positive elements in this column into the corresponding numbers in the last column. Select the row with the smallest quotient. (The case of two such quotients being equal is considered later.)
3. The column and row found in steps 1 and 2 locate the pivot. It is always positive. Exchange its row and column variables.
4. Replace the pivot by its reciprocal p.
5. Multiply the other elements in the pivot row by p.
6. Multiply the other elements in the pivot column by $-p$.
7. Now work column by column. In each incomplete column one element is known. Each of the others is obtained from the old value as follows. Multiply this known element by the old element in the pivot column and the required row, and subtract the product from the old element.

Fig. 5.6 illustrates these steps for the transformation carried out in section 5.7. The original table is reproduced at (a).

Figure 5.6

	x_1	x_2	
u_1	①	1	10 000 ←
u_2	2	3	24 000
u_3	3	5	45 000
$-z$	30	36	0

(a)

	u_1	x_2	
x_1	1	1	10 000
u_2	-2		
u_3	-3		
$-z$	-30		

(b)

	u_1	x_2	
x_1	1	1	10 000
u_2	-2	1	4 000
u_3	-3	2	15 000
$-z$	-30	6	-300 000

(c)

Step 1 requires us to select an element in the bottom row that is positive. In the present case both elements (30 and 36) are positive. Suppose we choose 30. Following step 2 we divide the other elements in this column into the numbers on the right. The quotients are $10\,000/1 = 10\,000$, $24\,000/2 = 12\,000$ and $45\,000/3 = 15\,000$. The first answer is the smallest and, in accordance with step 3, the pivot is in the u_1 row and x_1 column, circled in the table.

We can now start to construct the new table (Fig. 5.6(b)). The pivot variables u_1 and x_1 are exchanged and the pivot 1 is replaced by its reciprocal p, also 1. The remaining elements in the pivot row are multiplied by $p(=1)$ and the remaining elements in the pivot column by $-p(=-1)$. This completes steps 1–6 of the algorithm.

We now deal with the incomplete columns. In the x_2 column, one element is known, 1. The other elements in this column are found using step 7 in the algorithm. For instance, the new element in the second row of this column is obtained by multiplying the known element, 1, by the old element in the pivot column and required row, 2, and subtracting from the old element, thus

$$3 - (1 \times 2) = 1$$

The other new elements in this column are found in the same way:

$$5 - (1 \times 3) = 2$$
$$36 - (1 \times 30) = 6$$

In the right-hand column the known element is 10 000 and, using the same rule, the other new elements are

$$24\,000 - (10\,000 \times 2) = 4000$$
$$45\,000 - (10\,000 \times 3) = 15\,000$$
$$0 - (10\,000 \times 30) = -300\,000$$

The completed table (Fig. 5.6(c)) is identical to that of Fig. 5.5(b).

The simplex method was discovered in 1947 on the basis of work by Dantzig[1,2] and others.[3,4] A complete proof is lengthy and is not attempted here, but the steps for selecting the pivot are easily understood. Each element in the bottom row is the coefficient of a variable in the objective function. It represents the change in the value of z if one unit of that variable is incorporated into the solution. In the book production example, 30p is the profit obtained for each paperback that is produced. To improve a solution, therefore, we must choose a column with a positive element in the bottom row.

The other elements in the column are the resources needed in each department to produce one unit. In our initial solution (Fig. 5.4) one paperback requires 1 unit of printing (out of a total capacity of 10 000), 2 units of binding (out of 24 000) and 3 units of warehouse resources (out of 45 000). The quotients calculated in step 2 are therefore the limits on the numbers imposed by the capacities of the three departments. The smallest of these is selected to keep within the capacity of every department. In our present example, it is the printing department that restricts the number at this stage. This rule for selecting the pivot row is known as the *bottleneck criterion*.

5.10 THE OPTIMAL SOLUTION

To improve the solution further we carry out another transformation of the simplex table. The details are given in Fig. 5.7, the table at (a) being a copy of Fig. 5.6(c).

The only positive element in the bottom row is 6 and this establishes the pivot column. The quotients obtained by dividing the other elements in this

Figure 5.7

	u_1	x_2			u_1	u_2			u_1	u_2	
x_1	1	1	10 000	x_1		−1		x_1	3	−1	6 000
u_2	−2	(1)	4 000 ←	x_2	−2	1	4 000	x_2	−2	1	4 000
u_3	−3	2	15 000	u_3		−2		u_3	1	−2	7 000
−z	−30	6	−300 000	−z		−6		−z	−18	−6	−324 000

(a)   (b)   (c)

column into the numbers in the last column are $10\,000/1 = 10\,000$, $4000/1 = 4000$ and $15\,000/2 = 7500$. The second answer is the smallest and, by the bottleneck criterion, the pivot (shown circled) is in the second row.

The pivot variables u_2 and x_2 are exchanged, the pivot 1 is replaced by its reciprocal, also 1. If we now multiply the other elements in the pivot row by 1 and the other elements in the pivot column by -1, we obtain the partially completed new table in Fig. 5.7(b).

We now apply step 7 of the simplex algorithm. The known element in the second column is -2 and the other elements are therefore

$$1 - (-2 \times 1) = 3$$
$$-3 - (-2 \times 2) = 1$$
$$-30 - (-2 \times 6) = -18$$

In the last column the known element is 4000 and the others are therefore:

$$10\,000 - (4000 \times 1) = 6000$$
$$15\,000 - (4000 \times 2) = 7000$$
$$-300\,000 - (4000 \times 6) = -324\,000$$

The resulting table is shown in Fig. 5.7(c). From the properties of the simplex table, the elements in the top row are zero, and those in the left-hand column have the values in the last column. The solution is therefore:

$$u_1 = 0$$
$$u_2 = 0$$
$$x_1 = 6000 \qquad x_2 = 4000 \qquad u_3 = 7000 \qquad z = 324\,000$$

This solution gives a production schedule of 6000 paperbacks and 4000 hardbacks, and corresponds to the point E in Fig. 5.3. Since u_1 and u_2 are zero, the capacities of the printing and binding departments are fully used. On the other hand, there is spare capacity in the packing and dispatching department (7000 'units' out of 45 000). The profit z, given by the element in the bottom right-hand corner (with the sign changed), is 324 000 pence or £3240.

The elements in the bottom row of the table are now all negative and no further improvement is possible. The solution is therefore optimal.

The three simplex tables obtained in the analysis correspond to the points O, A and E respectively in Fig. 5.3. The first table (Fig. 5.6(a)) contained two positive elements in the bottom row and either could have been chosen for the pivot column. The selection of 30 led to a second basic feasible solution at A. Had the other element, 36, been chosen the second table would have corresponded to point D, but the third table would again have given the solution at point E.

5.11 APPLICATION TO SEVERAL PRODUCTS

The simplex method has been demonstrated using an example with a mixture of two products. For this it has proved to be more complicated and time consuming than the graphical approach. Its importance lies in the fact that the same algorithm can be used with mixtures of three or more products, to which the graphical method cannot be applied. In addition, the simplex method can be the basis of a computer program.

Example 5.2
A manufacturer of cookers is planning the production of three models. The production capacities in operator-hours per week of the various departments are machining, 3600; welding, 3000; assembly, 3000; painting, 2400.

The following table gives the production requirements and the expected profit for each model:

| Model | Production requirements (operator hours) | | | | Profit z |
	Machining	Welding	Assembly	Painting	(£)
Diana	2	2	4	1	12
Helen	3	3	3	1	14
Pandora	4	3	3	3	18

If all the production can be sold, and the profit is to be maximized, determine:

(a) how many of each model should be produced;
(b) the corresponding profit;
(c) how much production capacity is unused.

Solution
If we denote the numbers of Dianas, Helens and Pandoras by x_1, x_2 and x_3 respectively, the manufacturing constraints can be written:

$$\begin{aligned}
\text{Machining} \quad & 2x_1 + 3x_2 + 4x_3 \leq 3600 \\
\text{Welding} \quad & 2x_1 + 3x_2 + 3x_3 \leq 3000 \\
\text{Assembly} \quad & 4x_1 + 3x_2 + 3x_3 \leq 3000 \\
\text{Painting} \quad & x_1 + x_2 + 3x_3 \leq 2400
\end{aligned}$$

With the introduction of slack variables u_1, u_2, u_3 and u_4, these inequalities become:

$$\begin{aligned}
u_1 + 2x_1 + 3x_2 + 4x_3 &= 3600 \\
u_2 + 2x_1 + 3x_2 + 3x_3 &= 3000 \\
u_3 + 4x_1 + 3x_2 + 3x_3 &= 3000 \\
u_4 + x_1 + x_2 + 3x_3 &= 2400
\end{aligned}$$

The objective (profit) function to be maximized is

$$z = 12x_1 + 14x_2 + 18x_3$$

from which

$$-z + 12x_1 + 14x_2 + 18x_3 = 0$$

The simplex tables are given in Fig. 5.8 with the bottleneck ratios on the right. Three transformations are needed to reach the optimum solution. At each stage, the greatest positive element in the bottom row is used to select the pivot column and the pivot is circled for reference. The fourth table is optimal since all the elements in the bottom row are negative.

Figure 5.8

	x_1	x_2	x_3		bottleneck ratios
u_1	2	3	4	3600	3600/4 = 900
u_2	2	3	3	3000	3000/3 = 1000
u_3	4	3	3	3000	3000/3 = 1000
u_4	1	1	(3)	2400 ←	2400/3 = 800
$-z$	12	14	18	0	

	x_1	x_2	u_4		
u_1	0.667	(1.667)	-1.333	400 ←	400/1.667 = 240
u_2	1	2	-1	600	600/2 = 300
u_3	3	2	-1	600	600/2 = 300
x_3	0.333	0.333	0.333	800	800/0.333 = 2400
$-z$	6	8	-6	-14 400	

	x_1	u_1	u_4		
x_2	0.4	0.6	-0.8	240	240/0.4 = 600
u_2	0.2	-1.2	0.6	120 ←	120/0.2 = 600
u_3	(2.2)	-1.2	0.6	120	120/2.2 = 54.5
x_3	0.2	-0.2	0.6	720	720/0.2 = 3600
$-z$	2.8	-4.8	0.4	-16 320	

	u_3	u_1	u_4	
x_2	-0.182	0.818	-0.909	218.2
u_2	0.091	-1.091	0.545	109.1
x_1	0.455	-0.545	0.273	54.5
x_3	-0.091	-0.091	0.545	709.1
$-z$	-1.273	-3.273	-0.364	-16 472.7

From the final table, the optimal solution is

$$x_1 = 54.5 \qquad x_2 = 218.2 \qquad x_3 = 709.1 \qquad z = 16\,472.7$$
$$u_1 = 0 \qquad u_2 = 109.1 \qquad u_3 = 0 \qquad u_4 = 0$$

If we work on the basis that only whole numbers of cookers are practical (no carry forward from one week to the next), and we round the values down, we have 54 Dianas, 218 Helens and 709 Pandoras. Sometimes this rounding process will release enough resources to produce an extra unit of one model. In the present case, the rounded numbers use 3598 hours of machining, 2889 hours of welding, 2997 hours of assembly and 2399 hours of painting. The unused capacities of the four processes are therefore 2, 111, 3 and 1 hours respectively. These are insufficient to produce an extra unit of any of the three models. The answers to the three parts of the question are therefore:

(a) **54 Dianas, 218 Helens and 709 Pandoras**;
(b) **2 hours of machining, 111 hours of welding, 3 hours of assembly and 1 hour of painting** (in the 'exact' solution, the only unused capacity is 109.1 hours of welding);
(c) **£16 462** (£16 472.70 in the 'exact' solution).

5.12 THE NORMAL FORM

In Example 5.2, all the constraints are of the less-than-or-equal-to type and all the numbers on the right-hand sides of the inequalities are positive. A maximization problem of this kind is said to be of the normal form. This type is important because other linear programming problems can be transformed to the normal form. Constraints that lead to equations or inequalities of the greater-than-or-equal-to kind can be modified and the simplex method then applied.

For instance, we can easily ensure that minimum quantities of the various products are achieved. Suppose, in Example 5.2, the production schedules must include at least 100 Dianas, 200 Helens and 300 Pandoras. We first deduct from the capacities of the various departments the resources, in terms of operator-hours, needed for these minimum numbers. You will find that the right-hand sides of the inequalities then become 1600, 1300, 1100 and 1200 respectively. The revised simplex tables are given in Fig. 5.9.

Figure 5.9

	x_1	x_2	x_3		bottleneck ratios
u_1	2	3	4	1600	1600/4 = 400
u_2	2	3	3	1300	1300/3 = 433.3
u_3	4	3	③	1100 ←	1100/3 = 366.7
u_4	1	1	3	1200	1200/3 = 400
$-z$	12	14	18	0	

	x_1	x_2	u_3	
u_1	-3.333	-1	-1.333	133.3
u_2	-2	0	-1	200
x_3	1.333	1	0.333	366.7
u_4	-3	-2	-1	100
$-z$	-12	-4	-6	-6600

After the first transformation, all the elements in the bottom row are negative and the second solution is therefore optimal. It is

$$x_1 = 0 \qquad x_2 = 0 \qquad x_3 = 366.7$$
$$u_1 = 133.3 \quad u_2 = 200 \quad u_3 = 0 \qquad u_4 = 100$$
$$z = 6600$$

We must now increase the x-values by 100, 200 and 300 respectively to allow for the minimum orders specified at the beginning. The objective function z is also increased, to include the profit from these orders. The additional amount is $100 \times 12 + 200 \times 14 + 300 \times 18 = £9400$.

The answers rounded down to whole numbers as before are

(a) 100 Dianas, 200 Helens, 666 Pandoras;
(b) £15 988;
(c) in operator-hours: machining, 136; welding, 202; assembly, 2; painting, 102.

5.13 DEGENERATE SOLUTION

A solution is degenerate if one or more of the basic variables is zero. In the transportation problem (Ch. 4) it is a solution that uses fewer routes than the critical number. In the simplex table the basic variables have the values shown in the right-hand column; the solution is degenerate, therefore, if one or more zeros appear in this column (apart from the value of $-z$ in the bottom right-hand corner).

Degeneracy can appear in the initial solution or after several transformations. Take, for instance, constraint (e) in the book production problem of Example 5.1. This requires the number of hardback copies to be at least one-quarter of the total and, in the last line of Eq. 5.1, this is represented by the inequality

$$x_1 - 3x_2 \leqslant 0$$

By introducing a slack variable u_4, we obtain the equation

$$u_4 + x_1 - 3x_2 = 0$$

In the initial solution $x_1 = 0$ and $x_2 = 0$ so that u_4, which is an incorporated element at this stage, is zero and the solution is degenerate.

If the simplex table of Fig. 5.3(a) is extended to include this result we obtain the tables of Fig. 5.10(a) and (b). At this stage both elements in the bottom row are positive and either may be chosen for the pivot column. If we select the x_1 column we obtain the sequence of solutions shown in Fig. 5.10(c), (e) and (g). In Fig. 5.10(a) the smallest bottleneck ratio is 0 and the pivot is located in the u_4 row. The first transformation then leads to a second degenerate solution (Fig. 5.10(c)).

Although x_1 is now incorporated its value is still zero. However the next solution (Fig. 5.10(e)) is not degenerate and one further transformation achieves the optimal solution at Fig. 5.10(g).

If the initial choice of pivot column (Fig. 5.10(b)) is x_2 the degeneracy disappears in the next solution (Fig. 5.10(d)) and one further transformation leads to the same optimal solution at Fig. 5.10(f).

It is possible for the value of the objective function z to remain constant through several transformations, even though it is not optimal, and for an

Figure 5.10

(a)

	x_1	x_2		bottleneck ratios
u_1	1	1	10 000	10 000
u_2	2	3	24 000	12 000
u_3	3	5	45 000	15 000
u_4	(1)	-3	0 ←	0
$-z$	30 ↑	36	0	

(b)

	x_1	x_2		bottleneck ratios
u_1	1	1	10 000	10 000
u_2	2	(3)	24 000 ←	8 000
u_3	3	5	45 000	9 000
u_4	1	-3	0	-
$-z$	30	36 ↑	0	

(c)

	u_4	x_2		
u_1	-1	(4)	10 000 ←	2 500
u_2	-2	9	24 000	2 667
u_3	-3	14	45 000	3 214
x_1	1	-3	0	
$-z$	-30	126 ↑	0	

(d)

	x_1	u_2		
u_1	(0.333)	-0.333	2 000 ←	6 000
x_2	0.667	0.333	8 000	12 000
u_3	-0.333	-1.667	5 000	
u_4	3	1	24 000	8 000
$-z$	6 ↑	-12	-288 000	

(e)

	u_4	u_1		
x_2	-0.25	0.25	2 500	
u_2	(0.25)	-2.25	1 500 ←	6 000
u_3	0.5	-3.5	10 000	20 000
x_1	0.25	0.75	7 500	30 000
$-z$	1.5 ↑	-31.5	-315 000	

(f)

	u_1	u_2	
x_1	3	-1	6 000
x_2	-2	1	4 000
u_3	1	-2	7 000
u_4	-9	4	6 000
$-z$	-18	-6	-324 000

(g)

	u_2	u_1	
x_2	1	-2	4 000
u_4	4	-9	6 000
u_3	-2	1	7 000
x_1	-1	3	6 000
$-z$	-6	-18	-324 000

earlier table to recur. This condition is known as *cycling*. In a manual analysis we then need to make a different choice for the pivot column. In writing a computer program for the simplex method, however, care is needed to ensure that the machine does not continue in an unending cycle.

5.14 THE EXISTENCE OF SOLUTIONS

So far in this chapter it has been assumed that feasible solutions exist. This is not always the case.

Consider the constraints of Example 5.1. As given in the question they lead to the feasible region shown in Fig. 5.1. Suppose, however, the capacities of the various departments were reduced or the advance orders were increased. The feasible region would become smaller, its new size depending on the changes in the resources. It might be reduced to a single point, which would then represent the only feasible solution. Further reduction of the departmental capacities would make the constraints contradictory and no feasible solution would exist.

In contrast, it is possible for the feasible region to become infinite, as in the next example.

Example 5.3
Maximize

$$3x_1 + 5x_2$$

subject to

$$x_1, \quad x_2 \geqslant 0$$
$$x_1 - 4x_2 \leqslant 0$$
$$-2x_1 + x_2 \leqslant 3$$

Solution
Since there are only two 'products', a graphical approach is possible (Fig. 5.11).

Figure 5.11

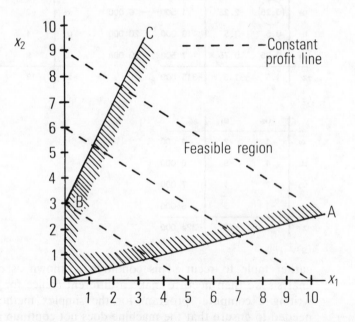

From the first of the less-than-or-equal-to constraints, $4x_2$ must not be less than x_1, or x_2 must not be less than $x_1/4$. The graph of $x_2 = x_1/4$ is a straight line through the origin, OA in the diagram. Feasible solutions must lie on or above this line.

From the last constraint, x_2 must be less than or equal to $2x_1 + 3$. The graph of $2x_1 + 3$ is another straight line, BC, intersecting the vertical axis at $x_2 = 3$. Feasible solutions must lie on or below this line.

As the diagram shows, the region between OA and BC extends indefinitely. It follows that a constant profit line can be drawn at any distance from the origin, however great, and there is no limit to the value of z.

The initial simplex table and the first transformation are shown in Fig. 5.12.

Figure 5.12

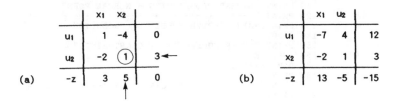

(a)   (b)

The initial solution is degenerate since there is a zero in the last column (apart from the bottom right-hand corner). The pivot must be positive and, if we choose x_2 as the pivot column, it can only be the element 1. Exchanging u_2 and x_2, and applying the usual rules, we obtain the first transformation (Fig. 5.12(b)). This represents the following solution:

$$x_1 = 0 \quad x_2 = 3 \quad u_1 = 12 \quad u_2 = 0 \quad z = 15$$

It corresponds to the point B in Fig. 5.11.

There is a positive element, 13, in the bottom row so the value of the objective function can be increased. However, the other elements in the column are both negative and we have no pivot.

The outcome is similar if, in the initial solution, we select the x_1 column for the pivot. In this case, the second table is also degenerate. Again the second table has one positive element in the bottom row, the other elements in the same column being negative.

A problem of this kind is said to be *unbounded*. It occurs when the last row of the simplex table contains a positive element, without a positive element in its column that could be selected as the pivot.

5.15 COMPUTER PROGRAM FOR THE NORMAL FORM

A computer solution for the normal form of the maximization problem is given in Fig. 5.13. It is based on the simplex method and, when run, it produces a screen display that matches closely the layout given in section 5.6. The main sequence is given in lines 10–750, with subroutines at lines 1000, 1200 and 1400.

Lines 10–90 introduce the notation and store the headings for the columns and rows of the simplex tables. Up to 10 products (columns) and 10 rows (constraints) are allowed for but these numbers can easily be increased by adjustments in lines 40–90. A practical limitation is the computer screen format. A maximum of 5 products can be accommodated within 40 columns of text and this can be increased to 11 products if an 80 column format is available. The size of the second array in line 40 is 11, rather than 10, to provide a row for the objective function in addition to the constraints.

Lines 100–380 print the heading and call for the data, and the initial table

Figure 5.13

```
10 REM    C,R          NUMBERS OF COLUMNS (PRODUCTS), ROWS (CONSTRAINTS)
20 REM    M$(), N$()   COLUMN, ROW HEADINGS
30 REM    P(X,Y)       ELEMENT AT ROW X, COLUMN Y
40 DIM M$(10):DIM N$(11)
50 FOR I=1 TO 10
60 READ M$(I):READ N$(I)
70 NEXT I
80 DATA X1,U1,X2,U2,X3,U3,X4,U4,X5,U5
90 DATA X6,U6,X7,U7,X8,U8,X9,U9,X10,U10
100 PRINT "---------------------------------------"
110 PRINT "LINEAR PROGRAMMING - NORMAL FORM"
120 PRINT "---------------------------------------"
130 PRINT:PRINT "ENTER NUMBER OF PRODUCTS"
140 INPUT C
150 PRINT "ENTER NUMBER OF <= CONSTRAINTS"
160 INPUT R
170 DIM P(R+1,C+1)
180 N$(R+1)="-Z"
190 PRINT:PRINT "ENTER X COEFFS. IN THE <= CONSTRAINTS"
200 PRINT
210 FOR I=1 TO R
220 PRINT "CONSTRAINT NO.";I
230 FOR J=1 TO C
240 PRINT "---COEFFICIENT OF X";J
250 INPUT P(I,J)
260 NEXT J
270 NEXT I
280 PRINT "ENTER X COEFFS. IN OBJECTIVE FUNCTION"
290 FOR J=1 TO C
300 PRINT "---COEFFICIENT OF X";J
310 INPUT P(R+1,J)
320 NEXT J
330 PRINT:PRINT "ENTER CONSTRAINT CAPACITIES"
340 FOR I=1 TO R
350 PRINT "---CAPACITY OF CONSTRAINT NO.";I
360 INPUT P(I,C+1)
370 NEXT I
380 P(R+1,C+1)=0
390 GOSUB 800
400 PRINT:PRINT "DO YOU WISH TO CHANGE AN ITEM (Y/N)"
410 INPUT Q$
420 IF Q$="N" OR Q$="n" THEN GOTO 480
430 PRINT "ENTER ROW, COLUMN NUMBERS OF THE ITEM"
440 INPUT X,Y
450 PRINT "PRESENT VALUE IS ";P(X,Y);"; ENTER NEW VALUE"
460 INPUT P(X,Y)
470 GOTO 390
480 GOSUB 1000
490 IF PR=0 THEN PRINT "UNBOUNDED SOLUTION": GOTO 740
500 IF T<=0 THEN GOTO 570
510 PRINT "CONTINUE (Y/N)"
520 INPUT Q$
530 IF Q$="N" OR Q$="n" THEN GOTO 740
540 GOSUB 1200
550 GOSUB 800
560 GOTO 480
570 PRINT
580 IF T=0 THEN PRINT "THIS IS ONE OF SEVERAL OPTIMAL SOLUTIONS":GOTO 600
590 PRINT:PRINT "THIS IS THE OPTIMAL SOLUTION"
600 PRINT
610 FOR J=1 TO R
620 PRINT N$(J);" = ";P(J,C+1)
630 NEXT J
640 GOSUB 1400
740 PRINT "---------------------------------------"
750 END
800 REM    PRINT TABLE
810 PRINT
820 FOR J=1 TO C
830 PRINT TAB(6*J-2);M$(J);
840 NEXT J
850 PRINT:PRINT
860 FOR I=1 TO R+1
870 IF I=R+1 THEN PRINT
880 PRINT N$(I);
890 FOR J=1 TO C+1
900 PRINT TAB(6*J-2);INT(100*P(I,J)+0.5)/100;
910 NEXT J
920 PRINT
```

```
 930 NEXT I
 940 RETURN
1000 REM       FIND PC, PIVOT COLUMN
1010 T=-1:PC=0
1020 FOR J=1 TO C
1030 IF T<P(R+1,J) THEN T=P(R+1,J):PC=J
1040 NEXT J
1050 IF T<=0 THEN GOTO 1180
1060 REM       FIND PR, PIVOT ROW
1070 Q1=1E10:PR=0
1080 FOR I=1 TO R
1090 IF P(I,PC)<=0 THEN GOTO 1130
1100 LET Q=P(I,C+1)/P(I,PC)
1110 IF Q<0 THEN GOTO 1130
1120 IF Q1>Q THEN Q1=Q:PR=I
1130 NEXT I
1140 PRINT
1150 IF PR=0 THEN GOTO 1170
1160 PRINT "PIVOT IS AT ROW ";PR;", COLUMN ";PC
1170 PRINT
1180 RETURN
1200 REM        TRANSFORM TABLE
1210 S$=N$(PR):N$(PR)=M$(PC):M$(PC)=S$
1220 P(PR,PC)=1/P(PR,PC)
1230 FOR J=1 TO C+1
1240 IF J=PC THEN GOTO 1260
1250 P(PR,J)=P(PR,J)*P(PR,PC)
1260 NEXT J
1270 FOR J=1 TO C+1
1280 IF J=PC THEN GOTO 1330
1290 FOR I=1 TO R+1
1300 IF I=PR THEN GOTO 1320
1310 P(I,J)=P(I,J)-P(PR,J)*P(I,PC)
1320 NEXT I
1330 NEXT J
1340 FOR I=1 TO R+1
1350 IF I=PR THEN GOTO 1370
1360 P(I,PC)=(-1)*P(I,PC)*P(PR,PC)
1370 NEXT I
1380 RETURN
1400 REM     VALUES OF NON-BASICS, Z
1410 PRINT:PRINT "ALL OTHER VARIABLES ARE ZERO"
1420 PRINT:PRINT "OBJECTIVE FUNCTION Z = ";(-1)*P(R+1,C+1)
1430 PRINT:RETURN
```

is displayed at line 390, using the subroutine at line 800.

Lines 400–470 provide an opportunity to check and amend the values in the initial table.

Lines 480–570 carry out the transformation of the table using the various subroutines. This section of the program is repeated until the solution is found to be unbounded at line 490 or optimal at line 500.

Lines 580–750 print the closing statements and the values of the variables in the optimal solution. (The gap in the line numbering between 650 and 730 will be used later.)

Lines 800–940 form the subroutine for printing the simplex tables. In order to keep the table to a reasonable size the numerical values are displayed to an accuracy of 0.01. However, the values are stored to the maximum accuracy of which the computer is capable and these are used in displaying the optimal solution at the end.

Lines 1000–1180 locate the pivot by the usual simplex rules. The control variable T is given an initial value of -1 and this is amended during the search for the pivot column. If the final value is positive the solution can be further improved. Otherwise, the value of T is used at lines 500, 580 and 590 to select the appropriate closing statement.

Lines 1200–1380 are the transformation subroutine. Line 1210 interchanges the row and column headings corresponding to the pivot and line 1220 replaces the pivot by its reciprocal. Lines 1230–1260 transform the other elements in the pivot row. The transformation of the other elements in the pivot column is delayed because the old values are needed for completing the non-pivot columns in lines 1270–1330. The transformation of the rest of the pivot column is carried out in lines 1350–1370.

Lines 1400–1430 are a subroutine for printing the values of the non-basic variables in the optimal solution, and the objective function.

As it stands the program is limited to problems in which the constraints are of the less-than-or-equal-to type, and the right-hand sides of the inequalities are non-negative. It does not overcome the problem of cycling but, when run, it halts after every transformation so that degeneracy and cycling are easily detected. A powerful, but longer, program that avoids these limitations is given by Bunday.[5]

The printout shown in Fig. 5.14 was obtained when the program was run with the data of Example 5.2.

In the next section the program is extended to cover minimization problems with greater-than-or-equal-to constraints.

Figure 5.14

```
----------------------------------------
LINEAR PROGRAMMING - NORMAL FORM
----------------------------------------

ENTER NUMBER OF PRODUCTS
?3
ENTER NUMBER OF <= CONSTRAINTS
?4

ENTER X COEFFS. IN THE <= CONSTRAINTS

CONSTRAINT NO.1
---COEFFICIENT OF X1
?2
---COEFFICIENT OF X2
?3
---COEFFICIENT OF X3
?4
CONSTRAINT NO.2
---COEFFICIENT OF X1
?2
---COEFFICIENT OF X2
?3
---COEFFICIENT OF X3
?3
CONSTRAINT NO.3
---COEFFICIENT OF X1
?4
---COEFFICIENT OF X2
?3
---COEFFICIENT OF X3
?3
CONSTRAINT NO.4
---COEFFICIENT OF X1
?1
---COEFFICIENT OF X2
?1
---COEFFICIENT OF X3
?3
ENTER X COEFFS. IN OBJECTIVE FUNCTION
---COEFFICIENT OF X1
?12
---COEFFICIENT OF X2
?14
---COEFFICIENT OF X3
?18
```

```
ENTER CONSTRAINT CAPACITIES
---CAPACITY OF CONSTRAINT NO.1
?3600
---CAPACITY OF CONSTRAINT NO.2
?3000
---CAPACITY OF CONSTRAINT NO.3
?3000
---CAPACITY OF CONSTRAINT NO.4
?2400
       X1    X2    X3

U1  2       3      4     3600
U2  2       3      3     3000
U3  4       3      3     3000
U4  1       1      3     2400

-Z  12     14     18     0

DO YOU WISH TO CHANGE AN ITEM (Y/N)
?N

PIVOT IS AT ROW 4, COLUMN 3

CONTINUE (Y/N)
?Y

       X1    X2    U4

U1  0.67  1.67  -1.33 400
U2  1     2     -1     600
U3  3     2     -1     600
X3  0.33  0.33  0.33   800

-Z  6     8     -6     -14400

PIVOT IS AT ROW 1, COLUMN 2

CONTINUE (Y/N)
?Y

       X1    U1    U4

X2  0.4   0.6   -0.8   240
U2  0.2   -1.2  0.6    120
U3  2.2   -1.2  0.6    120
X3  0.2   -0.2  0.6    720

-Z  2.8   -4.8  0.4    -16320

PIVOT IS AT ROW 3, COLUMN 1

CONTINUE (Y/N)
?Y
       U3    U1    U4

X2  -0.18 0.82  -0.91 218.18
U2  -9E-2 -1.09 0.55  109.09
X1  0.45  -0.55 0.27  54.55
X3  -9E-2 -9E-2 0.55  709.09

-Z  -1.27 -3.27 -0.36 -16472.73


THIS IS THE OPTIMAL SOLUTION

X2 = 218.181818
U2 = 109.090909
X1 = 54.5454545
X3 = 709.090909

ALL OTHER VARIABLES ARE ZERO

OBJECTIVE FUNCTION Z = 16472.7273

-------------------------------------
```

5.16 DUALITY

In the initial simplex table the x variables are zero and the slack u variables have their greatest values. During the transformations, x- and u-values are interchanged as the value of the objective function increases towards its greatest possible amount.

It can be shown that every maximization problem, formulated in terms of the x variables, is accompanied by a minimization problem, expressed in terms of the u variables. Furthermore the optimal values of the two objective functions are equal. The problems are said to be dual.

The relationships between the two problems can be illustrated with the data of Example 5.1. Constraints (a), (b) and (c) and the objective function are summarized on the left of Eq. 5.3, the corresponding minimization problem being shown on the right.

$$
\begin{aligned}
x_1, \quad x_2 &\geqslant 0 & u_1, \quad u_2, \quad u_3 &\geqslant 0 \\
x_1 + x_2 &\leqslant 10\,000 \\
2x_1 + 3x_2 &\leqslant 24\,000 & u_1 + 2u_2 + 3u_3 &\geqslant 30 \\
3x_1 + 5x_2 &\leqslant 45\,000 & u_1 + 3u_2 + 5u_3 &\geqslant 36
\end{aligned}
$$

$$
\text{Maximize } 30x_1 + 36x_2 \qquad \text{Minimize } 10\,000u_1 + 24\,000u_2 + 45\,000u_3
$$

$$[5.3]$$

A comparison of the two problems shows that the numbers on the right-hand sides of the inequalities in one are the coefficients in the objective function of the other. Furthermore, the coefficients of the x variables in the maximization problem, taken row by row, become those of the u variables in the minimization problem, taken column by column.

The optimal simplex tables for the two problems are also closely related, Fig. 5.15. The table for the maximization problem at (a) is repeated from Fig. 5.7(c). It can be converted to that for the minimization problem at (b) by interchanging the rows and columns and changing the sign of every element. Note that the number in the bottom right-hand corner is now z, the objective function, rather than $-z$.

Figure 5.15

(a)

	u_1	u_2	
x_1	3	-1	6 000
x_2	-2	1	4 000
u_3	1	-2	7 000
$-z$	-18	-6	-324 000

(b)

	x_1	x_2	u_3	
u_1	-3	2	-1	18
u_2	1	-1	2	6
z	-6000	-4000	-7000	324 000

The optimal solution to the minimization problem is therefore:

$$
\begin{aligned}
u_1 &= 18 & u_2 &= 6 & u_3 &= 0 \\
x_1 &= 0 & x_2 &= 0 & z &= 324\,000
\end{aligned}
$$

This solution has no practical significance for the book production problem of Example 5.1, but the mathematical relationship between dual problems is of great importance. It enables us to solve a minimization problem by applying the simplex method to the dual problem. Furthermore, the optimum solution can be read direct from the final simplex table.

In the tables displayed by the computer program of Fig. 5.13 the elements are rounded to the nearest 0.01, and reading the dual solution from the screen may not give sufficient accuracy in some examples. However, the computer stores the values to a greater accuracy and they can be displayed in this form by adding the lines given in Fig. 5.16 to the previous listing.

Figure 5.16

```
650 PRINT "DUAL PROBLEM SOLUTION (Y/N)"
660 INPUT Q$
670 IF Q$="N" OR Q$="n" THEN GOTO 740
680 PRINT:PRINT "DUAL PROBLEM OPTIMAL SOLUTION IS:"
690 PRINT
700 FOR J=1 TO C
710 PRINT M$(J);" = ";(-1)*P(R+1,J)
720 NEXT J
730 GOSUB 1400
```

Most micros will ensure that the additional lines automatically appear in the correct sequence according to their line numbers, but other computers (including the Amstrad PC) require that they are typed in the appropriate position within the original program. When the program is run a positive response to the prompt in line 650 will cause the computer to display the dual problem solution to the machine's full accuracy. The amended program can be tested using the data of Eq. 5.3. It confirms the solution $u_1 = 18$, $u_2 = 6$ and $z = 324\,000$.

5.17 THE NUTRITION PROBLEM

A classic minimization problem is that of obtaining a satisfactory diet at the least possible cost. It was investigated in 1945 by Stigler[6] who considered 77 food items. His work preceded the discovery of the simplex method and he used a trial-and-error approach because, in his words, 'there does not appear to be any direct method of finding the minimum of a linear function subject to linear conditions'. Vadja[7] points out that Stigler's result is, nevertheless, within 1 per cent of the true minimum cost.

The following, very simplified, example shows how the principle of duality and the simplex method can be applied to problems of this kind.

Example 5.4
The table below shows the nutritional contents of five foods, in grams per 100 g, together with their costs and, in the bottom line, the minimum weekly requirements for an adult.

	Grams per 100 g			Cost in pence per 100 g
	Proteins	Fats	Carbohydrates	
1. Wholemeal bread	8	1	56	8
2. Margarine	—	84	—	16
3. Cheese	25	35	—	38
4. Breakfast cereal	10	2	77	24
5. Diet snack bar	10	—	49	40
Weekly requirements (g)	500	600	2100	

Determine the smallest weekly cost of achieving the minimum requirements from the given food items.

Solution

It is convenient to use u for the variables in the minimization problem and x for the variables in the dual maximization problem. The minimization problem can be expressed as

$$u_1, \qquad u_2, \qquad u_3, \qquad u_4, \qquad u_5 \geq 0$$

$$\begin{array}{llll}
\text{Proteins} & 8u_1 & + 25u_3 + 10u_4 + 10u_5 \geq 500 \\
\text{Fats} & u_1 + 84u_2 + 35u_3 + 2u_4 & \geq 600 \\
\text{Carbohydrates} & 56u_1 & + 77u_4 + 49u_5 \geq 2100 \\
\text{Minimize} & 8u_1 + 16u_2 + 38u_3 + 24u_4 + 40u_5
\end{array}$$

and the dual maximization problem becomes

$$x_1, \qquad x_2, \qquad x_3 \geq 0$$

$$\begin{array}{lll}
8x_1 + & x_2 + & 56x_3 \leq 8 \\
 & 84x_2 & \leq 16 \\
25x_1 + & 35x_2 & \leq 38 \\
10x_1 + & 2x_2 + & 77x_3 \leq 24 \\
10x_1 & + & 49x_3 \leq 40
\end{array}$$

$$\text{Maximize} \quad 500x_1 + 600x_2 + 2100x_3$$

A manual analysis leads to some tedious arithmetic and a computer solution is recommended. Figure 5.17 shows the tables and optimum solution as given by the program of Figs 5.13 and 5.16.

In the first table the pivot is located in the third column and the first row. During the transformation, therefore, x_3 is incorporated and u_1 (the wholemeal bread) becomes a free element. In the second table, the pivot occurs in the second row of the second column, making u_2 (the margarine) a free element. The third transformation does not change the positions of the u variables but does, of course, change their values.

The final table represents the optimal solution for the maximization problem. The solution is

$$\begin{array}{lll}
x_1 = 0.98 & x_2 = 0.19 & x_3 = 0 \\
u_1 = 0 & u_2 = 0 & u_3 = 6.93 \quad u_4 = 13.86 \quad u_5 = 30.24 \\
z = 602.38
\end{array}$$

The interpretation of the same table for the dual minimization problem is

Figure 5.17

```
          X1    X2     X3
U1    8    1     56     8
U2    0    84    0      16
U3   25    35    0      38
U4   10    2     77     24
U5   10    0     49     40

-Z  500   600   2100   0

DO YOU WISH TO CHANGE AN ITEM (Y/N)
?N

PIVOT IS AT ROW 1, COLUMN 3

CONTINUE (Y/N)
?Y

       X1    X2     U1

X3   0.14  2E-2   2E-2  0.14
U2   0     84     0     16
U3   25    35     0     38
U4   -1    0.63   -1.37 13
U5   3     -0.87  -0.87 33

-Z   200   562.5  -37.5 -300

PIVOT IS AT ROW 2, COLUMN 2

CONTINUE (Y/N)
?Y

       X1    U2     U1

X3   0.14  0      2E-2  0.14
X2   0     1E-2   0     0.19
U3   25    -0.42  0     31.33
U4   -1    -1E-2  -1.37 12.88
U5   3     1E-2   -0.87 33.17

-Z   200   -6.7   -37.5 -407.14

PIVOT IS AT ROW 1, COLUMN 1

CONTINUE (Y/N)
?Y
       X3    U2     U1

X1   7     0      0.12  0.98
X2   0     1E-2   0     0.19
U3   -175  -0.38  -3.12 6.93
U4   7     -1E-2  -1.25 13.86
U5   -21   1E-2   -1.25 30.24

-Z   -1400 -6.4   -62.5 -602.38


THIS IS THE OPTIMAL SOLUTION

X1 = 0.976190476
X2 = 0.19047619
U3 = 6.92857143
U4 = 13.8571429
U5 = 30.2380952

ALL OTHER VARIABLES ARE ZERO

OBJECTIVE FUNCTION Z = 602.380952

DUAL PROBLEM SOLUTION (Y/N)
?Y

DUAL PROBLEM OPTIMAL SOLUTION IS:

X3 = 1400
U2 = 6.39880952
U1 = 62.5

ALL OTHER VARIABLES ARE ZERO

OBJECTIVE FUNCTION Z = 602.380952

----------------------------------------
```

obtained by interchanging the rows and columns and changing the sign of each element. From the table the optimum solution is

$$u_1 = 62.5 \qquad u_2 = 6.4 \qquad u_3 = 0 \qquad u_4 = 0 \qquad u_5 = 0$$
$$x_1 = 0 \qquad x_2 = 0 \qquad x_3 = 1400$$
$$z = 602.38$$

If the dual solution option is chosen the same results are obtained, the value of u_2 being displayed to greater accuracy.

Since u_3, u_4 and u_5 are all zero, only two foods are used, bread and margarine; not a very appetizing diet! As the foods are measured in units of 100g, the weekly amounts in the solution are **6250 g of bread** and **640 g of margarine**. The requirements for proteins and fats are met exactly ($x_1 = 0$ and $x_2 = 0$), but there is an excess of 1400 g of carbohydrates ($x_3 = 1400$). The weekly cost is 602 p, or **£6.02**.

5.18 SUMMARY

Many linear programming examples are equivalent to that of manufacturing two or more products with limited resources. The constraints are then the capacities of the various production departments and the objective is to maximize profit. Such constraints lead to inequalities of the less-than-or-equal-to kind; others may define minimum quantities that must be produced.

With two products a graphical analysis is possible, the constraints being represented by straight lines which define a feasible region. Lines of constant profit are also straight, and the optimal solution is given by the one which is furthest from the origin and intersects the feasible region, normally at one of its corners.

For three or more products the simplex method is widely used. The inequalities are transformed to equations by the inclusion of slack variables. An initial basic feasible solution is established at one corner of the feasible region, and the simplex algorithm then provides a systematic method of testing other corners until the optimum is found.

Every maximization problem can be interpreted as a complementary minimization problem. The objective functions of such dual problems have the same optimal value.

REFERENCES

1. Dantzig G B 1949 Programming in a linear structure. *Econometrica* **17**: 73
2. Dantzig G B 1957 Maximisation of a linear function of variables subject to linear inequalities. In Koopmans T C (ed) *Activity Analysis of Production and Allocation* John Wiley and Sons; Chapman and Hall, London, Ch. 21
3. Kantorovich L V 1939 *Matematicheskie metody organizatsii planirovania proizvodstva* Leningrad (quoted by Kreko B 1968 *Linear Programming* Pitman p. 11)

4. Lemke C E 1954 The dual method of solving linear programming problems. *Naval Research Logistics Quarterly* **1**: 36
5. Bunday B D 1984 *Basic Linear Programming* Edward Arnold, pp 127–34
6. Stigler G J 1945 The cost of subsistence *Journal of Farm Economics* **27**: 303
7. Vadja S 1973 *Planning by Mathematics* Pitman 2nd edn, pp 39–40

BIBLIOGRAPHY

Dantzig G 1963 *Linear Programming and Extensions* Princeton University Press

Kreko B 1968 *Linear Programming* (English translation) Pitman

Loomba N P 1964 *Linear Programming, an Introductory Analysis* McGraw-Hill

Taha H A 1987 *Operations Research* 4th edn Collier-Macmillan

Vajda S 1973 *Planning by Mathematics* 2nd edn Pitman

PROBLEMS

1. A manufacturer of television receivers is planning the production at one of its factories. The factory produces a portable set in two versions, colour and monochrome. The cabinets and audio sections are the same for both models and can be made at a maximum rate of 10 000 per month.

The video sections can be manufactured at maximum monthly rates of 6000 for colour and 15 000 for monochrome, or combinations of both in proportion. The assembly and test departments can deal with 7000 colour sets or 12 000 monochrome sets per month, or combinations of both in proportion.

There are standing orders for 1000 colour and 3000 monochrome sets that must be fulfilled each month.

Show these constraints on a suitable diagram and state whether each of the following production schedules is feasible:

(a) 3200 colour, 6600 monochrome;
(b) 3600 colour, 5600 monochrome;
(c) 4500 colour, 4000 monochrome;
(d) 4750 colour, 3000 monochrome.

Answer (b) and (d) are feasible.

2. If, in the previous problem, the profit margins are £30 for each colour set and £10 for each monochrome, what are the total monthly profits for each of the specified feasible solutions?

Find the maximum profit under these conditions and the corresponding production schedule.

Answer (b) £164 000; (d) £172 500. £174 000 with 4800 colour and 3000 monochrome.

3. Repeat No. 2 with the profit margins changed to £24 for each colour set and £14 for each monochrome.
Answer (b) £164 800; (d) £156 000. The maximum profit is £168 000 and this is achieved by a series of schedules as follows:

Colour	2800	2807	2814	2821	. . . 3815
Monochrome	7200	7188	7176	7164	. . . 5460

4. The Midshire Bus Company is planning to re-equip its fleet of buses with a mixture of two models – the 20 seat Shuttle costing £40 000, and the 50-seat Jumbo at £60 000. There are the following constraints:

(a) the total capital cost must not exceed £4 800 000;
(b) there is garaging for a maximum of 100 vehicles altogether;
(c) at least 30 Shuttles and 20 Jumbos are required;
(d) a total capacity of at least 2000 seats is needed;
(e) not less than one quarter of the buses must be Jumbos.

Draw a diagram on squared paper to show these constraints and mark the feasible region.
Determine the numbers of Shuttles and Jumbos that will achieve
 (i) the greatest number of Shuttles;
 (ii) the greatest total of seats;
 (iii) the maximum total operating profit, if the profit from a Jumbo is 40 per cent greater than from a Shuttle.
Answer (i) 75 Shuttles and 25 Jumbos; (ii) 30 Shuttles and 60 Jumbos; (iii) 60 Shuttles and 40 Jumbos.

5. The Ambridge Alchemy Company has enough raw material to produce a total of 400 units of a certain chemical compound. The compound can be sold in two qualities – standard and high purity. The profit is £7 on each standard unit and £10 on each high-purity unit. Production is subject to the following constraints:

(a) the manufacturing capacity is sufficient for a maximum of 480 units of the standard quality alone or 320 units of high purity alone, or proportions of each, totalling 1;
(b) at least 120 units of standard quality must be produced;
(c) for marketing reasons, at least one-fifth, but not more than one-half, of all production must be high purity.

Show the constraints on a suitable diagram and determine the respective quantities of standard and high-purity products that will lead to:
 (i) the greatest amount of the standard product;
 (ii) the greatest amount of the high-purity product;
(iii) the greatest total profit.
 What is the total profit in each case?
Answer (i) 320 units of standard and 80 units of high purity; (ii) 192 units of each; (iii) 240 units of standard and 160 units of high purity. Total profits are (i) £3040; (ii) £3264; (iii) £3280.

6. A massive housing scheme is planned by the Ambridge New Town

Development Corporation. A total of £36 million has been earmarked for housing units over the next 3 years and the programme includes houses with a building cost of £48 000 and flats costing £30 000 per unit. A site of 20 ha is available and the maximum density is to be 40 houses or 50 flats to the hectare.

The scheme must include a minimum of 200 houses and 100 flats that are needed for staff of the Tardy Timepiece Company, soon to move to the nearby industrial estate.

How many houses and flats should be built

(a) to house the greatest number of families, one per house or flat;
(b) to house the greatest number of people, assuming an average of three per flat and four and a half per house;
(c) to produce the greatest rental income, with flats at £30 per week and houses at £50 per week?

Determine the total number of families, total number of people and total rental income for each of the solutions (a), (b) and (c).

Answer The results are given in the following table:

	(a)	(b)	(c)
Houses	200	570	688
Flats	750	286	100
Number of families	950	856	788
Number of people	3150	3423	3396
Total weekly rent (£)	32 500	37 080	37 400

7. Draw a diagram to represent the following problem, in which x_1, $x_2 \geqslant 0$, and find the optimal solution.

$$x_1 + x_2 \leqslant 10$$
$$x_1 - 4x_2 \leqslant 0$$
$$-3x_1 + 4x_2 \leqslant 4$$
$$-x_1 + 2x_2 \leqslant 4$$
$$\text{Maximize} \quad 5x_1 + 6x_2$$

What happens if the first constraint is removed?

Answer $x_1 = 5.333$; $x_2 = 4.667$; $z = 54.667$. (Note that, if the simplex method is used, three transformations of the table may be needed, even though there are only two x variables.) If the first constraint is removed the solution is unbounded.

8. Solve each of the following 'two product' problems for $x_1, x_2 \geqslant 0$.

(a)
$$6x_1 + 5x_2 \leqslant 300$$
$$9x_1 + 15x_2 \leqslant 675$$
Maximize $x_1 + x_2$

(b)
$$x_1 + x_2 \leqslant 9$$
$$12x_1 + 7x_2 \leqslant 84$$
$$8x_1 + 13x_2 \leqslant 104$$
Maximize $9x_1 + 11x_2$

(c)
$$x_1 - 3x_2 \leqslant 1$$
$$-x_1 + x_2 \leqslant 2$$
Maximize $4x_1 + 5x_2$

(d)
$$4x_1 + x_2 \geqslant 14$$
$$3x_1 + 11x_2 \geqslant 11$$
$$x_1 + 4x_2 \geqslant 10$$
Minimize $x_1 + x_2$

Answer (a) $x_1 = 25$, $x_2 = 30$; $z = 55$ (b) $x_1 = 2.6$, $x_2 = 6.4$; $z = 93.8$
(c) Unbounded solution (d) $x_1 = 3.067$, $x_2 = 1.733$; $z = 4.8$.

9. A manufacturer of pocket calculators produces three models and estimates the weekly production requirements under four headings. These are given in the following table in some convenient units, together with the total resources available under each heading and the unit profit on each model.

Model	Resources required under heading				Unit profit z (£)
	A	B	C	D	
Euclid	4	2	2	6	5
Newton	3	5	4	6	8
Einstein	6	3	1	5	6
Total resources available	1800	1200	1500	2400	

Assuming that all production can be sold determine, for maximum total profit,

(a) how many of each model should be made;
(b) the corresponding total weekly profit;
(c) the number of units of unused resources.

Answer (a) 225 Euclids, 85 Newtons, 107 Einsteins; (b) £2447; (c) 3 units of resource A, 4 units of B, 603 of C, 5 of D.

10. What are the answers in No. 9 if the production schedule must include at least 100 of each model?
Answer (a) 200 Euclids, 100 Newtons, 100 Einsteins; (b) £2400; (c) 100 units of A, 600 of C, 100 of D.

11. Solve the following problems for non-negative values of the variables:

(a)
$$x_1 + 3x_2 + 2x_3 \leqslant 20$$
$$2x_1 + x_2 + x_3 \leqslant 8$$
$$4x_1 + 2x_2 + 5x_3 \leqslant 30$$
Maximize $x_1 + x_2 + x_3$

(b)
$$3x_1 + 2x_2 + 4x_3 + x_4 \leqslant 100$$
$$2x_1 + x_2 + 2x_3 + 2x_4 \leqslant 80$$
$$x_2 + x_4 \leqslant 20$$
$$2x_1 - x_2 - x_3 - x_4 \leqslant 0$$
Maximize $4x_1 + 7x_2 + 3x_3 + 9x_4$

Answer (a) There is a range of optimal solutions including $x_1 = 0$, $x_2 = 4$, $x_3 = 4$ and $x_1 = 0$, $x_2 = 3.333$, $x_3 = 4.667$; $z = 8$; (b) $x_1 = 13.333$, $x_2 = 0$, $x_3 = 6.667$, $x_4 = 20$; $z = 253.333$.

12. A fund manager is planning the investment of £6 000 000 so as to maximize its yield. The following stocks are considered:

Stock	A	B	C	D	E
Annual percentage yield	15	12	7	6	8

Stocks A and B are reckoned to be high risk and together must not carry more than 40 per cent of the total investment. In addition, neither A nor B must carry more than half as much as C, D and E taken together.

Of the three low-yield stocks, none must account for more than the other two put together.

Working in units of £100 000, express the data as a maximization problem of the normal form, and solve it. What is the overall percentage yield?

Answer Investments are: A, £1 800 000; B, £600 000; C, £1 800 000; D, 0; E, £1 800 000. Overall yield, 10.2 per cent.

13. The Well-tempered Wine Company is planning to clear one of its cellars by means of special Christmas offers. Stocktaking reveals the following numbers of cases (1 case = 12 bottles): 65 red wine, 65 white wine, 45 champagne, 40 each of sherry, port and whisky, and 25 each of gin and brandy.

The bottles are to be mixed in five selection packs called Taster, Celebration, Connoisseur, Epicure and Director's Special, selling at £35, £70, £70, £70 and £270 respectively. The contents of the packs, in numbers of bottles, are given in the following table:

	Red wine	White wine	Champagne	Sherry	Port	Whisky	Gin	Brandy
Taster	1	1	1	1	1	1	—	—
Celebration	4	2	1	2	—	1	1	1
Connoisseur	2	4	4	2	3	—	—	—
Epicure	3	1	1	1	1	1	1	1
Director's special	3	3	3	3	6	6	6	6

Assuming that all the packs can be sold, find the number of each that will maximize the revenue. What is the corresponding revenue, and how many bottles are unused?

Answer 180 Tasters, 45 Celebrations, 15 Connoisseurs, 105 Epicures and 25 Director's Specials. £24 600; 270 bottles of white wine and 75 bottles of champagne.

14. What are the answers in the previous example if, for marketing reasons, at least 30 packs of each selection are to be made?

Answer 150 Tasters, 60 Celebrations, 30 Connoisseurs, 60 Epicures and 30 Director's Specials. £23 850; 60 bottles of red wine, 240 bottles of white wine, 60 bottles of champagne and 30 bottles of whisky.

6 PROBABILITY AND STATISTICS

'Almost all human life depends on probabilities.'

Voltaire *Essay on Probabilities (1772)*

6.1 THE PROBABILITY SCALE

In the earlier chapters we looked at some of the OR techniques that can help in decision-making. In the numerical examples we were given details of resources, costs and other factors and, in order to find solutions, we had to assume that this information could be relied on.

In practice we may face major uncertainties. The progress of a building project through the winter months can be greatly affected by the weather, and the durations of some activities may turn out to be very different from the values used in the critical path analysis at the planning stage. Again, in present value calculations we may be making assumptions about interest rates for many years ahead and experience shows that these are far from predictable.

We learn to live with uncertainties in everyday life and we have many words and phrases to describe them. We talk about events being 'highly probable', 'unlikely', '90 per cent certain', 'a chance in a million' or having 'a 50–50 chance'. We use the term probability, denoted by p, for a numerical scale of likelihood and we give it values from 0 to 1. The highest value, $p = 1$, represents absolute certainty and the lowest, $p = 0$, corresponds to impossibility. It is clear that certain events – the sun will rise tomorrow, if I waved my arms I could fly in the air – lead to one or other of these extreme values.

6.2 FINDING PROBABILITY VALUES

Common sense enables us to determine the probabilities for some events such as throwing a six when rolling dice, obtaining a particular number when spinning a roulette wheel or drawing an ace from a pack of cards. We count the number of *possibilities* and we assume that they all have the same *probability*. This implies that there is no bias in the dice or roulette wheel, of course.

In each case, one of the possibilities must occur and the total probability is therefore $p = 1$. This value is shared equally between all the possibilities. The probability of obtaining a particular number when rolling a six-sided dice is therefore 1/6, and from a roulette wheel with 36 numbers it is 1/36. In many examples it will be convenient to convert such fractions to decimals, thus 0.1667 and 0.0278.

Drawing an ace from a pack of cards is slightly different. Of the 52 possibilities, 4 are aces and the probability of drawing an ace is therefore $4/52 = 1/13$ or, as a decimal, 0.0769. Values obtained by reasoning of this kind are called *a priori* probabilities.

Example 6.1
What is the probability of obtaining a total of 5 when two six-sided dice are rolled?

Solution
There are six possible outcomes for the first dice and six for the second. Since each possibility for the first can be combined with each for the second we have 36 possible outcomes altogether. Of these, four will produce a total 'score' of 5, namely, 1 and 4, 2 and 3, 3 and 2, 4 and 1.

The probability of obtaining the total 5 is therefore $4/36 = 1/9$ or, as a decimal, **0.1111**.

6.3 EXPERIMENTAL PROBABILITY

There are many cases in which we cannot deduce probabilities by reasoning alone. Sometimes we can carry out a series of trials and count the number of times the particular outcome occurs. The probability p can then be expressed as

$$p = \frac{\text{Number of occurences of the specified outcome}}{\text{Number of trials}}$$

We could carry out such an experiment for the rolling dice problem of Example 6.1. Our a priori reasoning gave a probability of 1/9 for throwing a total of 5 when two dice are rolled. Suppose we rolled the dice 900 times? We would not expect the total of 5 to occur exactly 100 times; indeed, we might be surprised if it did. But we would expect the number of occurrences to be in the region of 100. It represents some kind of average, and we call it the *expected* value. In the present case it is one possible value but if we had made 800 trials, instead of 900, the expected value would have been 88.89 and this could not have occurred under any circumstances.

We must also be clear about average and expected values when we discuss risks. A '50-year storm' or '50-year tide' means that there is an average interval of 50 years between one such occurrence and the next. It does not mean that, after 49 years without such an event, there is bound to be one in the following year. If we started keeping records now, the first occurrence of the event could be in the first year or the hundredth. Probabilities may tell us about the frequency at which events occur, but they cannot help us to predict the time or date of a particular occurrence. Nevertheless, probabilities and averages can help us make decisions.

Example 6.2
A small company offering a parcels delivery service kept a record of its

operations for a period of 100 days. It found that the number of vans required to operate the service was as follows:

Number of vans required	0	1	2	3	4 or more
Number of days	23	36	27	14	0

(a) What is the average daily cost if the vans are hired when required at an all-in cost of £40.00 per day each?

(b) The company is offered a contract under which it can pay a retaining fee of £5 per van per day plus a reduced rental of £30 for each day on which it is needed. Would it pay the company to accept this contract and, if so, for how many vans?

Solution

(a) The daily costs for 0, 1, 2 and 3 vans are £0.00, £40.00, £80.00 and £120.00. Hence, taking the total cost for 100 days, and dividing by 100, we obtain:

$$\text{Average daily cost} = \frac{23 \times £0.00 + 36 \times £40.00}{100}$$

$$+ \frac{27 \times £80.00 + 14 \times £120.00}{100}$$

$$= £52.80$$

There is no single day on which this cost occurs, of course, but an average (or 'expected') value can be useful in planning an operation of this kind. Note that the calculation can be approached in a slightly different way. The probabilities of 0, 1, 2 and 3 vans being required are 0.23, 0.36, 0.27 and 0.14. If we multiply these values by the corresponding daily costs and add the results we obtain the same answer.

(b) The offer of a reduced rental in return for a retaining fee will affect the daily costs for all possible numbers of vans, the amounts depending on the number of vans retained under the contract.

(i) Suppose 1 van is leased under the terms of the contract. Then, on days when no van is used the cost is £5.00. When 1 van is used the cost is £5.00 + £30.00 = £35.00. For 2 and 3 vans, the corresponding amounts are £35.00 + £40.00 = £75.00 and £35.00 + £80.00 = £115.00.

Combining these values with the corresponding probabilities, we have:

$$\text{Average daily cost} = 0.23 \times £5.00 + 0.36 \times £35.00$$
$$+ 0.27 \times £75.00 + 0.14 \times £115.00$$
$$= £50.10$$

(ii) If 2 vans are leased under the contract the daily costs for 0, 1, 2 and 3 vans are £10.00, £40.00, £70.00 and £110.00 respectively. Hence:

$$\text{Average daily cost} = 0.23 \times £10.00 + 0.36 \times £40.00$$
$$+ 0.27 \times £70.00 + 0.14 \times £110.00$$
$$= £51.00$$

(iii) With 3 vans leased the corresponding daily costs are £15.00, £45.00, £75.00 and £105.00. Hence:

$$\text{Average daily cost} = 0.23 \times £15.00 + 0.36 \times £45.00$$
$$+ 0.27 \times £75.00 + 0.14 \times £105.00$$
$$= £54.60$$

It follows from these results that it would save money if 1 or 2 vans were leased under the contract. To achieve the minimum cost **one van should be leased** in this way.

This is an average result, of course. Days on which no vans are required are now more expensive than under the daily hire arrangement, but this is more than compensated by the savings made when 1, 2 or 3 vans are needed.

6.4 DECISION TREES

In the last example the probabilities were based on the results of 100 observations. In many practical cases there is no opportunity to obtain the probability values by experiment. In these circumstances we have to make the best estimates we can, based on experience.

There is another complication. In the van-renting example it would be reasonable to assume that the operation would continue for many days and we could expect the average daily cost to become established in the long run. What can we do if we have to make a decision about a single event? It is argued that we should apply exactly the same principles and base our decision on the 'expected' values of the possible outcomes. The reasoning is that over a long period of time we shall face many such choices and, on average, this approach will give us the best return. We must be cautious when we apply this principle to extreme cases, as the solution to Example 6.4 will show.

In complex examples it is convenient to represent the various possiblities on a branching diagram, as in Fig. 6.1. This is called a decision tree. Junctions where we have to make a choice are called *decision points* and are represented by squares. Those that mark the meeting points of possibilities over which we have no control are called *chance points* and are shown by circles. At each chance point the cost or benefit of each branch is multiplied by the corresponding probability and the answers totalled. This gives the 'expected' value for the point. At decision points the most favourable choice is made. The process is continued from right to left across the diagram until we reach the initial decision point.

Example 6.3
An engineering company is planning its operations for the next 5 years and has to decide between a large and a small initial expansion. It is estimated that there is a 0.4 probability of a large increase in orders and a 0.6 probability that the market growth will be small.

The directors believe that a large initial expansion would bring an annual profit of £20 million if there were a large increase in orders, but an annual loss of £4 million if market growth were small. A small initial expansion is expected to bring an annual profit of £8 million irrespective of the extent of market growth.

Figure 6.1

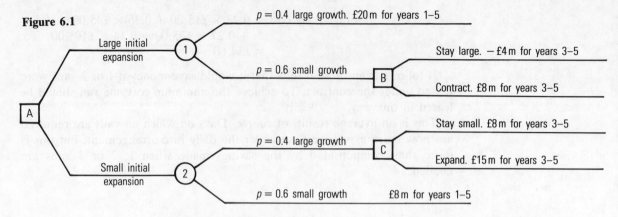

The size of the company could be readjusted after 2 years. If the initial expansion were large and market growth proved to be small, its size could be reduced and the annual profit would become £8 million for years 3, 4 and 5. Conversely, if the initial expansion were small and market growth were large a further expansion would increase the annual profit to £15 million for the last 3 years of the period.

What should the initial decision be if the cost of capital is

(a) ignored;
(b) taken as 15 per cent per annum?

Solution

The decision tree is shown in Fig. 6.1. The initial decision point is $\boxed{\text{A}}$, and the decisions to be made after 2 years are the branches that meet at $\boxed{\text{B}}$ and $\boxed{\text{C}}$. The chance points occur at $①$ and $②$.

At both $\boxed{\text{B}}$ and $\boxed{\text{C}}$ the better choice is to change the size from that selected at $\boxed{\text{A}}$ and the other options at these points are therefore discarded.

Figure 6.2

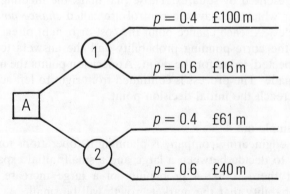

(a) Taking the four branches of the diagram in turn, the total profits for the 5 years (all in £ million) are therefore:

$$20 \times 5 = 100$$
$$-4 \times 2 + 8 \times 3 = 16$$

$$8 \times 2 + 15 \times 3 = 61$$
$$8 \times 5 \qquad\qquad = 40$$

These results are the basis of the reduced diagram (Fig. 6.2). Combining these results with the probability values, we have

Expected total profit at ① $= 0.4 \times 100 + 0.6 \times 16$
$$= £49.6 \text{ million}$$
Expected total profit at ② $= 0.4 \times 61 + 0.6 \times 40$
$$= £48.4 \text{ million}$$

Since ① gives the higher return the initial decision, on the basis of the information given in the question, should be the large expansion. However, the results are very close and, in practice, more detailed analysis would be called for. As in the previous example, the expected values will certainly not occur! If a large expansion is selected at the outset, the figure will be either 100 or 16, depending on the subsequent level of work. With a small initial expansion it will be 61 or 40. The expected value is a weighted average that would be achieved if it were possible to carry out the operation many times.

(b) If the cost of capital is to be allowed for, the various sums of money must be reduced to their present values. By the methods of Chapter 2 and with the given interest rate of 15 per cent, the factors for single payments are

Year	1	2	3	4	5
Factor	0.8696	0.7561	0.6575	0.5718	0.4972

By adding the factors for the appropriate years the repeated payment factors are

Years 1–2: factor $= 0.8696 + 0.7561 \qquad\quad = 1.6257$
Years 3–5: factor $= 0.6575 + 0.5718 + 0.4972 = 1.7265$
Years 1–5: factor $= 1.6257 + 1.7265 \qquad\quad = 3.3522$

Using these factors the present values of the four branches of Fig. 6.2 become

$$20 \times 3.3522 \qquad\qquad\qquad = 67.044$$
$$-4 \times 1.6257 + \;\; 8 \times 1.7265 = 7.309$$
$$8 \times 1.6257 + 15 \times 1.7265 = 38.903$$
$$8 \times 3.3522 \qquad\qquad\qquad = 26.818$$

Combining these results with the probability factors, we obtain:

Expected present value at ① $= 0.4 \times 67.044 + 0.6 \times 7.309$
$$= £31.2 \text{ million}$$
Expected present value at ② $= 0.4 \times 38.903 + 0.6 \times 26.818$
$$= £31.6 \text{ million}$$

The greater expected return is now achieved with the smaller initial expansion, the reverse of (a), but the two values are again very close. This example illustrates how sensitive the answers are to changes in the initial data.

Example 6.4

A wine merchant has a number of mail-order customers. The average value of each order is £80 and insurance against loss or breakage in the post costs £2 per order. If the probability of an order being lost or broken is reckoned to be 0.02, should the goods be insured?

Solution

If the goods are not insured, the average or 'expected' cost of loss or damage is obtained by combining the probability with the value of the order. Hence, for each order,

$$\text{Expected cost of not insuring} = 0.02 \times £80$$
$$= £1.60$$

This is a lower figure than the insurance premium of £2 and, on average, it is cheaper not to insure. However, a single loss leads to a high cost and, if there are few orders, **it would be prudent to insure**. This, of course, is the basis of all insurance. A relatively small premium enables us to insure against the heavy costs that would arise from remote possibilities such as a house fire, a car accident or untimely death. As individuals we hope that we shall not have to make a claim. In contrast, the insurance company receives a large number of premiums and these enable it to meet the large claims made by a small number of policyholders.

6.5 COMBINING PROBABILITIES

In many projects or systems there are many, or at least several, components. The performance of each component may be given in terms of probability values and we need to combine these to determine the overall outcome. A fire protection system may consist of several units each with its own probability of failure. Then again, in a building or civil engineering project the durations of individual activities may be expressed in terms of probabilities.

Suppose I travel to work each day along a road which has a number of junctions. Consider two such junctions (Fig. 6.3(a)) at which I may be delayed. To simplify the analysis, ignore the lengths of the delays and use the terms 'STOP' and 'GO' to signify being, and not being, delayed. For the two junctions taken together, there are four possible outcomes – GO at the first followed by GO at the second, GO followed by STOP, STOP followed by GO and STOP followed by STOP – as shown in Fig. 6.3(b).

Suppose, too, that I keep records of the number of delays and I find that it is GO at the first junction on 4 days out of 5. Then the probability of GO for this junction is $p = 4/5 = 0.8$. For STOP the probability is $p = 1/5 = 0.2$. If the GOs and STOPs occur randomly, so that they do not follow a pattern, we cannot predict what will happen on a particular day. We can only speak about what will happen on average.

At the second junction there are again two possibilities, but their probabilities may be different. Suppose, for this one, it is GO 3 days out of 4. Then the probabilities of GO and STOP are $p = 3/4 = 0.75$ and $p = 1/4 = 0.25$ respectively.

Figure 6.3

(a)

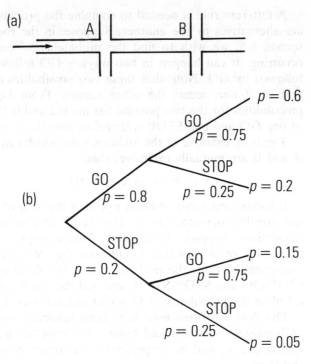

(b)

If there is no connection between the two junctions so that the outcome at the second is not affected by what happens at the first, then there will be four possibilities in all, as shown in Fig. 6.3(b).

On 4 days out of 5 it will be GO at the first junction, and on 3 days out of 4 GO at the second. It follows that, on average, it will be GO at both junctions on 3 days out of 5. The probability of two GOs is therefore $p = 3/5 = 0.6$. We can obtain this result by noting that it is the product of the two separate GO probabilities, that is, $p = 0.8 \times 0.75 = 0.6$. Similarly,

For GO followed by STOP, $p = 0.8 \times 0.25 = 0.2$
For STOP followed by GO, $p = 0.2 \times 0.75 = 0.15$
For STOP followed by STOP, $p = 0.2 \times 0.25 = 0.05$

The results are shown on the diagram and it will be seen that the sum of the probabilities for the four possible outcomes is 1.

Although we cannot say what the outcome will be on a particular day, the results can be useful. For example, if delay at both junctions means I am late for work, then the probability of being late is 0.05. In other words I shall be late 1 day in 20, on average.

6.6 MULTIPLICATION AND ADDITION RULES

The calculations carried out in the previous section are examples of the multiplication rule. This can be stated as follows. If A and B are independent events then the probability of both occurring is the product of their separate probabilities. In symbols,

$$p(A \text{ and } B) = p(A) \times p(B)$$

A different rule is needed to combine the probabilities of outcomes that are alternatives to one another. Suppose, in the road junction example of section 6.5, we wish to find the probability of one GO and one STOP occurring. It can happen in two ways − GO followed by STOP or STOP followed by GO. Note that these two possibilities are mutually exclusive, that is, if one occurs the other cannot. From Fig. 6.3(b) the separate probabilities for the two possibilities are 0.2 and 0.15. The total probability of one GO and one STOP is therefore $p = 0.2 + 0.15 = 0.35$.

This is an example of the addition rule, which can be stated as follows. If A and B are mutually exclusive, then

$$p(\text{A or B}) = p(\text{A}) + p(\text{B})$$

It follows from the addition rule that the sum of the probabilities of all the possible outcomes is 1. This result can often be used to simplify calculations. Suppose, in the traffic light example, we wished to know the probability of at least one STOP occurring. We could calculate (using the multiplication rule) the probabilities of the three possibilities GO–STOP, STOP–GO and STOP–STOP, and add the results. Alternatively, we could calculate the probability of GO–GO and subtract it from 1.

This device is often used in systems reliability calculations. Suppose the probabilities of success and failure in a complex mechanical or electronic system are p_s and p_f respectively. No other possibilities can exist and therefore

$$p_s + p_f = 1$$

This result is useful in examples where one outcome can occur in many ways but the other in only one.

Example 6.5

An industrial plant for the continuous production of a certain gas is protected by a system comprising a sensor, a microprocessor and a shutdown valve arranged in series, as shown in Fig. 6.4(a). The sensor responds to the purity of the gas and sends a signal to the microprocessor. If the gas is substandard the microprocessor triggers the mechanism to close the shutdown valve. All three units must perform satisfactorily if the system is to operate correctly.

For a given operating period, the probabilities of failure of the three units are 0.1, 0.05 and 0.02 respectively. What is the probability of system failure if

(a) the system contains one of each unit as shown in Fig. 6.4(a);
(b) a second sensor is added as shown in Fig. 6.4(b);
(c) a second parallel system is added as shown in Fig. 6.4(c);
(d) cross-connections are added as shown in Fig. 6.4(d)?

Solution

(a) Figure 6.5 is a branching diagram showing the possible outcomes. There are eight in all, and seven of them contain at least one failure. The system can therefore fail in seven ways. We could calculate the probability of each

Figure 6.4

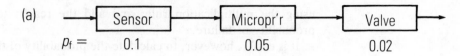

(a)

	Sensor	Micropr'r	Valve
$p_f =$	0.1	0.05	0.02

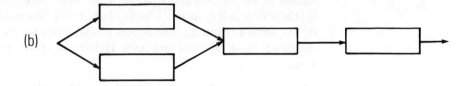

(b)

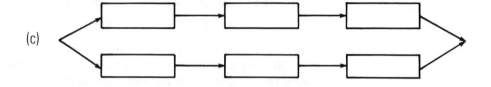

(c)

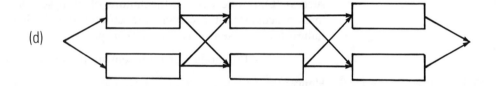

(d)

Figure 6.5

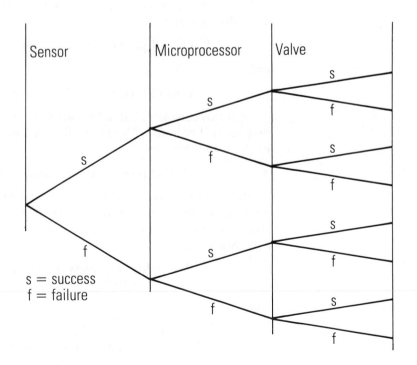

Sensor   Microprocessor   Valve

s = success
f = failure

using the multiplication rule, and add the results to obtain the overall probability of failure.

It is easier, however, to calculate the probability of the system succeeding and this can only occur in one way — success of the first unit combined with success of the second and success of the third. Since the failure probability for the sensor is 0.1, its probability of operating successfully is $1 - 0.1 = 0.9$. By the same reasoning, the success probabilities for the microprocessor and shutdown valve are 0.95 and 0.98. Hence, using the multiplication rule, we have:

Overall probability of success $= 0.9 \times 0.95 \times 0.98 = 0.838$

For the system as a whole there can only be two possibilities — success or failure — and their probabilities must total 1. Hence:

Overall probability of failure $= 1 - 0.838 = \mathbf{0.162}$

(b) The reliability of a system (its probability of success) can be increased by duplicating individual units. If there are two sensors, as shown in Fig. 6.4(b), there are four possible outcomes at the first stage — both sensors can fail, both can succeed or one can fail and one succeed, the last being possible in two ways. Of these four outcomes, three include at least one success. Only one case — the failure of both sensors — will result in the microprocessor not receiving the correct signal. Since the probability of failure for each sensor is 0.1, we can put:

Probability of both sensors failing $= 0.1 \times 0.1 = 0.01$

Hence:

Probability of at least one sensor succeeding $= 1 - 0.01 = 0.99$

Combining this result with the success probabilities for the microprocessor and valve, we obtain:

Overall probability of success $= 0.99 \times 0.95 \times 0.98 = 0.922$

and

Overall probability of failure $= 1 - 0.922 = \mathbf{0.078}$

(c) If two complete, but independent, systems are used overall failure will only occur if both fail. The probability of failure for each is, from the result in (a), 0.162. Hence:

Overall probability of failure $= 0.162 \times 0.162 = \mathbf{0.026}$

(d) If there are cross-connections, as shown in Fig. 6.4(d), the reliability is increased. The success of either unit at each of the three stages will ensure success overall. From (b) the probability of at least one sensor succeeding is 0.99. Similarly:

Probability of success of at least one microprocessor
$= 1 - (0.05 \times 0.05) = 0.9975$

and

Probability of success of at least one shutdown valve
$= 1 - (0.02 \times 0.02) = 0.9996$

Combining these results,

$$\text{Overall probability of success} = 0.99 \times 0.9975 \times 0.9996$$
$$= 0.987$$

and

$$\text{Overall probability of failure} = 1 - 0.987 = \mathbf{0.013}$$

The following points are worth noting in connection with this example:

1. It is difficult to obtain precise data on the failure probabilities of components. Therefore, we cannot justify the use of several significant figures in our answers.
2. If enough parallel units are introduced, the probability of failure can be reduced to any desired level — except zero. The risk of failure in an aircraft or nuclear power station can be made very small, but it cannot be eliminated completely.
3. Although the systems shown in (c) and (d) employ the same numbers of components, the cross connections in (d) give it a lower probability of failure.

Example 6.6

There are 30 cars in a supermarket car park each having a registration number in the range 1–999. What is the probability that there will be at least two cars with the same number?

How many cars will have to be present if the probability of this occurring is 0.5?

Solution

It is assumed that every number in the range has the same probability of appearing. The probability of a given number occurring is therefore 1/999. If we consider the cars one at a time the first can take any of the 999 numbers without producing duplication. The probability of this may be thought of as 999 out of 999. For the second car there is a probability of 1/999 that it will have the same number as the first and hence 998/999 that it will not. Similarly, the probability of the third having a number different from the first two is 997/999. Using the multiplication rule, the probability of the first three cars having different numbers is, therefore,

$$p = \frac{999}{999} \times \frac{998}{999} \times \frac{997}{999}$$

If the calculation is extended to allow for 30 cars the last term is 970/999 and the expression for p becomes

$$p = \frac{999}{999} \times \frac{998}{999} \times \frac{997}{999} \times \ldots \times \frac{970}{999}$$

$$= \frac{999 \times 998 \times 997 \times \ldots \times 970}{999 \times 999 \times 999 \times \ldots \times 999}$$

This result can be expressed more concisely using the factorial notation in which $n!$ represents the product of all numbers from 1 to n. Thus

$$999! = 999 \times 998 \times 997 \times \ldots \times 3 \times 2 \times 1$$

To eliminate all the numbers below 970 we divide by 969!. The numerator is therefore represented by 999!/969!. Furthermore the denominator of the expression for p can be written 999^{30}. Using these results we can write

$$p = \frac{999!}{999^{30} \times 969!}$$

Although many pocket calculators have single-stroke factorial and power functions they can only deal with numbers up to 10^{100}. Each of the three terms in the last fraction will exceed this value and we must return to the previous expression in which the numerator and denominator are both products of 30 numbers. By multiplying and dividing alternately the intermediate values are all less than 1. The result gives the probability of every car number being different. If it is subtracted from 1 we obtain the probability of at least two cars having the same number. The arithmetic is tedious and mistakes are easily made. It is therefore worth while writing a computer program and a suitable listing is given in Fig. 6.6.

Figure 6.6

```
10 P=1:N=999:C=0
20 P=P*N/999
30 C=C+1
40 N=N-1
50 IF C<30 THEN GOTO 20
60 PRINT "PROBABILITY IS ";1-P
70 END

>RUN
PROBABILITY IS 0.3558
```

Line 10 sets the initial values of P, the probability that the cars have different numbers, the numerator N and a car counter C.

Line 20 modifies the value of P, multiplying by the current numerator and dividing by 999.

Line 30 records the number of cars considered and line 40 reduces the numerator by 1 in preparation for the next stage of the calculation.

Line 50 ensures that the process is repeated 30 times and line 60 then prints the answer.

When the program is RUN the probability of at least two cars having the same registration number is found to be **0.3558**.

The program can be used for solving the second question by changing lines 50 and 60 to the following:

```
50 IF P>0.5 THEN GOTO 20
60 PRINT "REQUIRED NUMBER OF CARS IS ";C
```

Line 50 now ensures that the calculation of P continues until its value falls to 0.5 or less. The probability of two cars having the same number is then 0.5 or more.

Line 60 then prints the answer.

When the program is RUN it is found that **38 cars** are sufficient to ensure that the probability of at least two having the same registration number is 0.5.

The program is easily adapted to solve related problems. If the cars have four-figure registration numbers, for example, the value 999 in lines 10 and 20 should be changed to 9999.

6.7 SAMPLING AND THE BINOMIAL EXPANSION

In factories making components in large numbers, the production is often checked by testing samples taken at random. Suppose we know that 20 per cent of the components coming from a certain production line are faulty. If one component is taken at random, the probability of it being faulty is 0.2 and the probability of being OK is 0.8. What is the probability of finding one or more faulty components in a sample of, say, three?

Figure 6.7

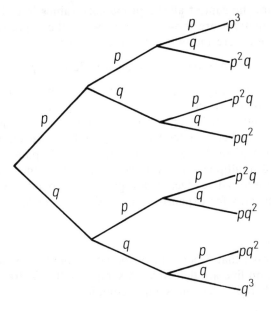

The analysis is similar to that used in the solution to the systems reliability question of Example 6.5. Suppose p and q are the probabilities of a component being faulty and OK respectively. With the present figures $p = 0.2$ and $q = 0.8$. The sum $(p + q)$ is always equal to 1. Figure 6.7 shows a branching diagram for a sample of three components. For each one there are two possibilities and, for the group of three, eight possibilities in all. The probabilities of these eight outcomes can be calculated by the multiplication rule and it is convenient to work in symbols for the time being.

The probability of all three components being faulty is $p \times p \times p$, which we can write as p^3, and this is shown at the end of the top path through the diagram. The next path represents the case of components 1 and 2 being faulty, with the third OK; this has a probability of $p \times p \times q = p^2q$. The next result is given by $p \times q \times p$, which is also p^2q. In each of the eight results the power of p corresponds to the number of faulty components and the power of q gives the number that are OK. In every case the two powers must total 3, the number of components in the sample.

We can use the results to find the probability of a specified number of components being faulty. For example the probability of there being two faulty components is given by the p^2q terms. There are three of these and hence the probability of two components in the sample being faulty is $3p^2q$.

Similarly, the probability of one being faulty is $3pq^2$, and the probability of none is q^3. Collecting results, and substituting the numerical values for p and q, we find:

Probability of three faulty components $= p^3 \quad = (0.2)^3 \quad\quad\quad\quad = 0.008$
Probability of two faulty components $= 3p^2q = 3 \times (0.2)^2 \times (0.8) = 0.096$
Probability of one faulty component $\quad = 3pq^2 = 3 \times (0.2) \times (0.8)^2 = 0.384$
Probability of zero faulty components $= q^3 \quad = (0.8)^3 \quad\quad\quad\quad = 0.512$

$$1.000$$

Again, the sum of all the probability values is 1. The four terms used in the calculations are those that arise when the expressions $(p + q)$, $(p + q)$ and $(p + q)$ are multiplied together. Thus:

$$(p + q)^3 = p^3 + 3p^2q + 3pq^2 + q^3$$

This result is an example of a general relationship known as the binomial expansion, see section A.9. It enables us to deal with other sample sizes and other numbers of faulty components. For example, the probability of three components being defective in a sample of seven is given by the term containing p^3 in the expansion of $(p + q)^7$. Expanding such expressions by repeated multiplication is tedious and the binomial theorem offers an efficient alternative. Details are given in Appendix A together with a table of coefficients for expansions up to the power 15.

Example 6.7

It is known that 5 per cent of the components produced on a certain mass production line are defective. A sample of five is drawn at random. What is the probability that the sample contains:

(a) one defective component;
(b) two defective components;
(c) at least two defective components?

Solution

If p and q are the probabilities of a component being defective and OK then $p = 0.05$ and $q = 0.95$. The required probabilities can be found from the expansion of $(p + q)^5$. Applying the binomial theorem,

$$(p + q)^5 = p^5 + 5p^4q + 10p^3q^2 + 10p^2q^3 + 5pq^4 + q^5$$

(a) The probability of one component being defective is given by the term containing one p. Thus

$$\text{Probability} = 5pq^4 = 5 \times (0.05) \times (0.95)^4 = \mathbf{0.2036}$$

(b) For two defective components,

$$\text{Probability} = 10p^2q^3 = 10 \times (0.05)^2 \times (0.95)^3 = \mathbf{0.0214}$$

(c) The probability of at least two components being defective can be found by summing the probabilities for two, three, four and five faulty components. It is easier, however, to find the probability of zero or one being defective, and then subtract the result from 1. From (a), the probability of one component being defective is 0.2036. The probability of the sample containing no defective components is

$$q^5 = (0.95)^5 = 0.7738$$

The probability of the sample containing zero or one defective component is therefore $0.2036 + 0.7738 = 0.9774$. Hence

Probability of two or more defective components $= 1 - 0.9774$
$$= \mathbf{0.0226}$$

Example 6.8

A multiple-choice examination paper contains 10 questions each with four possible answers, only one of which is correct. A candidate, who has not revised for the exam, decides to select the answers at random.

(a) What is the probability of the candidate selecting exactly four correct answers?
(b) If six or more correct answers are required for a pass, what is the probability of the candidate passing this paper?
(c) If the candidate sits three papers of this kind, what is the probability that he or she will pass in at least one?

Solution

Let p and q be the probabilities of selecting correct and incorrect answers for a particular question. With four answers to choose from, $p = 1/4 = 0.25$ and $q = 3/4 = 0.75$. Since there are 10 questions on the paper, the probability of selecting a specified number of correct answers is given by the appropriate term in the expansion of $(p + q)^{10}$.

Using the values given in Table A.1 we can write

$$(p = q)^{10} = p^{10} + 10p^9q + 45p^8q^2 + 120p^7q^3 + 210p^6q^4$$
$$+ 252p^5q^5 + 210p^4q^6 + 120p^3q^7 + 45p^2q^8$$
$$+ 10pq^9 + q^{10}$$

(a) The probability of selecting four correct answers is given by the term containing p^4. Hence

Probability $= 210p^4q^6 = 210 \times (0.25)^4 \times (0.75)^6 = \mathbf{0.1460}$

(b) The probability of selecting at least six correct answers is given by the terms containing p^6 and higher powers. These are the first five terms in the expansion and thus

Probability $= p^{10} + 10p^9q + 45p^8q^2 + 120p^7q^3 + 210p^6q^4$
$$= (0.25)^{10} + 10 \times (0.25)^9 \times 0.75$$
$$+ 45 \times (0.25)^8 \times (0.75)^2$$
$$+ 120 \times (0.25)^7 \times (0.75)^3$$
$$+ 210 \times (0.25)^6 \times (0.75)^4$$
$$= 0.000\,001 + 0.000\,029 + 0.000\,386 + 0.003\,090$$
$$+ 0.016\,222$$
$$= \mathbf{0.019\,728}$$

(c) With the possibility of pass or fail on each of three papers, there are eight possible outcomes altogether. Seven of these will each contain at least one pass and it is therefore easier to determine the probability of failing all three papers. Using the result in (b),

$$\text{Probability of failing one paper} = 1 - (\text{probability of passing})$$
$$= 1 - 0.019728$$
$$= 0.980272$$

Thus, by the multiplication rule,

$$\text{Probability of failing all three papers} = (0.980272)^3 = 0.941976$$

and

$$\text{Probability of passing at least one paper} = 1 - 0.941976$$
$$= \textbf{0.058024}$$

The answers show that there is little hope of success for the candidate who selects the answers randomly. The chance of picking four correct answers is roughly 1 in 7, and the chance of passing a paper (six or more correct answers) is only 1 in 50. If three such papers are taken the chances of passing at least one are still worse than 1 in 17. Perhaps there is a moral in this example; revise for your exams!

6.8 SIMULATION

In section 6.5 we looked at a journey through two road junctions in which there were two possibilities (GO and STOP) at each. By using the multiplication and addition rules we were able to calculate the probabilities for the four outcomes GO/GO, GO/STOP, STOP/GO and STOP/STOP. There is another way of obtaining the results; we can carry out an experiment 'on paper'.

At the first junction, it was GO on 4 days out of 5. Suppose we took 50 cards, wrote GO on 40 of them, STOP on the other 10 and then shuffled the pack thoroughly. We could then decide the outcome at the first junction by drawing a card at random – as in a lottery. We could do the same for the second junction, the only change being that we would need different proportions of GO and STOP cards.

If we repeated the process many times and kept records of our results, we could expect the various outcomes to occur in roughly the proportions we found earlier by combining the separate probabilities. The technique of running an 'experiment' to find answers in problems of this kind is called *simulation*. It is particularly valuable in cases that cannot be analysed by conventional mathematical methods.

Drawing cards from a pack is not the only random way of deciding the outcomes. Consider the second junction in which the probabilities of GO and STOP were 0.75 and 0.25. Suppose we take the numbers 1 to 36 and divide the range into two parts that are proportional to these probabilities. We assign 27 numbers to GO and 9 to STOP. Any numbers in the range will do but we might as well use the first 27 (1–27) for GO and the remainder (28–36) for STOP. Whenever we wish to simulate the journey through the second junction we take a number in the range 1–36 at random. If it falls between 1 and 27 we interpret the outcome as GO, and if it is between 28 and 36 we call it STOP.

But how can we select the number at random? As it happens, there are 36 numbers on a roulette wheel (ignoring the zeros) and if we had such a wheel, properly levelled and balanced, we could spin it each time we needed to simulate the journey through the second junction. We could then use the 'winning' number to decide whether the outcome were GO or STOP.

The number 36 is not always convenient. At the first junction, for example, it is GO on 0.8 of the days and $0.8 \times 36 = 28.8$, not a whole number. As an approximation, however, take the range 1–29 to represent GO at the first junction, 1–27 representing GO at the second. Suppose the numbers in Table 6.1 were obtained when the roulette wheel was spun 200 times. (In fact they were generated by a computer, as explained in the next section).

Table 6.1 200 random numbers in the range 1–36

13	32	11	19	13	28	5	16	11	19	9	16	2	27	5	35	17	23	35	22
32	33	8	10	29	25	31	22	3	2	29	21	26	33	36	26	34	36	8	27
25	24	26	18	24	26	15	20	35	17	16	14	7	8	4	19	25	9	19	14
6	25	25	25	9	2	19	17	10	19	22	12	22	20	26	8	29	21	9	1
25	13	28	31	13	5	27	14	28	8	25	30	35	25	4	19	18	24	7	20
31	5	10	11	2	26	8	31	35	36	9	34	34	1	10	10	23	35	3	9
27	32	17	32	32	10	23	30	16	19	22	31	17	31	14	1	34	36	24	2
16	7	20	32	8	25	23	20	7	5	15	29	11	14	19	17	2	5	33	21
23	13	2	11	34	29	10	30	7	30	22	15	10	3	25	36	30	3	12	2
7	16	7	7	5	20	6	12	10	28	27	20	30	25	35	34	22	36	21	11

We can use these numbers to simulate 100 journeys. Take the numbers in turn to decide the outcome at the two junctions alternately. The first number, 13, is in the range 1–29, which gives GO, and the second number, 32, is in the range 28–36, which is STOP at the second junction. The outcome of the first day's journey is therefore GO/STOP.

For the second day we take the next two numbers, 11 and 19. These give GO and GO respectively for the two junctions. If we continue in this way, and note the results, we obtain the outcomes for 100 journeys. It is a tedious process and, in practice, we can delegate it to a computer. With the present figures the totals for the four possibilities GO/GO, GO/STOP, STOP/GO and STOP/STOP are 62, 21, 11 and 6. Dividing by 100 the corresponding probabilities are 0.62, 0.21, 0.11 and 0.06. These compare with the calculated values of 0.6, 0.2, 0.15 and 0.05 obtained in section 6.5.

Spinning a roulette wheel may be no quicker than drawing cards from a pack, but the idea of assigning ranges of numbers to different outcomes, and using random numbers to decide which has occurred, is an important one in modern mathematics. The technique is sometimes called Monte Carlo – a reminder of the days when the town was the fashionable gambling centre of Europe.

6.9 RANDOM NUMBERS

To use the simulation method described in the previous section we need a long list of numbers that are distributed uniformly throughout the range of interest. If we are using whole numbers in the range 1–36, for example, we want each one to appear with the same frequency on average, but with no pattern whatsoever. This is not easy to achieve but there are methods of producing pseudo-random numbers that are suitable for most purposes. The usual approach is to obtain each number by carrying out some arithmetical process on the previous one. The first number in the sequence is called the *seed* and, if the same seed is used each time, we obtain the same sequence. This can be an advantage when work has to be checked.

Most computers and many pocket calculators are programmed to produce pseudo-random numbers in the range 0–0.9999. . . . If a different range is required the numbers are multiplied by a suitable factor. The 200 'random' numbers shown in section 6.8 were obtained by this means. A simple but very powerful formula consists of multiplying the current number by 997 and taking the fractional part of the result as the next number. With a suitable seven-figure seed, such as 0.528 416 3, this produces a sequence that is uniformly distributed and has a period (that is, the length before it repeats) of about 500 000 numbers.

On many computers the keyword RND will call up a random number in the range 0–0.9999. . . . In BBC BASIC use RND(1) and on the Casio pocket computer use RAN#. The function can be used within programs so that the computer can quickly carry out simulations with hundreds of trials.

Simulation, used in conjunction with random numbers, has many applications. It can be used, for example, to obtain an experimental value for π. Suppose a quadrant of a circle, radius 1 unit, is drawn within a square of side 1, as shown in Fig. 6.8. By Pythagoras, the equation of the circle is $x^2 + y^2 = 1$.

Next, imagine that the square is 'sprayed' with a large number of random points. The ratio of the number of 'hits' on the quadrant to 'hits' on the whole square will be the same as the ratio of their areas. The area of a circle, radius r, is πr^2 so for a quadrant of radius 1, the area is $\pi/4$. Hence

$$\frac{\text{Number of hits on quadrant}}{\text{Number of hits on square}} = \frac{\text{Area of quadrant}}{\text{Area of square}} = \frac{\pi/4}{1} = \frac{\pi}{4}$$

Figure 6.8

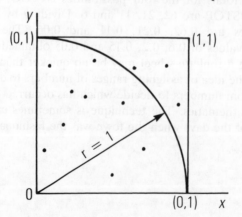

The short computer program listing of Fig. 6.9 uses this result and the RND function to determine a value for π.

Figure 6.9

```
10 N=400:C=0
20 FOR I=1 TO N
30 IF RND^2+RND^2<1 THEN C=C+1
40 NEXT I
50 PRINT "EXPERIMENTAL VALUE OF PI = ";4*C/N
60 END
```

Line 10 sets N, the total number of hits on the square, at 400 and the counter C at an initial value 0.

Lines 20–40 determine the number of hits on the quadrant. Pairs of random numbers (representing the coordinates x and y) are taken; if the sum of their squares is less than 1 the corresponding point is within the quadrant and the counter C is increased by 1.

Line 50 prints the value obtained for π. Ten successive runs on one computer gave the results 3.18, 3.15, 3.10, 3.24, 3.12, 3.21, 3.18, 3.12, 2.95 and 3.07.

Note that in BBC BASIC the keyword RND must be changed to RND(1) so that line 30 becomes:

$$30 \text{ IF RND(1)}^2 + \text{RND(1)}^2 < 1 \text{ THEN C=C+1}$$

The number of trials can be changed by altering the value of N in line 10. Does an increase in N produce answers closer to the value 3.141 59?

For many purposes it is convenient to have a range of 100 numbers. Since it is usual to display them as two-digit numbers we take the range from 00 to 99 and prefix those below 10 with a zero. Table C.5 gives a total of 700 random numbers in this format.

6.10 AVERAGES

The idea of an average value is a familiar one. We assess our salary, the size of a family or the fuel consumption of a car by comparing it with the 'average'. We think of the average as a representative or typical value, somewhere between the extremes.

In some examples the average value is one that cannot possibly apply to any of the occurrences; a report that the average family has 2.2 children and lives in a house with 3.1 bedrooms may prompt some humorous comments, but we realize that averages of this kind can be useful if they are interpreted correctly.

The most familiar kind of average is that in which a set of values is totalled and then divided by the number in the set. This is called the *arithmetic mean*. If there are n values in the set and they are denoted by x_1, x_2, $x_3 \ldots x_n$, the mean, usually written $\bar{x}$, is given by

$$\bar{x} = \frac{x_1 + x_2 + x_3 \ldots x_n}{n}$$

We use the symbol Σ (upper case sigma) to mean 'the sum of all the values of' and we can therefore shorten the result to

$$\bar{x} = \frac{\Sigma x}{n}$$

The arithmetic mean can be thought of as the value that would give the same total if it replaced every value in the set. There are other kinds of mean value. The *geometric mean* is based on the product of all the values rather than their sum. If it replaced every value in the set it would lead to the same answer when they are all multiplied together.

If the geometric mean is denoted by G, the relationship is

$$G \times G \times G \times \ldots (n \text{ times}) = x_1 \times x_2 \times x_3 \times \ldots \times x_n$$

or

$$G^n = x_1 \times x_2 \times x_3 \times \ldots \times x_n$$

and

$$G = {}^n\sqrt{(x_1 \times x_2 \times x_3 \times \ldots \times x_n)}$$

A third kind of average is the *harmonic mean*, sometimes denoted by H, which is based on the total of the reciprocal of all the values. Thus, $1/H$ is the arithmetic mean of the reciprocals of the values and we can write

$$\frac{1}{H} = \frac{1/x_1 + 1/x_2 + 1/x_3 + \ldots + 1/x_n}{n} = \frac{\Sigma(1/x)}{n}$$

from which

$$H = \frac{n}{\Sigma(1/x)}$$

Example 6.9
Find the arithmetic, geometric and harmonic means of the numbers 5, 14, 9, 6 and 8.

Solution
In each case $n = 5$. Using the appropriate formulae,

(a) Arithmetic mean $\bar{x} = \dfrac{5 + 14 + 9 + 6 + 8}{5} = \mathbf{8.4}$

(b) Geometric mean $G = {}^5\sqrt{(5 \times 14 \times 9 \times 6 \times 8)}$
$= {}^5\sqrt{(30\,240)} = \mathbf{7.87}$

(c) Harmonic mean $H = \dfrac{5}{1/5 + 1/14 + 1/9 + 1/6 + 1/8}$

$= \dfrac{5}{0.6742} = \mathbf{7.42}$

Each form of mean value has its uses but, in this book, the term average or mean will normally denote the arithmetic mean. Sometimes the values in a set are not all treated equally; they are said to be 'weighted'. An example of this occurs in critical path analysis, section 3.12. A mean time t for the duration of an activity is obtained from three estimates a, m and b, with m being given four times the weighting of the others. In effect, m is counted four times so that $t = (a + 4m + b)/6$.

6.11 CONTINUOUS AND DISCONTINUOUS FUNCTIONS

We often use graphs to display the results of experiments. If we allow a kettle of boiling water to cool, and we measure its temperature at convenient intervals, we can plot a graph of temperature against time from which we can deduce something about the cooling process. We can use the graph to estimate the temperature at intermediate times – a process called interpolation. We can also project the graph beyond our last reading to try and predict the temperature at a later time. The second process – extrapolation – is, for obvious reasons, less reliable.

Table 6.2 Women's world records for running

Distance (metres)	100	200	400	800	1500	2000
Time (seconds)	10.5	21.7	47.6	113.3	232.5	328.7

Table 6.2 gives the women's world records for running[1] at the end of 1988 and the results are shown graphically in Fig. 6.10.

Figure 6.10

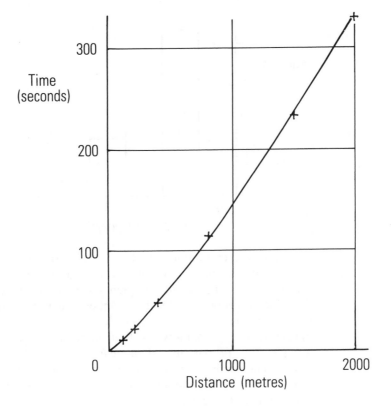

We can use the curve drawn through the points to make predictions for other distances. By interpolation, we would expect the record for 1000 m to be in the region of 150 seconds (2 minutes 30 seconds). For 1 mile (1609 m), a time of 250 seconds (4 minutes 10 seconds) seems attainable. We would have less confidence in predicting the times for 3000 or 5000 m from the data available here.

A function of this kind is called continuous. For every distance there is a corresponding time and the graph runs smoothly with no sudden changes in value. In contrast, consider Table 6.3. This gives a breakdown of the 165 goals scored by the soccer teams playing in the English and Scottish Leagues on 12 November 1988. Of the 122 teams playing on that day 29 did not score, 44 scored one goal, 30 scored two, 15 scored three and 4 scored four. No team scored more than four goals. The number of times a particular outcome occurs is called its frequency, denoted by f.

Table 6.3 Frequency distribution of soccer goal-scoring

Number of goals scored	0	1	2	3	4
Number of teams (frequency)	29	44	30	15	4

The relationship between the number of goals and the frequency is discontinuous. Intermediate values have no meaning; it is pointless to ask how many teams scored 2.3 or 3.7 goals. On the other hand, we shall not be surprised if the average number of goals per team is not a whole number.

Figure 6.11

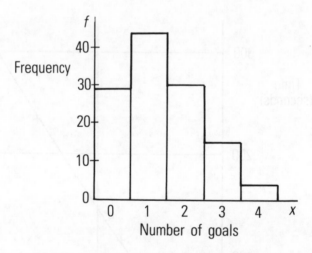

Instead of a continuous graph we display the results in a block diagram, as shown in Fig. 6.11. It is called a histogram. The number of goals, x, is shown horizontally and the frequency f is plotted vertically. The height of each block is proportional to the number of teams scoring the corresponding number of goals. If all the blocks have the same width, the area of each represents the probability of that number of goals being scored. For example the probability of a team scoring more than one goal is proportional to the combined areas of the blocks for two, three and four goals. This concept that the area represents a probability is the basis of many statistical calculations.

The numbers of goals that may be scored or the numbers of faults that may occur are examples of *discrete variables*. They can take only certain values (in the present case, integers such as 0, 1, 2, 3 . . .). In contrast the heights and weights of people are continuous variables. In quoting the height of a person we are not confined to whole numbers such as 161 or 162 cm; it could be 161.3 cm or, if we could measure accurately enough, possibly 161.37. When we are dealing with discrete variables, we can only speak about the probabilities of individual values occurring. With continuous variables, we talk of the probability of a value falling within a specified range.

Some statistical concepts apply equally to discrete and continuous variables. In addition, some mathematical results that apply to discrete variables give good approximations to continuous functions.

6.12 FREQUENCY DISTRIBUTION CURVES

The histogram of Fig. 6.11 is based on a total of 122 'trials' and only five different values of x. If there were many more trials and values the histogram might approximate to a curve, as in Fig. 6.12. This is called a frequency distribution curve and many examples in industry and everyday life exhibit this characteristic of a concentration of results in one region, with a tailing off on each side.

Figure 6.12

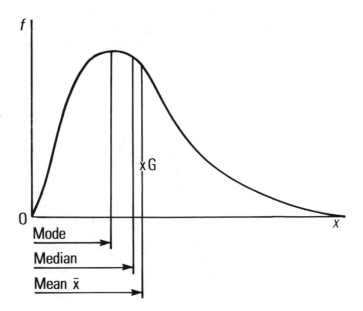

Some distributions, such as the heights of people, are symmetrical about the central values. Others, as in Fig. 6.12, are said to be *skewed*. If the longer tail is towards the larger values of x, as in this case, the distribution is said to be *positively skewed*. If it is towards the smaller values of x the skew is negative.

The diagram shows three kinds of central value – *mean*, *mode* and *median*. Mean is the arithmetic mean or average, as defined in section 6.10. In the soccer example, 165 goals were scored by 122 teams, giving a mean of $165/122 = 1.352$. The mean corresponds to the centroid (or centre of gravity) G for the area under the frequency distribution curve.

The mode, or modal value, is the value of x that occurs most frequently; in the soccer example this was clearly 1. In Fig. 6.12, it is the value that gives the highest point of the curve.

The median is the value that comes midway in the list of values when they are sorted into increasing or decreasing order. It is of little significance when there are few different values of x but is a useful measure when there are many. For example, the median mark in an examination is the one that divides the list of candidates in half when they are placed in rank order. A vertical line at this value divides the area under the frequency distribution curve into two equal parts.

In many skewed distributions the difference between the mean and the mode is found to be three times the difference between the mean and the median. In a symmetrical distribution, the mean, mode and median are equal.

6.13 VARIANCE AND STANDARD DEVIATION

Suppose we wished to compare house prices in different parts of the country. We could collect large numbers of values in the various regions and draw a frequency distribution curve for each. Imagine that the results for two regions, London and Midshire, are represented by the curves of Fig. 6.13.

Figure 6.13

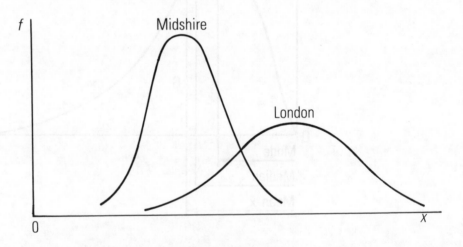

Each curve has a symmetrical bell shape but they differ in two major respects. The values for London have a higher mean and are more spread out than those for Midshire. In making comparisons, we need some measure of this dispersion or *scatter*. There is more than one possibility. One method is to calculate the *deviation* of every value, in other words, how far away it is from the mean and then take the average of the results. This is called the *mean deviation*. In making the calculation we consider all deviations as positive whether the value of x is greater or less than $\bar{x}$. Otherwise the negative deviations would tend to cancel the positive ones and, in a symmetrical case, their average would be zero. We write the absolute difference between x and $\bar{x}$ as $|x - \bar{x}|$. This means that it is only the numerical difference that is required and the sign is ignored.

With this notation we can write

$$\text{Mean deviation} = \frac{\Sigma|x - \bar{x}|}{n}$$

where n is the number of values.

Although mean deviation has some practical applications it is usual to work on the squares of the differences rather than the differences themselves. One advantage of this is that we do not need to distinguish between values above and below the mean. Negative differences become positive when squared. The average of the squares of the differences is called the variance. We can therefore write

$$\text{Variance} = \frac{\Sigma(x - \bar{x})^2}{n}$$

It is useful for many purposes to have an equivalent or mean difference that would give the same result if it replaced every value of x. This equivalent deviation is denoted by σ (sigma), or sometimes s. It follows that

$$n.\sigma^2 = \Sigma(x - \bar{x})^2$$

and

$$\sigma = \sqrt{\frac{\Sigma(x - \bar{x})^2}{n}}$$

This result is called the *root-mean-square deviation* or, more simply, the *standard deviation*. The standard deviation is the square root of the variance and each is readily obtained from the other. We can emphasize the relationship by using σ^2 to denote the variance.

Example 6.10
Calculate the arithmetic mean, the mean deviation, the variance and standard deviation for the set of values 6, 14, 9, 6 and 8.

Solution
With a small number of values the work can be set out in a table as follows:

x	$x - \bar{x}$	$|x - \bar{x}|$	$(x - \bar{x})^2$
6	−2.6	2.6	6.76
14	5.4	5.4	29.16
9	0.4	0.4	0.16
6	−2.6	2.6	6.76
8	−0.6	0.6	0.36
43		11.6	43.20

The given values are listed in the first column, the total being 43. Since $n = 5$, the mean value is

$$\bar{x} = \frac{\Sigma x}{n} = \frac{43}{5} = \mathbf{8.6}$$

With this result the other columns can be completed. The second column records the differences between the separate values and the mean, the results being negative for values below the mean. The next column gives the numerical differences, ignoring the signs. The total for this column is 11.6 and therefore:

$$\text{Mean deviation} = \frac{\Sigma|x - \bar{x}|}{n} = \frac{11.6}{5} = \textbf{2.32}$$

The fourth column shows the squares of the differences, the total being 43.20. This gives

$$\text{Variance } \sigma^2 = \frac{\Sigma(x - \bar{x})^2}{n} = \frac{43.20}{5} = \textbf{8.64}$$

Finally the standard deviation is obtained as the square root of the variance. Thus

$$\sigma = \sqrt{8.64} = \textbf{2.94}$$

6.14 POPULATION AND SAMPLE DEVIATIONS

The word 'population' is used to mean every member of a group and it is applied equally to people and objects. In many practical examples, such as the testing of mass produced components, we cannot include the whole population and we therefore draw a sample of n items. It can be shown that, under these conditions the value n should be replaced by $n - 1$ in the formula for standard deviation. Comparing the results we have

$$\text{Population } \sigma = \sqrt{\frac{\Sigma(x - \bar{x})^2}{n}} \qquad \text{Sample } \sigma = \sqrt{\frac{\Sigma(x - \bar{x})^2}{n - 1}}$$

For a large sample the difference is small. With a sample of 50, the result is only 1 per cent more than that given by the first formula. In the rest of this chapter the standard deviation will be calculated by the population formula.

6.15 GROUPED FREQUENCIES

In Example 6.10 one of the values in the group, 6, occurred twice. This caused no particular difficulty, but if a value occurs several times we can save time by dealing with all its occurrences at once. Suppose a value x occurs f times. In summing all the values this one adds fx to the total. For the complete set, the sum is Σfx and the total number of values n is Σf. Substituting these results in the expression given in section 6.10, the arithmetic mean becomes

$$\bar{x} = \frac{\Sigma fx}{\Sigma f}$$

In the same way, the sum of the squares of the deviations for all the instances of the value x is $f(x - \bar{x})^2$ and the standard deviation formula becomes

$$\sigma = \sqrt{\frac{\Sigma f(x - \bar{x})^2}{\Sigma f}}$$

Using these results with the goal-scoring data of Table 6.3, we have

x	f	fx	$x - \bar{x}$	$(x - \bar{x})^2$	$f(x - \bar{x})^2$
0	29	0	-1.352	1.828	53.01
1	44	44	-0.352	0.124	5.46
2	30	60	0.648	0.420	12.60
3	15	45	1.648	2.716	40.74
4	4	16	2.648	7.012	28.05

$$\Sigma f = 122 \quad \Sigma fx = 165 \qquad \Sigma f(x - \bar{x})^2 = 139.86$$

The mean value, obtained from the totals of the second and third columns, is

$$\bar{x} = \frac{\Sigma fx}{\Sigma f} = \frac{165}{122} = 1.352$$

This result is used to complete the remaining columns and the standard deviation is

$$\sigma = \sqrt{\frac{\Sigma f(x - \bar{x})^2}{\Sigma f}} = \sqrt{\frac{139.86}{122}} = \sqrt{1.146} = 1.071$$

The same technique can be used for groups in which there are many different values of x. The total range is divided into a few convenient intervals or classes and the occurrences within each class are all placed at its midpoint. The midpoint value is then taken as x for all the values in the class.

Example 6.11
The following values show the weekly sales of sundials by the Tardy Timepiece Company over a period of 50 weeks. Find the mean value and standard deviation.

102	132	132	104	78	110	144	91	135	92
135	109	106	103	101	82	129	112	163	114
112	106	151	141	124	146	77	153	129	134
108	118	118	123	98	111	106	117	127	136
146	153	130	125	129	154	131	157	114	138

Solution
The lowest and highest values are 77 and 157. It is convenient to divide this range into five equal classes, 70–89, 90–109, 110–129, 130–149 and 150–169. The midpoints of the classes are 79.5, 99.5, 119.5, 139.5 and 159.5. Tabulating as before,

Class boundaries	x	f	fx	$x - \bar{x}$	$(x - \bar{x})^2$	$f(x - \bar{x})^2$
70–89	79.5	3	238.5	-42.8	1831.8	5496
90–109	99.5	12	1194.0	-22.8	519.8	6238
110–129	119.5	16	1912.0	-2.8	7.8	125
130–149	139.5	13	1813.5	17.2	295.8	3846
150–169	159.5	6	957.0	37.2	1383.8	8303

$$\Sigma f = 50 \quad \Sigma fx = 6115.0 \qquad \Sigma f(x - \bar{x})^2 = 24008$$

From the column totals,

$$\bar{x} = \frac{\Sigma fx}{\Sigma f} = \frac{6115.0}{50} = \mathbf{122.3}$$

and

$$\sigma = \sqrt{\frac{\Sigma f(x - \bar{x})^2}{\Sigma f}} = \sqrt{\frac{24008}{50}} = \sqrt{(480.16)} = \mathbf{21.9}$$

6.16 COMPUTER PROGRAM FOR STANDARD DEVIATION

In using the formulae given above for variance and standard deviation it is first necessary to calculate the mean value x. This is not always convenient and for ease of computation a modified version is used. Noting that $(x - \bar{x})^2 = x^2 - 2x\bar{x} + x^2$, the group frequency formula for variance becomes

$$\sigma^2 = \frac{\Sigma f(x - \bar{x})^2}{\Sigma f} = \frac{\Sigma f(x^2 - 2x\bar{x} + \bar{x}^2)}{\Sigma f}$$

$$= \frac{\Sigma fx^2}{\Sigma f} - \frac{2\bar{x} \cdot \Sigma fx}{\Sigma f} + \frac{\bar{x}^2 \cdot \Sigma f}{\Sigma f}$$

But the mean value $\bar{x} = \Sigma fx/\Sigma f$ and the result can be written

$$\sigma^2 = \frac{\Sigma fx^2}{\Sigma f} - 2\left(\frac{\Sigma fx}{\Sigma f}\right)\left(\frac{\Sigma fx}{\Sigma f}\right) + \left(\frac{\Sigma fx}{\Sigma f}\right)^2 = \frac{\Sigma fx^2}{\Sigma f} - \left(\frac{\Sigma fx}{\Sigma f}\right)^2$$

This result is implemented in the computer program of Fig. 6.14, the three summations Σf, Σfx and Σfx^2 being denoted by S1, S2 and S3.

Figure 6.14

```
10 REM X,F    VALUE, FREQUENCY
20 REM V,S    VARIANCE, STANDARD DEVIATION
25 PRINT "----------------------------------------"
30 PRINT "MEAN, VARIANCE AND STANDARD DEVIATION"
35 PRINT "----------------------------------------"
40 S1=0:S2=0:S3=0
50 PRINT
60 PRINT "ENTER EACH VALUE AND ITS FREQUENCY"
70 PRINT "(0,0 TO FINISH)"
80 INPUT X,F
90 IF X=0 AND F=0 THEN GOTO 150
100 S1=S1+F
110 S2=S2+F*X
120 S3=S3+F*X*X
130 PRINT "NEXT?"
140 GOTO 80
150 V=S3/S1-(S2/S1)^2
160 PRINT
170 PRINT "MEAN                = ";S2/S1
180 PRINT "VARIANCE            = ";V
190 PRINT "STANDARD DEVIATION = ";SQR(V)
200 PRINT:PRINT "OPTIONS (ENTER CHOICE BY NUMBER):"
210 PRINT "  ADD FURTHER VALUES ..............1"
220 PRINT "  BEGIN NEW CALCULATION ..........2"
230 PRINT "  QUIT .........................3"
240 INPUT Q
250 IF Q=1 THEN GOTO 60
260 IF Q=2 THEN GOTO 40
270 PRINT "----------------------------------------"
280 END
```

Lines 10–20 specify the notation and line 30 prints the heading. Line 40 sets the initial values of the summations at zero.

Lines 60–80 call for the values and their frequencies, one by one. If the closing values (0, 0) are used the program jumps at line 90 to the calculation of the variance and the results sequence.

Lines 100–140 modify the summations and return the program to line 80 for the next input.

Line 150 calculates the variance and lines 160–190 display the results.

Lines 200–240 offer the choice of adding to the current set of values, starting a new calculation or ending. The selected option causes the program to branch at lines 250–270. To extend the current calculation, the program returns from line 250 to line 60. For a new calculation it returns to line 40. If neither is specified the program ends at lines 270–280.

The printout of Fig. 6.15 was obtained when the program was RUN with the goal-scoring data of Table 6.3.

Figure 6.15

```
--------------------------------------------
MEAN, VARIANCE AND STANDARD DEVIATION
--------------------------------------------

ENTER EACH VALUE AND ITS FREQUENCY
(0,0 TO FINISH)
?0
?29
NEXT?
?1
?44
NEXT?
?2
?30
NEXT?
?3
?15
NEXT?
?4
?4
NEXT?
?0
?0

MEAN              = 1.35245902
VARIANCE          = 1.14626445
STANDARD DEVIATION = 1.0706374

OPTIONS (ENTER CHOICE BY NUMBER):
   ADD FURTHER VALUES .............1
   BEGIN NEW CALCULATION ..........2
   QUIT .........................3
?3
--------------------------------------------
```

6.17 BINOMIAL DISTRIBUTION

A number of mathematical relationships have been put forward to represent frequency distribution curves. Note that:

1. They are not derived from experimental results but they are often in close agreement with observed values;
2. They are arranged so that the sum of the probabilities of all the possible outcomes is 1;
3. They are continuous functions which lead to smooth curves, in contrast to observed results which generally lead to histograms.

One such distribution is derived from the binomial expansion. If p and q are the probabilities of success and failure in each trial then, as shown in section 6.7, the terms in the expansion of $(p + q)^n$ give the probabilities of all the possible outcomes. Since $(p + q) = 1$, then $(p + q)^n = 1$, for all values of n. The expansion therefore satisfies the requirement that the sum of all the probabilities is 1.

In particular the probability of r successes is given by the term in which p is raised to the power r. The probability of 3 successes occurring in 10 trials, for example, is given by the term containing $p^3 q^7$. Since $p + q = 1$, we can write this result as $p^3(1 - p)^7$. The general result for the probability of r successes in n trials is $Cp^r(1 - p)^{n-r}$, where the coefficient C is obtained from Table A.1 or the computer program of Fig. A.2. This result forms the basis of the computer program of Fig. 6.16, which will determine the probabilities for the various outcomes, given the values of n and p. A display width of 40 columns is assumed. If fewer columns are available, the headings should be abbreviated and the TAB values in line 180 reduced.

Figure 6.16

```
10 REM  T    VALUE OF RTH TERM
20 REM  G,L  PROBABLITIES OF NOT MORE/NOT LESS THAN R SUCCESS
30 PRINT "----------------------------------------"
40 PRINT "BINOMIAL DISTRIBUTION"
50 PRINT "----------------------------------------"
60 PRINT
70 PRINT "ENTER NUMBER OF TRIALS (N) AND"
80 PRINT "PROBABILITY OF SUCCESS IN EACH (P):"
90 INPUT N,P
100 PRINT
110 PRINT "    PROBABILITY THAT THE NUMBER OF"
120 PRINT "    SUCCESSES IS:"
130 PRINT "    EXACTLY    NOT MORE    NOT LESS"
140 PRINT "    R          THAN R      THAN R"
150 PRINT "R="
160 T=(1-P)^N:G=T:L=1:F=1E5
170 FOR R=1 TO N+1
180 PRINT TAB(1);R-1;TAB(5);INT(T*F+0.5)/F;TAB(15);INT(G*F+0.5)/F;TAB(26);INT(
L*F+0.5)/F
190 L=L-T
200 T=T*P*N/(R*(1-P))
210 G=G+T
220 N=N-1
230 NEXT R
240 PRINT "----------------------------------------"
250 END
```

Lines 10–20 introduce the notation and 30–60 print the heading.

Lines 70–90 call for the number of trials and the probability of success in each. Lines 100–150 print the headings for the columns of results.

Line 160 sets the value of the first probability T, corresponding to no successes at all, and the corresponding 'not more than' and 'not less than' probabilities.

Line 170 ensures that the number of probability values is N + 1, the number of terms in the expansion.

Line 180 prints the values of T, M and L for each value of R. These are rounded to five decimal places, using the INTeger routine. This is a cumbersome process but it is available on nearly all computers. Many machines offer the automatic rounding of results and this results in a much neater listing.

Lines 190–220 modify the values of L, T and M in preparation for the next value of R.

When all the values have been displayed the program closes at lines 240–250.

The printout of Fig. 6.17 was obtained when the program was run with the data of Example 6.8. The answers to parts (a) and (b) of the question appear in the table. The probability of the candidate selecting four correct answers appears in the second column at R = 4 and the probability of selecting six or more correct answers is given in the fourth column at R = 6.

Figure 6.17

```
-----------------------------------------
BINOMIAL DISTRIBUTION
-----------------------------------------

ENTER NUMBER OF TRIALS (N) AND
PROBABILITY OF SUCCESS IN EACH (P):
?10
?0.25

        PROBABILITY THAT THE NUMBER OF
        SUCCESSES IS:
        EXACTLY    NOT MORE    NOT LESS
        R          THAN R      THAN R
R=
   0    5.631E-2   5.631E-2    1
   1    0.18771    0.24403     0.94369
   2    0.28157    0.52559     0.75597
   3    0.25028    0.77588     0.47441
   4    0.146      0.92187     0.22412
   5    5.84E-2    0.98027     7.813E-2
   6    1.622E-2   0.99649     1.973E-2
   7    3.09E-3    0.99958     3.51E-3
   8    3.9E-4     0.99997     4.2E-4
   9    3E-5       1           3E-5
  10    0          1           0
-----------------------------------------
>
```

To use the binomial distribution we need to know the number of trials and the probability of success at each. In Example 6.8 the values are given, but what figures do we use in a case such as the goal-scoring example of section 6.12? What is then a 'trial'?

Scoring a goal depends on many factors, but suppose we say that each team has 10 opportunities of scoring in a match. (We can try other values later.) Since the average number of goals scored by a team is 1.352 then the proportion of opportunities that are turned into goals is 1.352/10 = 0.1352. Each team therefore has 10 'trials' and a 'success probability' of 0.1352 for each. With these values the computer program obtained the probabilities shown in Table 6.4.

Table 6.4 Binomial distribution of soccer goal-scoring

Number of goals (successes)	Binomial probability	Number of teams	
		Calculated	Actual
0	0.233 97	29.5	29
1	0.365 78	44.6	44
2	0.257 33	31.4	30
3	0.107 28	13.1	15
4	0.029 35	3.6	4
5	0.005 51	0.7	—
6	0.000 72	0.1	—
7	0.000 06	—	—

The third column is obtained by multiplying each probability by 122, the number of teams. As we would expect, the results are not whole numbers. The probabilities for 7, 8, 9 and subsequent numbers of goals are each less than 0.00001. The number of teams scoring 10 goals, for instance, is 0.000 000 249.

There is good agreement between the calculated and observed results, but does this depend on the original choice for n? We can try other values. If we change n to 20 the probability of success $p = 1.352/20 = 0.0676$ and the calculated numbers of teams scoring 0, 1, 2, 3 and 4 goals become 30.1, 43.6, 30.0, 13.1 and 4.0 respectively; these are not very different from the values in Table 6.4 and the results do not seem very sensitive to changes in n.

Repeat the calculation for other values of n. What happens, for example, if we put $n = 4$, implying that each team has only four goal-scoring opportunities?

In section 6.18 we see what happens if n is made very large.

6.18 POISSON DISTRIBUTION

In section 6.17 we used the binomial distribution to predict the goal-scoring probabilities of soccer teams, based on the average number of goals per team and an artificial number of scoring opportunities or trials. We can generalize the analysis by introducing symbols.

Let m = mean (average) number of goals per team;
n = number of goal-scoring opportunities per team;
p = probability of success (scoring) from each opportunity;
q = probability of failure (not scoring).

The probabilities of 0, 1, 2, 3, 4 . . . successes (goals) are given by the terms in the expansion of $(q + p)^n$. We put q first so that the terms in the expansion contain p^0, p^1, p^2, p^3 . . . in that order. The probability of success from each opportunity is $p = m/n$ and, with this substitution the expansion becomes

$$(q + p)^n = q^n + \frac{n}{1} q^{n-1} \left(\frac{m}{n}\right) + \frac{n(n - 1)}{1 \times 2} q^{n-2} \left(\frac{m}{n}\right)^2$$
$$+ \frac{n(n - 1)(n - 2)}{1 \times 2 \times 3} q^{n-3} \left(\frac{m}{n}\right)^3 + \ldots$$

$$= q^n + \frac{n}{n} \cdot \frac{q^{n-1}m}{1} + \frac{n(n - 1)}{n^2} \cdot \frac{q^{n-2}m^2}{2!}$$
$$+ \frac{n(n - 1)(n - 2)}{n^3} \cdot \frac{q^{n-3}m^3}{3!} + \ldots$$

Now suppose that n becomes very large. The probability of success, p, becomes very small and q, which equals $1 - p$, will be nearly equal to 1. Furthermore, the fractions $n(n - 1)/n^2$, $n(n - 1)(n - 2)/n^3$ . . . will each be nearly equal to 1. In the limiting case, as n tends to infinity, these become exact values and the expansion can be written

$$1 + \frac{m}{1!} + \frac{m^2}{2!} + \frac{m^3}{3!} + \ldots$$

This is an example of the exponential series. It is shown in section A.10 that its sum to infinity is e^m. As in the binomial expansion, the terms in the series can be used to find the probabilities of $0, 1, 2, 3, \ldots$ successes. Since the sum is e^m and not 1, we must divide each term by e^m to ensure that the sum of all the probabilities is 1. For r successes we need the term containing m^r. This is $m^r/r!$ and the corresponding probability is

$$p(r \text{ successes or events}) = \frac{m^r}{r!e^m} = \frac{e^{-m}m^r}{r!}$$

This result is known as the Poisson distribution. For a given value of r the Poisson probability depends only on the mean value m; we do not have to make any assumptions about n, the number of trials. The symbols a, z and μ are also used by some authors to denote the mean value in the Poisson formula.

Note that when $r = 0$, $m^r = m^0 = 1$ and $r! = 0! = 1$ (see section A.6).

If we apply the Poisson formula to the goal-scoring example of section 6.11, the only value required is the mean number of goals per team, $m = 1.352$. The probability of a team scoring , say, three goals is therefore:

$$p(r = 3) = \frac{e^{-m}m^r}{r!} = \frac{e^{-1.352} \times 1.352^3}{3!} = \frac{0.2587 \times 2.4713}{6}$$
$$= 0.1066$$

On this basis the number of teams expected to score three goals is $0.1066 \times 122 = 13.0$. If we repeat the calculation for other numbers of goals we obtain the values in the third row of Table 6.5.

Table 6.5 Comparison of binomial and Poisson frequencies for goal-scoring example

Number of goals	0	1	2	3	4
Number of teams:					
Binomial ($n = 10$)	28.5	44.6	31.4	13.1	3.6
Poisson	31.6	42.7	28.8	13.0	4.4
Actual	29	44	30	15	4

The differences between the binomial and Poisson results are small and it could not be claimed that the observed values in the bottom line support one formula rather than the other. The Poisson results are easier to calculate; to convert the binomial data we simply put $m = np$. It has been suggested[2] that the Poisson distribution may be taken as a close approximation to the binomial when n is greater than 50 and np is less than 5.

The computer program of Fig. 6.18 will determine the probabilities according to the Poisson distribution. It follows the pattern of the listing given in Fig. 6.16 for the binomial distribution and the comments on the formatting of the results table and the rounding of numerical answers apply equally here. One difference is the number of terms. In the binomial expansion there are $n + 1$ terms altogether and the program loops until they are all calculated. In contrast, the exponential series has an infinite number

PROBABILITY AND STATISTICS

Figure 6.18

```
 10 REM T    VALUE OF RTH TERM
 20 REM G,L  PROBABILITIES OF NOT MORE/NOT LESS THAN
 30 PRINT "----------------------------------------"
 40 PRINT "POISSON DISTRIBUTION"
 50 PRINT "----------------------------------------"
 60 PRINT
 70 PRINT "ENTER AVERAGE VALUE (M):"
 80 INPUT M
 90 PRINT
100 PRINT "      PROBABILITY THAT THE NUMBER OF"
110 PRINT "      OCCURRENCES IS:"
120 PRINT "      EXACTLY    NOT MORE    NOT LESS"
130 PRINT "      R          THAN R      THAN R"
140 PRINT "R="
150 R=0:T=EXP(-M):G=T:L=1:F=1E5
160 PRINT TAB(1);R;TAB(6);INT(F*T+0.5)/F;TAB(16);INT(F*G+0.5)/F;TAB(27);INT(F*
L+0.5)/F
170 L=L-T
180 R=R+1
190 T=T*M/R
200 G=G+T
210 IF T>0.001 THEN GOTO 160
220 PRINT "----------------------------------------"
230 END
```

of terms and the program stops when the probability falls below a specified value.

Line 70 calls for the mean value M and the probabilities relating to 0 occurrences are determined in line 150 and printed in line 160.

Lines 170–200 modify the answers to give the results for the next value of R.

Line 210 returns the program to line 160 until the probability of exactly R occurrences falls below 0.001. This limit can easily be amended if more terms are required. The program ends at lines 220–230.

Figure 6.19

```
----------------------------------------
POISSON DISTRIBUTION
----------------------------------------

ENTER AVERAGE VALUE (M):
?1.352

      PROBABILITY THAT THE NUMBER OF
      OCCURRENCES IS:
      EXACTLY    NOT MORE    NOT LESS
      R          THAN R      THAN R
R=
 0    0.25872    0.25872     1
 1    0.34979    0.60851     0.74128
 2    0.23646    0.84497     0.39149
 3    0.10656    0.95154     0.15503
 4    3.602E-2   0.98756     4.846E-2
 5    9.74E-3    0.9973      1.244E-2
 6    2.19E-3    0.99949     2.7E-3
----------------------------------------
```

The printout in Fig. 6.19 was obtained when the program was run for a mean value of 1.352, the figure for the goal-scoring example.

6.19 NORMAL DISTRIBUTION

Many groups of experimental data, such as the heights and weights of people, lead to frequency distribution curves having a symmetrical bell shape, as shown in Fig. 6.13. The quantity being measured is plotted horizontally as the x variable. The vertical axis represents the frequency and, for a continuous variable, these are counted by the grouped frequency

Figure 6.20

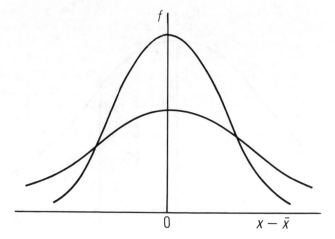

technique. As the diagram indicates, such curves may differ in position and in their proportions. We can bring them all to the same axis of symmetry by taking the horizontal axis as $x - \bar{x}$ instead of x, as shown in Fig. 6.20.

The horizontal axis now represents how far a particular value is from the mean. Although the two curves in the diagram now have the same axis of symmetry, they display different amounts of scatter or dispersion. One is taller and thinner than the other. Suppose we change the horizontal variable from $x - \bar{x}$ to z, where

$$z = \frac{x - \bar{x}}{\sigma}$$

The new variable z represents the difference between a value and the mean as a proportion of the standard deviation σ. It is the number of standard deviations that x is away from the mean value $\bar{x}$, and we speak of values that are, for example, 'within half a standard deviation' or 'more than two standard deviations' from the mean.

If results are plotted on this basis it is found that many groups of observations – such as human heights and weights and test results on materials and components – fall on the same curve. The vertical ordinate is denoted by $f(z)$, meaning 'a function of z', and the equation to the curve is

$$f(z) = \frac{1}{\sqrt{(2\pi)}} \, e^{-z^2/2}$$

The curve corresponding to this formula is shown in Fig. 6.21 and it is known as the *normal curve* because results that did not fit it were once regarded as 'abnormal'. The alternative name 'Gaussian' is used, after the mathematician Gauss, but credit is also due to De Moivre and Laplace. The formula was not derived from experimental results; it should be thought of as a mathematical relationship which fits many experimental observations.

Mathematically, the curve extends to infinity in both directions. Nevertheless, the total area under the curve is finite and the factor $1/\sqrt{(2\pi)}$ ensures that this area equals 1. The function $f(z)$ is called the frequency density and the area under a section of the curve is the probability that the variable z has a value within that range. Thus, the area between z_1 and z_2 is

Figure 6.21

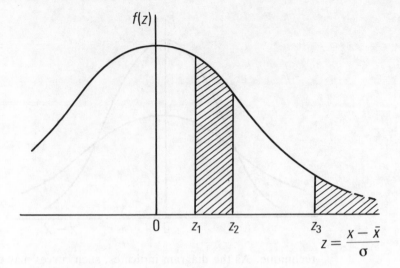

the probability that z falls between these two values. The distribution therefore meets the requirement that the total probability for all possible values is 1.

The probability of the variable having a value greater than, say, z_3 is the area under the curve between this value and infinity, as indicated in the figure. This is known as the *one-tail area*. Although it is easy to apply the results in examples the calculation of the area itself is not straightforward and values are usually taken from tables. Table C.3 gives the one-tail area for values of z from 0 to 3.00 in increments of 0.01.

Example 6.12
A manufacturer of light bulbs claims that they have a life of 1000 hours. When a batch was tested it was found that the mean life was 1070 hours, with a standard deviation of 40. Assuming a normal distribution, find the probability of a bulb lasting for (a) 1150 hours, (b) 1000 hours.

If 100 of these bulbs were installed, when could the first failure be expected?

Solution
With the usual notation, $\bar{x} = 1070$ and $\sigma = 40$.

(a) Putting $x = 1150$ the value of z is

$$z = \frac{x - \bar{x}}{\sigma} = \frac{1150 - 1070}{40} = 2$$

From Table C.3 the corresponding one-tail area is 0.022 75.
The required probability is therefore **0.022 75** or 2.275 per cent.

(b) With $x = 1000$ the value of z becomes

$$z = \frac{1000 - 1070}{40} = -1.75$$

Since the curve is symmetrical the one-tail area to the left of $z = -1.75$ is the same as that to the right of $z = 1.75$. From Table C.3 this area is

0.040 07 and, since the total area under the curve is 1, the area to the right of $z = -1.75$ is $1 - 0.040 07 = 0.959 93$.

The probability of a bulb lasting for 1000 hours is therefore **0.959 93** or almost 96 per cent.

If one bulb in a hundred fails the corresponding probability is 0.01. From Table C.3 the nearest value of the one-tail area is 0.009 90, the corresponding value of z being 2.33. Hence the first failure can be expected at 2.33 standard deviations below the mean. With a standard deviation of 40 this amounts to $2.33 \times 40 = 93.2$ hours. The first failure can therefore be expected at $1070 - 93.2 =$ **976.8 hours**.

As in other statistical calculations the word 'expected' must be interpreted in the sense of average or likelihood.

6.20 PROPERTIES OF THE NORMAL CURVE

In the last example the standard deviation was only a small proportion of the mean value. Had the mean value been 70 hours, instead of 1070, and the standard deviation 40, the normal distribution would have predicted a negative life for some of the light bulbs! We can see why this does not occur in practice by considering typical values of z.

From Table C.3, the one-tail area for $z = 1$ is 0.1587. By symmetry the area to the left of $z = -1$ is the same. Thus, the total area that is more than one standard deviation from the mean is $0.1587 + 0.1587 = 0.3174$ and the area within one standard deviation of the mean is $1 - 0.3174 = 0.6826$. Therefore, over 68 per cent of all values are within one standard deviation of the mean.

By similar reasoning, over 95 per cent of all values are within two standard deviations and about 99.7 per cent are within three standard deviations.

In the light bulb example a value of zero would be $1070/40 = 26.75$ standard deviations below the mean and the probability of this is too small to be worth considering.

As the solution to Example 6.12 showed, Table C.3 can be interpolated to find the value of z when the one-tail area is known. This may not be convenient when the area is very small and rounded values are specified. Table C.4 gives the value of z directly for selected tail areas.

6.21 COMPUTER PROGRAM FOR ONE-TAIL AREAS

Finding the area under a curve is the calculus process of integration. In the case of the normal curve there is no simple form for the integral. One way round the difficulty is to express the function $f(z)$ as an infinite series, using the expansion of e^x, and to integrate term by term. The converse process of finding z for a given area can then be tackled on a trial-and-error basis.

Cohen[3] has devised two short BASIC programs using this approach. The terms in the infinite series are calculated one by one until the effect of considering further terms is negligible. The method is 'exact' in the mathematical sense but is limited by the accuracy to which the computer can work.

An alternative is to use some of the ingenious formulae that have been devised to give the answers directly. This is a quicker process and the results can be at least as accurate. The following relationships between A, the one-tail area, and z are based on a paper by Derenzo.[4]

$$A = \frac{1}{2} \exp\left[-\frac{(83z + 351)z + 562}{703/z + 165}\right]$$

If z is in the range 0–5.5 the error is less than 0.042 per cent. The paper gives a second formula for values of z greater than 5.5.

The formula for finding z from A is

$$z = \sqrt{\frac{[(4y + 100)y + 205]y^2}{[(2y + 56)y + 192]y + 131}}$$

where $y = -\ln(2A)$.

This formula can be applied to one-tail areas as small as 1×10^{-7} without the error in z exceeding 0.00013. A further formula is given for one-tail areas down to 10^{-112}.

The above formulae are used in the computer program of Fig. 6.22. It will determine A or z, given the other, and will also print tables of values. Type the listing in the following four stages, and RUN it after each as a check.

1. Lines 10–250 and 600–650. RUN the program at this stage, select the first option from the menu, and find the area for various values of z. Check the results against Table C.3.
2. Add lines 300–350 and 700–740. Test the new sections by RUNning the program to find z for various areas. Check the results using Table C.4.
3. Add lines 400–490 and check by selecting option 3 from the menu.
4. Add lines 500–580 and check by selecting option 4.

Lines 10–100 print the heading and menu, and lines 110–140 call up the subroutine corresponding to the chosen option.

Lines 150–170 provide the opportunity for a further calculation. If this is not taken up the program ends at lines 180–190.

Lines 200–250 are a subroutine for finding A. Lines 210–220 ask for the value of z and line 230 calls up a further subroutine which performs the calculation. The result is printed at line 240 and the main program is rejoined.

Lines 300–350 are the corresponding subroutine for finding z, when the area A is known.

Lines 400–490 form the subroutine for printing a table of areas. Line 410 prints the heading and line 420 sets the initial value of the counter C. Line 430 sets the range of values and the increment and line 440 calls up the subroutine for calculating z. Line 470 ensures that there is a gap in the table after every fifth entry and the main program is rejoined at line 490.

Lines 500–580 carry out the corresponding steps for a table of z values. It is convenient to have different increments for A in different parts of the range and the initial value D is specified in line 520. Line 560 increases the increment by a factor of 10 after every 10 calculations. When A reaches the

Figure 6.22

```
 10 REM    Z,A COORDINATE, AREA
 20 PRINT "-----------------------------------"
 30 PRINT "NORMAL CURVE - ONE TAIL AREA"
 40 PRINT "-----------------------------------"
 50 PRINT:PRINT "ENTER CHOICE BY NUMBER:":PRINT
 60 PRINT "FIND AREA A FOR GIVEN Z . . . . . . 1"
 70 PRINT "FIND Z FOR GIVEN AREA A . . . . . . 2"
 80 PRINT "PRINT TABLE OF AREAS  . . . . . . . 3"
 90 PRINT "PRINT TABLE OF Z FOR SELECTED AREAS 4"
100 PRINT:INPUT N
110 IF N=1 THEN GOSUB 200
120 IF N=2 THEN GOSUB 300
130 IF N=3 THEN GOSUB 400
140 IF N=4 THEN GOSUB 500
150 PRINT:PRINT "ANOTHER CALCULATION (Y/N)"
160 INPUT Q$
170 IF Q$="Y" OR Q$="y" THEN GOTO 50
180 PRINT "-----------------------------------"
190 END
200 REM    FIND A FOR GIVEN Z
210 PRINT "ENTER VALUE OF Z (0-5)"
220 INPUT Z
230 GOSUB 600
240 PRINT:PRINT "ONE TAIL AREA A = ";A
250 RETURN
300 REM    FIND Z FOR GIVEN A
310 PRINT "ENTER AREA A (0.000001-0.5)"
320 INPUT A
330 GOSUB 700
340 PRINT:PRINT "Z = ";Z
350 RETURN
400 REM    PRINT TABLE OF AREAS
410 PRINT TAB(1);"Z";TAB(8);"ONE TAIL AREA"
420 PRINT:C=4
430 FOR Z=0 TO 3.5 STEP 0.1
440 GOSUB 600
450 C=C+1
460 PRINT TAB(1);Z;TAB(8);A
470 IF C=5 THEN PRINT:C=0
480 NEXT Z
490 RETURN
500 REM    TABLE OF Z FOR SELECTED AREAS
510 PRINT TAB(1);"AREA";TAB(10);"Z"
520 PRINT:C=0:A=0:D=1E-4
530 A=A+D:C=C+1
540 GOSUB 700
550 PRINT TAB(1);A;TAB(10);Z
560 IF C=9 THEN D=10*D:A=0:C=0:PRINT
570 IF A=0.5 THEN RETURN
580 GOTO 530
600 REM    CALCULATE A
610 X=1/(2*EXP(((83*Z+351)*Z*Z+562*Z)/(703+165*Z)))
620 A=INT(1E4*X+0.5)/1E4
630 IF X<0.01 THEN A=INT(1E6*X+0.5)/1E6
640 IF X<0.0001 THEN A=INT(1E8*X+0.5)/1E8
650 RETURN
700 REM    CALCULATE Z
710 Y=-LN(2*A)
720 Z=SQR(((((4*Y+100)*Y+205)*Y*Y)/(((2*Y+56)*Y+192)*Y+131)))
730 Z=INT(1E4*Z+0.5)/1E4
740 RETURN
```

value 0.5 line 570 causes the subroutine to end, otherwise line 580 returns it to line 530 for the next value.

Lines 600–650 perform the calculation for finding A. The value is determined in line 610 as an interim variable X and lines 620–640 round the result to four, six or eight decimal places depending on its magnitude.

Lines 700–740 are the subroutine for calculating z from A. Note that the natural logarithm is required in line 710. Some machines use the keyword LN but with others LOG is needed. In the latter case change the line to

710 Y=-LOG(2*A)

The numbers of decimal places in the answers should prove sufficient for most practical purposes. If more are required, change the factors within the INTeger statements in lines 620–640 and 730. If smaller increments are needed in the table of areas change the STEP value in line 430 from 0.1 to 0.01.

The tables are displayed in long vertical columns and these can be accommodated on all computer screens. Some machines and printers offer formats with 80 or more columns of characters and these can be used to produce displays such as Tables C.3 and C.4. The details will vary from one computer to another.

Example 6.13

A transport manager finds that one brand of tyre used on a particular model of car has a mean life of 26 600 miles with a standard deviation of 846 miles. What are the probabilities of a tyre wearing out

(a) before 26 000 miles;
(b) between 26 000 and 27 000 miles;
(c) between 27 000 and 28 000 miles?

Solution

Figure 6.23 shows how the mileages are related to the normal curve. The one-tail areas can be found using the computer program of Fig. 6.22 or by interpolation of Table C.3.

Figure 6.23

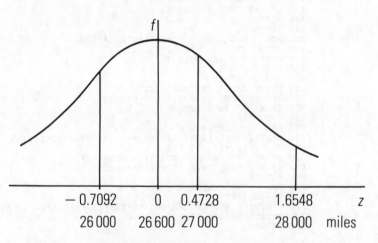

(a) With $x = 26\,000$, the value of z is given by

$$z = \frac{x - \bar{x}}{\sigma} = \frac{26\,000 - 26\,600}{846} = -0.7092$$

The negative sign indicates that the value is below the mean and the one-tail area corresponding to $z = 0.7092$ is to the left of this value. From the computer or tables the area is 0.2392.

Hence the probability of the tyre wearing out before reaching 26 000 miles is **0.2392**.

(b) For 27 000 miles the value of z is $(27\,000 - 26\,600)/846 = 0.4728$ and the corresponding one-tail area (this time to the right) is 0.3182. The probability of a tyre wearing out between 26 000 and 27 000 miles is given by the area under the curve between these two values. This is found by subtracting the two one-tail areas from the whole area, 1. Hence

$$\text{Probability} = 1 - (0.2392 + 0.3182) = \mathbf{0.4426}$$

(c) By similar calculations the value of z for 28 000 miles is 1.6548 and the corresponding one-tail area is 0.0490. The area between the values for 27 000 and 28 000 miles is the difference between their one-tail areas, since they are on the same side of the mean. Thus

$$\text{Required probability} = 0.3182 - 0.0490 = \mathbf{0.2692}$$

6.22 LINEAR REGRESSION

In the earlier sections of this chapter we have looked at examples with single variables — such as the number of goals scored by a soccer team or the life of a light bulb. The variables have had several or many values and we have been concerned with finding the mean, the standard deviation and the probabilities of particular values occurring.

Many practical problems involve several variables at the same time. The deflection of a beam will depend on the forces that act on it, its shape and size, the elasticity of its material and the way in which it is supported. The time taken to build a house will be a function of many things — its design, the form of construction, the labour available, the delivery of materials and the weather.

To test our theories in cases of this kind, or to obtain results when no theory exists, we carry out experiments. If the outcome depends on several factors, or 'parameters' as they are often called, we vary one at a time and note the effect. In the beam example, just mentioned, we might start by taking several values of the force and measuring the deflection for each. We then have several pairs of values and we can draw a graph to show how one variable affects the other.

The parameter that we are changing is usually plotted horizontally and the one that we measure, vertically. Suppose, in an experiment, we set several values of one variable x, and measured the corresponding values of another variable y, with the following results:

x	-5	-2	0	3	6	11
y	-4	1	3	5	10	15

These results are represented by the points in Fig. 6.24 and it appears that they can be represented reasonably well by a straight line. We can draw such a line 'by eye', but different experimenters will not necessarily draw exactly the same line. All such lines will, however, have the following form:

$$y = mx + c$$

where m is the slope and c the intercept on the y-axis (see section A.7). Once we have chosen the values for m and c we have defined the position of every point on the line. If we select a value for x we can predict the

Figure 6.24

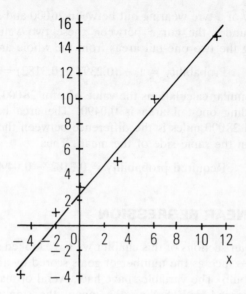

corresponding value of y in two ways; we can read it from the graph or we can substitute the value of x in the equation and calculate y.

We obviously want the best straight line, but what do we mean by 'best'? And, having defined best, how do we achieve it? Suppose we compare the values of y given in the table with those calculated from the equation. The smaller the differences the more closely the equation will fit the observed values. Since there are several points, we must settle for some form of average and the usual criterion is the method of least squares. This means that we choose m and c so that the sum of the squares of the differences between the calculated and observed values is as small as possible. It can be shown that this is achieved by calculating the values of m and c from the experimental results, using the following formulae

$$m = \frac{n\,\Sigma xy - (\Sigma x)(\Sigma y)}{n\,\Sigma x^2 - (\Sigma x)^2}$$

$$c = \frac{(\Sigma y)(\Sigma x^2) - (\Sigma x)(\Sigma xy)}{n\,\Sigma x^2 - (\Sigma x)^2}$$

where n is the number of experimental results.

To find m and c we need the summations of x, x^2 and xy. For the points shown in Fig. 6.24 these are obtained from Table 6.6. It also includes a column for y^2 which is needed later.

With these results and putting $n = 6$ the slope and intercept values are

$$m = \frac{6 \times 258 - 13 \times 30}{6 \times 195 - 13^2} = \frac{1158}{1001} = 1.157$$

and

$$c = \frac{30 \times 195 - 13 \times 258}{6 \times 195 - 13^2} = \frac{2496}{1001} = 2.494$$

Table 6.6 Linear
regression analysis

	x	y	x^2	xy	y^2
	-5	-4	25	20	16
	-2	1	4	-2	1
	0	3	0	0	9
	3	5	9	15	25
	6	10	36	60	100
	11	15	121	165	225
Totals	13	30	195	258	376

With these values the equation of the least-squares line is

$$y = 1.157x + 2.494.$$

We can use this result to predict intermediate values of y. What value of y can we expect when $x = 7$? From the equation,

$$y = 1.157 \times 7 + 2.494 = 10.59$$

We can use the equation to predict y for other values of x. If we put $x = 12$ it gives $y = 16.38$ and when $x = -1$, $y = 1.337$. Since this 'best' line does not pass through all the experimental points, the calculated values of y will not usually coincide with the measured values. When $x = 3$, for instance, the equation gives $y = 5.965$ against the observed value of 5. This technique for determining the straight line best suited to a group of experimental results is called *linear regression*.

However, the equation should not be used to predict the value of x for a given value of y. The reason for this is that it has been chosen to minimize the sum of the squares of the vertical distances from the points to the line. The equation for predicting x from y should be based on the horizontal distances from the points to the line. We can find it by exchanging x and y in the expressions for m and c. The two relationships are known as the 'y on x' and 'x on y' equations.

To find the x on y equation we have only to add the column for y^2 to Table 6.6, as anticipated earlier. Since the product yx is the same as xy, the only new terms are those involving y^2. Thus, using m' and c' for the new slope and intercept, we have

$$m' = \frac{n\,\Sigma yx - (\Sigma y)(\Sigma x)}{n\,\Sigma y^2 - (\Sigma y)^2} = \frac{6 \times 258 - 30 \times 13}{6 \times 376 - 30^2} = \frac{1158}{1356} = 0.854$$

and

$$c' = \frac{(\Sigma y^2)(\Sigma x) - (\Sigma y)(\Sigma yx)}{n\,\Sigma y^2 - (\Sigma y)^2} = \frac{376 \times 13 - 30 \times 258}{6 \times 376 - 30^2}$$

$$= \frac{-2852}{1356} - 2.103$$

The x on y equation is therefore

$$x = 0.854y - 2.103$$

The formulae for m and c lead to the best straight line by the least-squares criterion but how good is it? No matter how scattered the points are a straight-line equation will be obtained. Take the following pairs of values:

x	-3	-1	1	3	5	7
y	-2	-3	-2	1	6	13

If you perform the same calculations on these results you will find that the y on x equation is

$$y = 1.500x - 0.833$$

Now plot the points and, on the same axes, add the straight line given by this equation. You will see that the issue is not whether the equation gives the best straight line because the points define a smooth curve. In practice, it is always worth while plotting the points first; the outcome will often show whether linear regression is appropriate.

With a single variable we can obtain a measure of scatter by calculating the variance or its square root, the standard deviation. With two variables we need a measure of their correlation − how closely they are related. We would regard the relationship between x and y as perfect if all the points fell on the line and it is useful to have a measure of how near we are to this ideal. This is done by a relationship that involves the standard deviations of the variables x and y (denoted by σ_x and σ_y) and also a quantity called the covariance. The covariance of x and y is denoted by $\mathrm{cov}(x,y)$ and is defined as

$$\mathrm{cov}(x, y) = \frac{1}{n}\Sigma(x - \bar{x})(y - \bar{y})$$

How well the quantities x and y correlate is measured by a quantity called the *product moment correlation coefficient*, denoted by r. It is given by

$$r = \frac{\mathrm{cov}(x, y)}{\sigma_x \sigma_y}$$

and, for perfect correlation, $r = 1$ or -1.

The two variances and the covariance can be expressed in terms of the various summations. It can then be shown that the correlation coefficient becomes

$$r = \frac{n\,\Sigma xy - (\Sigma x)(\Sigma y)}{\sqrt{\{n\,\Sigma x^2 - (\Sigma x)^2\}\{n\,\Sigma y^2 - (\Sigma y)^2\}}}$$

The three relationships in this expression also appear in the formulae for m and m'. The extra arithmetic for calculating r is therefore small. With the values derived from Table 6.6, the numerator of the fraction is 1158 and the expressions within the square root sign are 1001 and 1356 respectively. Hence

$$r = \frac{1158}{\sqrt{(1001 \times 1356)}} = \frac{1158}{1165} = 0.994$$

It can also be shown that r is the geometric mean of the slope values, m and m'. The numerical value of r is therefore $\sqrt{(mm')}$ and its sign (positive or negative) will be the same as that of m and m'. In the present example the slopes are 1.157 and 0.854 and the coefficient is $\sqrt{(1.157 \times 0.854)} = 0.994$, as before.

6.23 COMPUTER PROGRAM FOR LINEAR REGRESSION ANALYSIS

The computer program shown in Fig. 6.25 determines the y on x and x on y equations, and the correlation coefficient. When the analysis has been completed the program will estimate y or x when the other is given.

Line 10 defines the five summations used in the calculations and lines 20–40 print the heading. Line 50 sets each of the summations and the number of results N at zero.

Lines 60–80 call for the pairs of values and line 90 sends the program to the calculation sequence if X and Y are both set at the wild value -99. In

Figure 6.25

```
10 REM    S1,S2,S3,S4,S5  SUMMATIONS OF X, Y, X*X, Y*Y, X*Y
20 PRINT "------------------------------------"
30 PRINT "LINEAR REGRESSION"
40 PRINT "------------------------------------"
50 S1=0:S2=0:S3=0:S4=0:S5=0:N=0
60 PRINT:PRINT ."ENTER X AND Y VALUES (X FIRST)"
70 PRINT "(-99,-99 TO FINISH)"
80 INPUT X,Y
90 IF X=-99 AND Y=-99 THEN GOTO 150
100 S1=S1+X:S2=S2+Y
110 S3=S3+X*X:S4=S4+Y*Y
120 S5=S5+X*Y:N=N+1
130 PRINT "NEXT?"
140 GOTO 80
150 E1=N*S5-S1*S2
160 E2=N*S3-S1*S1
170 E3=N*S4-S2*S2
180 E4=S1*S5-S2*S3
190 E5=S2*S5-S1*S4
200 M=E1/E2:M1=E1/E3
210 C=-E4/E2:C1=-E5/E3
220 R=E1/SQR(E2*E3)
230 PRINT:PRINT "Y ON X EQUATION:"
240 IF C<0 THEN PRINT "Y = ";M;"X";C:GOTO 260
250 PRINT "Y = ";M;"X+";C
260 PRINT:PRINT "X ON Y EQUATION:"
270 IF C1<0 THEN PRINT "X = ";M1;"Y";C1:GOTO 290
280 PRINT "X = ";M1;"Y+";C1
290 PRINT:PRINT "CORRELATION COEFFICIENT R = ";R
300 PRINT:PRINT "OPTIONS:"
310 PRINT "(ENTER CHOICE BY NUMBER)":PRINT
320 PRINT "ADD MORE RESULTS................1"
330 PRINT "BEGIN NEW CALCULATION..........2"
340 PRINT "ESTIMATE Y FOR GIVEN X.........3"
350 PRINT "ESTIMATE X FOR GIVEN Y.........4"
360 PRINT "QUIT...........................5"
370 INPUT Q
380 Q=INT Q
390 IF Q<1 OR Q>5 THEN GOTO 300
400 IF Q=1 THEN GOTO 60
410 IF Q=2 THEN GOTO 50
420 IF Q=3 THEN GOTO 450
430 IF Q=4 THEN GOTO 510
440 GOTO 570
450 PRINT:PRINT "ENTER VALUE(S) OF X (-99 TO FINISH)"
460 PRINT "X               ESTIMATE FOR Y"
470 INPUT U
480 IF U=-99 THEN GOTO 300
490 PRINT TAB(15);M*U+C
500 GOTO 470
510 PRINT:PRINT "ENTER VALUE(S) OF Y (-99 TO FINISH)"
520 PRINT "Y               ESTIMATE FOR X"
530 INPUT V
540 IF V=-99 THEN GOTO 300
550 PRINT TAB(15);M1*V+C1
560 GOTO 530
570 PRINT "------------------------------------"
580 END
```

the unlikely case of an experimental result having these values, this line in the program must be modified.

Lines 100–120 add the appropriate amounts to the five summations and increase N by 1.

Lines 130–140 cause the process to repeat until all the experimental results have been entered.

Lines 150–190 evaluate five expressions, E1, E2, E3, E4 and E5, that appear in the formulae and these are used in lines 200–220 to calculate the two slopes, the two intercepts and the correlation coefficient.

Lines 230–360 display the results and a table of options for further calculations.

Lines 370–390 check that the selection is valid and lines 400–440 cause the program to branch according to the choice that is made.

Lines 450–500 estimate y when x is given and lines 510–560 are used to find x when y is given. In both cases the program returns to the menu in line 300 when no further values are required.

Lines 570–580 close the program when the QUIT option is taken.

6.24 SUMMARY

Probability p is measured on a scale from 0 (representing impossibility) to 1 (absolute certainty). In some instances, such as rolling dice or drawing a card from a pack, we can calculate the probability of a particular outcome on common-sense grounds. Where the results cannot be obtained by reasoning, we conduct trials and count the number of occurrences of each outcome. In all cases the sum of the probabilities of all the possible outcomes is 1.

If a financial value can be placed on each of the different outcomes then the average or expected value from one trial is found by multiplying each of the separate values by its probability and summing the results. In complex examples, where there are several decision and chance points, we represent all the possibilities on a decision tree.

Where two outcomes are mutually exclusive, the probability of one or the other occurring is the sum of their probabilities. Where they are independent, the probability of both occurring is the product of the separate values.

If there are several trials, each with the same two possible outcomes, the probabilities of the various overall outcomes are given by the terms in the binomial expansion.

An alternative to calculations is the method of simulation in which trials are carried out on paper or by a computer. Each outcome is assigned a range of numbers which is proportional to its probability. At every chance point a random number is used to decide the outcome and results are collected for a large number of trials.

For a discrete variable the frequencies with which the values occur are shown by a histogram; each value is represented by a rectangular block whose height is proportional to its frequency. If the variable is continuous, the frequency distribution curve shows the frequency density of any value;

the area between two values represents the probability of the variable falling within that range.

The Poisson formula is often used to predict the frequencies for discrete variables. The binomial expansion is a good approximation to the Poisson distribution if the power of n is sufficiently large.

The normal distribution is widely used for continuous variables or discrete variables with a large number of values when the variation is symmetrical. The one-tail area represents the probability of the variable being further than a specified distance from the mean.

Linear regression analysis determines the equation of the best straight line for a set of two-variable experimental results, by the least squares criterion. The product moment correlation coefficient provides a measure of 'goodness-of-fit', how well the results are represented by the line.

REFERENCES

1. McFarlan D 1988 *The Guinness Book of Records 1989* Guinness Publishing p 297
2. Barnett S, Cronin T M 1971 *Mathematical Formulae for Engineering and Science Students* Bradford University Press and Crosby Lockwood p 49
3. Cohen S S 1985 *Operational Research* Edward Arnold, pp 134–6
4. Derenzo S E 1977 Approximations for hand calculators using small integer coefficients *Mathematics of Computation* **31** (137): 214–27 January

BIBLIOGRAPHY

Clarke G M, Cooke D 1983 *A Basic Course in Statistics* 2nd edn Edward Arnold

Cooke D, Craven A H, Clarke G M 1982 *Basic Statistical Computing* Edward Arnold

Green A E, Bourne A J 1972 *Reliability Technology* Wiley

Jardine A K S 1973 *Maintenance, Replacement and Reliability* Pitman

Levin R I 1987 *Statistics for Management* 4th edn Prentice-Hall

Moroney M J 1953 *Facts from Figures* 2nd edn Pelican Original, Penguin

Rees D G 1985 *Essential Statistics* Chapman and Hall

Rowntree D 1984 *Probability* Edward Arnold

Rowntree D 1981 *Statistics without Tears* Penguin

Sabine P, Plumpton C 1985 *Probability* Macmillan

Sabine P, Plumpton C 1985 *Statistics* Macmillan

Sincich T 1987 *Statistics by Example* 3rd edn Collier Macmillan

Spigel M R 1972 *Statistics* Schaum's Outline Series, McGraw-Hill

Topping J 1958 *Errors of Observation and their Treatment* Institute of Physics Monograph for Students

PROBLEMS

1. What is the probability of obtaining a value greater than 3 when a six-sided dice is rolled? If two such dice are rolled, what is the probability of obtaining a total that is

(a) exactly 7;
(b) greater than 6?

Answer 0.5; (a) 1/6 = 0.1667; (b) 7/12 = 0.5833.

2. In a normal pack of 52 playing cards, each of the four suits has three picture cards (jack, queen, king). What is the probability of drawing

(a) a picture card;
(b) two picture cards, one from each of two packs;
(c) two picture cards from one pack?

Answer (a) 3/13 = 0.2308; (b) 9/169 = 0.0533; (c) 11/221 = 0.0498.

3. A fruit machine displays three fruits, each being orange, lemon, cherry or apple. If the selection is completely random, what is the probability that the machine displays

(a) three different fruits;
(b) three fruits of the same kind;
(c) two fruits of the same kind;
(d) three citrus fruits?

Answer (a) 3/8 = 0.375; (b) 1/16 = 0.0625; (c) 9/16 = 0.5625; (d) 1/8 = 0.125.

4. The owner of a patisserie keeps records of the demand for pineapple cream pies over a period of 100 days. The results are as follows:

Daily demand	0	1	2	3	4	5	6 or more
Number of days	17	32	26	16	7	2	0

What is the average daily demand? The pies will not keep overnight and, at the end of each day, unsold stock is wasted. If the pies cost £1 each and sell for £2, how many should be ordered each day to maximize profit, and what is the corresponding average daily profit?
Answer 1.7; 2; £0.18.

5. A survey of schoolchildren in a certain district shows that 30 per cent of them require dental treatment. A sample of four children is taken at random. What is the probability that the sample will contain

(a) two children requiring treatment;
(b) at least one child requiring treatment?

Answer (a) 0.265; (b) 0.760.

6. A space vehicle carries two computer systems for controlling its rocket motors, each with a 1 in 40 probability of failing during the flight. If both fail

the crew have a 75 per cent chance of returning safely under manual control. What is the overall probability of disaster occurring?
Answer 0.000 156.

7. There are 20 guests at a party. What is the probability that two will share the same birthday? Ignore the effects of leap years. How many guests must there be for the probability to exceed 0.8?
Answer 0.4114; 35.

8. A widely quoted example that conforms closely to the Poisson distribution is the number of Prussian cavalrymen killed by a horse kick. The records for 10 corps in the 20-year period 1875–94 (200 results in all) showed that the observed frequencies for 0, 1, 2, 3, and 4 deaths were 109, 65, 22, 3 and 1 respectively.

Find the mean number of deaths per corps per year and use this value to calculate the corresponding Poisson frequencies. What are the binomial frequencies, taking $n = 10$?
Answer 0.61; 108.7, 66.3, 20.2, 4.1 and 0.6; 106.6, 69.2, 20.2, 3.5 and 0.4.

9. The numbers of years in the reigns of 41 English and British monarchs from William I to George VI were as follows:

21	13	35	19	35	10	17	56	35	20	50	22
13	9	39	22	0	2	24	38	6	0	5	44
22	24	36	3	13	6	12	13	33	59	10	7
63	9	25	1	15							

Calculate the mean, variance and standard deviation of these values.
Answer 21.6; 272.9; 16.52.

10. A superstore chain is reviewing its policy and planning its activities for the next 5 years. Management consultants have advised that there is a 0.3 probability of high growth in the market during this period, a 0.5 probability of low growth and a 0.2 probability of zero growth. Three courses of action are considered:

(a) Expansion now. By building new stores now the company would be in a strong position if growth were high, but this policy would lead to losses in the event of zero growth.
(b) No expansion. This would put the company at a disadvantage should the market grow but would enable it to operate economically if the market remained static.
(c) Reappraisal after 2 years. Under conditions of high growth this would lead to lower profits than (a) but it would enable the company to choose an appropriate level of expansion for the remainder of the period.

The estimated outcomes, in terms of average percentage profit, are as follows:

	High growth	Low growth	Zero growth
Expansion now	18	11	−2
No expansion	8	7	6
Reappraisal after 2 years	14	12	6

Represent the data on a tree diagram, recommend a course of action and state the corresponding expected percentage profitability.
Answer Wait 2 years; expected outcome 11.4 per cent.

11. An oil company plans to drill 15 wells in an area where there is a 0.35 probability that any one well will produce oil in commercial quantities. The cost of drilling each well is £200 000. Each successful well will produce a return of £1.2 million; unsuccessful wells produce no return. Calculate

(a) the expected profit from the 15 wells;
(b) the probability that the profit will exceed £4 million;
(c) the probability that the company will make a loss.

Answer (a) £3.3 million; (b) 0.4356; (c) 0.0617.

12. In a flood-prevention scheme a dyke is built to a height that is exceeded by the flood water once in 10 years. Find the probability that flooding will occur

(a) once in the first 20 years;
(b) not more than once in the first 20 years;
(c) more than three times in the first 20 years.

Answer (a) 0.271; (b) 0.406; (c) 0.143.

13. Figure 6.26 shows some communications networks that use three types of unit A, B and C. These have probabilities 0.8, 0.9 and 0.95 of relaying a message successfully. A network will operate successfully when one or more routes between the transmission and receiving stations P and Q contain units that are all functioning correctly. Find the probability that each of the networks shown will operate successfully.
Answer (a) 0.684; (b) 0.999; (c) 0.990; (d) 0.978.

14. Sketch each of the following curves over the range $x = 0$ to $x = 1$ and use the stochastic method of section 6.9 to estimate the area under each curve between these limits.

$$\text{(a) } y = \frac{1}{1 + x} \qquad \text{(b) } y = \frac{1}{1 + x^2}$$

$$\text{(c) } y = \frac{1}{\sqrt{(1 + x)}} \qquad \text{(d) } y = \frac{1}{\sqrt{(1 + x^2)}}$$

Answer The results depend on the random numbers generated by the computer. For comparison the answers obtained by calculus methods are (a) 0.693; (b) 0.785; (c) 0.828; (d) 0.881.

15. According to *Wisden Cricketers' Almanack* 1988 the following scores were achieved by the sides batting first in 40-over matches during the 1987 season:

Figure 6.26

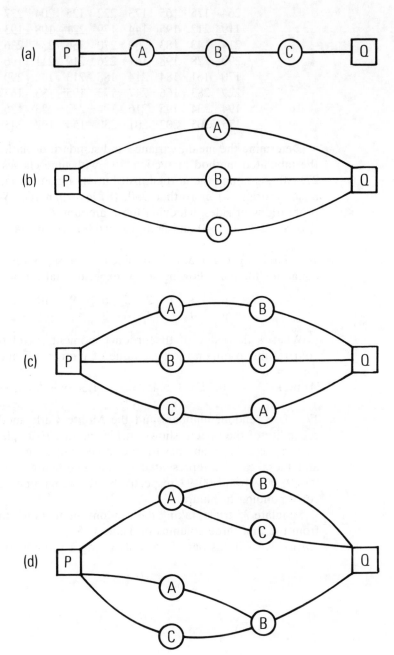

264	175	165	173	222	125	204	237	228	128
119	212	195	144	179	221	198	193	191	281
214	143	183	200	270	156	234	236	175	227
290	228	198	161	226	219	211	196	208	188
170	161	184	214	188	213	142	290	170	132
229	283	166	247	173	195	183	167	209	220
194	234	195	216	194	232	223	186	161	210
175	205	202	201	230	154	192	245	219	244

Determine the mean, variance and standard deviation of the scores using the tabulated method of section 6.15 with nine classes 111–30, 131–50 . . . 271–90. Assuming the normal distribution applies, what is the probability of a side scoring (a) more than 250, (b) less than 160? What were the actual proportions of sides achieving these amounts?
Answer   200.5, 1340 and 36.6; (a) 0.0881; (b) 0.1343; 0.075 and 0.1125.

16.   Find, by the methods of linear regression the y on x and x on y equations for the following set of experimental results:

x	-3	1	2	5	6	9	10	12
y	9	6	4	3	2	1	-1	-2

What is the value of the product moment correlation coefficient? Use your results to obtain the best value of y for $x = 7$ and the best value of x for $y = 5$.
Answer $y = -0.705x + 6.45$; $x = -1.383y + 9.05$; -0.987; 1.515; 2.135.

17.   Use random numbers and the Monte Carlo method to estimate the reliability of the system shown in Fig. 6.4(a), Example 6.5.

The success probabilities for the three components are 0.9, 0.95 and 0.98, and these can be represented by the two-figure random number ranges 00–89, 00–94 and 00–97 respectively, the remaining numbers in each case corresponding to failure.

Simulate 35 trials, taking the random numbers for the three components from the first three columns of Table C.5.
Answer   5 failures out of 35 trials giving a probability of failure of 0.143.

7 QUEUES

'Why should I be standing in line, just waiting for bread?'
Harburg, Gorney *'Brother, can you spare a dime?'*

7.1 TYPES OF QUEUE

Queueing (the second 'e' is optional) is a familiar feature of everyday life. We queue at the bus stop, the post office and the supermarket check-out. In a self-service restaurant we join a line of people shuffling up to the counter and at a top soccer match we must arrive early if we are to reach the turnstiles before the kick-off.

These queues may cause us no concern beyond a little frustration but there are others that lead to great distress – homeless families on a local authority housing list or patients waiting for hospital treatment.

We use the term *customers* for those in the queue and it can apply to objects as well as people. Aircraft waiting to land at a busy airport, letters stacked in an in-tray and broken machine tools awaiting repair in a factory are all examples of customers in a queueing system. Indeed, the early work on queueing theory by A K Erlang was a response to problems arising in the design of telephone systems.

Figure 7.1(a) shows a single queue, single-server system in which the customers form one line and are served at a single point. We distinguish between the queue of customers (those waiting to be served) and the system, which includes the customer being served.

If there are several servers, each performing the same function, we may have parallel queues as in Fig. 7.1(b) or a single queue from which the customer at the head moves to the first available service point as in Fig. 7.1(c).

In all three cases the customer leaves the system after being served but in some systems (Fig. 7.1(d)) the customer receives two or more kinds of service, passing different servers in series. In such cases a queue may form between each server and the next. This can arise at an airport, for example, where a passenger passes through the ticket check-in, customs and passport control in succession or in a factory where a component undergoes a sequence of several different processes.

Figure 7.1

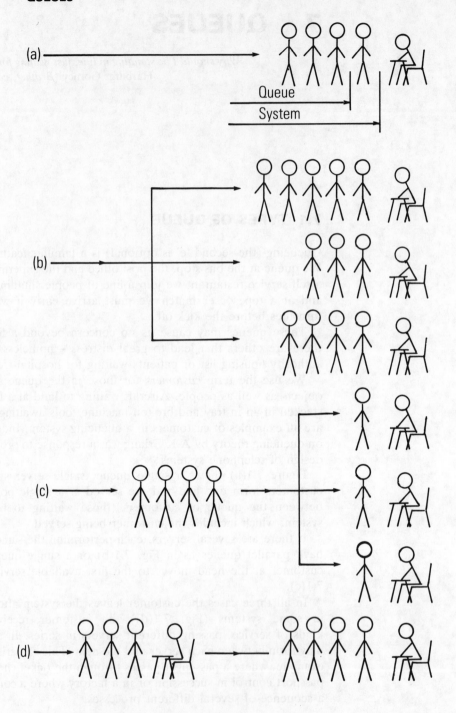

7.2 CHARACTERISTICS OF QUEUES

Queues can be classified by the following five properties:

(a) the pattern of customer arrivals;
(b) the pattern of service;
(c) the number of servers;
(d) the maximum customer capacity of the system;
(e) the order in which customers are served (the queue *discipline*).

The specification of a queue by these characteristics in the form a/b/c/d/e is known as Kendall's notation. It is convenient to discuss the last two first. In the case of (d), there may be a limit to the possible number of customers. This may be due to the capacity of the system or the potential number of customers requiring the service. Broken machine tools waiting to be repaired were mentioned earlier as an example of a queue; in this case the capacity of the system is limited to the total number of machine tools in use. In many practical examples the potential number of customers is so large that we can treat it as infinite. A busy roundabout, for instance, may be used by thousands of vehicles and, for calculations of queue size, it is reasonable to take the number as being unlimited.

There are several possibilities for (e) in the above list. The most common queue discipline is first-in, first-out (FIFO) and this is the usual rule when we are shopping or waiting for a bus. There are others, however. If letters are placed on top of an in-tray pile and are then dealt with from the top we have a last-in, first-out (LIFO) pattern. There are also queues in which certain customers have priorities; in a traffic queue, for example, we move aside and give way to ambulances, fire engines and police cars.

Unless otherwise stated it will be assumed in the rest of this chapter that the system has infinite capacity and a FIFO discipline. We can therefore omit the last two segments of the Kendall notation and express the characteristics of the system in the form a/b/c. The patterns of arrivals and service (a and b) are considered in section 7.4. The parameter c is simply the number of servers.

7.3 TERMINOLOGY

The time taken by a server to serve one customer is called the *service time*. In general there will be periods when there are no customers in the system and these constitute *idle time*. The *rate of service* is the number of customers that a server can deal with in a specified time, such as 1 hour, assuming there is no idle time.

The time between successive customers joining the system is known as the *inter-arrival time*. The *rate of arrival* is the number of customers joining the system in a specified time. Queueing is a random process and, in most cases, we have to work with average or mean values of all these times and rates.

Queues are also affected by the behaviour of the customers. The simplest pattern to analyse is that in which the customer joins the system whatever the length of the queue and remains until served, however long it takes.

However, customers may become impatient and a full analysis has to take account of the following possibilities:

Balking. The refusal of a customer to enter the system because the queue is too long.

Reneging. A customer may leave the system before being served because the waiting time proves too great.

Jockeying. This occurs when a customer leaves one queue to join a shorter parallel one.

As indicated earlier, 'customers' are not necessarily people. The concepts of balking and reneging can apply equally to vehicles joining a traffic queue or goods arriving at a warehouse.

There are two general approaches to the analysis of queues. We can make some (fairly drastic) assumptions and derive formulae for the average values of queue length, waiting time and other properties, and this method is adopted in the next few sections. Alternatively we can apply the technique of simulation, described in section 6.8; this is taken up in section 7.13 below.

7.4 THE SIMPLE OR M/M/1 QUEUE

A simple queue is defined as having the following properties:

1. Single queue, single server as in Fig. 7.1(a).
2. Customers are individuals (no fractions or groups).
3. No limit to the potential number of customers nor to the capacity of the system.
4. Variable arrivals.
5. Variable service times.
6. The variability of the number of customers arriving in a given time and of the number being served in that time, both follow a Poisson distribution.
7. First in, first out (FIFO) discipline.
8. No simultaneous arrivals.
9. No balking, reneging nor jockeying.
10. The system has been operating long enough to have settled down and the transient effects have died out.

The number of customers in the system can be thought of as a population in which a customer arriving represents a birth and one leaving corresponds to a death. It can be shown that, with assumption 6, the arrival and service patterns are examples of what is known as the Markov birth–death process.[1] For this reason the first two parameters in the Kendall notation are denoted by 'M' (for Markovian). Since there is a single server, the third parameter is $c = 1$ and the queue is described as an M/M/1 type. If we wish to stress the infinite capacity and FIFO discipline of the simple queue we can use the five parameter designation M/M/1/∞/FIFO.

It can also be shown that assumption 6 leads to the following results:

$$\text{Mean inter-arrival time} = \frac{1}{\text{Mean rate of arrival}}$$

and

$$\text{Mean service time} = \frac{1}{\text{Mean rate of service}}$$

It is usual to denote the mean rate of arrival and the mean rate of service by the Greek letters λ (lambda) and μ (mu) respectively. In this case the mean inter-arrival time is $1/\lambda$ and the mean service time is $1/\mu$.

All the results for simple queues depend on the ratio of the mean rate of arrival to the mean rate of service. This is called the *traffic intensity* (or sometimes traffic density) and is denoted by another Greek letter ρ (rho). It is also known as the *utilization factor*. Thus:

$$\text{Traffic intensity } \rho = \frac{\text{Mean rate of arrival}}{\text{Mean rate of service}} = \frac{\lambda}{\mu}$$

From the previous relationships between mean times and mean rates it follows that this result can also be written

$$\text{Traffic intensity } \rho = \frac{\text{Mean service time}}{\text{Mean inter-arrival time}}$$

For limited periods the rate of arrival may exceed the rate of service and the queue will then lengthen. For a queue to be stable, however, the mean rate of arrival must be less than the mean rate of service. This means that the traffic intensity must be less than 1.

Example 7.1
At a post office counter with a single server the average service time is 90 seconds and customers arrive at the rate of 24 per hour. Treating the system as a simple queue, find:

(a) the mean rate of service;
(b) the mean inter-arrival time;
(c) the traffic intensity.

Solution
(a) Since 1 hour = 3600 seconds, we have:

$$\text{Mean rate of service} = \frac{3600}{90} = \textbf{40 per hour}$$

$$\text{(b) Mean inter-arrival time} = \frac{3600}{24} = \textbf{150 seconds}$$

$$\text{(c) Traffic intensity } \rho = \frac{\text{Mean rate of arrival}}{\text{Mean rate of service}} = \frac{24}{40} = \textbf{0.6}$$

We can also obtain the result using times rather than rates. Thus

$$\text{Traffic intensity } \rho = \frac{\text{Mean service time}}{\text{Mean inter-arrival time}} = \frac{90}{150} = \textbf{0.6}$$

7.5 THEORY OF THE SIMPLE OR M/M/1 QUEUE

If we observed a simple queue over a period of time we would expect the number of customers in the system to vary. Theoretically it could take any value from zero to infinity. Since we cannot predict the number for a particular instant we have to work in terms of probabilities.

Suppose p_0, p_1, p_2, $p_3 \ldots p_n$ are the respective probabilities of there being 0, 1, 2, 3, . . . n customers in the system. Each probability value can also be thought of as the proportion of the total time for which there is the corresponding number of customers in the system.

Table 7.1 Queue length probabilities

Number in system	Number in queue	Probability	
0	0	p_0	p_0
1	0	p_1	ρp_0
2	1	p_2	$\rho^2 p_0$
3	2	p_3	$\rho^3 p_0$
. . .	. . .	. . .	. . .
n	$n-1$	p_n	$\rho^n p_0$
. . .	. . .	. . .	. . .

The first three columns of Table 7.1 show the number in the system, the number in the queue and the corresponding probability value. For most entries the number in the queue is one less than the number in the system; the exception occurs when the number in the system is zero. The average number in the system is therefore less than one more than the average number in the queue.

The various numbers of customers can be regarded as independent 'events' and, from the theory given in section 6.6, the sum of all their probability values is equal to 1. Thus

$$p_0 + p_1 + p_2 + p_3 + \ldots + p_n \ldots \text{ to infinity} = 1 \qquad [7.1]$$

Since the traffic density must be less than one the rate at which customers arrive is, on average, less than that at which they can be served. We can therefore expect the probability values to decrease as the number in the system increases. This is indeed the case and it can be shown that each probability value is ρ times the previous one.

Thus $p_1 = \rho p_0$ and $p_2 = \rho p_1$. Substituting the first of these results in the second we have $p_2 = \rho^2 p$. Similarly, $p_3 = \rho^3 p_0$, $p_4 = \rho^4 p_0$ and, in general, $p_n = \rho^n p_0$. All the probabilities can therefore be expressed in terms of p_0 as shown in the right-hand column of Table 7.1. If these results are substituted in Eq. 7.1 it becomes

$$p_0 + \rho p_0 + \rho^2 p_0 + \rho^3 p_0 + \ldots + \rho^n p_0 \ldots \text{ to infinity} = 1$$

This is a geometric series (or progression) and it is shown in Appendix A that its sum to infinity, S, is given by $S = a/(1 - r)$, where a is the first term and r is the common ratio of each term to the previous one, provided $|r| < 1$. In the present case the first term is p_0 and the common ratio is the traffic intensity ρ. The expression on the left-hand side is therefore equal to $p_0/(1 - \rho)$ and we can write

$$\frac{p_0}{1 - \rho} = 1$$

from which

$$p_0 = 1 - \rho \qquad\qquad\qquad [7.2]$$

The probability of there being no customer in the system, and therefore the probability of a customer not having to wait is $1 - \rho$. It follows that the probability of there being at least one customer in the system, and therefore the probability of a new customer having to wait, is ρ, since the two probabilities (not having to wait and having to wait) must total 1.

Using Eq. 7.2 and the expressions in the right-hand column of Table 7.1, the probabilities of there being 1, 2, 3 . . . customers in the system are respectively $\rho(1 - \rho)$, $\rho^2(1 - \rho)$, $\rho^3(1 - \rho)$ . . ., and the general result is

$$P_n = \rho^n(1 - \rho) \qquad\qquad\qquad [7.3]$$

It is of interest to know the likelihood of a queue exceeding a certain length. If P is the probability of the number in the system being equal to or greater than n, we can write:

$$P = p_n + p_{n+1} + p_{n+2} + \ . \ . \ . \ \text{to infinity}$$

and, using Eq. 7.3, this becomes

$$P = \rho^n(1 - \rho) + \rho^{n+1}(1 - \rho) + \rho^{n+2}(1 - \rho) \ . \ . \ . \ \text{to infinity}$$

This is another geometric series, the first term being $\rho^n(1 - \rho)$ and the common ratio ρ. The sum to infinity is therefore:

$$P = \frac{\rho^n(1 - \rho)}{(1 - \rho)} = \rho^n \qquad\qquad\qquad [7.4]$$

Example 7.2
For the simple queue of Example 7.1 find the probabilities that

(a) a customer does not have to wait for service;
(b) there are exactly two customers in the system;
(c) there are exactly four customers in the system;
(d) there are more than three customers in the system.

Solution
(a) The probability of not having to wait is the probability of there being no customer in the system. Thus

$$\text{Probability of not having to wait} = 1 - \rho = 1 - 0.6$$
$$= \mathbf{0.4}$$

(b) Using Eq. 7.3,

$$\text{Probability of two customers in the system} = \rho^2(1 - \rho)$$
$$= 0.6^2(1 - 0.6)$$
$$= \mathbf{0.144}$$

(c) Similarly, the probability of four customers in the system is

$$p_4 = \rho^4(1 - \rho) \quad = 0.6^4(1 - 0.6)$$
$$= \mathbf{0.05184}$$

(d) The probability of there being more than three customers in the system is the probability that there are four or more. Using Eq. 7.4,

$$\text{Probability of more than three in the system} = \rho^4 = 0.6^4$$
$$= \mathbf{0.1296}$$

7.6 COMPUTER PROGRAM FOR SYSTEM SIZE PROBABILITIES

The BASIC listing given in Fig. 7.2 calculates the probabilities of various numbers of customers being in the system. It determines these values for (a) a specified number of customers and (b) at least that number, using the formulae of Eq. 7.3 and 7.4.

Figure 7.2

```
10 PRINT "------------------------------------------"
20 PRINT "SIMPLE QUEUE - SYSTEM SIZE PROBABILITY"
30 PRINT "------------------------------------------"
40 PRINT:PRINT "ENTER TRAFFIC INTENSITY (LESS THAN 1)"
50 INPUT R
60 IF R>=1 THEN PRINT "INFINITE QUEUE":GOTO 150
70 PRINT
80 PRINT "NUMBER        PROBABILITY OF THIS NUMBER"
90 PRINT "IN SYSTEM    EXACTLY      AT LEAST"
100 PRINT
110 N=0:P=1-R:A=1:F=1E5
120 PRINT TAB(1);N;TAB(12);INT(F*P+0.5)/F;TAB(25);INT(F*A+0.5)/F
130 N=N+1:P=P*R:A=A*R
140 IF P>0.001 THEN GOTO 120
150 PRINT:PRINT "ANOTHER CALCULATION (Y/N)"
160 INPUT Q$
170 IF Q$="Y" OR Q$="y" THEN GOTO 40
180 PRINT "------------------------------------------"
190 END
>
```

Lines 10–30 print the heading and 40–50 call for the value of R, the traffic intensity. Line 60 displays an 'infinite queue' message if R is not less than 1; otherwise lines 70–100 print a heading for the table of results.

Line 110 specifies initial values of N, the number in the system; E, the probability of exactly this number, and A, the probability of at least this number. Line 120 displays these values, the INTeger routine being used to round the results to five places of decimals.

Line 130 modifies the values to give the next line of the table and line 140 checks whether the probability value has fallen below 0.001. If it has not the program is returned to line 120. Otherwise the calculation ends and a new one is offered in line 150. A positive response returns the program to line 40; otherwise the program ends at lines 180–190.

Other levels of accuracy can be obtained by changing the factor 1E5 (= 100000) in line 120 and the cut-off probability value can be altered in line 140 if desired.

The printout obtained with a traffic intensity of 0.6 is shown in Fig. 7.3. It includes the answers obtained in the solution to Example 7.2.

Figure 7.3

```
----------------------------------------
SIMPLE QUEUE - SYSTEM SIZE PROBABILITY
----------------------------------------

ENTER TRAFFIC INTENSITY (LESS THAN 1)
?0.6

NUMBER      PROBABILITY OF THIS NUMBER
IN SYSTEM   EXACTLY      AT LEAST

0           0.4          1
1           0.24         0.6
2           0.144        0.36
3           8.64E-2      0.216
4           5.184E-2     0.1296
5           3.11E-2      7.776E-2
6           1.866E-2     4.666E-2
7           1.12E-2      2.799E-2
8           6.72E-3      1.68E-2
9           4.03E-3      1.008E-2
10          2.42E-3      6.05E-3
11          1.45E-3      3.63E-3

ANOTHER CALCULATION (Y/N)
?N
----------------------------------------

  >
```

7.7 AVERAGE NUMBERS OF CUSTOMERS IN THE QUEUE AND SYSTEM

The proportion of the total time for which there is a given number of customers in the system is equal to the probability of that number being in the system. It is convenient to consider a total time of 1. Hence if N_1 is the average number in the system we can write

$$N_1 = \frac{0 \times p_0 + 1 \times p_1 + 2 \times p_2 + 3 \times p_3 + \ldots \text{to infinity}}{p_0 + p_1 + p_2 + p_3 + \ldots \text{to infinity}}$$

From Eq. 7.1 the denominator of this fraction equals 1. Also, the first term in the numerator is zero and, using Eq. 7.3, we can write

$$N_1 = \rho p_0 + 2\rho^2 p_0 + 3\rho^3 p_0 + \qquad \ldots \text{to infinity} \qquad [7.5]$$

Furthermore, if we multiply through this result by ρ and shift each term on the right-hand side to the right, we obtain:

$$\rho N_1 = \qquad \rho^2 p_0 + 2\rho^3 p_0 + 3\rho^4 p_0 + \ldots \text{to infinity}$$

If the last result is subtracted from the previous one, the left-hand side becomes $N_1 - \rho N_1$ and the coefficient of each term on the right-hand side becomes 1. Hence

$$N_1 - \rho N_1 = \rho p_0 + \rho^2 p_0 + \rho^3 p_0 + \qquad \ldots \text{to infinity}$$

The right-hand side is another convergent geometric series, the first term being ρp_0 and the common ratio ρ. Its sum to infinity is therefore $\rho p_0 / (1 - \rho)$ which equals ρ, since from Eq. 7.2, $p_0 = 1 - \rho$. Thus

$$N_1(1 - \rho) = \rho$$

and, finally,

$$N_1 = \frac{\rho}{1 - \rho} \qquad [7.6]$$

The analysis for the average number in the queue is very similar, the difference being that the probability values in Table 7.1 are associated with the corresponding numbers in the second column rather than the first. If the average number in the queue is N_2 then, by modifying the series for N_1, we have:

$$N_2 = 0 \times p_0 + 0 \times p_1 + 1 \times p_2 + 2 \times p_3 + \ldots \text{ to infinity}$$

the denominator being equal to 1 as before. The first two terms are now zero and the result is

$$N_2 = \rho^2 p_0 + 2\rho^3 p_0 + 3\rho^4 p_0 + \ldots \text{ to infinity}$$

This result is similar to Eq. 7.5, the only difference being that each term on the right-hand side is multiplied by the factor ρ. This factor is carried through the analysis and hence, using Eq. 7.6, we have

$$N_2 = \rho N_1 = \frac{\rho^2}{1 - \rho} \qquad\qquad [7.7]$$

This average is based on the total time including those periods when there is no customer in the queue. Suppose, however, that N_3 is the average number in the queue when there is a queue. The total time of interest is no longer 1 but is reduced by the amounts p_0 and p_1, the proportions of the time for which there is no customer or only one customer in the system. We can obtain N_3 by an analysis similar to that used previously with the original denominator 1 being replaced by $1 - p_0 - p_1$. Thus

$$N_3 = \frac{N_2}{1 - p_0 - p_1}$$

Since $p_0 = 1 - \rho$ and $p_1 = \rho(1 - \rho)$ we can put

$$N_3 = \frac{N_2}{1 - (1 - \rho) - \rho(1 - \rho)} = \frac{N_2}{1 - 1 + \rho - \rho + \rho^2} = \frac{N_2}{\rho^2}$$

Finally, substituting for N_2 from Eq. 7.7, the result becomes

$$N_3 = \frac{1}{1 - \rho} \qquad\qquad [7.8]$$

Example 7.3

For the queue of Example 7.1 calculate the average number of customers:

(a) in the system;
(b) in the queue (including times when there is no queue);
(c) in the queue when there is a queue.

Solution

The traffic intensity $\rho = 0.6$. Using Eqs 7.6, 7.7 and 7.8 we have

(a) average number in the system $= \dfrac{\rho}{1 - \rho} = \dfrac{0.6}{1 - 0.6} = \mathbf{1.5}$

(b) average number in queue $= \dfrac{\rho^2}{1 - \rho} = \dfrac{0.6^2}{1 - 0.6} = \mathbf{0.9}$
(including idle time)

(c) average number in queue when there is a queue $= \dfrac{1}{1-\rho} = \dfrac{1}{1-0.6} = \mathbf{2.5}$

7.8 AVERAGE TIME IN THE QUEUE AND SYSTEM

A customer joining the system has to wait in the queue while everyone already in the system is served. Thus

$$\text{Average time in queue} = \text{(average number in system)} \times \text{(mean service time)}$$

$$= \frac{\rho}{1-\rho} \times \frac{1}{\mu}$$

The total time in the system is made up of the time in the queue and the service time. Thus

$$\text{Average time in system} = \text{(average time in queue)} + \text{(mean service time)}$$

$$= \frac{\rho}{1-\rho} \times \frac{1}{\mu} + \frac{1}{\mu}$$

$$= \left(\frac{\rho}{1-\rho} + 1 \right) \times \frac{1}{\mu}$$

$$= \frac{\rho + 1 - \rho}{1-\rho} \times \frac{1}{\mu}$$

$$= \frac{1}{1-\rho} \times \frac{1}{\mu}$$

Example 7.4

For the queue of the previous example find the average time a customer is

(a) in the queue;
(b) in the system.

Solution

It is not necessary to use the formulae if the answers to the previous examples are assumed. Thus

(a) average time in the queue $=$ (average number in system)
$\times$ (mean service time)
$= 1.5 \times 90$
$= \mathbf{135 \ seconds}$.

(b) average time in the system $=$ (average time in queue)
$+$ (mean service time)
$= 135 + 90$
$= \mathbf{225 \ seconds}$.

7.9 SUMMARY OF RESULTS

The formulae obtained in sections 7.5–7.7 all depend on the traffic intensity ρ. Finding its value is therefore the key to all numerical examples on simple queues. Collecting the results, we have the following:

Probability that system is idle	$= 1 - \rho$
Probability of customer not having to wait	$= 1 - \rho$
Probability of customer having to wait	$= \rho$
Probability of exactly n customers in system	$= \rho^n(1 - \rho)$
Probability of n or more customers in system	$= \rho^n$

$$\text{Average number of customers in system} = \frac{\rho}{1 - \rho}$$

$$\text{Average number in queue (including times when there is no queue)} = \frac{\rho^2}{1 - \rho}$$

$$\text{Average number in the queue when there is a queue} = \frac{1}{1 - \rho}$$

$$\text{Average time a customer is in the queue} = \frac{\rho}{1 - \rho} \times \frac{1}{\mu}$$

$$\text{Average time a customer is in the system} = \frac{1}{1 - \rho} \times \frac{1}{\mu}$$

7.10 QUEUEING COSTS

When we have to queue at the bus stop or supermarket check-out we may feel frustrated but we probably do not put a monetary value on our waiting time. In contrast, the queues that can arise in a factory or office add directly to the costs through lost working time. The costs of a queue can be reckoned under two headings:

(a) providing the service;
(b) customers' waiting time.

If more money is spent under (a) in providing a faster service we can expect waiting times to be reduced and savings to be made under (b). If one organization has to bear both parts there is an incentive to minimize the total cost.

No general formulae exist for determining the optimum conditions in all cases and numerical examples may have to be solved by trial and error.

Example 7.5

A hypermarket chain distributes goods to its stores in its own lorries. For one particular store the lorries are dispatched from the warehouse at 30 minute intervals. It would take one unloader an average of 48 minutes to unload a lorry and it may be assumed that the speed of unloading is proportional to the number of unloaders employed.

The cost of employing an unloader is £6.00 per hour and the cost of each lorry and its driver is £36.00 per hour.

If the system may be regarded as a simple queue, how many unloaders should be employed?

Solution

Table 7.2 shows the times and costs for one to six unloaders. The mean rate of arrival, row ②, is constant at 2 per hour. The rate of service, row ③, is $60/48 = 1.25$ per hour for one unloader and proportional to the number employed. The traffic intensity, row ④, is obtained by dividing row ② by row ③. With one unloader the traffic intensity is greater than 1 and the queue is unstable. No further calculations are given in this column, therefore.

Row ⑤ shows the values of the factor $1/(1 - \rho)$ used in calculating the time in the system.

Table 7.2 Queue costs

① Number of unloaders		1	2	3	4	5	6
② Mean rate of arrival		2	2	2	2	2	2
③ Mean rate of service		1.25	2.5	3.75	5	6.25	7.5
④ Traffic intensity (ϱ)		1.6*	0.8	0.533	0.4	0.32	0.267
⑤ Mean service time (minutes)		—	24	16	12	9.6	8
⑥ $1/(1 - \varrho)$		—	5	1.875	1.667	1.471	1.364
⑦ Average time in system (minutes)		—	120	30	20	14.1	10.91
⑧ Average lorry cost per hour (£)		—	144	36	24	16.92	13.09
⑨ Unloaders cost per hour (£)		—	12	18	24	30	36
⑩ Total cost per hour (£)		—	156	54	48	46.92	49.09

*This value leads to an infinite queue

Row ⑥ is the reciprocal of row ③ and shows the average service time (in hours). Row ⑦ is the average time each lorry is in the system, found by multiplying row ⑤ by row ⑥. Since two lorries are unloaded per hour the hourly cost of waiting, shown in row ⑧, is found by doubling this result and multiplying by the all-in lorry cost of £36.00 per hour.

Row ⑨ shows the hourly cost of employing the unloaders and row ⑩ the total (waiting + unloading) cost.

It will be seen that the smallest total cost, £46.92 per hour, is obtained when five unloaders are employed.

7.11 THE SINGLE-CHANNEL, MULTIPLE-SERVER OR M/M/k QUEUE

If there is more than one server the system can be arranged as a multichannel queue (Fig. 7.1(b)) or as a single channel feeding all the servers (Fig. 7.1(c)). The latter arrangement ensures that a long line of people is not held up by one long-winded customer and it eliminates jockeying. This is the system considered here.

It is assumed that the arrival and service patterns conform to the same Markovian processes as before and, if k is the number of servers, the system is described as an M/M/k queue in Kendall's notation.

Let λ be the rate of arrival as before and μ the rate of service for each server. With k servers the total rate of service is $k\mu$ and the traffic intensity becomes

$$\rho = \frac{\lambda}{k\mu}$$

Some authors define μ as the combined rate of service for all the servers; in this case $\rho = \lambda/\mu$. As before the traffic intensity must be less than 1 for the system to be stable.

The analysis of the M/M/k queue is more complicated than that for the simple queue and the formulae for average times and numbers are relatively complex. In this book we shall obtain the results by the computer program given in the next section. The formulae are quoted without proof by Makower and Williamson[2] and they all involve p_0, the probability that there are no customers in the system. This quantity requires the summation of a series containing k terms. These terms contain the factorials of numbers from 0 to $k - 1$ and it should be noted that 0! and 1! are both equal to 1 (see Appendix A). A rigorous analysis of the M/M/k queue can be found in the book by Bunday.[3]

7.12 COMPUTER PROGRAM FOR THE MULTI-SERVER M/M/k QUEUE

The computer program of Fig. 7.4 determines, for the multi-server queue,

- the idle time;
- probabilities of having and not having to wait;
- the average numbers in the queue and in the system;
- the average times in the queue and in the system (in terms of the mean service time).

Figure 7.4

```
 10 PRINT "------------------------------------"
 20 PRINT "SINGLE AND MULTI-SERVER QUEUES"
 30 PRINT "------------------------------------"
 40 PRINT:PRINT "ENTER NUMBER OF SERVERS,"
 50 PRINT "SERVICE RATE AND ARRIVAL RATE"
 60 INPUT N,S,A
 70 D=A/(N*S)
 80 IF D>=1 THEN PRINT "<ERROR>":GOTO 40
 90 K=D*N/(1-D):L=1:M=0
100 IF N=1 THEN GOTO 160
110 FOR I=1 TO N-1
120 K=K*D*N/(I+1)
130 L=L*D*N/I
140 M=M+L
150 NEXT I
160 P=1/(K+M+1)
170 X=P:GOSUB 350
180 PRINT:PRINT "SYSTEM IS IDLE FOR ";100*Z;"% OF THE TIME"
190 X=K*P:GOSUB 350
200 PRINT:PRINT "PROBABILITY OF HAVING TO WAIT = ";Z
210 PRINT "PROB'TY OF NOT HAVING TO WAIT = ";1-Z
220 X=X*D/(1-D):GOSUB 350
230 PRINT:PRINT "AVERAGE NUMBER IN QUEUE  = ";Z
240 X=X+D*N:GOSUB 350
250 PRINT "AVERAGE NUMBER IN SYSTEM = ";Z
260 X=X/(D*N)-1:GOSUB 350
270 PRINT:PRINT "AVERAGE TIME IN QUEUE  = ";Z;" X (MST)"
280 PRINT "AVERAGE TIME IN SYSTEM = ";1+Z;" X (MST)"
290 PRINT "WHERE (MST) = THE MEAN SERVICE TIME"
300 PRINT:PRINT "ANOTHER CALCULATION (Y/N)"
310 INPUT Q$
320 IF Q$="Y" OR Q$="y" THEN CLS:GOTO 40
330 PRINT "------------------------------------"
340 END
350 Z=INT(1000*X+0.5)/1000
360 RETURN
```

If required, the program can be used for a simple queue by specifying the number of servers as 1.

Lines 10–30 print the heading and lines 40–60 call for the number of channels, the mean service rate for each channel and the mean arrival rate. Line 70 calculates the traffic intensity, R (for rho), and line 80 checks that it is less than 1 before allowing the program to proceed.

The main calculations are carried out in lines 90–160, the probability, P, that there are no customers in the system being obtained in line 160.

The results are rounded and displayed in lines 170–290. Each is first denoted by X and is then rounded to three decimal places as Z in the subroutine at lines 350–360.

Lines 300–320 offer the chance of a new calculation. If this is accepted the program returns to line 40; otherwise it ends at lines 330-340.

Example 7.6

In the photocopying section of a busy office 'customers' arrive at the rate of 10 per hour. Compare the following systems:

(a) three standard copiers each able to serve customers at the rate of 5 per hour;
(b) a single high-speed copier with a service rate of 15 per hour.

Solution

For (a) the number of servers, the service rate and the arrival rate are 3, 5 and 10 respectively. For (b) the corresponding values are 1, 15 and 10. Figure 7.5 shows the output from the computer program of Fig. 7.4 when these values are entered.

Figure 7.5

```
(a)  ------------------------------------
     SINGLE AND MULTI-CHANNEL QUEUES
     ------------------------------------

     ENTER NUMBER OF CHANNELS,
     SERVICE RATE AND ARRIVAL RATE
     ?3
     ?5
     ?10

     SYSTEM IS IDLE FOR 11.1% OF THE TIME

     PROBABILITY OF HAVING TO WAIT = 0.444
     PROB'TY OF NOT HAVING TO WAIT = 0.556

     AVERAGE NUMBER IN QUEUE  = 0.889
     AVERAGE NUMBER IN SYSTEM = 2.889

     AVERAGE TIME IN QUEUE  = 0.444 X (MST)
     AVERAGE TIME IN SYSTEM = 1.444 X (MST)
     WHERE (MST) = THE MEAN SERVICE TIME

     ANOTHER CALCULATION (Y/N)
     ?N
     ------------------------------------
```

```
(b)  ------------------------------------
     SINGLE AND MULTI-CHANNEL QUEUES
     ------------------------------------

     ENTER NUMBER OF CHANNELS,
     SERVICE RATE AND ARRIVAL RATE
     ?1
     ?15
     ?10

     SYSTEM IS IDLE FOR 33.3% OF THE TIME

     PROBABILITY OF HAVING TO WAIT = 0.667
     PROB'TY OF NOT HAVING TO WAIT = 0.333

     AVERAGE NUMBER IN QUEUE  = 1.333
     AVERAGE NUMBER IN SYSTEM = 2

     AVERAGE TIME IN QUEUE  = 2 X (MST)
     AVERAGE TIME IN SYSTEM = 3 X (MST)
     WHERE (MST) = THE MEAN SERVICE TIME

     ANOTHER CALCULATION (Y/N)
     ?N
     ------------------------------------
```

The results show that the idle time and the probability of having to wait are both greater in the case of (b). In the case of (a), however, idle time means that all three machines are idle. The average number in the queue is also greater for (b).

In (a) the mean service time for each machine is 60/5 = 12 minutes. In

(b) it is $60/15 = 4$ minutes for the single machine. Combining these values with the computer results we obtain

for (a): average time in the queue $= 0.444 \times 12 =$ **5.33 minutes**,
          average time in the system $= 1.444 \times 12 =$ **17.33 minutes**,
for (b): average time in the queue $= \quad 2 \times 4 \ =$ **8 minutes**,
          average time in the system $= \quad 3 \times 4 \ =$ **12 minutes**.

So although in (b) there is a greater probability of having to wait, the time in the system is less because of the much faster service. On these grounds (b) is superior. In practice we would have to consider the cost of providing this superior service and the effect of a breakdown when the service is dependent on a single machine.

7.13 QUEUE SIMULATION

When we use the formulae given in the earlier sections of this chapter we must remember that they all depend on certain assumptions about the patterns of arrival and service. In practice the patterns may be very different. Furthermore, the queue discipline may differ from the FIFO rule that we have used so far.

In such cases we can use simulation. This is a particularly valuable technique when we are planning a new service or the modification of an existing one. Simulation enables us to experiment with different types of service and see how effective they are before putting them into practice. From observations on the existing queue we can express the arrival and service patterns in terms of probabilities. Then we can use random numbers (see section 6.9) to simulate the operation of the queue over a period of time. If we limit the exercise to a few customers we can carry out the simulation 'by hand' but for a large number we can program a computer.

Example 7.7

Observations on a car wash show that the inter-arrival times of customers are distributed with the following probabilities:

Range of inter-arrival times (minutes)	0–2	2–4	4–6	6–8	8–10
Probabilities	0.06	0.20	0.47	0.23	0.04

Investigate the operation of the system assuming that the car wash offers a 4-minute standard programme only.

Solution

The service time, 4 minutes, is the same for all customers and this is an example of a deterministic service pattern. In order to assign inter-arrival times to customers we take the midpoint of each range to represent all values in that range. On this basis, the inter-arrival time can be 1, 3, 5, 7 or 9 minutes. By combining these values with the corresponding probability values we can obtain the average inter-arrival time. Thus

$$\text{Average inter-arrival time} = 0.06 \times 1 + 0.20 \times 3 + 0.47 \times 5$$
$$+ 0.23 \times 7 + 0.04 \times 9$$
$$= \textbf{4.98 minutes}$$

Since this is greater than the service time the system appears to be stable.

Table 7.3 Inter-arrival time probabilities

Midpoint inter-arrival time (minutes)	1	3	5	7	9
Probability	0.06	0.20	0.47	0.23	0.04
Random number range	00–05	06–25	26–72	73–95	96–99

The probability values are given to two places of decimals and it is convenient to represent them by two-figure random numbers as shown in Table 7.3, the total range being 00–99. Thus the first probability value, 0.06, is represented by the first 6 numbers, that is 00–05, the next value, 0.20, by the next 20 numbers, 06–25 and so on. A simulation for a series of 10 cars is shown in Table 7.4.

Table 7.4 Car wash simulation

Car no.	Random number	Inter-arrival time (minutes)	Clock time (minutes) Arrival	Enter	Depart
1	—	—	0	0	4
2	76	7	7	7	11
3	21	3	10	11	15
4	22	3	13	15	19
5	30	5	18	19	23
6	01	1	19	23	27
7	61	5	24	27	31
8	03	1	25	31	35
9	28	5	30	35	39
10	62	5	35	39	43

We have to make an assumption about the initial state of the system. It is convenient to start with an idle system and assume that the first car arrives at time 0. Since the system is empty the car enters the wash immediately and departs after 4 minutes. This is shown by the first line of Table 7.4. The behaviour of the system then depends on the inter-arrival times between successive cars and these are determined by the sequence of random numbers. Suppose the random numbers, taken from a calculator or from a table such as Table C.5, are as shown in the second column. The random number for car 2 is 76 and, referring to Table 7.3, this is in the range 73–95 giving an inter-arrival time of 7 minutes. The next two random numbers, 21 and 22, are both in the range 6–25, giving intervals of 3 minutes each and the next, 30, is in the range 26–72, corresponding to an interval of 5 minutes. By continuing this process we complete the third column of Table 7.4.

The right-hand side of Table 7.4 shows the times at which each car arrives, enters the car wash and departs. Working in minutes, car 1 leaves at time 4 and the system is idle until the arrival of car 2 at time 7. This car goes straight into the car wash and leaves 4 minutes later at time 11.

Meanwhile car 3 has arrived at time 10, 3 minutes after the arrival of car 2. It has to wait 1 minute for car 2 to depart and then enters the car wash, leaving at time 15. Car 4 is only 3 minutes behind and arrives at time 13. Therefore, it has to wait 2 minutes before entering the car wash at time 15 and leaving at time 18. The inter-arrival time for car 5 is 5 minutes and therefore, it has to wait only 1 minute. If the calculation is continued it is found that the tenth car leaves the car wash at time 43.

From Table 7.4, it is possible to determine the number of cars in the system at any given time. For the period 0–4 minutes only car 1 is in the system. When it departs the system is idle until the arrival of car 2 at time 7. For the period 7–10 car 2 is alone in the system but the arrival of car 3 at time 10 means that there are two cars in the system – one in the car wash and one waiting – until time 11. By comparing the values in the last three columns, the number in the system at any given time can be found. For instance, car 6 does not depart until time 27, by which time cars 7 and 8 have arrived. For the period 25–27, therefore, there are three cars in the system. The same thing occurs in period 30–31 when cars 7, 8 and 9 are all in the system.

When the inter-arrival time is 1 or 3 minutes the number of cars in the system increases, but if it is 5, 7 or 9 minutes the number decreases.

Table 7.5 Car wash queue and system sizes

Number in system	Number in queue	Periods (minutes)	Total time (minutes)
0	0	4–7	3
1	0	0–4, 7–10, 11–13, 15–18, 23–24, 39–43	17
2	1	10–11, 13–15, 18–23, 24–25, 27–30, 31–39	20
3	2	25–27, 30–31	3

Table 7.5 shows the periods for which various numbers of cars are in the system and in the queue. There is no car in the system for a total of 3 minutes, one for a total of 17 minutes, two for a total of 20 minutes and 3 for a total of 3 minutes. Hence

$$\text{Average number in system} = \frac{0 \times 3 + 1 \times 17 + 2 \times 20 + 3 \times 3}{43}$$

$$= \frac{66}{43} = \mathbf{1.535}$$

Similarly,

$$\text{Average number in queue} = \frac{0 \times 3 + 0 \times 17 + 1 \times 20 + 2 \times 3}{43}$$

$$= \frac{26}{43} = \mathbf{0.605}$$

The times spent by the cars in the queue, in minutes, are respectively 0, 0, 1, 2, 1, 4, 3, 6, 5 and 4. The total for the 10 cars is 26 minutes or an average of 2.6 minutes per car. Since every car has a service time of 4 minutes the average time in the system is 2.6 + 4 = 6.6 minutes.

All these results must be treated with caution. They are based on a sequence of only 10 cars and, furthermore, the simulation has been arranged to start and end with a single car in the system.

7.14 COMPUTER PROGRAM FOR THE CAR WASH EXAMPLE

The simulation exercise can be extended to a large number of cars by using the computer program of Fig. 7.6. This will construct a table similar to Table 7.4 for any specified number of cars and will calculate the average times in the queue and in the system.

Figure 7.6

```
10 PRINT "------------------------------------"
20 PRINT "CAR WASH SIMULATION"
30 PRINT "------------------------------------"
40 PRINT:PRINT "ENTER NUMBER OF CARS"
50 INPUT N
60 DIM A(N):DIM E(N):DIM D(N)
70 A(1)=0:E(1)=0:D(1)=4
80 X=0:Y=4
90 PRINT:PRINT "CAR";TAB(5);"INTER-ARRIVAL";TAB(21);"CLOCK TIMES:"
100 PRINT "NO.";TAB(5);"TIME";TAB(21);"ARR.";TAB(28);"ENTER";TAB(35);"DEP."
110 PRINT:PRINT TAB(1);1;TAB(5);"-";TAB(21);0;TAB(28);0;TAB(35);4
120 C=0
130 FOR I=2 TO N
140 C=C+1
150 IF C>4 THEN PRINT:C=0
160 R=INT(RND*100)
170 G=1
180 IF R>5 THEN G=3
190 IF R>25 THEN G=5
200 IF R>72 THEN G=7
210 IF R>95 THEN G=9
220 A(I)=A(I-1)+G
230 E(I)=A(I)
240 IF E(I)<D(I-1) THEN E(I)=D(I-1)
250 D(I)=E(I)+4
260 X=X+E(I)-A(I)
270 Y=Y+D(I)-A(I)
280 PRINT TAB(1);I;TAB(5);G;TAB(21);A(I);TAB(28);E(I);TAB(35);D(I)
290 NEXT I
300 X=INT(100*X/N+0.5)/100
310 Y=INT(100*Y/N+0.5)/100
320 PRINT:PRINT "AVERAGE TIME IN QUEUE  = ";X
330 PRINT "AVERAGE TIME IN SYSTEM = ";Y
340 PRINT "------------------------------------"
350 END
```

The program follows closely the method used in analysing Example 7.7. It uses the following notation:

$$N = \text{number of cars,}$$
$$A(I), \text{ and } D(I) = \text{arrival and departure times of the Ith car,}$$
$$E(I) = \text{time of entry to the car wash of the Ith car,}$$
$$X \text{ and } Y = \text{accumulated times spent by cars in the queue and in the system,}$$
$$G = \text{time gap between successive arrivals.}$$
$$R = \text{random number between 0 and 99,}$$
$$C = \text{row counter used in formatting the table.}$$

Lines 10–30 print the title and 40–50 call for the number of cars to be used in the simulation. Line 60 sets up arrays for the arrival, entry and departure times and line 70 specifies the values of these quantities for the first car. Line 80 sets the initial values of the times in the queue and in the system.

Lines 90–110 print the heading for the table and its first row, and line 120 sets the initial value of the row counter.

Lines 130–290 determine and print the rest of the table. Line 150 ensures that there is a gap in the table after every five rows.

Line 160 gives a random number in the range 0–99. Note that in BBC BASIC the function RND must be replaced by RND(1) so that the line reads:

$$160 \ R=INT(RND(1)*100)$$

Lines 170–210 use the value of R to set the inter-arrival time and lines 220–250 use the result to calculate the arrival, entry and departure times for the current car, which are printed at line 280.

Lines 260–270 add the times in the queue and in the system to the running totals. When the sequence has been completed, these values are averaged in lines 300–310 and displayed in lines 320–330. Since the service time is the same for all cars at this stage it is not essential to calculate these times separately. However, the extra lines in the program are used later when variations in service times are considered.

The program ends at lines 340–350.

Figure 7.7

```
----------------------------------------
CAR WASH SIMULATION
----------------------------------------

ENTER NUMBER OF CARS
?20

CAR   INTER-ARRIVAL    CLOCK TIMES:
NO.   TIME             ARR.    ENTER   DEP.

 1     -                0       0       4
 2     5                5       5       9
 3     3                8       9      13
 4     7               15      15      19
 5     5               20      20      24

 6     3               23      24      28
 7     3               26      28      32
 8     7               33      33      37
 9     5               38      38      42
10     5               43      43      47

11     3               46      47      51
12     7               53      53      57
13     5               58      58      62
14     5               63      63      67
15     7               70      70      74

16     1               71      74      78
17     5               76      78      82
18     7               83      83      87
19     5               88      88      92
20     3               91      92      96

AVERAGE TIME IN QUEUE  = 0.55
AVERAGE TIME IN SYSTEM = 4.55
----------------------------------------
```

The printout of Fig. 7.7 was obtained when the program was run for 20 cars. If the program is run for large numbers of cars the printing of the individual times can be eliminated by deleting lines 90–110, 150 and 280. The average times in the queue for five successive runs, each with 500 cars, were 0.71, 1.03, 1.11, 0.95 and 0.81 minutes. The corresponding average times in the system were all 4 minutes longer, since the service time is constant.

Example 7.8

Suppose, in the previous example, the motorists are offered a choice of (a) the standard 4-minute wash or (b) a 6-minute 'wash and wax' programme. Investigate the operation of the system if one quarter of the customers select (b).

Solution

The probabilities of (a) and (b) are respectively 0.75 and 0.25. Combining these with the corresponding service times, we obtain

$$\text{Average service time} = 0.75 \times 4 + 0.25 \times 6 = 4.5 \text{ minutes.}$$

This is still less than the average inter-arrival time so we can expect the system to remain stable, albeit with longer average times in the queue and in the system.

Since the service pattern is no longer deterministic, we use random numbers to decide whether a customer selects (a) or (b). The probabilities of (a) and (b) can be represented by the number ranges 0–74 and 75–99. To work 'by hand' we need two extra columns in Table 7.4, one for a second sequence of random numbers and the other to show the corresponding service times, either 4 or 6 minutes.

In the computer program we need to add 2 minutes to the departure time for one-quarter of the customers. This can be achieved by a single line between 250 and 260, thus

$$255 \text{ IF RND}>=0.75 \text{ THEN } D(I)=D(I)+2$$

or, in BBC BASIC,

$$255 \text{ IF RND}(1)>=0.75 \text{ THEN } D(I)=D(I)+2$$

When the program was run five times with this modification, again using a sequence of 500 cars, the average times in the queue were found to be 3.01, 4.88, 2.30, 2.83 and 4.52 minutes. The corresponding average times in the system were 7.47, 9.42, 6.81, 7.38 and 9.08 minutes. In each case, the average time in the system is greater than the average time in the system by approximately 4.5 minutes, the calculated average service time. Note that the program still specifies the first car as having the 4-minute service time.

If half the customers opt for the 'wash and wax' programme the average service time becomes 5 minutes. This is longer than the average inter-arrival time and we can expect the system to become unstable. Try the effect of changing the value 0.75 in line 255 to 0.6, then to 0.5 and finally to 0.4. In each case, run the simulation with sequences of, say, 100 and 500 cars. With an unstable queue the average times will tend to lengthen as the number of cars in the sequence is increased.

7.15 SUMMARY

Queueing is a random process and we can only express the results of our calculations as probabilities and averages. A queue develops through the interaction of the patterns of arrivals and service. A key concept is traffic intensity, the ratio of the mean rate of arrival to the mean rate of service.

For the queue to be stable, this ratio must be less than 1.

A simple queue consists of a single channel and single server, in which the arrival and service patterns follow certain statistical distributions and the queue discipline is FIFO. It is also assumed that customers arrive and are served singly, and that there is no limit to the potential number of customers. For these conditions there are formulae for the average numbers of customers in the queue and in the system, and the average times spent by customers in the queue and the system, all in terms of the traffic intensity.

The corresponding results for a single channel, multi-server system are more complex but are easily evaluated by computer. In terms of the average times in the queue and in the system, a queue with k servers is inferior to a single queue having k times the mean rate of service.

Queues that are not amenable to simple mathematical analysis can be investigated by simulation techniques. The progress of a series of customers through the system is represented by a probabilistic model in which the values of inter-arrival times, service times and other variables are determined by the use of random numbers. Computers can quickly establish average results for large numbers of customers and can predict the effects of changing the rate of service or queue discipline.

REFERENCES

1. Bronson R 1982 *Operations Research* Schaum's Outline Series, McGraw-Hill Ch 21
2. Makower M S, Williamson E 1985 *Operational Research* 4th edn Teach Yourself Books, Hodder and Stoughton pp 104–5
3. Bunday B D 1986 *Basic Queueing Theory* Edward Arnold Ch 3

BIBLIOGRAPHY

Cooper R B 1981 *Introduction to Queueing Theory* 2nd edn Edward Arnold
Murdoch J 1977 *Queueing Theory* Macmillan
Newell G F 1982 *Applications of Queueing Theory* Chapman and Hall

PROBLEMS

1. In a workshop stores run by a single storekeeper, the inter-arrival and service times of customers are observed and classified into 2-minute ranges. The probabilities of the various values are shown in the following table:

Range (minutes)	0–2	2–4	4–6	6–8	8–10	10–12
Midpoint of range	1	3	5	7	9	11
Probability of this						
Inter-arrival time	0.04	0.11	0.35	0.35	0.11	0.04
Service time	0.09	0.19	0.37	0.30	0.05	—

Calculate the mean inter-arrival and service times.

Answer 6.0 and 5.06 minutes.

2. For a simple queue calculate the average numbers (a) in the system, (b) in the queue when there is a queue and (c) in the queue (including times when there is no queue) for traffic intensities of 0.5, 0.8, 0.9 and 0.95. *Answer* (a) 1; 4; 9; 19; (b) 2; 5; 10; 20; (c) 0.5; 3.2; 8.1; 18.05.

3. For the traffic intensities of the previous example and a mean service time of 24 seconds, calculate the average time a customer is (a) in the queue and (b) in the system.
Answer (a) 24, 96, 216, 456 seconds; (b) 48, 120, 240, 480 seconds.

4. A rail commuter buys a ticket every morning and notes that on average he has to wait in a queue 3 days out of 5. He also finds that the average time to be served when he reaches the head of the queue is 20 seconds. Treating the system as a simple queue and assuming that the figures are the same for other passengers, find:

(a) the average number of customers in the queue (including occasions when the queue length is zero);
(b) the average time in the system.

Answer (a) 0.9; (b) 50 seconds.

5. At a post office counter with a single server it is observed that the average number of customers in the queue (apart from the person being served) is five, including times when the queue length is zero. The mean rate of arrival is 20 per hour. Assuming the system to be a simple queue, find:

(a) the traffic intensity;
(b) the average time a customer is in the queue,
(c) the average time a customer is in the system.

Answer (a) 0.854; (b) 15 minutes; (c) 17.6 minutes.

6. The breakdown and repair of machines in a large production workshop may be regarded as a simple queueing system. The average repair time for each machine is 40 minutes and it is found that for 40 per cent of the total time there is no machine under repair. Calculate:

(a) the average number of machines that are out of action;
(b) the average time a machine is waiting to be repaired when it breaks down;
(c) the probability of three or more machines being broken down at the same time.

Answer (a) 1.5; (b) 60 minutes; (c) 0.216.

7. A study was made of the operation of a goods reception bay throughout a working week of 40 hours. The number of vehicles arriving was 117 and, with two persons employed on unloading, the average unloading time was 15 minutes. Treating the system as a simple queue, calculate:

(a) the probability that a vehicle does not have to wait to be unloaded;
(b) the average number of vehicles in the system;
(c) the average time a vehicle is in the system.

For a trial period the number of unloaders was varied and it was found that with three, four and five persons the average unloading times were 12, 10 and 9 minutes respectively, there being no appreciable reduction with more than five. If the waiting time of a vehicle and driver costs £20 per hour and the all in cost of each unloader is £6 per hour, how many should be employed?

Answer   (a) 0.269; (b) 2.72; (c) 55.8 minutes; four unloaders.

8.   (a) At the head office of the Tardy Timepiece Company there is a stationery store which is open for 30 hours a week and is run by a single storekeeper. The average number of customers in the store (including the person being served) is three and the average time to serve a customer is 2½ minutes. Treating the system as a simple queue, find:

  (i) the traffic intensity;
 (ii) the average time a customer is in the system;
(iii) the probability of a customer not having to wait;
(iv) the average number of customers per hour;
 (v) the probability of there being five or more customers in the store.

  (b) Sir Tempus Tardy is looking for ways to reduce office costs. At present the storekeeper prepares a handwritten invoice for each customer. He estimates that the installation of a computer to undertake the paperwork would reduce the average service time to 2 minutes. The waiting time of each customer is reckoned to cost £3 per hour and the leasing of the computer would cost £100 per week. Will it pay Sir Tempus to lease the computer and, if so, what weekly saving could be expected?

Answer   (a) (i) 0.75; (ii) 10 minutes; (iii) 0.25; (iv) 18 per hour; (v) 0.237.
(b) Yes; saving of £35 per week.

9.   If, in a simple queue, the traffic intensity is 0.7 what are the probabilities that the number of customers in the system is (a) less than four, (b) four or more?

  A shopkeeper wants to ensure that the probability of there being more than two customers in the queue (apart from the person being served) is less than 2 per cent. What is the maximum traffic density that will ensure this?

Answer   (a) 0.76; (b) 0.24; 0.376.

10.   A single server queueing system has room for a maximum of m customers (including the person being served). When the system is full new customers go elsewhere. In all other respects the system behaves as a simple queue and, in particular, the probability of there being n customers in the system is given by $p_n = \rho^n p_0$. Show, by modifying the analysis of section 7.5, that:

  (i) the probability of there being no customer in the system is given by

$$p_0 = \frac{1 - \rho}{1 - \rho^{m+1}}$$

  (ii) the probability of the system being full (this occurs when there are m customers in the system) is

$$p_m = \rho^m p_0 = \frac{\rho^m(1 - \rho)}{1 - \rho^{m+1}}$$

In a single-server barber's shop there are three chairs for waiting customers. If these are all occupied new customers go elsewhere. The mean service time is 12½ minutes and customers arrive at the rate of three per hour. Calculate:

(a) the proportion of idle time;
(b) the proportion of the time for which the system is full;
(c) the probabilities of there being one, two, and three customers in the system;
(d) the average number in the queue;
(e) the average number in the system;
(f) the average time in the queue;
(g) the average time in the system.

Compare the results with those for an infinite capacity queue having the same traffic intensity.
Answer (a) 0.415; (b) 0.063; (c) 0.259, 0.162 and 0.101; (d) 0.391; (e) 1.138; (f) 14.2 minutes; (g) 26.7 minutes. For the corresponding simple queue: (a) 0.375; (b) 0; (c) 0.234, 0.146 and 0.092; (d) 1.042; (e) 1.667; (f) 20.8 minutes; (g) 33.3 minutes.

11. In a queueing system customers arrive at the rate of eight per hour, with a Poisson distribution. Service can be provided in one of the following ways:

(a) a single server with a mean service time of 5 minutes;
(b) two servers, each with a mean service time of 10 minutes;
(c) four servers, each with a mean service time of 20 minutes.

Find, for each method of service,

(i) the probability of the system being idle;
(ii) the probability of a customer having to wait;
(iii) the average number of customers in the system;
(iv) the average time a customer is in the system.

Answers	(a)	(b)	(c)
(i) probability of idle system	0.333	0.2	0.06
(ii) probability of having to wait	0.667	0.467	0.378
(iii) average number in system	2	2.4	3.424
(iv) mean time in system (minutes)	15	18	25.68

12. The service at a bank operates on a single channel multi-server system. There are three tellers and the mean service time is 4 minutes. If customers arrive at the rate of 24 per hour find, making the usual assumptions about the distribution of arrivals and service times,

(a) the percentage of the time for which the system is idle;
(b) the average number of customers in the queue;
(c) the average number in the system;
(d) the average time in the queue;
(e) the average time in the system.

Answer (a) 18.7 per cent; (b) 0.313; (c) 1.913; (d) 0.78 minutes; (e) 4.78 minutes.

13. In a travel agent's office customers arrive at the rate of 10 per hour. Three booking staff are employed and the mean service time is 15 minutes. Treating the system as a single-channel multi-server queue, and making the usual assumptions, find:

(a) the average number in the queue;
(b) the average time a customer is waiting to be served;
(c) how many staff should be employed if the average waiting time is to be less than 3 minutes;
(d) the proportions of the time for which the system is idle when there are three staff and also for the number found in (c).

Answer   (a) 3.511; (b) 21.1 minutes; (c) 5; (d) 0.045 and 0.08.

14.   (a) An office that is open for 40 hours a week has two photocopiers that are leased at an all-in cost of £50 per week each. Staff arrive to use the machines at the rate of 33 per hour and the mean service time is 3 minutes. Making the usual assumptions, find:

 (i) the average number of staff waiting to use a photocopier;
 (ii) the average time a customer is in the queue;
(iii) the average time a customer is in the system.

(b) The hourly cost to the company of staff using the photocopiers is £7.50 per hour, including overheads. Should the number of photocopiers be increased and, if so, to what figure?

(c) An improved photocopier, costing £80 per week, runs 50 per cent faster and would give a mean service time of 2 minutes. Would it pay to change to the new model and, if so, how many should be leased?

Answer (a) (i) 3.516; (ii) 6.393 minutes; (iii) 9.393 minutes. (b) Yes; 4. (c) Yes; 3.

15.   Observations of a supermarket check-out show that the times between successive arrivals (to the nearest minute) are distributed as follows:

Inter-arrival time	0	1	2	3	4	5	6	7	8	9
Percentage of cases	3	5	12	21	26	16	8	5	3	1

The service times, including giving change and processing cheques and credit cards, also to the nearest minute are as follows:

Service time	1	2	3	4	5	6	7
Percentage of cases	12	22	33	17	11	4	1

Simulate the passage of 30 customers through the check-out. Start the simulation with the arrival of the first customer and use the first column of random numbers in Table C.5 to determine the subsequent inter-arrival times. Take the numbers in the second column to give the service times.

Use your simulation to estimate:

(a) the average number of customers in the system;
(b) the average time a customer is in the system.

Answer   (a) 2.4; (b) 8.47 minutes.

16.   Modify the computer program of Fig. 7.6 to incorporate the data of the previous problem and run it to simulate the passage of several hundred customers.

Compare the average time in the system with that obtained from the 'hand' simulation.

Answer Running the program several times for 1000 customers gave mean times in the system between 4.76 and 5.79 minutes.

8   STOCK CONTROL

'When she got there, the cupboard was bare,
And so the poor dog had none.'

Sarah Catherine Martin,
The Comic Adventures of Old Mother Hubbard
(*from* The Concise Oxford Dictionary of Quotations)

8.1 THE NEED TO HOLD STOCKS

Every organization has to maintain stocks of materials if it is to run smoothly. Note that in industry the alternative term *inventory* is often used. Factories hold stocks of raw materials, components and spare parts to meet the needs of the production departments. An office needs a stationery store, even if it is merely a cupboard to hold the paper, pens, pencils and other items used by staff. At home we store food in the fridge or larder so that we do not have to go shopping every time we want to prepare a meal. And shops themselves exist because we cannot go to the manufacturers for everything we need.

As these examples show stockholding can be regarded as a means of decoupling demand from supply. Some industries have attempted to dispense with stockholding by asking suppliers to deliver components only when they are needed. This 'just-in-time' system[1] has been adopted by large car manufacturers, but it means that an interruption in the supply of a single component can bring a production line to a halt.

Failures in stock control can have spectacular and sometimes disastrous consequences. The over-production of food can lead to huge stocks being held in some countries at times when there is famine in other parts of the world.

8.2 CATEGORIES OF STOCK

It is convenient to classify stocks under three headings:

1. *Active* stocks are the quantities held to meet the average requirements.
2. *Buffer* (or *safety*) stocks are the additional amounts that are held to meet variations in demand.
3. *Strategic* stocks are those which are purchased in anticipation of shortages or price rises.

224

8.3 THE COSTS OF STOCKHOLDING

Holding stocks of goods gives rise to costs under several headings, in addition to the direct purchase cost.

(a) *Ordering cost* Every time an order is placed with a supplier there is a cost arising from the preparation and dispatch of the order and the checking of the goods on delivery. In addition there may be a delivery charge. These costs rise as the number of orders increases.

(b) *Storage or holding cost* This is the cost associated with the storage of goods while they are waiting to be used. It includes interest on the capital tied up in the stocks, insurance, the rent and rates on warehouses and storage areas, and the cost of maintaining the correct temperature and humidity for perishable items. Costs under this heading increase as stock levels rise.

(c) *Stockout costs* Running out of stock can prove costly. Factory production can be halted by a shortage of a single component or the lack of spare parts for broken machine tools. Shops will lose business and, in the long run, customers if they cannot supply goods when required.

(d) *Discounts* Some suppliers offer discounts if items are purchased in large batches. Buying in bulk will lead to higher storage costs but the increase may be outweighed by the savings on the purchase price.

Example 8.1

A householder living in a remote area uses bottled gas at the rate of one cylinder a week. The cylinders have to be collected from a supplier and each return journey costs £12.00. If the supplier charges a rental of £1.50 per week for each cylinder and the householder's car can carry a maximum of five, how many should be collected on each visit?

Solution

It is convenient to tabulate all the possibilities and work out the costs on a weekly basis. Since one cylinder is used each week the number of weeks between visits equals the number of cylinders collected. Hence with batches of one, two, three, four and five cylinders, the weekly transport costs are £12.00, £6.00, £4.00, £3.00 and £2.40 respectively. The results are:

Number of cylinders	Weekly cost (£)		
	Rental	Transport	Total
1	1.50	12.00	13.50
2	3.00	6.00	9.00
3	**4.50**	**4.00**	**8.50**
4	6.00	3.00	9.00
5	7.50	2.40	9.90

The table shows that the total cost is least when the cylinders are collected in **batches of three**.

8.4 ECONOMIC BATCH SIZE

The last example shows that there is an intermediate batch size for which the total cost is a minimum. A simple theory for determining the optimum size of order can be constructed from the following assumptions:

1. The demand is steady;
2. The supplier is reliable;
3. The ordering cost is the same for all batch sizes;
4. The price per item is constant (no discounts for bulk buying);
5. There is sufficient ordering and storage capacity.

The first two assumptions lead to a variation in stock level of the kind shown in Fig. 8.1. The level falls steadily until the stocks are exhausted. A new batch is then received and the process is repeated.

Figure 8.1

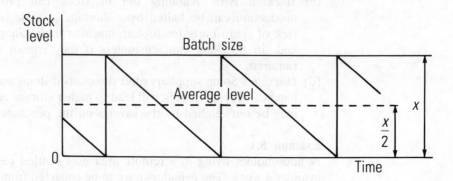

The notation used in the analysis varies from one book to another. The following symbols are used here:

x = batch size or order quantity;
Q = quantity used per annum;
p = unit price of each item;
i = storage cost per annum as a fraction of the average value of the stocks held;
S = cost of placing each order.

Although the symbols are defined in terms of annual costs the results can be used on a monthly or weekly basis provided they are applied consistently. From Fig. 8.1 it can be seen that the average stock level is $\frac{1}{2}x$ and the storage cost is therefore $\frac{1}{2}xpi$. The number of orders placed during the period of a year, month or week is Q/x and the corresponding cost is QS/x. The total cost C (storage plus ordering) is therefore given by

$$C = \tfrac{1}{2}xpi + \frac{QS}{x} \qquad [8.1]$$

Differentiating to find the minimum cost, we obtain

$$\frac{dC}{dx} = \tfrac{1}{2}pi - \frac{QS}{x^2}$$

For maximum or minimum this equals zero and

$$\frac{QS}{x^2} = \tfrac{1}{2}pi$$

or

$$x = \sqrt{\frac{2QS}{pi}}$$

[8.2]

The positive root corresponds to a minimum and this value of x is the batch size for which the total cost is least. It is called the economic batch size or economic order quantity.

The corresponding minimum cost is obtained by substituting this value of x in Eq. 8.1. It gives

$$\begin{aligned}
C_{min} &= \tfrac{1}{2}pi\sqrt{\frac{2QS}{pi}} + QS\sqrt{\frac{pi}{2QS}} \\
&= \tfrac{1}{2}\sqrt{(2piQS)} + \tfrac{1}{2}\sqrt{(2piQS)} \\
&= \sqrt{(2piQS)}
\end{aligned}$$

[8.3]

The result shows that, at the economic batch size, the storage and ordering costs are equal. Figure 8.2 shows the variation of the storage, ordering and total costs with batch size. The relationships are similar to those for the inverse cost model discussed in Chapter 1 (see section 1.9 and Fig. 1.9).

Figure 8.2

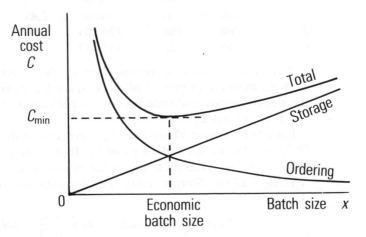

Example 8.2
In a large office there is a steady demand for typing paper at the rate of 40 reams a week. A stationery supplier delivers weekly and will supply the paper at an all-in cost of £12.00 per ream against an official company order. The cost of placing each order is £18.00 including all the paperwork and checking the delivery, irrespective of the batch size. The storage cost amounts to 0.3 per cent per week of the average value of the stocks held.

Find the economic batch size for this item, the corresponding stockholding cost and the frequency at which orders should be placed.

228 STOCK CONTROL

Solution

In the notation given above and working in £ and weeks, $Q = 40$, $p = 12.00$, $i = 0.3/100 = 0.003$ and $S = 18.00$. From Eq. 8.1 the economic batch size is

$$x = \sqrt{\frac{2 \times 40 \times 18.00}{12.00 \times 0.003}} = \sqrt{(40\,000)} = \mathbf{200}$$

The corresponding cost (storage + ordering) is, from Eq. 8.3,

$$C_{min} = \sqrt{(2 \times 12.00 \times 0.003 \times 40 \times 18.00)}$$
$$= \sqrt{51.84} = \textbf{£7.20 per week}$$

With a batch size of 200 and a demand of 40 per week an order should be placed **every 5 weeks**.

Alternatively, we can use a tabulation method similar to that in the solution to Example 8.1. Taking a range of ordering intervals from 1 to 6 weeks, we obtain the following:

Interval between orders (weeks)	Batch size	Average stock Level	Average stock Value (£)	Storage	Ordering	Total
1	40	20	240.00	0.72	18.00	18.72
2	80	40	480.00	1.44	9.00	10.44
3	120	60	720.00	2.16	6.00	8.16
4	160	80	960.00	2.88	4.50	7.38
5	**200**	**100**	**1200.00**	**3.60**	**3.60**	**7.20**
6	240	120	1440.00	4.32	3.00	7.32

The table confirms the results given by the formulae. They can also be deduced from the properties of this cost model, namely that the product of the weekly storage and ordering costs is constant and at the economic batch size they are equal.

For a batch size of 40 and one order every week the weekly storage cost is £0.72 and the weekly ordering cost is £18.00. The product of these costs is $(0.72 \times 18.00) = 12.96$. Hence, at the economic batch size, each is equal to $\sqrt{12.96} = £3.60$. Storage costs are proportional to the batch size and therefore:

$$\text{Economic batch size} = 40 \times \frac{3.60}{0.72} = \mathbf{200}$$

as before.

8.5 COMPUTER PROGRAM FOR ECONOMIC BATCH SIZE

A BASIC program for determining economic batch size is given in Fig. 8.3. It includes some lines that are needed later for calculations involving discounts and batch manufacturing. The program offers a choice of units for money and time. The batch size is calculated to the nearest whole number and the other results – the interval between orders, the frequency of orders and the costs – to two places of decimals.

Figure 8.3

```
10 REM    M$,T$          COST AND TIME UNITS
20 REM    Z              MENU CONTROL VARIABLE
30 REM    D,T,Y          DISCOUNT NUMBER, THRESHOLD AND RATE
40 REM    C1,C2,C3,C     STORAGE, ORDERING COSTS, DISCOUNT SAVING, TOTAL COST
50 REM    X1,C4,C5,Y1    VALUES OF X,C,C3,Y USED IN DISCOUNT CALCULATIONS
60 PRINT "-------------------"
70 PRINT "ECONOMIC BATCH SIZE"
80 PRINT "-------------------"
90 PRINT
100 PRINT "ENTER COST UNIT (£,$)"
110 INPUT M$
120 PRINT "ENTER TIME UNIT (WEEK, MONTH, YEAR)"
130 INPUT T$
140 PRINT
150 PRINT "ENTER CALCULATION TYPE BY NUMBER"
160 PRINT "PLACING ORDERS . . . . . . . . 1"
170 PRINT "BATCH MANUFACTURING. . . . . . 2"
180 INPUT Z
190 IF Z<>1 AND Z<>2 THEN PRINT "<ERROR>":GOTO 140
200 PRINT
210 PRINT "ENTER:  DEMAND PER ";T$
220 INPUT Q
230 PRINT "UNIT PRICE OR MANUFACTURING COST IN ";M$
240 INPUT P
250 PRINT "STORAGE COST PER ";T$;" AS PERCENTAGE OF"
260 PRINT "AVERAGE VALUE OF STOCKS HELD"
270 INPUT I
280 I=I/100
290 PRINT "ORDERING/CHANGEOVER COST PER BATCH IN ";M$
300 INPUT S
310 D=0:C3=0:Y=0
320 IF Z=1 THEN GOTO 340
330 GOSUB 900
340 X=SQR(2*Q*S/(P*I))
350 IF Z=2 THEN GOTO 380
360 PRINT "NUMBER OF DISCOUNT LEVELS (0 IF NONE)"
370 INPUT D
380 GOSUB 800
390 IF D<>0 THEN GOSUB 600
400 REM   DISPLAY RESULTS
410 PRINT:PRINT "RESULTS:"
420 PRINT "ECONOMIC BATCH SIZE    = ";X
430 PRINT "ORDER/BATCH INTERVAL   = ";INT(100/N+0.5)/100;" ";T$;"S"
440 PRINT "NO. OF ORDERS/BATCHES  = ";INT(100*N+0.5)/100;" PER ";T$
450 PRINT "COSTS (";M$;" PER ";T$;"):"
460 PRINT "  STORAGE             = ";C1
470 PRINT "  ORDERING/CHANGEOVER = ";C2
480 IF Z=2 OR D=0 THEN GOTO 500
490 PRINT "  DISCOUNT            = ";C3
500 PRINT "  TOTAL (NET)         = ";C
510 PRINT "------------------------------------------"
520 END

800 REM     COST CALCULATION
810 X=INT(X+0.5)
820 N=Q/X
830 C1=INT(X*P*(1-Y)*I*50+0.5)/100
840 C2=INT(N*S*100+0.5)/100
850 C=C1+C2-C3
860 RETURN
```

The notation of section 8.4 is used for the input values, except that all symbols are in upper case. Lines 10–90 define some additional variables and print the heading.

Lines 100–140 call for the units in which costs and time are to be measured. Note that on some computer/printer combinations the £ sign is obtained with the hash (#) key.

Lines 150–200 offer the choice of ordering or batch manufacturing calculations. At this stage the second choice is not available. Line 190 ensures that a valid response is given.

Lines 210–300 call for the demand and cost figures in the units selected earlier. Line 310 specifies some initial values for variables that are used later.

For ordering calculations the program jumps from line 320 to 340 where the economic batch size is determined using the formula of Eq. 8.2.

Lines 360–370 call for the number of discount levels. At present the response is zero and, at line 380, the program goes to the subroutine at line 800. This evaluates the costs and the results are displayed by lines 400–510, the program ending at line 520.

In the subroutine, the economic batch size is rounded to the nearest whole number in line 810. Line 820 determines the frequency of orders and lines 830–850 calculate the storage, ordering and total costs, each to two places of decimals.

Figure 8.4

```
-------------------
ECONOMIC BATCH SIZE
-------------------

ENTER COST UNIT (£,$)
?£
ENTER TIME UNIT (WEEK, MONTH, YEAR)
?WEEK

ENTER CALCULATION TYPE BY NUMBER
PLACING ORDERS . . . . . . . . 1
BATCH MANUFACTURING. . . . . . 2
?1

ENTER:  DEMAND PER WEEK
?40
UNIT PRICE OR MANUFACTURING COST IN £
?12
STORAGE COST PER WEEK AS PERCENTAGE OF
AVERAGE VALUE OF STOCKS HELD
?0.3
ORDERING/CHANGEOVER COST PER BATCH IN £
?18
NUMBER OF DISCOUNT LEVELS (0 IF NONE)
?0

RESULTS:
ECONOMIC BATCH SIZE   = 200
ORDER/BATCH INTERVAL  = 5 WEEKS
NO. OF ORDERS/BATCHES = 0.2 PER WEEK
COSTS (£ PER WEEK):
   STORAGE            = 3.6
   ORDERING/CHANGEOVER = 3.6
   TOTAL (NET)        = 7.2
-----------------------------------------
```

Figure 8.4 shows the printout obtained when the program was run for the data of Example 8.2.

8.6 THE EFFECT OF DISCOUNTS

Many suppliers offer discounts for large orders and these should be taken into account when determining the economic batch size. Suppose (Fig. 8.5) two levels of discount are offered at thresholds above the economic batch size in the no-discount case. By increasing the batch size to the minimum value that qualifies for a discount, the saving in the purchase price may outweigh the increase in the combined ordering and storage cost. No simple formula exists to cover all possibilities and each example must be tackled from first principles.

Figure 8.5

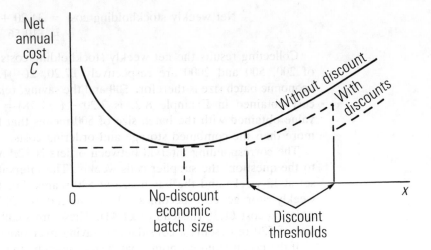

Example 8.3

Suppose, in Example 8.2, the supplier offers a discount of 2.5 per cent on orders of 500 or more and 5 per cent on orders of 2000 or more. What is now the economic batch size and what saving is made compared with the no-discount result?

Solution

Using the demand and cost figures of Example 8.2 we have, for a batch size of 500:

Discount per item	$= \dfrac{2.5}{100} \times 12.00 = £0.30$
Discount price	$= 12.00 - 0.30 = £11.70$
Average stock level	$= \dfrac{500}{2} = 250$
Ordering interval	$= \dfrac{500}{40} = 12.5$ weeks

Hence,

Weekly storage cost	$= 250 \times 11.70 \times \dfrac{0.3}{100}$
	$= £8.78$
Weekly ordering cost	$= \dfrac{18.00}{12.5} = £1.44$
Weekly discount	$= 40 \times 0.30 = £12.00$

and

$$\text{Net weekly stockholding cost} = 8.78 + 1.44 - 12.00$$
$$= £(-)1.78$$

Similarly, for a batch size of 2000, the discount per item is £0.60, the discount price is £11.40, the average stock level is 1000 and the interval between orders is 50 weeks.

With these results the weekly storage cost is £34.20, the weekly ordering cost is £0.36 and the weekly discount is £24.00. Thus

$$\text{Net weekly stockholding cost} = 34.20 + 0.36 - 24.00$$
$$= £10.56$$

Collecting results the net weekly stockholding costs for ordering batches of 200, 500 and 2000 are respectively £7.20, £(−)1.78 and £10.56. The economic batch size is therefore **500** and the saving, relative to the minimum cost obtained in Example 8.2, is 7.20 − (−1.78) = **£8.98**. The negative value obtained with the batch size of 500 means that the discount is worth more than the combined storage and ordering costs.

The corresponding interval between orders is 12.5 weeks but, according to the question, the supplier calls weekly. The interval should therefore be set at 13 weeks and the batch size at 520 reams. For this size of order the weekly storage cost becomes £9.13 (instead of £8.78) and the weekly ordering cost £1.38 (instead of £1.44). These are small changes and a batch size of 520 represents a considerable saving over batches of 200 and 2000.

If the no-discount economic batch size, given by the formula of Eq. 8.2, is below the threshold at which the first discount is offered the method used in this solution is usually adequate. There are two exceptions and these are illustrated in Fig. 8.6.

Figure 8.6

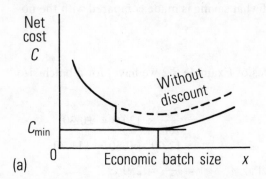

(a)

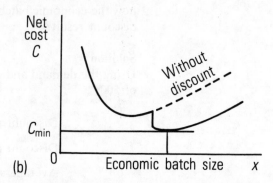

(b)

In Fig. 8.6(a) the discount becomes available at a batch size below the value given by the formula. In this case the formula must be evaluated again with the price p reduced by the amount of the discount. The second possibility is shown in Fig. 8.6(b). Here, the economic batch size without a discount is just below the discount threshold, but the reduction in unit cost is sufficient to make it a little above. In this case the formula of Eq. 8.2 must again be evaluated, using the reduced unit price.

Figure 8.7

```
600 REM      DISCOUNT CALCULATION
610 X1=X:C4=C:C5=0:Y1=0
620 PRINT "FOR EACH DISCOUNT GIVE MINIMUM BATCH
630 PRINT "SIZE AND PERCENTAGE PRICE REDUCTION
640 FOR K=1 TO D
650 PRINT "---DISCOUNT NO. ";K
660 INPUT T,Y
670 C3=INT(Q*P*Y+0.5)/100
680 Y=Y/100
690 X=SQR(2*Q*S/((1-Y)*P*I))
700 IF X<T THEN X=T
710 GOSUB 800
720 IF C4>C THEN C4=C:X1=X:C5=C3:Y1=Y
730 NEXT K
740 X=X1:C3=C5:Y=Y1
750 GOSUB 800
760 RETURN
```

The computer program of Fig. 8.3 can be extended to allow for discounts by adding the subroutine shown in Fig. 8.7. With many machines the lines may be added to the end of the program and the computer will sort them into the correct numerical order. Other machines will not do this and the new lines must be entered in the correct numerical sequence.

Line 610 sets the initial values of some additional variables used for storing intermediate results. Lines 620–660 call for the threshold batch size and percentage reduction in price for each of the discounts. The calculation in lines 670–700 determines whether the economic batch size for the current level of discount occurs at the threshold size.

Line 710 calls up the cost calculation subroutine and line 720 records the details if the cost is less than the previous best. Line 730 causes the program to loop until all the discount levels have been considered and line 750 ensures that the cost calculation is repeated for the optimum batch size. Line 760 returns the computer to the main program and the results are displayed as before.

Figure 8.8 shows the printout that was obtained when the expanded program was run with the data of Example 8.3.

Figure 8.8

```
--------------------
ECONOMIC BATCH SIZE
--------------------

ENTER COST UNIT (£,$)
?£
ENTER TIME UNIT (WEEK, MONTH, YEAR)
?WEEK

ENTER CALCULATION TYPE BY NUMBER
PLACING ORDERS . . . . . . . . 1
BATCH MANUFACTURING. . . . . . 2
?1

ENTER:  DEMAND PER WEEK
?40
UNIT PRICE OR MANUFACTURING COST IN £
?12
STORAGE COST PER WEEK AS PERCENTAGE OF
AVERAGE VALUE OF STOCKS HELD
?0.3
ORDERING/CHANGEOVER COST PER BATCH IN £
?18
NUMBER OF DISCOUNT LEVELS (0 IF NONE)
?2
FOR EACH DISCOUNT GIVE MINIMUM BATCH
SIZE AND PERCENTAGE PRICE REDUCTION
---DISCOUNT NO. 1
?500
?2.5
---DISCOUNT NO. 2
?2000
?5

RESULTS:
ECONOMIC BATCH SIZE   = 500
ORDER/BATCH INTERVAL  = 12.5 WEEKS
NO. OF ORDERS/BATCHES = 8E-2 PER WEEK
COSTS (£ PER WEEK):
   STORAGE            = 8.78
   ORDERING/CHANGEOVER = 1.44
   DISCOUNT           = 12
   TOTAL (NET)        = -1.78
------------------------------------------
```

8.7 BATCH PRODUCTION

In manufacturing industries it often proves economical to make products in batches and then to draw from stock as required. If the batch is produced very rapidly and the demand for the product is uniform, the stock level variation is similar to that shown in Fig. 8.1.

The corresponding costs are of the same two kinds as those encountered when stock is bought and stored. Each time a batch is made there is a setting-up or change-over cost equivalent to the ordering and delivery cost. In addition there is the storage cost and this is calculated, as before, on the average value of the stocks held. The economic batch size can therefore be determined by the formula of Eq. 8.2 with the ordering cost S being taken as the change-over or setting-up cost.

Example 8.4

A bicycle manufacturer finds that there is a steady demand for a particular machine at the rate of 4000 a year. The unit cost of manufacture is £80.00 and the storage cost is 24 per cent per annum of the average value of the stocks held. Production is to be organized on a batch basis and the setting-up cost is £600.00 for each batch.

What is the economic batch size, and the annual setting-up and storage costs, if the production rate is

(a) very large compared to the sales rate;
(b) 7200 a year?

Solution

(a) With a very rapid production rate the economic batch size is given by the formula of Eq. 8.2, with S being the setting-up cost. Working in £ and year units, $Q = 4000$, $p = 80$, $i = 0.24$ and $S = 600$. Hence, the economic batch size is given by

$$x = \sqrt{\frac{2QS}{pi}} = \sqrt{\frac{2 \times 4000 \times 600}{80 \times 0.24}} = \mathbf{500}$$

This corresponds to eight batches a year and an average stock level of 250. Thus

$$\text{Annual setting-up cost} = 8 \times 600 = \mathbf{£4800}$$

$$\text{Annual storage cost} = 250 \times 80 \times \frac{24}{100} = \mathbf{£4800}$$

 Figure 8.9

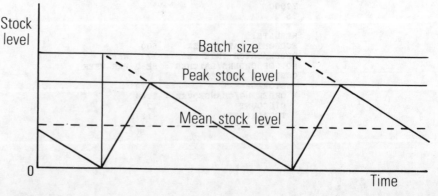

(b) If the batch is not produced 'instantaneously' the stock level variation is modified to that shown in Fig. 8.9. The peak level of stock is now lower than the batch size because part of the batch is sold during the production period. With the values given for the demand and production rates, the proportion of the batch sold in this period is 4000/7200 or 5/9 and the maximum stock level is reduced to $(1 - \frac{5}{9}) = \frac{4}{9}$ of the batch size.

The average stock level is reduced in the same proportion and this can be allowed for by a corresponding reduction in the denominator of the formula. The calculation for the economic batch size is now

$$x = \sqrt{\frac{2 \times 4000 \times 600}{80 \times 0.24 \times (4/9)}} = \mathbf{750}$$

This corresponds to 5.333 batches a year or one batch every 10 weeks approximately. During each production period the number of bicycles sold is $\frac{5}{9}$ of the batch size (750), approximately 417. The peak level of stock is therefore $750 - 417 = 333$, and the average level is one-half of this value, 166.5. Using these results,

$$\text{Annual setting-up cost} = 5.333 \times 600 = \mathbf{£3200}$$
$$\text{Annual storage cost} = 166.5 \times 80 \times \frac{24}{100} = \mathbf{£3200}$$

Figure 8.10

```
900 REM      BATCH MANUFACTURING
910 PRINT "ENTER MANUFACTURING RATE PER ";T$
920 PRINT "(0 IF VERY LARGE)"
930 INPUT R
940 IF R<>0 THEN I=I*(1-Q/R)
950 RETURN
```

The computer program for economic batch size given in Figs. 8.3 and 8.7 can be extended to cover batch production by adding the lines shown in Fig. 8.10. These form a short subroutine that is called up from the main program if the batch manufacturing option is selected. Lines 910–920 call for the manufacturing rate and the response 0 is required, rather illogically, for a very large rate. This will ensure in line 940 that the calculation is continued in the main program without modification. Otherwise, the effect of a finite production rate is achieved by modifying the interest rate in line 940.

The printout of Fig. 8.11 was obtained when the extended program was run with the data of Example 8.4(b).

8.8 MANUFACTURING CYCLE

The analysis of section 8.6 applies to a single product, the production facility being idle between the manufacturing of one batch and the next. Suppose that several products are made in batches on the same production line in a manufacturing cycle. There are so many possible variations that numerical examples should be worked from first principles.

Example 8.5
A hi-fi manufacturer makes three types of midi units known as the *Mozart*,

Figure 8.11

```
---------------------
ECONOMIC BATCH SIZE
---------------------

ENTER COST UNIT (£,$)
?£
ENTER TIME UNIT (WEEK, MONTH, YEAR)
?YEAR

ENTER CALCULATION TYPE BY NUMBER
PLACING ORDERS . . . . . . . .1
BATCH MANUFACTURING. . . . . .2
?2

ENTER:  DEMAND PER YEAR
?4000
UNIT PRICE OR MANUFACTURING COST IN £
?80
STORAGE COST PER YEAR AS PERCENTAGE OF
AVERAGE VALUE OF STOCKS HELD
?24
ORDERING/CHANGEOVER COST PER BATCH IN £
?600
ENTER MANUFACTURING RATE PER YEAR
(0 IF VERY LARGE)
?7200

RESULTS:
ECONOMIC BATCH SIZE   = 750
ORDER/BATCH INTERVAL  = 0.19 YEARS
NO. OF ORDERS/BATCHES = 5.33 PER YEAR
COSTS (£ PER YEAR):
   STORAGE            = 3200
   ORDERING/CHANGEOVER = 3200
   TOTAL (NET)        = 6400
----------------------------------------
```

Beethoven and *Mahler*. There is a single assembly line and production is organized on a batch basis so that the different types follow each other in a manufacturing cycle.

The quantities and costs are as follows:

	Sales (per week)	Production rate in isolation (per week)	Cost per item (£)
Mozart	250	750	60
Beethoven	150	600	100
Mahler	100	240	150

The stockholding cost is $\frac{1}{2}$ per cent per week of the average cost of the stocks held, and the cost of changing the assembly line from one product to another is £400.

Determine the economical manufacturing cycle period in terms of stockholding and changeover costs, and the corresponding costs involved.

Solution

For the Mozart model the sales and production rates are 250 and 750 respectively. Hence the proportion of the time that must be devoted to making this model is $250/750 = \frac{1}{3}$. The corresponding fractions for the Beethoven and Mahler models are $\frac{1}{4}$ and $\frac{5}{12}$. The three fractions total 1 and, in consequence, there is no idle time.

The variation in stock level for each of the three models is shown in Fig. 8.12. There can be no idle time and the change-over from one model to the next is assumed to be instantaneous.

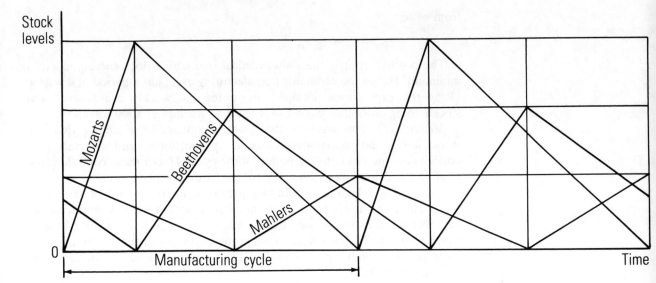

Stock levels

Mozarts

Beethovens

Mahlers

0

Manufacturing cycle

Time

Figure 8.12

Method (a) Working from first principles, let x weeks be the time of the complete manufacturing cycle. Since there are three change-overs per cycle the total change-over cost is $3 \times £400 = £1200$ and

$$\text{Weekly changeover cost} = £\frac{1200}{x}.$$

In order to meet sales demands the numbers of units to be made in the cycle are $250x$ Mozarts, $150x$ Beethovens and $100x$ Mahlers. Since the sales rates for the three models are respectively $\frac{1}{3}$, $\frac{1}{4}$ and $\frac{5}{12}$ of the manufacturing rates the peak stock levels are $\frac{2}{3}$, $\frac{3}{4}$ and $\frac{7}{12}$ of the three batch sizes. The average stock levels will be half as much, namely $250x/3$ Mozarts, $450x/8$ Beethovens and $700x/24$ Mahlers. Combining each of these values with the corresponding cost and using the given stockholding cost of $\frac{1}{2}$ per cent per week, we obtain

$$\begin{aligned}\text{Weekly stockholding cost} &= \frac{\frac{1}{2}}{100}\left(\frac{250x}{3} \times 60 + \frac{450x}{8} \times 100 + \frac{700x}{24} \times 150\right) \\ &= \frac{\frac{1}{2}}{100}\left(\frac{120\,000x + 135\,000x + 105\,000x}{24}\right) \\ &= £75x\end{aligned}$$

Working in £ units, the total weekly cost C is therefore

$$C = \frac{1200}{x} + 75x$$

Differentiating to find a minimum (or maximum),

$$\frac{\mathrm{d}C}{\mathrm{d}x} = -\frac{1200}{x^2} + 75$$

and, equating this result to zero,

$$x^2 = \frac{1200}{75} = 16$$

from which

$$x = \pm 4.$$

The positive root is the only practical one and it does correspond to a minimum. Hence the economic manufacturing cycle has a period of **4 weeks**. Using the expressions obtained above for the weekly change-over and stockholding costs the result $x = 4$ leads to a value of **£300** for each.

Method (b) The answers can also be obtained by noting that the stockholding and change-over costs are proportional, and inversely proportional, respectively to the period of the cycle. Under these conditions the total cost is a minimum when the two separate costs are equal.

We start by selecting an arbitrary period and it is convenient to take 12 weeks since this leads to an exact number of weeks for the production of each batch. The proportions of the total time required for the Mozarts, Beethovens and Mahlers were found at the beginning of the solution to be $\frac{1}{3}$, $\frac{1}{4}$ and $\frac{5}{12}$ respectively. With a total of 12 weeks these lead to batch times of 4, 3 and 5 weeks.

The change-over cost per period is $3 \times £400 = £1200$ and, for a 12-week period,

$$\text{Weekly changeover cost} = 1200/12 = £100$$

In a 4-week production period the number of Mozarts made is $4 \times 750 = 3000$ and the number sold is $4 \times 250 = 1000$. Hence the peak stock level is 2000 and the average is 1000.

In the same way, the average stock level of Beethovens is $3(600 - 150)/2 = 675$ and, for Mahlers it is 350. With these values,

$$\text{Weekly stockholding cost} = \frac{\frac{1}{2}}{100} (1000 \times 60 + 675 \times 100 + 350 \times 150)$$
$$= £900$$

The product of the weekly change-over and stockholding costs is the same for all cycle lengths and, since they are equal at the optimum conditions, we can say

$$\text{Cost of each at the economic level} = \sqrt{(100 \times 900)} = £300$$

The stockholding cost is proportional to the cycle period and, by proportion,

$$\text{Economic manufacturing cycle period} = \frac{300}{900} \times 12 = \textbf{4 weeks}$$

as before.

8.9 RE-ORDER SYSTEMS

The variation in stock level shown in Fig. 8.1 is based on the assumptions that demand is uniform and the supplier is reliable. In practice the demand is liable to fluctuate and the stock level variation is more complex (Fig. 8.13). Allowance must also be made for *lead time*, the period between

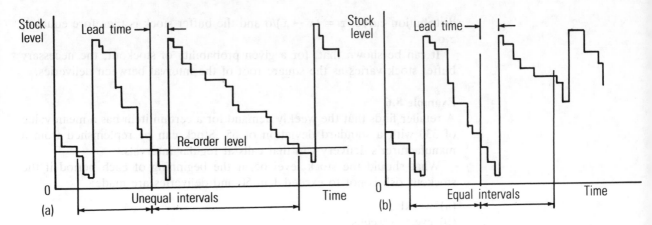

Figure 8.13

taking a decision to order stock and having the items available to meet demand.

There are two general approaches to the matter of reordering. One is the *two-bin* or *re-order level* (ROL) system. Suppose the stock is held in two bins, not necessarily the same size, and that demand is met by drawing from the first until it is empty. At this stage we place an order for new stock and, until it is delivered, we meet demand from the second bin. It should therefore be large enough to meet the requirements during the lead time period. The size of the order must be chosen to replenish both bins. Separate containers are not necessary and the two-bin concept can be achieved by setting a stock level which triggers the placing of an order (Fig. 8.13(a)). Demand will fluctuate during the lead time period and successive orders will not produce exactly the same peak level of stock.

An alternative to the re-order level system is the *fixed-interval* approach (Fig. 8.13(b)). In this system orders are placed at regular intervals but the size of the order varies, depending on the stock level at the time. It is sometimes known as the *re-order cycle* (ROC) system.

For a single item in isolation the reorder level system is likely to prove more economical. However, where several items are purchased together – during a weekly visit to a supermarket, for instance – the fixed interval system may be cheaper. If demand is uniform the two systems are equivalent; successive orders are of the same size and are placed at the same intervals.

8.10 BUFFER STOCKS

If demand fluctuates the stock level may fall to zero while we are waiting for a delivery of new stock. The probability of being out of stock, or *stockout* as it is called, is related to the size of the buffer stock. If the mean demand is large compared with the standard deviation, it is usual to assume that the pattern of demand follows the normal or Gaussian distribution. From a table of one-tail areas we can determine the necessary buffer stock for a given stockout risk.

If x is the level of stock at the beginning of the period and $\bar{x}$ is the mean demand, the buffer stock is $x - \bar{x}$. In the usual notation for the normal distribution curve, $z = (x - \bar{x})/\sigma$ and the buffer stock is therefore equal to $z.\sigma$.

It can be shown that, for a given probability of stockout, the necessary buffer stock varies as the square root of the interval between deliveries.

Example 8.6
A retailer finds that the weekly demand for a certain item has a mean value of 330 with a standard deviation of 55. Stock can be replenished from a manufacturer's delivery van that calls at regular intervals.

What should the stock level be at the beginning of each period if the stockout risk is not to exceed 1 in 50 and deliveries are made:

(a) weekly;
(b) every 3 weeks?

Solution
(a) A stockout risk of 1 in 50 corresponds to a probability, and hence a one-tail area, of 0.02. From Table C.3 the corresponding value of z is 2.054. The buffer stock required is therefore:

$$x - \bar{x} = z.\sigma = 2.054 \times 55 = 113$$

At the beginning of each week the required stock level is $330 + 113 =$ **443**.

(b) Using the square root rule the buffer stock required for a 3-week period is $113 \times \sqrt{3} = 196$. The mean demand is $3 \times 330 = 990$ and the initial stock level should be $990 + 196 =$ **1186**.

8.11 BUFFER STOCKS WITH POISSON DEMAND DISTRIBUTION

It is reasonable to use the normal distribution when the mean demand is large compared with the standard deviation. With a small mean demand the Poisson distribution is more appropriate. For a given mean demand, m, the probability, p, of the demand, r, occurring is given by the formula in section 6.18, namely

$$p = \frac{e^{-m}m^r}{r!}$$

In particular the probability of the demand being zero is e^{-m}. The probabilities of successive demands (1, 2, 3 . . .) can then be calculated in turn by multiplying this result by m/r.

Example 8.7
In a medical practice the mean demand for a certain vaccine is five per week. Assuming a Poisson type distribution what buffer stock is needed at the beginning of each week if the risk of stockout is not to exceed 1 in 30?

Solution
With a mean demand $m = 5$, the probability of the demand being zero is

$$p_0 = e^{-m} = e^{-5} = 0.006738$$

It follows that the probability of the demand being greater than zero is $1 - 0.006738 = 0.993262$. The following table gives the corresponding probabilities for other demands, rounded to four places of decimals. Each value in the second column is found by the iterative method given above. It is then subtracted from the value in the third column of the previous line to give the new value in that column.

		Probability of:
Demand	This demand	More than this demand
0	0.0067	0.9933
1	0.0337	0.9596
2	0.0842	0.8754
3	0.1404	0.7350
4	0.1755	0.5595
5	0.1755	0.3840
6	0.1462	0.2378
7	0.1044	0.1334
8	0.0653	0.0681
9	0.0363	0.0318

A risk of 1 in 30 corresponds to a probability of 0.0333. The table is continued until the figure in the third column falls below this value. It is reached with a weekly demand of 9 and hence a buffer stock of $9 - 5 = $ **4**.

Figure 8.14

```
 10 PRINT "------------------------------------------"
 20 PRINT "STOCKOUT RISK FOR POISSON TYPE DEMAND"
 30 PRINT "------------------------------------------"
 40 PRINT "ENTER MEAN DEMAND"
 50 INPUT M
 60 PRINT "ENTER BUFFER STOCK, STOCKOUT RISK"
 70 PRINT "(-1 FOR THE UNKNOWN)"
 80 INPUT B,R
 90 IF B<>-1 AND R<>-1 THEN PRINT "<ERROR>":GOTO 60
100 P=1/EXP(M)
110 P1=1-P
120 X=0
130 X=X+1
140 P=P*M/X
150 P1=P1-P
160 IF B=-1 AND P1<=R THEN PRINT "BUFFER STOCK = ";X-M:GOTO 190
170 IF R=-1 AND X>=M+B THEN PRINT "STOCKOUT RISK = ";INT(P1*1E4+0.5)/1E4:GOTO 190
180 GOTO 130
190 PRINT "------------------------------------------"
200 END
```

These results can also be obtained using the computer program for the Poisson distribution given in Fig. 6.18. It is convenient to have a separate buffer stock program, and a suitable listing is given in Fig. 8.14. If the buffer stock is specified it will determine the probability of stockout and vice versa. The mean demand, buffer stock and stockout risk are denoted by M, B and R. The probabilities of the demand being respectively equal to X, and greater than X, are P and P1. Lines 10–80 print the heading and call for the values of M, B and R. The value -1 must be assigned to either B or R; otherwise an error message is printed at line 90. The calculation is carried out in lines 100–180 and the program loops between lines 130 and 180 until the required result is obtained and printed at line 160 or 170.

The program should not be used for large values of the mean demand M, lest the numerical range of the computer is exceeded at line 100. If the result for B is not a whole number it should be rounded up to the next integer.

Figure 8.15

```
-----------------------------------------
STOCKOUT RISK FOR POISSON TYPE DEMAND
-----------------------------------------
ENTER MEAN DEMAND
?8
ENTER BUFFER STOCK, STOCKOUT RISK
(-1 FOR THE UNKNOWN)
?3
?-1
STOCKOUT RISK = 0.1119
-----------------------------------------
```

Figure 8.15 shows the printout obtained when the program was used to find the stockout risk for a mean demand of 8 and a buffer stock of 3.

8.12 SUMMARY

Stock (or inventory) can be classified as active, buffer (or safety) and strategic. The purpose of stock control is to ensure that goods are available when required and at the least total cost.

When demand is uniform and the supplier is reliable the storage cost and ordering/delivery cost averaged over a given time period are respectively proportional to, and inversely proportional to, the batch size. Under these conditions, and in the absence of discounts, the economic batch size is that which makes these two costs equal. The square root formula offers a direct method of calculating it.

A discount on the unit price for larger orders may outweigh the increase in the combined storage and ordering/delivery cost, but this depends on the figures in each case.

The optimum quantity for batch production can be obtained by similar methods, the ordering cost being replaced by the change-over or setting-up cost. If the manufacturing rate is high compared with the sales rate, the square root formula can be used without modification. With a finite production rate, some stock will be sold during the manufacturing period and the formula must be adjusted to allow for the resulting reduction in the peak stock level.

The two principal reordering systems are based on fixed quantities or fixed intervals. The fixed quantity system is known as the ROL or two-bin system. In this, an order is placed when the stock level falls to a specified value. In the fixed interval, or periodic review, system successive orders are placed at equal intervals but the size of the order depends on the stock level at the time.

The level of buffer stocks is set to bring the risk of stockout within a specified value. With a large mean demand the variation is assumed to follow the normal or Gaussian distribution but with a small value, the Poisson distribution is used.

REFERENCE

1. Hall R W 1989 *Zero Inventories* Dow Jones-Irwin

BIBLIOGRAPHY

Battersby A 1970 *A Guide to Stock Control* 2nd edn Pitman
Lewis C D 1981 *Scientific Inventory Control* 2nd edn Butterworths
Thomas A B 1980 *Stock Control in Manuafacturing Industries* 2nd edn
Gower Press

PROBLEMS

1. In a workshop stores there is a steady demand for a small component at the rate of 800 per week. The item costs 50 p and the storage cost is reckoned to be 26 per cent per annum of the average value of the stocks held. If the ordering and delivery cost is £9.00 per order, how many should be ordered at a time? What is the frequency at which the orders should be placed and what are the weekly ordering and storing costs?
Answer   2400; every 3 weeks; £3.00 each.

2. What are the results in question 1 if the demand increases to 7200 per week?
Answer   7200; every week; £9.00.

3. What are the results in question 1 for a demand of 800 per week if the unit price is increased to 90 p?
Answer   Approximately 1800; every 2.25 weeks; £4.00.

4. Suppose, in question 1, the supplier offers a discount of 1.5 per cent on the price of 50 p for orders of 10 000 or more. Should the size and frequency of orders be changed? What is the minimum discount that will justify ordering in batches of 10 000?
Answer   No; about 1.75 per cent.

5. A jewellery manufacturer uses gold at the rate of 750 ounces a year. It costs £300 per ounce and, because of high insurance charges, the delivery of each order costs £180. If the storage costs amount to 25 per cent per annum of the average value of the stocks held, what is the economic ordering quantity and the annual costs of delivery and storage?
Answer   60 ounces; £2250 each.

6. A travel agency presents each of its customers with a gift pack costing £3.00. The demand is steady at 9000 per year. The ordering and delivery cost is £12.00 per order and the storage cost, including overheads, is reckoned to be 20 per cent per annum of the average value of the stocks held.

How many orders should be placed each year and of what size? What are

244   **STOCK CONTROL**

the annual costs of delivery and storage for this item?
Answer   15; 600; £180 each.

7.   (a) A manufacturer buys in a component with a unit cost of £1.20.
There is a steady demand within the firm at the rate of 4000 per year, the
ordering and delivery cost is £4.00 for each batch and the cost of storing
stocks is 15 per cent per annum of their average value. What is the economic
batch size?

(b) Two suppliers offer the component at the same basic price but with
different discounts. One offers a discount of 3 per cent on orders of 1000 or
more and the other offers 4 per cent on orders of 2000 or more. Which
should be used with an annual consumption of 4000? At what level of
consumption does it pay to order from the supplier offering the larger
discount?
Answer   (a) 422; (b) the one offering 3 per cent on orders of 1000; 6100.

8.   A manufacturer of batteries for calculators finds that there is a steady
demand for a particular type at the rate of 60 000 per year. The unit cost of
manufacture is £1.20 and production is to be organized on a batch basis, the
setting-up cost being £50 per batch. The cost of holding stocks is 20 per cent
per annum of their average value. Find the economic manufacturing batch
size and the corresponding number of batches per year, assuming that the
production rate is

(a) very large compared with the sales rate;
(b) 200 000 per annum.

What is the combined annual setting-up and holding cost in each case?
Answer   (a) 5000; 12; £1200; (b) approximately 6000; 10; £1000.

9.   The Tardy Timepiece Company is diversifying. Its 'Gardenpride' range
now includes three products – sundials, weather-vanes and flag-poles. The
weekly sales and production rate (in isolation), together with the unit cost of
manufacture, for each product, are given in the following table:

Product	Sales (per week)	Production rate (per week)	Unit cost (£)
Sundials	200	400	120
Weather-vanes	100	500	80
Flag-poles	180	600	100

Production is organized on a batch basis so that the three products follow
one another in a manufacturing cycle. The cost of changing from one
product to another is £1000 and the cost of holding stocks is 0.5 per cent per
week of their average value. Assume that no production time is lost when
changing from one product to another.

Show that there is no idle time during the cycle and determine the most
economical manufacturing cycle period (to the nearest whole week) in terms
of the combined storage and change-over cost.

What is the weekly cost of each under this condition?
Answer   6 weeks; £465 and £500.

10. A manufacturer of camping equipment makes three models of lightweight tent – known as the Alpine, the Pennine and the Grampian. Their unit manufacturing costs are respectively £60, £40 and £55, the corresponding weekly sales are 120, 150 and 90, and each can be made at the rate of 360 per week. The tents are made in batches and there is a setting-up cost of £160 each time a batch is started. The tents can be held in stock at a cost of 0.5 per cent per week of the average value of the stocks held.

(a) What is the economic batch size, the interval between batches and the corresponding combined weekly setting-up and storage cost for each model if it can be made in isolation?
(b) Suppose, however, the three models are produced in turn in a manufacturing cycle. What is then the economic cycle period, the numbers of the respective models produced per cycle and the total weekly setting-up and storage cost?

Answer (In practice the batch sizes would be rounded to convenient values.)

(a) Alpine: 438; 3.65 weeks; £87.64
Pennine: 641; 4.27 weeks; £74.83
Grampian: 374; 4.16 weeks; £77.07
(b) 4 weeks; 480 Alpines, 600 Pennines and 360 Grampians; £240.

11. A supplier of industrial chemicals notes the weekly demand for a particular solvent for a period of 100 weeks and obtains the following results:

Sales (litres)	400–500	500–600	600–700	700–800	800–900	900–1000	1000–1100	1100–1200
Number of weeks	2	8	15	23	27	14	6	5

Determine the mean weekly demand and the necessary buffer stocks if the stockout risk is not to exceed 1 in 200. Assume weekly deliveries, zero lead time and a normally distributed demand.

What are the corresponding buffer stocks if deliveries are made at 3-week intervals?
Answer 806 and 407 litres; 705 litres.

12. A retail photographer finds that the mean demand for a particular projector bulb is five per week. Assuming that this demand varies according to the Poisson distribution what is the probability that it will exceed (a) six; (b) nine?

What is the probability that it will be exactly nine?
What should the stock level be at the beginning of each week if the risk of stockout is not to exceed 1 in 100?
Answer (a) 0.238; (b) 0.0318; 0.0363; 11.

9 GAMES AND STRATEGIES

'Play up, play up! And play the game!'

Sir Henry Newbolt
Vitae Lampada

9.1 COMPETITION AND CONFLICT

Operational research is concerned with optimization. We are seeking the course of action that leads to the best outcome – in whatever way we define it. Topics such as linear programming lead to deterministic models; in others, queueing and stock control for example, there are random factors such as the choices made by other people. In these cases our answers can only be expressed in terms of averages and probabilities.

In business and industry there is a further consideration. The outcome in many cases will depend partly on the choices made by our competitors and their objectives are likely to conflict with our own. The branch of OR that deals with problems of this kind is known as the *theory of games*. Despite its name it is applied to very serious problems – including those of military strategy, an example of OR being used in its original context.

The characteristics of games, in the OR sense, can best be explained by means of a numerical example. Consider the following, somewhat fanciful, story.

Example 9.1
The Technological University of Ambridge has been saddened by the sudden death of its first chancellor and great benefactor, Sir Tempus Tardy. Under the terms of his will a sum of money has been set aside to erect a large statue of himself somewhere on the campus.

There is a curious condition to the bequest. The university has been planned on a gridiron pattern (Fig. 9.1) with roads running north–south and east–west, the figures alongside the intersections being their altitudes in metres above sea-level. The statue is to be erected at one of these intersections, to be determined as follows. Lady Tardy is to select one of the east–west roads, and the Vice-Chancellor, Professor Hy Tech, one of the north–south roads, each choosing without knowing the other's decision.

Unfortunately they have conflicting objectives. Lady Tardy wants the statue to be placed as high as possible on the campus, but Professor Tech, who has very modern tastes, regards the design as heavy and lifeless, detracting from the adventurous architecture of the new buildings. He would like to see it located at the lowest possible point.

What are their respective strategies?

Figure 9.1

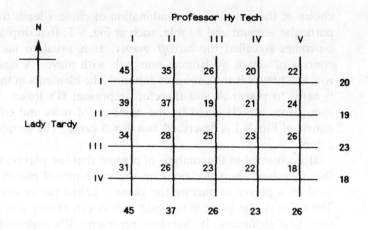

Professor Hy Tech

Solution

First we examine the figures from Lady Tardy's point of view. She might be attracted to east–west road I which contains the highest value of all, 45. However, Professor Tech is not likely to select north–south road I and the outcome would be as low as 20 if he selected road IV. Suppose, therefore, she records the lowest value from each of the possibilities open to her. The results are shown on the right-hand side of the diagram. Of these, the highest value is 23, corresponding to east–west road III. If Lady Tardy selects this road she can be sure that the statue will be located at a height of at least 23 m.

Now look at the problem from Professor Tech's point of view. He might be attracted by roads III or V which contain values as low as 19 and 18 m respectively. However, they each have intersections at greater altitudes, up to 26 m. For the Vice-Chancellor, the worst outcome corresponds to the highest value and, for each of the north–south routes, this is shown at the bottom. He will regard the best of these values as 23, the one corresponding to road IV. If he chooses this road the statue cannot be located at an intersection higher than 23 m.

This is the same value as 'best of the worst' for Lady Tardy. In circumstances like these, it is argued, each protagonist can do no better than select the road that leads to this value. This will ensure a certain minimum 'benefit' for each of them. With other choices they could be worse off.

Therefore, Lady Tardy chooses road III and Professor Hy Tech selects road IV.

9.2 DEFINITIONS

A competitive situation such as that described in the above example is known as a *game* and the persons or groups involved are called the *players*. This chapter is confined to games in which there are only two players and in which the gain of one is the loss of the other. These are known as *two-person zero-sum games*.

Each player can choose from a number of *courses of action* and a *play* occurs when they simultaneously make their choices, neither knowing the choice of the other. Each combination of choices leads to an outcome of a particular amount and a table, such as Fig. 9.1, that displays all the possible outcomes is called the *payoff matrix*. It is usual to identify the possible courses of action by Roman numerals with player A having the choice of row and player B the choice of column. The elements in the matrix show the benefits to player A and therefore represent B's losses. Two-person zero-sum games are classified by the numbers of rows and columns so that the matrix of Fig. 9.1 is described as a 4 × 5 game. The simplest type is a 2 × 2 game.

It is assumed in the analysis of a game that the players are intelligent and that they base their decisions on the same payoff matrix. The set of rules used by a player in playing the game is called the *strategy* for that player. The *value* of the game is the gain that A can expect when both players use their best strategies. It therefore represents B's expected loss. A negative value will be a loss for A and a gain for B.

The *solution* of a game is a statement of the best strategies for A and B, and the resulting value.

9.3 PURE STRATEGY

The general approach to the solution of games was formulated by von Neumann and Morgenstern and first published in 1944. It consists essentially of taking a pessimistic view and evaluating the worst outcome for each possible strategy. The best strategy is then the one which leads to the best of these worst outcomes. This method for finding the best strategy is known as the *minimax criterion*.

In the solution to Example 9.1 it was found that the best of the worst outcomes of the various courses of action was the same for both players. Where this occurs the game is said to have a *saddle point*. Under this condition the best strategy for each player is to select the course of action leading to this point. If this game were played several times the players should make the same choices each time. This constitutes a *pure strategy* and the game is said to be *stable*. The value of the game is the outcome corresponding to the saddle point.

The solution to the game of Example 9.1 can therefore be stated as: Lady Tardy plays III, Professor Tech plays IV and the value is 23.

9.4 MIXED STRATEGY

Suppose you and I play a game with the following rules. (It is known as 'matching coins'.) We each reveal a coin, the two having the same denomination. If we both play heads or both play tails you win and take both coins. If we play opposites I win. What should our strategies be?

The matrix of Fig. 9.2(a) shows your gains (and my losses) for the four possible outcomes. Negative values represent losses for you and gains for me.

First, examine the matrix for a saddle point. The worse outcome for you when you play heads is −1 and the worse outcome when you play tails is

Figure 9.2

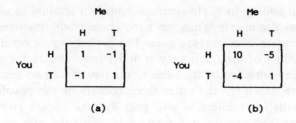

(a)   (b)

also −1. Hence the 'best of the worst' for you is −1. By similar reasoning the best of the worst for me is 1 (your gain and my loss when we both play heads or both play tails). Hence, by the minimax criterion there is no saddle point and no pure strategy.

This is confirmed by considering what would happen if we played the game several times and one of us made the same choice each time. If I played heads repeatedly you would always play heads and win. However, if you played heads repeatedly I could always play tails and then I would win. Such a game is said to be *unstable*. A player who attempts a pure strategy in a game like this will lose steadily.

We must therefore play a mixture of heads and tails and, since the game is symmetrical, each of us should play heads and tails in equal proportions. If I were to play tails more frequently than heads you could play tails all the time and, on average, you would win more than you would lose. Furthermore, we must avoid any pattern in our play. If I played H H H T T T H H H T T T . . . consistently you could adopt the same sequence and win every time.

The same arguments apply to you and the best strategy for each of us is therefore to play heads and tails at random but in equal proportions. With the present rules we can achieve this by tossing the coins each time we play. A strategy of this kind in which we establish the proportions in which we play our different courses of action is known as a *mixed strategy*.

The value of the game is the average or expected outcome. With the matrix of Fig. 9.2(a) the four possibilities would occur in equal proportions and the value of the game is 0. A game having the value 0 is said to be *fair*.

9.5 AN UNFAIR GAME

Next suppose we change the rules to the following. If we both play heads you win 10, if we both play tails you win 1, if you play tails and I play heads I win 4 (and you therefore lose 4) and if you play heads and I play tails I win 5 (your gain being −5). This game is represented by the matrix of Fig. 9.2(b).

First consider what would happen if we merely tossed the coins as before. On average the four outcomes in the matrix would occur with the same probability, 0.25. Hence your average gain would be $0.25 \times (10 - 5 - 4 + 1) = 0.5$. On this basis the game appears to be in your favour.

As in the previous case there is no saddle point. If either of us adopted a pure strategy it would be exploited by the other who would then win consistently. Hence, we must each adopt a mixed strategy.

We each have to choose two fractions (one for heads and one for tails)

250   **GAMES AND STRATEGIES**

that add up to 1. (In simple examples it is usual to work in fractions rather than decimals.) When we have chosen our fractions we can use them to calculate your average gain. The probability of obtaining two heads is the product of the fractions you and I have chosen for heads. This product is then multiplied by the value of the payoff for two heads, 10. The calculation is repeated for the other three corners of the payoff matrix and the four results are totalled to give your average gain. I now invite you to choose your fractions for heads and tails, with the aim of achieving the highest average gain.

I have already chosen mine! After a short calculation I have decided to play heads and tails in the proportions $\frac{3}{10}$ and $\frac{7}{10}$ respectively. Use these fractions in combination with the ones you have chosen and calculate your average or expected gain from playing the game. Then try other fractions for your proportions of heads and tails to see whether you can produce a result that is more favourable from your point of view.

In fact you will find that, whatever fractions you choose for heads and tails, the average outcome from your point of view is -0.5. This result is a consequence of the fractions I have chosen ($\frac{3}{10}$ for heads and $\frac{7}{10}$ for tails) and it cannot be changed by you. This can be appreciated by considering what happens, on average, when you play heads and when you play tails. On the occasions when you play heads, you will gain 10 when I play heads ($\frac{3}{10}$ of the occasions) and lose 5 when I play tails ($\frac{7}{10}$ of the occasions). Hence

$$\text{Average gain when you play heads} = \frac{3}{10} \times 10 + \frac{7}{10} \times (-5)$$
$$= -0.5$$

The calculation is similar when you play tails. Thus

$$\text{Average gain when you play tails} = \frac{3}{10} \times (-4) + \frac{7}{10} \times 1$$
$$= -0.5$$

On average, therefore, you lose 0.5 when you play heads and 0.5 when you play tails. No matter what proportions you assign to heads and tails you will lose (and I shall gain) an average of 0.5. The value of the game (from your point of view) is -0.5 and it is not a fair one.

9.6 THE DETERMINATION OF MIXED STRATEGIES

A mixed strategy is defined by the proportions of the occasions on which each of the courses of action is chosen by a player. The individual choices are made at random (by using a table of random numbers, for instance) but in accordance with these proportions. Figure 9.3 shows a payoff matrix for a 2×2 game in which the four possible outcomes are e, f, g and h. As usual, these quantities represent A's gains and B's losses. If they do not lead to a saddle point then a mixed strategy is required.

Suppose A plays course of action I for a proportion x of the occasions and II for $(1 - x)$ of the occasions. Combining these proportions with the elements of the payoff matrix,

Average outcome when B plays I $= x.e + (1 - x).g$

and

Average outcome when B plays II $= x.f + (1 - x).h$

Now consider these two results from B's point of view, remembering the assumption that B, like A, is an intelligent player and possesses the same information as A in the form of the payoff matrix. If the first result is smaller than the second then B can reduce A's average gain by playing column I more frequently than II. If the first result is greater then B can choose to play II more frequently. If the two results are equal, however, B's choice of proportions cannot influence the average outcome. For this condition, therefore:

$$x.e + (1 - x).g = x.f + (1 - x).h$$

and

$$x(e + h - f - g) = h - g$$

from which

$$x = \frac{h - g}{(e + h) - (f + g)}$$

This is the proportion of the occasions for which A should play row I. The corresponding proportion for row II is therefore:

$$1 - x = 1 - \frac{h - g}{(e + h) - (f + g)}$$

$$= \frac{(e + h) - (f + g) - (h - g)}{(e + h) - (f + g)}$$

$$= \frac{e - f}{(e + h) - (f + g)}$$

The denominator is the same for both results. It follows that the values of x and $(1 - x)$, and hence the proportions of the occasions on which A should play rows I and II, are in the ratio $(h - g)$ to $(e - f)$.

By similar reasoning it can be shown that B should play columns I and II in the ratio $(h - f)$ to $(e - g)$. A simple rule for remembering these results is given in the next section.

Once the proportions are known, the value of the game can be found by applying A's proportions to the elements in either column or B's proportions to the elements in either row. The result will be the same in all four cases.

The results can be illustrated using the matrix of Fig. 9.2(b) in which you were player A and I was player B. In the notation of Fig. 9.3, $e = 10$,

Figure 9.3

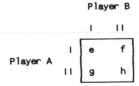

$f = -5$, $g = -4$ and $h = 1$. My best strategy (as player B) is to play columns I and II in the ratio $(h - f)$ to $(e - g)$, that is 6:14, or 3:7. I therefore play $\frac{3}{10}$ of I and $\frac{7}{10}$ of II.

Your best strategy (as player A) would be to play rows I and II in the ratio $(h - g)$ to $(e - f)$, that is 5:15 or 1:3. You should therefore play $\frac{1}{4}$ of I and $\frac{3}{4}$ of II. Using your proportions with the elements in the first column,

$$\text{Value of the game} = \frac{1}{4} \times 10 + \frac{3}{4} \times (-4) = -\frac{1}{2}$$

or -0.5 as obtained earlier. Although the formula for x enables the players to determine their best strategies they cannot change the value of the game. This is governed by the payoff matrix.

Remember, too, that a mixed strategy only specifies the proportions in which the courses of action should be played; for each individual play the choice should be a random one. This can be achieved by assigning ranges of numbers to the two courses of action that represent these proportions. Then, for each occasion, the choice is made on the basis of a random number generated by a computer or calculator, or taken from a table of random numbers.

This may seem a hazardous policy, especially if the game is to be played only once, but the argument is that we have used our best judgement in arriving at the payoff matrix and we should therefore adopt the strategy that results from it. Nevertheless, we may well be apprehensive at the thought of military decisions being taken in this way!

9.7 SADDLE-POINT TEST AND THE MIXED STRATEGY RULE

If the greatest and second greatest elements in a 2×2 payoff matrix are diagonally opposite, there is no saddle point and the solution to the game consists of mixed strategies.

It will then be found that the results $(h - g)$ and $(e - f)$ used in finding A's strategy are both positive or both negative. But $(h - g)$ is the difference of the elements in the second row and $(e - f)$ is the difference of those in the first row. To find A's strategy, therefore, we take the numerical differences in the rows and play them in the reverse ratio.

The method is illustrated in Fig. 9.4 using the payoff matrix of the

Figure 9.4

		Me		row differences	row differences reversed	proportions
		H	T			
You	H	10	-5	15	5	$^5/_{20}$
	T	-4	1	5	15	$^{15}/_{20}$
column differences		14	6			
column differences reversed		6	14			
proportions		$^6/_{20}$	$^{14}/_{20}$			

matching coins game shown in Fig. 9.2(b). My strategy (as player B) is determined by taking the column differences and playing them in the reverse ratio.

Example 9.2
Solve the following games and state whether they are fair.

(a)

Player B

		I	II
	I	-1	-2
Player A	II	1	3

(b)

Player B

		I	II
	I	1	-3
Player A	II	-1	3

Solution
(a) From A's point of view the worse outcomes in rows I and II are -2 and 1 respectively. The 'best of the worst' is therefore 1. From B's point of view the worse outcomes in columns I and II are 1 and 3, and the best of the worst is again 1. Hence there is a saddle point.

The same conclusion is reached by noting that the greatest and second greatest elements in the matrix (3 and 1) are not diagonally opposite.

The solution is A plays II, B plays I and the value of the game is 1. The game is therefore in A's favour and is not a fair one.

(b) The greatest and next greatest elements (3 and 1) are now diagonally opposite. There is no saddle point and a mixed strategy is required. The differences in rows I and II are 4 and 4. Hence A plays I and II equally ($\frac{1}{2}$ and $\frac{1}{2}$). The differences in the columns are 2 and 6 respectively. Reversing these, B plays I and II in the ratio $6:2$, that is $\frac{3}{4}$ and $\frac{1}{4}$ respectively. Applying A's proportions to column I, the average outcome is zero.

The solution is A plays $\frac{1}{2}$ of I and $\frac{1}{2}$ of II, B plays $\frac{3}{4}$ of I and $\frac{1}{4}$ of II. The value of the game is 0 and it is therefore a fair one.

9.8 DOMINANCE

A matrix larger than 2×2 can be reduced in size if, for one of the players, one course of action is always inferior to another. The second course of action is then said to dominate the first, which can be eliminated from the matrix. It occurs if all the elements in one row or column are greater than the corresponding elements in a parallel row or column.

Example 9.3
Solve the following game.

Player B

		I	II	III
	I	1	-1	3
	II	2	-1	2
Player A	III	-1	0	0
	IV	-2	0	4

Solution

Each element in column I is less than (or equal to) the corresponding element in column III. Whatever A does, therefore, column I is always a better choice for B than column III. Both players know this and column III is eliminated. This reduces the game to the following 4 × 2 matrix:

Player B

		I	II
	I	1	-1
	II	2	-1
Player A	III	-1	0
	IV	-2	0

Now consider A's viewpoint. The first element in row II is greater than the first in row I and the second in row II is equal to the second in row I. In all cases, therefore, A will do better (or at least as well) by preferring row II to row I. Hence row I is eliminated. In the same way, row IV is dominated by III and is also eliminated. The game is now reduced to the 2 × 2 matrix shown below.

Player B

		I	II
	II	2	-1
Player A	III	-1	0

By the minimax criterion, or the diagonal test for the greatest and second greatest elements, there is no saddle point and no mixed strategy. Both players should therefore use mixed strategies.

The row differences for II and III are 3 and 1 respectively. Hence A should play these rows in the ratio 1:3, that is, $\frac{1}{4}$ and $\frac{3}{4}$. The column differences are also 3 and 1. Player B should therefore play I and II in the proportions $\frac{1}{4}$ and $\frac{3}{4}$ respectively.

The value of the game can be found by applying A's strategy to either column or B's strategy to either row. Using A's strategy and column I, we have

$$\text{Value} = \frac{1}{4} \times 2 + \frac{3}{4} \times (-1) = -0.25$$

and the game is not a fair one. The full solution is as follows:

A plays I, II, III, IV in the proportions 0, $\frac{1}{4}$, $\frac{3}{4}$, 0
B plays I, II, III in the proportions $\frac{1}{4}$, $\frac{3}{4}$, 0
Value of the game is -0.25

9.9 THE 2 × *n* GAME

The method of dominance does not reduce all games to a 2 × 2 matrix. Consider, for example, the game shown in Fig. 9.5(a).

Applying the minimax text, the best of the worst outcomes for A is 0 in

Figure 9.5

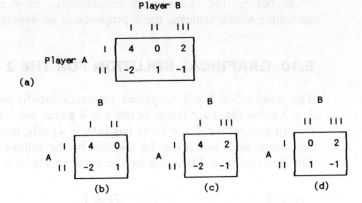

(a)

(b)   (c)   (d)

row I and column II, and for B is 1 in row II and column II. Since these elements do not coincide there is no saddle point and no pure strategy. Next we test for dominance. The first and third elements in row I are greater than the corresponding elements in row II but the second is less. Turning to the columns there is no dominance between columns I and II, II and III, and II and III. Therefore the matrix cannot be reduced.

Now consider B's strategy. Although none of the columns are dominated player B can choose to omit one. Figures 9.5(b), (c) and (d) show the 2 × 2 games that are left if columns III, II and I are omitted in turn. These are known as subgames. We next find the value of each subgame.

By the minimax criterion or the diagonal test the subgame shown in Fig. 9.5(b) has no saddle point. It therefore requires a mixed strategy. The row differences are 4 and 3 respectively, so A plays I and II in the ratio 3 : 4, that is, in the proportions $\frac{3}{7}$ and $\frac{4}{7}$. The column differences are 6 and 1 respectively, so B plays columns I and II in the proportions $\frac{1}{7}$ and $\frac{6}{7}$. The value of the game can be obtained by applying A's proportions to either column or B's proportions to either row. Using A's proportions and column I, we have

$$\text{Value} = \frac{3}{7} \times 4 + \frac{4}{7} \times (-2) = \frac{4}{7} \quad \text{or} \quad 0.571$$

For the subgame shown in Fig. 9.5(c) the minimax test shows that the best of the worst outcomes is the same for both players, namely, the element 2 in row I and column III. This subgame therefore has a saddle point and each player has a pure strategy. Player A plays I, B plays II and the value is 2.

The third subgame, Fig. 9.5(d), has no saddle point and therefore requires a mixed strategy. By the usual rules A plays I and II in the proportions $\frac{1}{2}$ and $\frac{1}{2}$, B plays II and III in the proportions $\frac{3}{4}$ and $\frac{1}{4}$, and the value is $\frac{1}{2}$.

Since player B can choose which column to omit, and therefore which subgame is played, it is the one with the lowest value that is selected. In the present example this is the last of the three, obtained by omitting column I, that is played. The full solution is as follows: A plays I and II in the proportions $(\frac{1}{2}, \frac{1}{2})$, B plays I, II and III in the proportions $(0, \frac{3}{4}, \frac{1}{4})$ and the value is $\frac{1}{2}$.

As before, the two players should make their choices by a random technique which achieves these proportions on average.

9.10 GRAPHICAL SOLUTION FOR THE 2 × n GAME

The number of 2 × 2 subgames increases rapidly as n increases. In the 2 × 3 game there are three, in the 2 × 4 game, six, and in the 2 × 5 game, ten. In general the 2 × n game has $\frac{1}{2}n(n-1)$ subgames. The arithmetic can become tedious and it can be avoided by the following graphical solution. The description is illustrated by the game of Fig. 9.5.

Figure 9.6

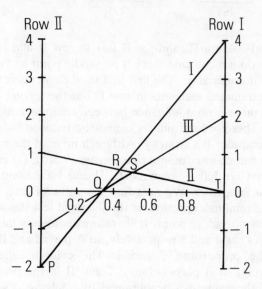

Draw two vertical scales (Fig. 9.6), each with a range that includes all the elements in the payoff matrix. For the game of Fig. 9.5 this range is from −2 to 4. Take a horizontal axis between the zero points and divide it into convenient intervals between 0 and 1.

Then for each column of the payoff matrix plot the elements in rows I and II on the right- and left-hand axes respectively and join them by a straight line. For column I the line runs from 4 to − 2, for column II from 0 to 1, and for column III from 2 to − 1 as shown in Fig. 9.6.

Join the lowest segments of these lines to form a boundary running between the vertical axes. It is PQST in Fig. 9.6. The vertical coordinate of the highest point on this boundary, S in the present case, gives the value of the game. In addition, the foot of the ordinate of this point divides the horizontal scale in the proportions which A should use for rows I and II.

If the line for column III is omitted the highest point of the boundary is R and this represents the solution of the subgame shown in Fig. 9.5(b). By measurement, the value is 0.57 and A's strategy would be to play rows I and II in the proportions 0.43 and 0.57.

There is a resemblance between this method and the graphical solution to the two-product linear programming problem described in Chapter 5. The region below the boundary PQST in Fig. 9.6 corresponds to a feasible region in the solution to the linear programming problem and in both cases the optimum solution is represented by a vertex on the boundary. It has been shown by Dantzig[1] that the linear programming and game problems are equivalent and this result is used in the next section for solving the $m \times n$ game.

9.11 THE $m \times n$ GAME

In the $2 \times n$ game, player A's strategy is limited to two courses of action but player B has n columns from which to choose two. It is therefore B who decides which 2×2 subgame is played. If A and B both have more than two courses of action the 2×2 subgame approach is not applicable. Instead we solve the $m \times n$ game by analysing the corresponding linear programming problem. The details of the method are best explained by reference to a numerical example.

Figure 9.7

		Player B			
		u_1	u_2	u_3	u_4
		I	II	III	IV
x_1	I	2	−1	−2	0
Player A x_2	II	−1	−1	1	−2
x_3	III	−2	0	−1	2

Consider the 3×4 game shown in Fig. 9.7. If you apply the minimax and dominance tests you will find that the game has neither a saddle point nor a dominant course of action. As a consequence the payoff matrix cannot be reduced. Suppose x_1, x_2 and x_3 are the proportions that player A uses for the courses of action corresponding to rows I, II and III, and u_1, u_2, u_3 and u_4 are the proportions used by player B for columns I, II, III and IV.

When B plays column I therefore the average outcome for A will be $(2x_1 - x_2 - 2x_3)$. Similarly, when A plays row II the average outcome for B will be $(+ u_1 + u_2 - u_3 + 2u_4)$, the signs being opposite to those shown in the matrix because A's gains are B's losses. There are corresponding linear expressions for the other rows and columns. In the equivalent linear programming problem the x-values are the quantities of the three 'products' and the u-values become the slack variables. The x-values in the solution will give A's strategy in terms of the proportions in which rows I, II and III are played. The u-values (with the signs reversed) will be the corresponding results for B. They form the solution to the dual problem. In both cases the optimum value of the objective function will correspond to the value of the game.

Some amendments must be made to the payoff matrix to ensure that the problem is cast in the normal linear programming form. First we eliminate all the negative quantities in the payoff matrix by adding a fixed number to every element. In the present example this number is 2 and the result is shown in Fig. 9.8 (a). This does not affect the optimum solution so far as the x- and u-values are concerned but, at the end, we shall have to reduce the optimum value of the objective function by the same number to find the true value of the game.

	u_1	u_2	u_3	u_4
x_1	4	1	0	2
x_2	1	1	3	0
x_3	0	2	1	4

(a)

	x_1	x_2	x_3
u_1	-4	-1	0
u_2	-1	-1	-2
u_3	0	-3	-1
u_4	-2	0	-4

(b)

With this payoff matrix the average outcome (for A) when B plays column I is $(4x_1 + x_2 + 0 \times x_3)$ and this must be greater than 0. The normal form of the linear programming problem requires less-than-or-equal-to constraints and this is achieved by changing the sign of every element in the matrix. The four constraints corresponding to the four columns of the payoff matrix therefore become

$$
\begin{aligned}
-4x_1 - x_2 - &\quad\ \ \leqslant 0 \\
-x_1 - x_2 - 2x_3 &\leqslant 0 \\
-3x_2 - x_3 &\leqslant 0 \\
-2x_1 \qquad\ - 4x_3 &\leqslant 0
\end{aligned}
$$

The coefficients in these inequalities are collected in the matrix of Fig. 9.10(b), the columns and rows being interchanged to match the layout of the simplex table. The zeros on the right-hand sides of these inequalities correspond to the 'capacities' of the constraints in the linear programming problem.

There are two further constraints. The variables x_1, x_2 and x_3 must total 1 since they are the proportions in which A plays I, II and III. This is achieved by the following equation:

$$x_1 + x_2 + x_3 + kx_4 + u_5 = 1$$

provided the x_4 coefficient, k, and the dual (slack) variable u_5 are both zero. In the dual problem the corresponding relationship is

$$u_1 + u_2 + u_3 + u_4 + k'u_5 + x_4 = 1$$

The last two results are incorporated in the problem by adding an extra row and extra column to the first simplex table as shown in Fig. 9.9. Note that the requirement for the coefficients of x_4 and u_5 to be zero is met by putting the row 5, column 4 element equal to zero. The additional variables x_4 and u_5 are ignored when we interpret the optimum solution at the end of the analysis.

The bottleneck ratios are shown on the right and each pivot is circled. In the first table there is only one positive (non-zero) element in the bottom row; it is in column 4. This locates the pivot column and the bottleneck test leads to a ratio of zero in each of the first four rows. An arbitrary choice has to be made and row 1 has been selected.

The second table is obtained by the usual rules. There are now two positive elements in the bottom row and the greater, 4, has been selected for

Figure 9.9

	x_1	x_2	x_3	x_4		bottleneck ratios
u_1	-4	-1	0	①	0	0
u_2	-1	-1	-2	1	0	0
u_3	0	-3	-1	1	0	0
u_4	-2	0	-4	1	0	0
u_5	1	1	1	0	1	infinity
$-z$	0	0	0	1	0	

	x_1	x_2	x_3	u_1		
x_4	-4	-1	0	1	0	
u_2	③	0	-2	-1	0	0
u_3	4	-2	-1	-1	0	0
u_4	2	1	-4	-1	0	0
u_5	1	1	1	0	1	1
$-z$	4	1	0	-1	0	

	u_2	x_2	x_3	u_1		
x_4	$^4/_3$	-1	$-^8/_3$	$-^1/_3$	0	
x_1	$^1/_3$	0	$-^2/_3$	$-^1/_3$	0	
u_3	$-^4/_3$	-2	⑤$/_3$	$^1/_3$	0	0
u_4	$-^2/_3$	1	$-^8/_3$	$-^1/_3$	0	
u_5	$-^1/_3$	1	$^5/_3$	$^1/_3$	1	$^3/_5$
$-z$	$-^4/_3$	1	$^8/_3$	$^1/_3$	0	

	u_2	x_2	u_3	u_1		
x_4	$-^4/_5$	$-2^1/_5$	$^8/_5$	$^1/_5$	0	
x_1	$-^1/_5$	$-^4/_5$	$^2/_5$	$-^1/_5$	0	
x_3	$-^4/_5$	$-^6/_5$	$^3/_5$	$^1/_5$	0	
u_4	$-^{14}/_5$	$-^{11}/_5$	$^8/_5$	$^1/_5$	0	
u_5	1	③	-1	0	1	$^1/_3$
$-z$	$^4/_5$	$2^1/_5$	$-^8/_5$	$-^1/_5$	0	

	u_2	u_5	u_3	u_1		
x_4	$^3/_5$	$^7/_5$	$^1/_5$	$^1/_5$	$^7/_5$	
x_1	$^1/_{15}$	$^4/_{15}$	$^2/_{15}$	$-^1/_5$	$^4/_{15}$	
x_3	$-^2/_5$	$^2/_5$	$^1/_5$	$^1/_5$	$^2/_5$	
u_4	$-3^1/_{15}$	$^{11}/_{15}$	$^{13}/_{15}$	$-^1/_5$	$^{11}/_{15}$	
x_2	$^1/_3$	$^1/_3$	$-^1/_3$	0	$^1/_3$	
$-z$	$-^3/_5$	$-^7/_5$	$-^1/_5$	$-^1/_5$	$-^7/_5$	

the pivot column. This time there are three bottleneck ratios of zero. Selecting the first of these (row 2) leads to the pivot of value 3.

In the present example it is convenient to work in fractions and the next table has three positive elements in the bottom row. If we take the greatest of these ($\frac{8}{3}$) the pivot is in the third column. The bottleneck test then locates the pivot in the third row.

The next table has two positive bottom row elements. Taking the greater ($\frac{21}{5}$) locates the pivot in the second column. There is only one other positive element in this column and the pivot is in row 5.

After the next transformation all the bottom row elements are negative and we have therefore reached the optimum. If we ignore x_4 the solution is

$$x_1 = \tfrac{4}{15} \qquad x_2 = \tfrac{1}{3} \qquad x_3 = \tfrac{2}{5} \qquad z = \tfrac{7}{5}$$

The solution to the dual problem, ignoring u_5, is

$$u_1 = \tfrac{1}{5} \qquad u_2 = \tfrac{3}{5} \qquad u_3 = \tfrac{1}{5} \qquad u_4 = 0$$

The solution to the game, therefore, is that A plays I, II and III in the proportions $\frac{4}{15}$, $\frac{1}{3}$ and $\frac{2}{5}$ and B plays I, II, III and IV in the proportions $\frac{1}{5}$, $\frac{3}{5}$, $\frac{1}{5}$ and 0. The value of the game is found by reducing z by 2 (the number which was added to all the elements in the payoff matrix at the beginning). The result is $-\frac{3}{5}$ and the game is not a fair one.

The solution can be checked by applying A's proportions to the elements in the columns of the original payoff matrix or B's proportions to the elements in the rows. Using A's solution ($\frac{4}{15}$, $\frac{1}{3}$, $\frac{2}{5}$) and the elements in column I we find

$$\text{Value} = \tfrac{4}{15} \times 2 + \tfrac{1}{3} \times (-1) + \tfrac{2}{5} \times (-2) = -\tfrac{3}{5}$$

The same result is obtained for the elements in columns II and III but not for column IV which is excluded from B's strategy. The same value is obtained by using B's proportions and the elements in row I or row II. The strategies of the two players therefore lead to the same average outcome and neither can improve on this value, provided both play intelligently.

A computer solution for the game can be found using the program given in Chapter 5 (Fig. 5.13). When the program is run the number of 'products' should be entered as 4 and the number of less-than-or-equal-to constraints as 5 to allow for the extra row and extra column in the simplex table. The coefficients are taken from the first table of Fig. 9.9. Figure 9.10 shows the last part of the printout that was obtained when the program was run. The results are the decimal equivalents of those found in the 'hand' solution.

The method is general and it can therefore be applied to any of the games analysed earlier in this chapter. In the 2×3 game of Fig. 9.5(a), for instance, the least element is -2. We therefore begin by adding 2 to all the elements and then changing their signs. Then, by exchanging the rows and columns and adding the extra row and extra column as before we obtain the first simplex table (Fig. 9.11). In the language of linear programming there are three products and four constraints.

By the usual hand or computer methods the solution is

$$x_1 = 0.5 \qquad x_2 = 0.5 \qquad z = 2.5$$

and the solution to the dual problem is

Figure 9.10

```
          U2     U5     U3     U1
X4    0.6    1.4    0.2    0.2    1.4
X1    7E-2   0.27   0.13   -0.2   0.27
X3    -0.4   0.4    0.2    0.2    0.4
U4    -2.07  0.73   0.87   0.2    0.73
X2    0.33   0.33   -0.33  0      0.33

-Z    -0.6   -1.4   -0.2   -0.2   -1.4

THIS IS THE OPTIMAL SOLUTION

X4 = 1.4
X1 = 0.266666667
X3 = 0.4
U4 = 0.733333333
X2 = 0.333333333

ALL OTHER VARIABLES ARE ZERO

OBJECTIVE FUNCTION Z = 1.4

DUAL PROBLEM SOLUTION (Y/N)
?Y

DUAL PROBLEM OPTIMAL SOLUTION IS:

U2 = 0.6
U5 = 1.4
U3 = 0.2
U1 = 0.2

ALL OTHER VARIABLES ARE ZERO

OBJECTIVE FUNCTION Z = 1.4

----------------------------------------
```

Figure 9.11

	x_1	x_2	x_3	
u_1	-6	0	1	0
u_2	-2	-3	1	0
u_3	-4	-1	1	0
u_4	1	1	0	1
-z	0	0	1	0

$$u_1 = 0 \quad u_2 = 0.75 \quad u_3 = 0.25$$

The x- and u-values correspond to the relevant proportions in the strategies for A and B respectively. The value of the game, obtained by deducting 2 from the value of the objective function z, is 0.5. The solution obtained earlier is therefore confirmed.

9.12 SUMMARY

The theory of games enables us to determine the best strategy for each player when two or more each have to select a course of action and the outcome depends on the combination of their choices. A two-person, zero-sum game is one in which there are two players (usually denoted by A and B) and A's gain is equal to B's loss. This is the only type covered in this book. The elements in the payoff matrix show the gains to A that arise from each of the combinations of their choices.

Games are classified by the numbers of choices available to the players. An $m \times n$ game is one in which player A has m courses of action and B has n. In the analysis of a game we first apply the minimax test. The players note the worst outcome from each of the courses of action open to them. If the best of the worst outcomes is the same for both players we have a saddle point. In this case each player can do no better than select the course of action that leads to the saddle point, however many times the game is played. This is called a pure strategy and the game is said to be stable.

The smallest game has a 2×2 matrix. If there is no saddle point the game is said to be unstable and a mixed strategy is required. Player A plays rows I and II in the ratio of the row differences reversed and B plays columns I and II in the ratio of the column differences reversed. Each time the game is played the choice should be a random one but based on these proportions.

The value of the game is reckoned as A's gain and therefore B's loss. For a game with a saddle point it is the corresponding element in the payoff matrix. With a mixed strategy it is the average outcome arising from the proportions in which A and B play their different courses of action.

Games larger than 2×2 can sometimes be reduced by dominance. If every element in a particular row or column is inferior to the corresponding element in a parallel row or column the player discards the former. It is then omitted from the strategy for that player.

A $2 \times n$ game (or one that can be reduced to this form by dominance) is analysed by considering all the 2×2 subgames. Player B then selects the subgame that gives the least value to A by omitting all the other columns. The strategies for the two players and the value are then determined on the basis of this 2×2 game.

Larger games that have no saddle point and cannot be reduced by dominance are analysed by solving the equivalent linear programming problem using the simplex method. The solution and dual solution represent the strategies for the two players and the optimum value of the objective function gives the value of the game.

REFERENCE

1. Dantzig G B, A proof of the equivalence of the programming problem and the game problem in Koopmans T C (ed), 1957, *Activity Analysis of Production and Allocation* Wiley Ch 20

BIBLIOGRAPHY

Berry J, Burghes D, Huntly I 1986 *Decision Mathematics* Ellis Horwood
Neumann J von, Morgenstern O 1953 *Theory of Games and Economic Behavior* 3rd edn Princeton University Press
Rasmusen E 1989 *Games and Information* Basil Blackwell
Thomas L C 1984 *Games Theory and Application* Ellis Horwood
Williams J D 1954 *The Compleat Strategyst* McGraw-Hill

PROBLEMS

1. Solve the following zero-sum, two-person games.

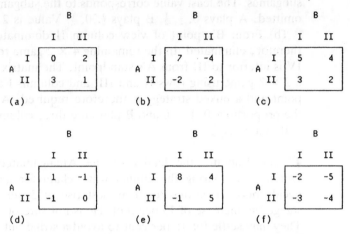

(a)

		B I	B II
A	I	0	2
	II	3	1

(b)

		B I	B II
A	I	7	-4
	II	-2	2

(c)

		B I	B II
A	I	5	4
	II	3	2

(d)

		B I	B II
A	I	1	-1
	II	-1	0

(e)

		B I	B II
A	I	8	4
	II	-1	5

(f)

		B I	B II
A	I	-2	-5
	II	-3	-4

Answer (a) Mixed strategy. A plays $\frac{1}{2}$, $\frac{1}{2}$. B plays $\frac{1}{4}$, .473. Value, $1\frac{1}{2}$.
(b) Mixed strategy. A plays $\frac{4}{15}$, $\frac{11}{15}$. B plays $\frac{2}{5}$, $\frac{3}{5}$. Value, $\frac{2}{5}$. (c) Pure strategy.
A plays I. B plays II. Value, 4. (d) Mixed strategy. A plays $\frac{1}{3}$, $\frac{2}{3}$. B plays $\frac{1}{3}$, $\frac{2}{3}$.
Value, $-\frac{1}{3}$. (e) Mixed strategy. A plays $\frac{3}{5}$, $\frac{2}{5}$. B plays $\frac{1}{10}$, $\frac{9}{10}$. Value, $\frac{22}{5}$.
(f) Pure strategy. A plays II. B plays II. Value, -4.

2. There is fierce competition for petrol sales between the two garages in
Ambridge. Ambridge Autocars have the better position on the main road,
but Midshire Motors sell the more widely promoted Zoom petrol.

Despite their intense rivalry the two firms have agreed a sales policy. At
the beginning of each month they announce in the *Borchester Gazette*,
independently of one another, whether they are giving 2p off or 4p off.

Ambridge Autocars have found that they make £100 a week profit if both
garages offer 2p off but this falls to £90 if both offer 4p off. Furthermore
their profit is £80 if they give 4p off when Midshire Motors are offering 2p
off, despite increased sales, and it falls to £70 if they give 2p off when their
rivals offer 4p off.

Construct a payoff matrix showing these profits and determine the best
strategy for Ambridge Autocars, treating the problem as a 2 × 2 zero-sum
game. On this basis what is the value of the game?
Answer Play 2p off and 4p off in the proportions $\frac{1}{4}$ and $\frac{3}{4}$. £85.00.

3. Solve the following games.

(a)

		B I	B II	B III
A	I	0	-4	2
	II	3	5	1
	III	1	-4	3

(b)

		B I	B II	B III
A	I	3	1	7
	II	5	1	4
	III	2	3	3
	IV	0	2	6

Answer (a) From A's point of view row III dominates row I which is therefore eliminated. The reduced matrix has no dominance nor saddle point. It must therefore be analysed as a 2×3 game with three 2×2 subgames. The least value corresponds to the subgame in which column II is omitted. A plays 0, $\frac{1}{2}$, $\frac{1}{2}$. B plays $\frac{1}{2}$, 0, $\frac{1}{2}$. Value is 2.

(b) From B's point of view column II dominates column III which is therefore eliminated. In the remaining 4×2 game row I is inferior to II and IV is inferior to III from A's standpoint. The matrix is therefore reduced to a 2×2 game using rows II and III, and columns I and II. It has no saddle point and a mixed strategy is therefore required. A plays the four rows in the proportions 0, $\frac{1}{4}$, $\frac{3}{4}$, 0 and B plays the three columns in the proportions $\frac{2}{5}$, $\frac{3}{5}$, 0. Value is $\frac{13}{5}$.

4. Joe Luddite, the leader of the Amalgamated Windmill Operatives Union, is preparing the annual wage claim for his members and has to decide between asking for a modest rise of 5 per cent and demanding a staggering increase of 15 per cent. He is not sure of the employer's attitude. They may settle for 15 per cent to avoid a strike but they could hold out for 5 per cent and risk industrial action. A third possibility is that they would be willing to compromise at 10 per cent.

Joe's standing in the union depends on his success in the negotiations. If he asked for, and won, a 15 per cent rise his stock would be high. On the other hand, a 5 per cent settlement after a 15 per cent claim would be taken as a sign of weakness. Worst of all would be a situation in which he asked for 5 per cent and it transpired that the employers would have settled for 15 per cent.

He draws up the following payoff matrix to represent the relative benefits to himself of the various possibilities.

		Employers willing to settle for:		
		5%	10%	15%
Union claim	5%	4	−5	−10
	15%	−5	2	10

Determine Joe's best strategy and the value of the game.

Answer There is no saddle point and no dominance. The three 2×2 subgames, obtained by omitting each of the three columns in turn, have values of 2 (pure strategy), $-\frac{10}{29}$ (mixed strategy) and $-\frac{17}{16}$ (mixed strategy). The last value is the least and the employers ensure that this is the game that is played by omitting the last column from their strategy. Joe therefore plays 5 per cent and 15 per cent in the proportions $\frac{7}{16}$ and $\frac{9}{16}$. The value is $-\frac{17}{16}$.

5. Solve the following 2×6 game:

		B					
		I	II	III	IV	V	VI
A	I	16	-12	8	0	-16	7
	II	-4	12	4	8	14	5

Answer There is neither dominance nor a saddle point initially. Since there are 15 2×2 subgames a graphical solution is recommended. The least-value subgame is that formed with columns I and V. A plays $\frac{9}{25}, \frac{16}{25}$ and B plays $\frac{3}{5}$, $0, 0, 0, \frac{2}{5}, 0$. The value is $\frac{16}{5}$.

6. Solve the following 3×4 game.

		B			
		I	II	III	IV
	I	2	4	5	2
B	II	-1	6	0	-6
	III	3	-2	-3	4

Answer There is neither dominance nor a saddle point. Mixed strategies are required and these are determined by solving the equivalent linear programming problem. Player A uses $(\frac{5}{7}, 0, \frac{2}{7})$; B uses $(\frac{6}{7}, \frac{1}{7}, 0, 0)$. The value is $\frac{16}{7}$.

7. In the two-person game known as 'scissors, paper and stone' each player selects one of these objects. Scissors defeats paper by cutting it, paper wins against stone by wrapping it and stone beats scissors by blunting them. The winner gains 1 point from the loser but if the two players choose the same object there is no gain to either. The payoff matrix is shown below at (a). Determine the strategies for each player and the value of the game.

		B		
		scissors	paper	stone
	scissors	0	1	-1
A	paper	-1	0	1
	stone	1	-1	0

(a)

		B		
		scissors	paper	stone
	scissors	0	3	-4
A	paper	-1	0	2
	stone	3	-3	0

(b)

What is the solution for the payoff matrix shown at (b)?

Answer (a) There is neither dominance nor a saddle point. Since the game is a fair one and the same for both players the strategy for each is $\frac{1}{3}, \frac{1}{3}, \frac{1}{3}$ and the value is 0.

(b) Although the sum of all the elements in the matrix is again zero, the game is not the same for the two players. Mixed strategies are required and

solving the equivalent linear programming problem by the simplex method
leads to $(\frac{15}{61}, \frac{33}{61}, \frac{13}{61})$ for A and $(\frac{24}{61}, \frac{22}{61}, \frac{15}{61})$ for B. The value is $\frac{6}{61}$. The game
therefore favours A to a small extent.

Appendix A
MATHEMATICAL NOTATION AND FORMULAE

A.1 DISPLAYING LARGE AND SMALL NUMBERS

Operational research is a quantitative subject. The data we use and the results we obtain are usually expressed in the form of numbers. Practical examples may lead to very large or very small values. A major construction project can cost billions of pounds or dollars; in contrast, the probability of failure in a potentially dangerous industrial process needs to be very small, perhaps less than one ten-millionth.

When such numbers are written out in full they contain many figures or digits. To make them easier to read we divide the digits into groups of three, starting at the decimal point. It is now recommended that the groups are separated by spaces rather than commas, as hitherto. To avoid having a single digit standing alone, we usually omit the space in numbers up to 9999 and down to 0.0001. These conventions have been used throughout this book. For example:

$$£47\,800\,000 \qquad £4780 \qquad 0.000\,004\,78 \qquad 0.0478$$

Neither spaces nor commas should be used when you enter numbers in a calculator or computer. As an alternative to writing long numbers in full, we can use scientific notation. This is explained in section A.5 and it is accepted by most computers and scientific calculators.

A.2 THE ROUNDING OF NUMBERS

We make considerable use of calculators and computers in operational research and these machines can work to a greater accuracy than is normally justified by the quality of the data. The answers should therefore be 'rounded' to a degree of accuracy that is merited by the original data and the nature of the problem.

Rounding is specified in one of two ways – the number of decimal places or the number of significant figures. To round the number 30.182 65 to two decimal places, we discard the last three figures, giving 30.18. However, to three decimal places it becomes 30.183, since we round up when the following figure (in this case, 6) is greater than 5. If the only figure to be discarded is a 5, we round upwards and, to four decimal places, the result

267

would be 30.1827. Many calculators and computers offer automatic rounding to a specified number of decimal places.

Significant figures are counted from the left, starting with the first non-zero digit. Thus, to three significant figures, 30.18265 becomes 30.2 and 0.003018265 becomes 0.00302.

Whole numbers are termed integers and, in some examples, only integer values have any meaning. The number of guests at a party, the number of cars in a household and the number of faults in a batch of manufactured items can only be integers. At the same time the average number for several parties, households or batches may well be a number containing a decimal portion. Some calculators and most computers offer a facility for extracting the integer portion of a number. In the BASIC computer language the keyword is INT. Note that this always rounds downwards so that

$$INT(15.87)=15 \quad and \quad INT(-15.87)=-16$$

If we wish to round to the nearest integer (up or down) we first add 0.5 to the number. If $X = 15.87$, for instance,

$$INT(X+0.5)=16$$

This device can be adapted to round results to any specified number of decimal places. If we wish to round the values of X to three decimal places we can multiply by 1000, add 0.5, take the integer value and divide by 1000. Thus, with $X = 0.3018$, we find

$$INT(1000*X+0.5)/1000=0.302$$

This routine is used in several computer programs in this book.

A.3 ABSOLUTE VALUES

Sometimes we need the size of a number irrespective of whether it is positive or negative. Its magnitude, with the sign removed, is called the *absolute value* or *modulus*. We show this by putting the number within vertical bars, thus

$$|15.87| = 15.87 \quad and \quad |-15.87| = 15.87$$

In computer programs, and on scientific calculators, the keyword is ABS so that

$$ABS(-15.87)=15.87$$

A.4 POWERS AND ROOTS

There are many calculations in which a number has to be multiplied by itself several times. Thus

$$3 \times 3 \times 3 \times 3 \times 3 = 243$$

This is described as 'raising 3 to the power 5' and we say that 243 is the fifth power of 3. The result of raising a number to a power is sometimes termed the *exponent* but it should not be confused with the exponential function e^x (see section A.11). It is written

$$3^5 = 243$$

The second and third powers are referred to as the square and cube of the number. Scientific calculators can determine powers by a single keystroke, usually shown as y^x. Computers use the circumflex symbol ^ (or ↑), as in 3^5 and Y^X. Note that calculations with large powers, such as 501^{43} (501^43 on a computer), exceed the capacity of most calculators and computers, and will produce error messages.

We can find a meaning for zero and negative powers by considering a sequence of calculations with decreasing powers. For example,

$$3^5 = 243 \quad 3^4 = 81 \quad 3^3 = 27 \quad 3^2 = 9$$

Each time the power is reduced by 1, the answer is divided by the number. Thus, taking the sequence further, $3^1 = 3$ and $3^0 = 1$. By the same reasoning, every number to the power 1 is equal to itself and every number to the power 0 is 1.

Extending this process we have

$$3^1 = 3 \quad 3^0 = 1 \quad 3^{-1} = 1/3^1 \quad \text{and} \quad 3^{-2} = 1/3^2$$

Thus, a number raised to a negative power is the reciprocal of the same number raised to the corresponding positive power.

The reverse process to calculating a power is finding a root. Since 243 is the fifth power of 3, then 3 is the fifth root of 243. The special cases of the second and third roots are called the square and cube roots respectively. Roots are shown by the symbol $^5\sqrt{}$, the index figure indicating which root is required. Where no index is given we assume that the square root is intended. Most calculators have a square root facility, shown as $\sqrt{x}$ or simply $\sqrt{}$. With computers the keyword is SQR so that:

$$SQR(576)=24 \quad \text{and} \quad SQR(287.93)=16.9685$$

Other roots are obtained by using the power function. To find the fifth root of 243, we raise 243 to the power one-fifth. Thus

$$^5\sqrt{243} = 243^{1/5} = 243^{0.2}$$

and, for the computer, this is expressed as 243^(1/5) or 243^0.2.

Any attempt to take the root of a negative number will produce an error message.

To find the power needed to raise one given number to another, we have to use logarithms (see section A.12).

A.5 SCIENTIFIC NOTATION

It is convenient to show very large or very small values as a number in the range 1–9.999999 . . . multiplied by a power of 10. For example, the mean distance between the earth and the sun is approximately 149 500 000 000 m and this is written 1.495×10^{11}. On the other hand the wavelength of blue light is in the region of 0.000 000 45 m and this is written 4.5×10^{-7}. This method of expressing numbers is called scientific notation or, sometimes, standard form.

Scientific calculators will handle numbers in this form; see the manual for your machine for details. Most computers use the letter E followed by the power of 10, so that the two values mentioned in the last paragraph will be displayed as 1.495E11 and 4.5E-7 respectively. Computers will also accept numerical data in this form; a value of 1 million may be entered as 1E6, for instance.

A.6 FACTORIALS

We sometimes need the product of all the integers up to a specified number. This is called the factorial of the number and is shown by putting an exclamation mark after it, thus 6! We usually write the integers in descending order so that

$$6! = 6 \times 5 \times 4 \times 3 \times 2 \times 1$$

Most scientific calculators offer factorials as a single keystroke, provided the answer is within the acceptable range of numbers. Most calculators are limited to numbers up to $9.9999 \ldots \times 10^{99}$ and the largest factorial in this range is 69!

Computers do not have a built-in factorial function and the answer must be obtained by writing a routine within the program to carry out the successive multiplications.

In some calculations we need the product of all the integers between two specified values. This can be obtained by dividing the factorial of the upper value by the factorial of the number that is one below the lower value. For example:

$$16 \times 15 \times 14 \times 13 \times 12 = \frac{16 \times 15 \ldots \times 12 \times 11 \times 10 \times \ldots \times 3 \times 2 \times 1}{11 \times 10 \times \ldots \times 3 \times 2 \times 1}$$

$$= \frac{16!}{11!}$$

Note that the factorial of an integer is equal to the factorial of the next higher number divided by that number. Thus

$$4! = 5!/5 \qquad 3! = 4!/4 \quad \text{and} \quad 2! = 3!/3$$

On this basis $1! = 2!/2 = 1$, and $0! = 1!/1 = 1$. The last result is required for certain calculations in queueing theory.

A.7 STRAIGHT-LINE GRAPHS

There are a number of examples in operational research in which two variables, such as x and y, are related by an equation of the form

$$y = mx + c$$

where m and c are constants.

Whenever this occurs, a graph of y plotted against x is a straight line and,

Figure A.1

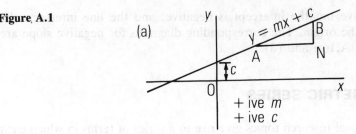

(a)

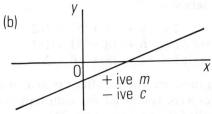

(b)

Figure A.1

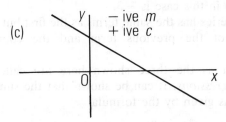

(c)

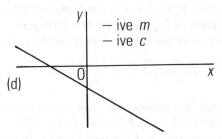

(d)

for this reason, the relationship is said to be linear. Some examples in linear programming (Ch. 5) can be solved graphically and the graphs are all straight lines.

We usually plot y vertically (positive upwards) and x horizontally (positive to the right) as shown in Fig. A.1. If this is done, the constant m is the slope or gradient of the graph. For two points such as A and B (Fig. A.1(a)), the slope m equals the difference in their y-values divided by the difference in x that is BN/AN. Furthermore, the constant c is the intercept on the y-axis, that is, the value of y when $x = 0$. The constants m and c can be positive or negative and the figure shows four possibilities.

At Fig. A.1(a), m and c are both positive, the slope is upwards to the right and the line cuts the y-axis above the origin O. At Fig. A.1(b) the slope is positive but the intercept is negative, and the line intersects the y-axis below the origin. The corresponding diagrams for negative slope are shown at Fig. A.1(c) and (d).

A.8 GEOMETRIC SERIES

Some operational research topics give rise to a series of terms in which each term is related to the previous one in a specified way. We may require the values of the separate terms, or the sum of the whole series. Consider the following three series:

$$S = 2 + 6 + 18 + 54 + 162$$
$$S = 2 - 6 + 18 - 54 + 162$$
$$S = 162 + 54 + 18 + 6 + 2 \qquad\qquad [A.1]$$

In the first of these each term, after the first, is three times the previous one. If the series were continued the sixth term would be $162 \times 3 = 486$. The factor 3 is called the *common ratio*. The terms in the second series have the same absolute values but are alternately positive and negative. The common ratio in this case is -3.

The third series has the same terms as the first but in reverse order. Each is one-third of the previous term and the common ratio is 1/3 or 0.3333 . . . .

Series such as the three shown here are called *geometric series* or *geometric progressions*. It can be shown that the sum of a geometric series with n terms is given by the formula

$$S = \frac{a(1 - r^n)}{1 - r}$$

where a is the first term and r is the common ratio.

In the first series of Eq. A.1, the first term a is 2, the common ratio r is 3 and the number of terms n is 5. Using the formula, the sum is

$$S = \frac{2(1 - 3^5)}{1 - 3} = \frac{2(1 - 243)}{-2} = \frac{2 \times (-242)}{-2} = 242$$

Check this result by adding the five terms and show that the formula confirms the sum of the second series to be 122.

Geometric series arise in Chapters 2 and 7. In section 2.4 the final value, FV, of a series of n payments, each A, is shown to be

$$FV = A(1 + i)^{n-1} + A(1 + i)^{n-2} + A(1 + i)^{n-3} + \ldots A$$

where i is the rate of interest. It is convenient to consider the terms in reverse order. If this is done, the first term $a = A$ and the common ratio $r = (1 + i)$. Hence the sum of the series is

$$FV = \frac{a(1 - r^n)}{1 - r} = \frac{A[1 - (1 + i)^n]}{1 - (1 + i)} = \frac{A[1 - (1 + i)^n]}{-i}$$

$$= \frac{A[(1 + i)^n - 1]}{i}$$

A second example occurs in section 2.7 where it is shown that the present value factor for a series of n payments is given by

$$F_4 = \frac{1}{(1 + i)^1} + \frac{1}{(1 + i)^2} + \frac{1}{(1 + i)^3} + \frac{1}{(1 + i)^4} + \dots$$
$$+ \frac{1}{(1 + i)^n}$$

where i is again the interest rate. The first term a and common ratio r are both equal to $1/(1 + i)$ and the sum is therefore:

$$F_4 = \frac{a(1 - r^n)}{1 - r} = \frac{1/(1 + i)[1 - 1/(1 + i)^n]}{1 - 1/(1 + i)}$$

Multiplying the numerator and denominator of this expression by $(1 + i)$ leads to the result

$$F_4 = \frac{(1 + i)/(1 + i)[1 - 1(1 + i)^n]}{(1 + i) - 1} = \frac{1}{i}\left[\frac{1}{(1 + i)^n}\right]$$

As they stand the third series in Eq. A.1 has the same total as the first. What happens, however, if we add further terms to them? The sum of the first series becomes larger and larger without limit. By adding enough terms we can make the sum greater than any value we choose. To exceed 1 million, for instance, 13 terms are required. A series of this kind in which there is no limit to the sum is said to be *divergent*.

The third series is different. Its sum also increases as further terms are added — but there is a limit. With five terms the sum is 242 and with 10 it is 242.996 (to three decimal places). By adding more terms we can approach the value 243 as closely as we like but we can never equal it exactly with a finite number of terms. The series is said to be *convergent* and the value 243 is called its *sum to infinity*.

For a geometric series to be convergent the absolute value of the common ratio must be less than 1. In symbols, $|r| < 1$. As n increases the value of r^n becomes smaller. In mathematical language, the limiting value of r^n, as n tends to infinity, is zero. With this value, the formula for S becomes

$$\text{Sum to infinity} = \frac{a}{1 - r}$$

Use this result to check that the sum to infinity of the series $162 + 54 + 18 + 6 + 2 \dots$ is 243. Show also that the corresponding result for the series $162 - 54 + 18 - 6 + 2 \dots$ is 121.5.

The formula for the sum to infinity is used in the theory of the simple queue, section 7.5.

A.9 BINOMIAL THEOREM

When two algebraic expressions are multiplied together, every term in one must be multiplied by every term in the other. Hence, if we multiply $(a + b)$ by $(c + d)$ we obtain four terms ab, ad, bc and bd. This is written

$$(a + b)(c + d) = ac + ad + bc + bd$$

Suppose the expressions are both $(a + b)$. The four terms in the result are now aa, ab, ba and bb. If we write aa as a^2 and bb as b^2, and note that $ba = ab$, the result can be written

$$(a + b)^2 = a^2 + 2ab + b^2$$

The process can be extended to higher powers. For $(a + b)^3$, we multiply the last result by another $(a + b)$. This gives

$$(a + b)^3 = (a^2 + 2ab + b^2)(a + b)$$
$$= a^3 + a^2b + 2a^2b + 2ab^2 + b^2a + b^3$$
$$= a^3 + 3a^2b + 3ab^2 + b^3$$

The general result for $(a + b)^n$ where n is a positive integer, can be found using the following rules:

1. There are $(n + 1)$ terms altogether.
2. The first term is a^n. This may be regarded as a^nb^0 since b^0 is equal to 1.
3. In each successive term the power of a is reduced by 1 and the power of b increased by 1, the final term being b^n.
4. The numerical coefficients of the terms, taken in order, are

$$1, \quad \frac{n}{1}, \quad \frac{n(n - 1)}{1 \times 2}, \quad \frac{n(n - 1)(n - 2)}{1 \times 2 \times 3}, \quad \ldots$$

With these rules the rth term in the series can be written

$$\frac{n(n - 1)(n - 2) \ldots (n - r + 2)}{1 \times 2 \times 3 \ldots (r - 1)} a^{n-r+1}b^{r-1}$$

The result is known as the binomial series or expansion. As an example of its use, consider the expansion of $(a + b)^5$. From the rules given above there are six terms altogether and, without the numerical coefficients, they are

$$a^5 \qquad a^4b \qquad a^3b^2 \qquad a^2b^3 \qquad ab^4 \qquad b^5$$

The corresponding numerical coefficients are given by

$$1, \quad \frac{5}{1}, \quad \frac{5 \times 4}{1 \times 2}, \quad \frac{5 \times 4 \times 3}{1 \times 2 \times 3}, \quad \frac{5 \times 4 \times 3 \times 2}{1 \times 2 \times 2 \times 4}, \quad \frac{5 \times 4 \times 3 \times 2 \times 1}{1 \times 2 \times 3 \times 4 \times 5}$$

The fractions equal 1, 5, 10, 10, 5 and 1 respectively. Therefore

$$(a + b)^5 = a^5 + 5a^4b + 10a^3b^2 + 10a^2b^3 + 5ab^4 + b^5$$

The symmetry of the terms, and their coefficients, is found in all binomial expansions of this kind. If n is even the middle term contains equal powers of a and b, and its coefficient is higher than any other in the expression.

Figure A.2

```
 10 PRINT "----------------------------"
 20 PRINT "BINOMIAL COEFFICIENTS"
 30 PRINT "----------------------------"
 40 INPUT "ENTER POWER OR INDEX N",N
 50 M=INT(N):C=1
 60 PRINT:PRINT "TERM   COEFFICIENT"
 70 FOR R=1 TO N+1
 80 PRINT TAB(1);R;TAB(10);C
 90 C=C*M/R
100 M=M-1
110 NEXT R
120 PRINT "----------------------------"
130 END
```

The coefficient of the term containing b^r in the expansion of $(a + b)^n$ is usually denoted by ^nC_r or $_nC_r$. The short computer program in Fig. A.2 will calculate all the coefficients for a given value of n. It can be tested by entering the value 5 in response to the initial prompt and comparing the results with the coefficients found for the expansion of $(a + b)^5$ above. Note that higher values can lead to very large coefficients. With $n = 30$, for example, the middle coefficient is 155 117 520.

Table A.1 Binomial coefficients

	r = 1	2	3	4	5	6	7	8	9	10	11	12	13	14	15	16
n = 1	1	1														
2	1	2	1													
3	1	3	3	1												
4	1	4	6	4	1											
5	1	5	10	10	5	1										
6	1	6	15	20	15	6	1									
7	1	7	21	35	35	21	7	1								
8	1	8	28	56	70	56	28	8	1							
9	1	9	36	84	126	126	84	36	9	1						
10	1	10	45	120	210	252	210	120	45	10	1					
11	1	11	55	165	330	462	462	330	165	55	11	1				
12	1	12	66	220	495	792	924	792	495	220	66	12	1			
13	1	13	78	286	715	1287	1716	1716	1287	715	286	78	13	1		
14	1	14	91	364	1001	2002	3003	3432	3003	2002	1001	364	91	14	1	
15	1	15	105	455	1365	3003	5005	6435	6435	5005	3003	1365	455	105	15	1

Table A.1 displays the coefficients for expansions up to $(a + b)^{15}$. It is known as *Pascal's triangle* and it can be constructed independently by the following rules. The first and last terms in each row equal 1, and the others can be obtained by noting that the sum of the rth and $(r + 1)$th terms in one row becomes the $(r + 1)$th term in the next. For example, the sum of the fourth and fifth terms in row 9, viz. 84 and 126, is the fifth term in row 10, 210. Starting at the top, the whole table can be constructed in this way.

A.10 THE EXPONENTIAL FUNCTION

The expansion of $(a + b)^n$ by means of the binomial theorem is the starting point for another important series. Suppose we put $a = 1$ and $b = 1/n$. The first few terms of the expansion are then as follows:

$$\left(1 + \frac{1}{n}\right)^n = 1 + n\left(\frac{1}{n}\right) + \frac{n(n-1)}{1 \times 2}\left(\frac{1}{n}\right)^2$$
$$+ \frac{n(n-1)(n-2)}{1 \times 2 \times 3}\left(\frac{1}{n}\right)^3 + \dots$$

In the second and subsequent terms the quantity n appears the same number of times in the numerator and denominator. By dividing each n in the denominator into one of the bracket expressions in the numerator the result becomes

$$\left(1 + \frac{1}{n}\right)^n = 1 + 1 + \frac{(1 - 1/n)}{1 \times 2} + \frac{(1 - 1/n)(1 - 2/n)}{1 \times 2 \times 3} + \dots$$

As n tends to infinity the fractions $1/n$, $2/n$, $3/n$ . . . all tend to zero. The result is another convergent infinite series. Its sum to infinity is denoted by e and we can therefore write:

$$e = 1 + \frac{1}{1!} + \frac{1}{2!} + \frac{1}{3!} + \ldots$$

the factorial 1! being introduced to maintain the pattern of the series. We can also write the first term as 1/0! The value of e found from this series is 2.7183 . . . and it is stored in scientific calculators and computers. It is interesting to examine the approximations obtained by evaluating the original expression $(1 + 1/n)^n$ for increasing values of n, using a scientific calculator. With $n = 2$, the result is $(1 + \frac{1}{2})^2 = 2.25$. With $n = 10$ it becomes $(1 + 0.1)^{10} = 2.5937$ and with $n = 100$ it is 2.7048. Try putting $n = 1000$ and $n = 10^6$.

A series for e^x can be deduced by similar reasoning to that used above. If we replace the power n by nx the expansion becomes

$$\left(1 + \frac{1}{n}\right)^{nx} = 1 + \frac{x}{1} + \frac{(1 - 1/n)(1 - 2/n)}{1 \times 2}x^2 \ldots .$$

As n tends to infinity the expression on the left becomes e^x and all the expressions in brackets on the right become 1. We can therefore write

$$e^x = 1 + \frac{x}{1!} + \frac{x^2}{2!} + \frac{x^3}{3!} + \ldots .$$

This series is convergent for all (finite) values of x. The function e^x is usually called the exponential function, although this term is sometimes applied to all power functions such as 2^x or 5^x. On a scientific calculator it is shown as e^x and in computer BASIC the keyword is EXP.

A.11 LOGARITHMS

For many years logarithms were used mainly to simplify multiplication, division and finding powers and roots. Nowadays we rely on calculators and computers to perform these calculations. Logarithms have other purposes, however. They occur as functions in their own right, and we still need to use them in finding the power to which one number has to be raised to equal another. We no longer need tables, however, because they are included in the functions built into scientific calculators and computers.

A logarithm is itself a power − the power to which one number, called the base, has to be raised to equal the given number. Two bases are widely used. Common logarithms have the base 10; these are convenient in many arithmetical processes because the common logarithms of 10, 100, 1000 . . . are 1, 2, 3 . . . respectively. Natural or Napierian logarithms have the exponential number e as their base.

In mathematical text a distinction is often made by writing $\log_{10}$ for common logarithms and $\log_e$ for natural logarithms. If no base is specified natural logarithms are assumed. Unfortunately there is no universally agreed notation on calculators and computers. Some machines use LOG for common logarithms and LN for natural logarithms. Others use LOG10 for common logarithms and LOG for natural logarithms. At least one machine, the Sinclair Spectrum home computer, offers natural logarithms only, but they can easily be converted to common logarithms within a program. In many instances we require the ratio of two logarithms and they can be common or natural provided the same base is used for both numbers.

A basic property of all logarithms is that the sum of their values for two numbers, such as a and b, is the logarithm of the product ab. In symbols,

$$\log (ab) = \log a + \log b$$

By an extension of this result we can find the value of the index or power n in the relationship $y = x^n$. If n is an integer,

$$y = x^n = x \times x \times x \times x \times x \times x \ldots (n \text{ times})$$

and

$$\log y = \log x + \log x + \log x \ldots (n \text{ times})$$
$$= n \log x$$

from which

$$n = \frac{\log y}{\log x}$$

The result is used in several calculations in this book and the logarithms can be common or natural. The relationship is also valid when n is not an integer. The need to find n in this way occurs frequently and it is surprising that most scientific calculators do not offer the function as a single keystroke.

If x is given the value 1, the relationship for n leads to division by zero and a calculator or computer will display an error message. Any attempt to find a logarithm of a negative number will also lead to an error message.

Appendix B
NOTES ON THE COMPUTER PROGRAMS

All variables in the program listings are denoted by upper case (capital) letters so that symbols such as x, y and z that are used in normal mathematical presentation become X, Y and Z. Furthermore, computers cannot recognize subscripts and x_1, x_2 and x_3 become X1, X2 and X3.

The standard typewriter keyboard has only a few mathematical symbols ($+$, $-$ and $=$). In computer programming, therefore, we use several symbols that differ from those to be found in conventional mathematical text. Multiplication is denoted by $*$ (the asterisk or 'star') instead of $\times$ and division is shown by / (the solidus or 'slash') instead of $\div$. The computer cannot interpret an index or superscript and raising a number to a power is achieved with the circumflex symbol ^ (or $\uparrow$). Note that the multiplication sign must be placed between each variable and the next in a compounded product. Thus the term $4x_1^3x_2$ will appear as 4*X1^3*X2 in a computer program. The square of a variable, e.g. x^2, can be shown as X^2 or X*X; either form requires three keystrokes.

Table B.1
Mathematical symbols and notation

Operation	Conventional symbol	Computer symbol
Multiplication	$\times$	$*$
Division	$\div$	/
x to the power y	x^y	X^Y
Exponential function	e^x	EXP(X)
Square root	$\sqrt{x}$	SQR(X)
Common logarithm	$\log_{10}x$	LOG(X) or LOG10(X)
Natural logarithm	$\log_e x$	LN(X) or LOG(X)
Absolute value or modulus	$\|x\|$	ABS(X)
Less than or equal to	$\leq$	<=
Greater than or equal to	$\geq$	>=
Not equal to	$\neq$	<>
Brackets	$[\{(\ldots)\}]$	$(((\ldots)))$

Some functions, such as square root or logarithm, can only be obtained by keywords. Table B.1 shows the conventional symbols used in this book and their computer equivalents.

In a few cases there are variations between computers. Some machines use LOG for common logarithms and LN for natural logarithms. Others use

278

LOG10 and LOG respectively. Where a ratio of two logarithms is required either common or natural logarithms may be used but in one or two programs natural logarithms are essential.

Computers cannot interpret fractions in which the denominator is displayed below the numerator. Expressions must therefore be arranged in a single line using brackets. We are also limited to round brackets. The hierarchy of square, curly and round brackets used in mathematics has to be achieved by the successive use of round brackets. We must therefore take care to ensure that the numbers of opening and closing brackets are equal. One result of these limitations is that mathematical expressions can take on a very different appearance in computer listings. The formula given in section 6.21, for calculating the variable z from the one-tail area of the normal curve is

$$z = \sqrt{\frac{[(4y + 100)y + 205]y^2}{[(2y + 56)y + 192]y + 131}}$$

In the computer listing of Fig. 6.22 this appears as

```
Z=SQR((((4*Y+100)*Y+205)*Y*Y)/(((2*Y+56)*Y+192)*Y+131))
```

The programs in this book have been written in a simple form of BASIC that should suit all home and personal computers. Many machines offer facilities that can shorten and simplify the listings. In some, a few small amendments to the listings may be needed and the following notes, read in conjunction with the owner's manual for your computer, will help you to make the necessary changes.

1. All keywords such as PRINT, GOTO, FOR and TO are given in upper-case letters. This form is used by all computers. In BBC BASIC abbreviations such as P. for PRINT and G. for GOTO may be used.
2. Variables have generally been denoted by single letters such as X. On some machines, such as the Casio pocket computers, this is the only acceptable form. In some programs double letters or letters and single numerals such as F1 have been used. Many machines will accept lower case letters and words such as factor1 as variables. In the BASIC 2 dialect used on the Amstrad PC all variables are changed to lower case automatically.
3. The keyword LET has been omitted from assignment statements so that LET X=X+1 appears as X=X+1. On the Spectrum computer LET is essential.
4. In branching statements such as IF . . . THEN GOTO or IF . . . THEN GOSUB the keywords THEN or GOTO/GOSUB may be optional on your computer. Consult your owner's manual if in doubt.
5. The programs are terminated by the keyword END. Some computers require STOP instead.
6. In some programs the numerical answers are rounded using the INTeger routine. This is universally available but it can prove cumbersome and some computers offer automatic rounding.
7. Upper case has been used for all text. This simplifies the typing of the

listings but changing to the more usual mixture of upper and lower case text can lead to a neater appearance.

8. All the text and tables appearing on the screen can be accommodated in 40 columns. By making a few abbreviations the displays will fit into 32 columns, the only format available on some machines. In contrast many computers offer 80 columns and some programs can be extended and improved by taking advantage of this layout.

9. The TAB function has been used to display tables of results with the columns numbered from 0 to 39. If your computer numbers the columns from 1 to 40 you should increase the TAB values given in the listings by 1. Some computers have an automatic tabulating facility.

10. In mathematical functions such as EXP(X) or SQR(X) the argument X has been placed in brackets. They can be omitted on some computers. If in doubt, include them.

11. Where data are to be entered using INPUT, the prompting text can be included in the same line or shown as a separate PRINT statement. Thus

```
170 INPUT "ENTER FIRST PRICE AND SALES";P1,S1
```

or

```
170 PRINT "ENTER FIRST PRICE AND SALES"
180 INPUT P1,S1
```

The second method should work with all computers.

12. Where a prompt calls for two or more values, some computers require them to be typed and entered one at a time, each on a separate line. With other machines the values must all be typed together on one line, separated by commas, and then entered simultaneously.

13. Where a program can branch in several ways, a separate IF . . . THEN statement is given for each. With some computers they can be combined in a single ON statement.

14. No graphics have been used in the programs because of the wide variations between machines.

15. In the longer programs the listings have been divided into sections that can be tested separately. When the first part has been typed in and found to run successfully, it should be saved to disc or tape. The remaining sections can be added and tested one at a time. The extra lines must appear at the correct places in the program according to their line numbers and most computers will sort them automatically. With the Amstrad PC, however, they must be inserted at the correct places in the program.

16. Some numerical answers have to be obtained by successive approximations and this is achieved by looping within the program until sufficient accuracy is obtained. Some computers offer a REPEAT . . . UNTIL function that can simplify the procedure.

17. Some of the programs used in probability and statistics require the

generation of random numbers in the range 0–0.999999.. On most computers this is achieved by the keyword RND. In BBC BASIC use RND(1). On the Casio pocket computer the keyword is RAN# (RND being used for the rounding of numerical values).

Appendix C
TABLES

Table C.1   Present value (PV) of unit sum paid or received after n periods
$PV = 1/(1 + i)^n$. Compound interest rate i from 0.01 to 0.10 (1–10%)

i= n=	0.01 1%	0.02 2%	0.03 3%	0.04 4%	0.05 5%	0.06 6%	0.07 7%	0.08 8%	0.09 9%	0.10 10%	n=
1	0.9901	0.9804	0.9709	0.9615	0.9524	0.9434	0.9346	0.9259	0.9174	0.9091	1
2	0.9803	0.9612	0.9426	0.9246	0.9070	0.8900	0.8734	0.8573	0.8417	0.8264	2
3	0.9706	0.9423	0.9151	0.8890	0.8638	0.8396	0.8163	0.7938	0.7722	0.7513	3
4	0.9610	0.9238	0.8885	0.8548	0.8227	0.7921	0.7629	0.7350	0.7084	0.6830	4
5	0.9515	0.9057	0.8626	0.8219	0.7835	0.7473	0.7130	0.6806	0.6499	0.6209	5
6	0.9420	0.8880	0.8375	0.7903	0.7462	0.7050	0.6663	0.6302	0.5963	0.5645	6
7	0.9327	0.8706	0.8131	0.7599	0.7107	0.6651	0.6227	0.5835	0.5470	0.5132	7
8	0.9235	0.8535	0.7894	0.7307	0.6768	0.6274	0.5820	0.5403	0.5019	0.4665	8
9	0.9143	0.8368	0.7664	0.7026	0.6446	0.5919	0.5439	0.5002	0.4604	0.4241	9
10	0.9053	0.8203	0.7441	0.6756	0.6139	0.5584	0.5083	0.4632	0.4224	0.3855	10
11	0.8963	0.8043	0.7224	0.6496	0.5847	0.5268	0.4751	0.4289	0.3875	0.3505	11
12	0.8874	0.7885	0.7014	0.6246	0.5568	0.4970	0.4440	0.3971	0.3555	0.3186	12
13	0.8787	0.7730	0.6810	0.6006	0.5303	0.4688	0.4150	0.3677	0.3262	0.2897	13
14	0.8700	0.7579	0.6611	0.5775	0.5051	0.4423	0.3878	0.3405	0.2992	0.2633	14
15	0.8613	0.7430	0.6419	0.5553	0.4810	0.4173	0.3624	0.3152	0.2745	0.2394	15
16	0.8528	0.7284	0.6232	0.5339	0.4581	0.3936	0.3387	0.2919	0.2519	0.2176	16
17	0.8444	0.7142	0.6050	0.5134	0.4363	0.3714	0.3166	0.2703	0.2311	0.1978	17
18	0.8360	0.7002	0.5874	0.4936	0.4155	0.3503	0.2959	0.2502	0.2120	0.1799	18
19	0.8277	0.6864	0.5703	0.4746	0.3957	0.3305	0.2765	0.2317	0.1945	0.1635	19
20	0.8195	0.6730	0.5537	0.4564	0.3769	0.3118	0.2584	0.2145	0.1784	0.1486	20
21	0.8114	0.6598	0.5375	0.4388	0.3589	0.2942	0.2415	0.1987	0.1637	0.1351	21
22	0.8034	0.6468	0.5219	0.4220	0.3418	0.2775	0.2257	0.1839	0.1502	0.1228	22
23	0.7954	0.6342	0.5067	0.4057	0.3256	0.2618	0.2109	0.1703	0.1378	0.1117	23
24	0.7876	0.6217	0.4919	0.3901	0.3101	0.2470	0.1971	0.1577	0.1264	0.1015	24
25	0.7798	0.6095	0.4776	0.3751	0.2953	0.2330	0.1842	0.1460	0.1160	0.0923	25
26	0.7720	0.5976	0.4637	0.3607	0.2812	0.2198	0.1722	0.1352	0.1064	0.0839	26
27	0.7644	0.5859	0.4502	0.3468	0.2678	0.2074	0.1609	0.1252	0.0976	0.0763	27
28	0.7568	0.5744	0.4371	0.3335	0.2551	0.1956	0.1504	0.1159	0.0895	0.0693	28
29	0.7493	0.5631	0.4243	0.3207	0.2429	0.1846	0.1406	0.1073	0.0822	0.0630	29
30	0.7419	0.5521	0.4120	0.3083	0.2314	0.1741	0.1314	0.0994	0.0754	0.0573	30
40	0.6717	0.4529	0.3066	0.2083	0.1420	0.0972	0.0668	0.0460	0.0318	0.0221	40
50	0.6080	0.3715	0.2281	0.1407	0.0872	0.0543	0.0339	0.0213	0.0134	0.00852	50
60	0.5504	0.3048	0.1697	0.0951	0.0535	0.0303	0.0173	0.00988	0.00568	0.00328	60
70	0.4983	0.2500	0.1263	0.0642	0.0329	0.0169	0.00877	0.00457	0.00240	0.00127	70
80	0.4511	0.2051	0.0940	0.0434	0.0202	0.00945	0.00446	0.00212	0.00101	0.00049	80

Table C.2. Present value (PV) of unit sum per period for n periods.
$PV = PV(1 - [1/(1+i)^n])/i$ Compound interest rate i from 0.01 to 0.10.
$$\frac{(1 - [1/i]^n)}{i}$$

Table C.1 (continued) Compound interest rate *i* from 0.11 to 0.20 (11–20%)

| i= | 0.11 | 0.12 | 0.13 | 0.14 | 0.15 | 0.16 | 0.17 | 0.18 | 0.19 | 0.20 | |
n=	11%	12%	13%	14%	15%	16%	17%	18%	19%	20%	n=
1	0.9009	0.8929	0.8850	0.8772	0.8696	0.8621	0.8547	0.8475	0.8403	0.8333	1
2	0.8116	0.7972	0.7831	0.7695	0.7561	0.7432	0.7305	0.7182	0.7062	0.6944	2
3	0.7312	0.7118	0.6931	0.6750	0.6575	0.6407	0.6244	0.6086	0.5934	0.5787	3
4	0.6587	0.6355	0.6133	0.5921	0.5718	0.5523	0.5337	0.5158	0.4987	0.4823	4
5	0.5935	0.5674	0.5428	0.5194	0.4972	0.4761	0.4561	0.4371	0.4190	0.4019	5
6	0.5346	0.5066	0.4803	0.4556	0.4323	0.4104	0.3898	0.3704	0.3521	0.3349	6
7	0.4817	0.4523	0.4251	0.3996	0.3759	0.3538	0.3332	0.3139	0.2959	0.2791	7
8	0.4339	0.4039	0.3762	0.3506	0.3269	0.3050	0.2848	0.2660	0.2487	0.2326	8
9	0.3909	0.3606	0.3329	0.3075	0.2843	0.2630	0.2434	0.2255	0.2090	0.1938	9
10	0.3522	0.3220	0.2946	0.2697	0.2472	0.2267	0.2080	0.1911	0.1756	0.1615	10
11	0.3173	0.2875	0.2607	0.2366	0.2149	0.1954	0.1778	0.1619	0.1476	0.1346	11
12	0.2858	0.2567	0.2307	0.2076	0.1869	0.1685	0.1520	0.1372	0.1240	0.1122	12
13	0.2575	0.2292	0.2042	0.1821	0.1625	0.1452	0.1299	0.1163	0.1042	0.0935	13
14	0.2320	0.2046	0.1807	0.1597	0.1413	0.1252	0.1110	0.0985	0.0876	0.0779	14
15	0.2090	0.1827	0.1599	0.1401	0.1229	0.1079	0.0949	0.0835	0.0736	0.0649	15
16	0.1883	0.1631	0.1415	0.1229	0.1069	0.0930	0.0811	0.0708	0.0618	0.0541	16
17	0.1696	0.1456	0.1252	0.1078	0.0929	0.0802	0.0693	0.0600	0.0520	0.0451	17
18	0.1528	0.1300	0.1108	0.0946	0.0808	0.0691	0.0592	0.0508	0.0437	0.0376	18
19	0.1377	0.1161	0.0981	0.0829	0.0703	0.0596	0.0506	0.0431	0.0367	0.0313	19
20	0.1240	0.1037	0.0868	0.0728	0.0611	0.0514	0.0433	0.0365	0.0308	0.0261	20
21	0.1117	0.0926	0.0768	0.0638	0.0531	0.0443	0.0370	0.0309	0.0259	0.0217	21
22	0.1007	0.0826	0.0680	0.0560	0.0462	0.0382	0.0316	0.0262	0.0218	0.0181	22
23	0.0907	0.0738	0.0601	0.0491	0.0402	0.0329	0.0270	0.0222	0.0183	0.0151	23
24	0.0817	0.0659	0.0532	0.0431	0.0349	0.0284	0.0231	0.0188	0.0154	0.0126	24
25	0.0736	0.0588	0.0471	0.0378	0.0304	0.0245	0.0197	0.0160	0.0129	0.0105	25
26	0.0663	0.0525	0.0417	0.0331	0.0264	0.0211	0.0169	0.0135	0.0109	0.00874	26
27	0.0597	0.0469	0.0369	0.0291	0.0230	0.0182	0.0144	0.0115	0.00912	0.00728	27
28	0.0538	0.0419	0.0326	0.0255	0.0200	0.0157	0.0123	0.00971	0.00767	0.00607	28
29	0.0485	0.0374	0.0289	0.0224	0.0174	0.0135	0.0105	0.00823	0.00644	0.00506	29
30	0.0437	0.0334	0.0256	0.0196	0.0151	0.0116	0.00900	0.00697	0.00541	0.00421	30
40	0.0154	0.0107	0.00753	0.00529	0.00373	0.00264	0.00187	0.00133	0.00095	0.00068	40
50	0.00542	0.00346	0.00222	0.00143	0.00092	0.00060	0.00039	0.00025	0.00017	0.00011	50
60	0.00191	0.00111	0.00065	0.00039	0.00023	0.00014					60
70	0.00067	0.00036	0.00019	0.00010							70
80	0.00024	0.00012									80

Table C.2 Present value (PV) of unit sum per period for n periods $PV = 1/i\{1 - 1/(1 + i)^n\}$. Compound interest rate i from 0.01 to 0.10 (1–10%)

i=	0.01 1%	0.02 2%	0.03 3%	0.04 4%	0.05 5%	0.06 6%	0.07 7%	0.08 8%	0.09 9%	0.10 10%	
n=											n=
1	0.990	0.980	0.971	0.962	0.952	0.943	0.935	0.926	0.917	0.909	1
2	1.970	1.942	1.913	1.886	1.859	1.833	1.808	1.783	1.759	1.736	2
3	2.941	2.884	2.829	2.775	2.723	2.673	2.624	2.577	2.531	2.487	3
4	3.902	3.808	3.717	3.630	3.546	3.465	3.387	3.312	3.240	3.170	4
5	4.853	4.713	4.580	4.452	4.329	4.212	4.100	3.993	3.890	3.791	5
6	5.795	5.601	5.417	5.242	5.076	4.917	4.767	4.623	4.486	4.355	6
7	6.728	6.472	6.230	6.002	5.786	5.582	5.389	5.206	5.033	4.868	7
8	7.652	7.325	7.020	6.733	6.463	6.210	5.971	5.747	5.535	5.335	8
9	8.566	8.162	7.786	7.435	7.108	6.802	6.515	6.247	5.995	5.759	9
10	9.471	8.983	8.530	8.111	7.722	7.360	7.024	6.710	6.418	6.145	10
11	10.368	9.787	9.253	8.760	8.306	7.887	7.499	7.139	6.805	6.495	11
12	11.255	10.575	9.954	9.385	8.863	8.384	7.943	7.536	7.161	6.814	12
13	12.134	11.348	10.635	9.986	9.394	8.853	8.358	7.904	7.487	7.103	13
14	13.004	12.106	11.296	10.563	9.899	9.295	8.745	8.244	7.786	7.367	14
15	13.865	12.849	11.938	11.118	10.380	9.712	9.108	8.559	8.061	7.606	15
16	14.718	13.578	12.561	11.652	10.838	10.106	9.447	8.851	8.313	7.824	16
17	15.562	14.292	13.166	12.166	11.274	10.477	9.763	9.122	8.544	8.022	17
18	16.398	14.992	13.754	12.659	11.690	10.828	10.059	9.372	8.756	8.201	18
19	17.226	15.678	14.324	13.134	12.085	11.158	10.336	9.604	8.950	8.365	19
20	18.046	16.351	14.877	13.590	12.462	11.470	10.594	9.818	9.129	8.514	20
21	18.857	17.011	15.415	14.029	12.821	11.764	10.836	10.017	9.292	8.649	21
22	19.660	17.658	15.937	14.451	13.163	12.042	11.061	10.201	9.442	8.772	22
23	20.456	18.292	16.444	14.857	13.489	12.303	11.272	10.371	9.580	8.883	23
24	21.243	18.914	16.936	15.247	13.799	12.550	11.469	10.529	9.707	8.985	24
25	22.023	19.523	17.413	15.622	14.094	12.783	11.654	10.675	9.823	9.077	25
26	22.795	20.121	17.877	15.983	14.375	13.003	11.826	10.810	9.929	9.161	26
27	23.560	20.707	18.327	16.330	14.643	13.211	11.987	10.935	10.027	9.237	27
28	24.316	21.281	18.764	16.663	14.898	13.406	12.137	11.051	10.116	9.307	28
29	25.066	21.844	19.188	16.984	15.141	13.591	12.278	11.158	10.198	9.370	29
30	25.808	22.396	19.600	17.292	15.372	13.765	12.409	11.258	10.274	9.427	30
40	32.835	27.355	23.115	19.793	17.159	15.046	13.332	11.925	10.757	9.779	40
50	39.196	31.424	25.730	21.482	18.256	15.762	13.801	12.233	10.962	9.915	50
60	44.955	34.761	27.676	22.623	18.929	16.161	14.039	12.377	11.048	9.967	60
inf.	100.000	50.000	33.333	25.000	20.000	16.667	14.286	12.500	11.111	10.000	inf.

Table C.2 (continued) Compound interest rate i from 0.11 to 0.20 (11–20%)

i=	0.11 11%	0.12 12%	0.13 13%	0.14 14%	0.15 15%	0.16 16%	0.17 17%	0.18 18%	0.19 19%	0.20 20%	
n=											n=
1	0.901	0.893	0.885	0.877	0.870	0.862	0.855	0.847	0.840	0.833	1
2	1.713	1.690	1.668	1.647	1.626	1.605	1.585	1.566	1.547	1.528	2
3	2.444	2.402	2.361	2.322	2.283	2.246	2.210	2.174	2.140	2.106	3
4	3.102	3.037	2.974	2.914	2.855	2.798	2.743	2.690	2.639	2.589	4
5	3.696	3.605	3.517	3.433	3.352	3.274	3.199	3.127	3.058	2.991	5
6	4.231	4.111	3.998	3.889	3.784	3.685	3.589	3.498	3.410	3.326	6
7	4.712	4.564	4.423	4.288	4.160	4.039	3.922	3.812	3.706	3.605	7
8	5.146	4.968	4.799	4.639	4.487	4.344	4.207	4.078	3.954	3.837	8
9	5.537	5.328	5.132	4.946	4.772	4.607	4.451	4.303	4.163	4.031	9
10	5.889	5.650	5.426	5.216	5.019	4.833	4.659	4.494	4.339	4.192	10
11	6.207	5.938	5.687	5.453	5.234	5.029	4.836	4.656	4.486	4.327	11
12	6.492	6.194	5.918	5.660	5.421	5.197	4.988	4.793	4.611	4.439	12
13	6.750	6.424	6.122	5.842	5.583	5.342	5.118	4.910	4.715	4.533	13
14	6.982	6.628	6.302	6.002	5.724	5.468	5.229	5.008	4.802	4.611	14
15	7.191	6.811	6.462	6.142	5.847	5.575	5.324	5.092	4.876	4.675	15
16	7.379	6.974	6.604	6.265	5.954	5.668	5.405	5.162	4.938	4.730	16
17	7.549	7.120	6.729	6.373	6.047	5.749	5.475	5.222	4.990	4.775	17
18	7.702	7.250	6.840	6.467	6.128	5.818	5.534	5.273	5.033	4.812	18
19	7.839	7.366	6.938	6.550	6.198	5.877	5.584	5.316	5.070	4.843	19
20	7.963	7.469	7.025	6.623	6.259	5.929	5.628	5.353	5.101	4.870	20
21	8.075	7.562	7.102	6.687	6.312	5.973	5.665	5.384	5.127	4.891	21
22	8.176	7.645	7.170	6.743	6.359	6.011	5.696	5.410	5.149	4.909	22
23	8.266	7.718	7.230	6.792	6.399	6.044	5.723	5.432	5.167	4.925	23
24	8.348	7.784	7.283	6.835	6.434	6.073	5.746	5.451	5.182	4.937	24
25	8.422	7.843	7.330	6.873	6.464	6.097	5.766	5.467	5.195	4.948	25
26	8.488	7.896	7.372	6.906	6.491	6.118	5.783	5.480	5.206	4.956	26
27	8.548	7.943	7.409	6.935	6.514	6.136	5.798	5.492	5.215	4.964	27
28	8.602	7.984	7.441	6.961	6.534	6.152	5.810	5.502	5.223	4.970	28
29	8.650	8.022	7.470	6.983	6.551	6.166	5.820	5.510	5.229	4.975	29
30	8.694	8.055	7.496	7.003	6.566	6.177	5.829	5.517	5.235	4.979	30
40	8.951	8.244	7.634	7.105	6.642	6.233	5.871	5.548	5.258	4.997	40
50	9.042	8.304	7.675	7.133	6.661	6.246	5.880	5.554	5.262	4.999	50
60	9.074	8.324	7.687	7.140	6.665	6.249	5.882	5.555	5.263	5.000	60
inf.	9.091	8.333	7.692	7.143	6.667	6.250	5.882	5.556	5.263	5.000	inf.

Table C.3 One-tail area of the normal curve

z	0.00	0.01	0.02	0.03	0.04	0.05	0.06	0.07	0.08	0.09
0.0	0.5000	0.4960	0.4920	0.4880	0.4840	0.4800	0.4760	0.4721	0.4681	0.4641
0.1	0.4601	0.4562	0.4522	0.4482	0.4443	0.4403	0.4364	0.4325	0.4285	0.4246
0.2	0.4207	0.4168	0.4129	0.4090	0.4051	0.4013	0.3974	0.3936	0.3897	0.3859
0.3	0.3821	0.3783	0.3745	0.3707	0.3669	0.3632	0.3594	0.3557	0.3520	0.3483
0.4	0.3446	0.3409	0.3373	0.3336	0.3300	0.3264	0.3228	0.3192	0.3156	0.3121
0.5	0.3086	0.3051	0.3016	0.2981	0.2946	0.2912	0.2878	0.2844	0.2810	0.2776
0.6	0.2743	0.2710	0.2677	0.2644	0.2611	0.2579	0.2547	0.2515	0.2483	0.2452
0.7	0.2420	0.2389	0.2358	0.2328	0.2297	0.2267	0.2237	0.2207	0.2178	0.2148
0.8	0.2119	0.2090	0.2062	0.2033	0.2005	0.1977	0.1950	0.1922	0.1895	0.1868
0.9	0.1841	0.1815	0.1789	0.1763	0.1737	0.1711	0.1686	0.1661	0.1636	0.1612
1.0	0.1587	0.1563	0.1539	0.1516	0.1492	0.1469	0.1446	0.1424	0.1401	0.1379
1.1	0.1357	0.1336	0.1314	0.1293	0.1272	0.1251	0.1231	0.1211	0.1190	0.1171
1.2	0.1151	0.1132	0.1113	0.1094	0.1075	0.1057	0.1039	0.1021	0.1003	0.0986
1.3	0.09684	0.09513	0.09345	0.09179	0.09016	0.08854	0.08695	0.08537	0.08382	0.08229
1.4	0.08078	0.07930	0.07783	0.07638	0.07496	0.07355	0.07217	0.07080	0.06946	0.06813
1.5	0.06683	0.06554	0.06427	0.06303	0.06180	0.06059	0.05940	0.05822	0.05707	0.05593
1.6	0.05481	0.05371	0.05263	0.05156	0.05051	0.04948	0.04847	0.04747	0.04649	0.04552
1.7	0.04457	0.04364	0.04272	0.04182	0.04094	0.04007	0.03921	0.03837	0.03754	0.03673
1.8	0.03594	0.03515	0.03438	0.03363	0.03289	0.03216	0.03145	0.03074	0.03006	0.02938
1.9	0.02872	0.02807	0.02743	0.02680	0.02619	0.02559	0.02500	0.02442	0.02385	0.02330
2.0	0.02275	0.02222	0.02169	0.02118	0.02067	0.02018	0.01970	0.01923	0.01876	0.01831
2.1	0.01786	0.01743	0.01700	0.01658	0.01618	0.01578	0.01539	0.01500	0.01463	0.01426
2.2	0.01390	0.01355	0.01321	0.01287	0.01254	0.01222	0.01191	0.01160	0.01130	0.01101
2.3	0.01072	0.01044	0.01017	0.00990	0.00964	0.00939	0.00914	0.00889	0.00865	0.00842
2.4	0.00820	0.00797	0.00776	0.00755	0.00734	0.00714	0.00695	0.00675	0.00657	0.00639
2.5	0.00621	0.00604	0.00587	0.00570	0.00554	0.00538	0.00523	0.00508	0.00494	0.00480
2.6	0.00466	0.00453	0.00440	0.00427	0.00414	0.00402	0.00391	0.00379	0.00368	0.00357
2.7	0.00347	0.00336	0.00326	0.00317	0.00307	0.00298	0.00289	0.00280	0.00272	0.00263
2.8	0.00255	0.00248	0.00240	0.00233	0.00226	0.00219	0.00212	0.00205	0.00199	0.00193
2.9	0.00187	0.00181	0.00175	0.00169	0.00164	0.00159	0.00154	0.00149	0.00144	0.00139
3.0	0.00135	0.00131	0.00126	0.00122	0.00118	0.00114	0.00111	0.00107	0.00103	0.00100

Table C.4   Values of *z* for selected one-tail areas of the normal curve

area	z	area	z	area	z	area	z	area	z
0.00001	4.2648	0.0001	3.7190	0.001	3.0903	0.01	2.3265	0.1	1.2816
0.00002	4.1074	0.0002	3.5401	0.002	2.8783	0.02	2.0539	0.2	0.8417
0.00003	4.0127	0.0003	3.4316	0.003	2.7479	0.03	1.8809	0.3	0.5244
0.00004	3.9443	0.0004	3.3528	0.004	2.6522	0.04	1.7508	0.4	0.2532
0.00005	3.8905	0.0005	3.2906	0.005	2.5760	0.05	1.6449	0.5	0.0000
0.00006	3.8461	0.0006	3.2389	0.006	2.5123	0.06	1.5549		
0.00007	3.8081	0.0007	3.1947	0.007	2.4574	0.07	1.4759		
0.00008	3.7750	0.0008	3.1560	0.008	2.4090	0.08	1.4052		
0.00009	3.7455	0.0009	3.1215	0.009	2.3657	0.09	1.3408		
0.00010	3.7190	0.0010	3.0903	0.010	2.3265	0.10	1.2816		

Table C.5 Random numbers

61 40 01 24 21	91 98 37 91 08	05 29 46 60 19	85 28 80 57 79
57 40 93 56 44	83 12 02 27 64	36 32 71 02 33	87 46 98 48 21
80 55 89 61 22	67 52 21 61 92	56 77 49 58 19	18 90 54 65 16
79 78 25 76 40	10 51 38 25 60	41 73 29 34 73	79 47 68 02 67
98 33 67 32 68	40 08 31 43 49	88 07 38 57 46	53 72 84 12 18
61 09 21 22 08	17 30 92 64 01	31 08 80 43 13	15 91 46 47 22
80 47 29 85 02	30 86 59 18 74	53 03 87 94 20	06 81 38 32 46
12 86 31 53 06	50 69 72 03 34	99 44 84 24 30	35 03 39 10 66
72 95 94 00 09	37 25 55 09 52	61 14 68 11 56	07 50 45 60 09
01 98 64 99 40	72 49 76 26 55	97 24 02 65 38	89 50 42 98 34
55 88 12 38 30	08 37 32 34 05	55 64 11 64 59	26 49 01 25 15
30 62 68 60 44	07 78 18 69 55	87 36 27 16 48	38 11 28 33 27
11 96 62 09 84	05 38 65 94 93	89 11 39 40 85	80 52 23 27 50
17 27 18 96 53	29 29 82 57 92	67 28 14 47 17	42 56 92 28 88
52 70 87 07 58	15 17 03 37 42	58 06 64 34 41	26 40 39 00 65
33 14 19 74 86	05 34 14 19 97	48 27 27 82 86	61 45 94 16 51
36 47 35 15 82	66 00 30 43 61	12 26 93 51 98	68 79 17 15 82
47 29 63 32 58	93 82 56 92 91	93 43 42 85 51	96 88 99 55 82
21 23 24 30 81	00 33 42 26 13	76 28 72 62 78	33 69 42 38 00
65 83 83 63 74	41 54 91 70 75	24 77 42 59 94	41 98 73 37 33
79 58 95 37 96	82 17 12 88 43	33 65 42 18 14	73 37 02 04 85
14 12 20 36 19	72 73 82 54 55	92 77 23 98 69	28 24 94 84 96
02 75 27 04 58	82 54 96 21 82	90 80 90 84 56	49 38 75 37 30
84 29 78 89 31	93 46 27 49 92	10 08 06 85 31	22 40 32 69 77
12 48 10 05 61	03 68 83 01 55	84 45 36 04 10	94 55 01 36 69
40 00 96 08 53	09 44 52 22 90	54 77 60 16 40	91 50 59 33 12
69 00 47 80 99	26 47 61 79 41	53 60 16 30 39	11 57 06 30 42
21 22 62 25 23	87 32 97 13 91	06 81 20 98 39	39 34 92 03 07
66 94 96 78 63	96 11 62 23 49	00 50 35 79 37	97 09 84 84 28
31 81 12 84 43	75 88 98 34 14	92 54 30 37 68	05 81 46 13 35
80 92 38 84 92	59 15 64 63 23	22 36 03 19 49	07 03 09 89 73
20 70 27 20 40	83 28 04 68 92	29 49 32 99 57	44 81 95 48 57
56 08 47 05 23	87 47 45 73 89	32 61 90 79 14	21 89 57 68 85
60 72 59 25 27	54 52 90 80 20	62 90 48 35 19	29 91 65 44 63
93 01 44 08 84	39 29 75 98 81	20 28 62 75 53	85 66 92 99 14

INDEX